Calling in the Soul

GENDER AND THE CYCLE OF LIFE

Calling in the Soul

IN A HMONG VILLAGE

PATRICIA V. SYMONDS

UNIVERSITY OF WASHINGTON PRESS

SEATTLE AND LONDON

University of Washington Press
P.O. Box 50096
Seattle, WA 98145-5096, USA
www.washington.edu/uwpress

Library of Congress Cataloging-in-Publication Data
Symonds, Patricia V.
Calling in the soul : gender and the cycle of life in a Hmong village /
Patricia V. Symonds.
p. cm.
Includes bibliographical references and index.
ISBN 0-295-98339-6 (pbk. : alk. paper)
1. Hmong (Asian people)—Thailand, Northern—Rites and ceremonies.
2. Women, Hmong—Thailand, Northern—Social conditions.
3. Sex role—Thailand, Northern.
4. Sexual division of labor—Thailand, Northern.
5. Patrilineal kinship—Thailand, Northern.
6. Thailand, Northern—Social life and customs.
7. Hmong Americans—Social life and customs.
I. Title.
DS570.M5S95   2003   305.895'9420593—DC22   2003049342

To my husband,
Alan Ellis Symonds

CONTENTS

CONTENTS

PREFACE

MY INTEREST IN HMONG birthing practices began in 1979, when I was collecting medical histories from women at a clinic for low-income patients in Providence, Rhode Island. Many of these women were Hmong refugees from the hills of Laos. Few of them spoke English, and even fewer came in for early prenatal care. They were apprehensive about the medical procedures, even those as simple as having their blood drawn or providing a urine sample. At the prospect of getting a physical examination by a male physician, they were frightened and resentful. All too often one of the health clinic's Hmong clients arrived at a local hospital with her newborn baby in her arms, having given birth at home or in the car on the way to the hospital.

With only one Hmong interpreter on duty, and only in the mornings, the women did not get much individual attention, and their responses remained a mystery to me. It was only when the interpreter and I had become close friends that I began to understand why Hmong women subjected themselves to the Western medical practices they obviously mistrusted: they wanted to become eligible for the federal Women, Infants, and Children Program (WIC),[1] which provided food vouchers; and to ensure that their babies became citizens, they needed to document birth in the United States.

Later I conducted research on adolescent pregnancy and its implications for Hmong in America. With my interpreter Iab Moua Yang, I visited many Hmong women and their husbands in the Providence Hmong community.[2]

One morning, Iab Moua Yang and I visited a pregnant woman at the home of her husband's parents, where the young couple lived. We wanted to interview the couple about their marriage, but the husband was not at home. The young woman invited us to sit down, her mother-in-law offered us Coca-Cola™, and the interview began. After about an hour, the young woman said that she was in labor and feeling uncomfortable. I was quite startled; she had given no indication that she was in pain. I immediately offered to take her and her mother-in-law to the local maternity hospital.

As soon as we arrived, the young woman was examined and then taken to the delivery room; meanwhile I obtained permission from both the doctor and the mother-in-law to observe the birth. When the nurse told the young woman to remove her clothing, she began to protest, but a few words from her mother-in-law made her comply with the nurse's instructions to undress and don the hospital johnny. The physician conferred with Iab Moua Yang to get permission to rupture the chorionic membrane and/or to perform an episiotomy if necessary.[3] Iab Moua Yang asked the mother-in-law, who refused permission for both procedures.

The young woman was not a participant in these discussions. If she gave any indication that she was in pain, such as moaning softly, her mother-in-law would silence her by saying that she was bringing shame upon her family. The mother-in-law's influence appeared to upset the physician, who said, "The girl is afraid of the mother. If I need to carry out these procedures, I will insist she leave the room." Fortunately, the infant was born without the need for medical intervention. The fact that this young woman was able to deliver her child without expressing pain pointed to the way in which childbirth is constructed by the Hmong.[4]

As I observed several more births in the Hmong community in Providence, I became acutely aware of the concerns of many Hmong women, especially their fears of an episiotomy or a Caesarean section. The Hmong believe that any surgical procedure disrupts the balance of the body in relation to its surroundings: that anesthesia causes soul loss; that one will never be physically or spiritually well in this world if something is taken from the body; that metal placed in the body—such as a pin in a bone—will prevent a person from peacefully entering the land of darkness at death; and that all of these ill effects will be borne throughout future incarnations.

I was also aware of the medical providers' concerns, in particular their questions as to why Hmong women would not come to the clinic for pre-natal care. The staff also wanted women to arrive at the hospital early enough in their labor that the child would be born in the hospital, but Hmong women arrived with newborn babies in their arms more and more often. Nor did the staff understand why Hmong women refused to eat hospital food or drink cold juices or water.

In 1986 I decided to undertake a study of Hmong birth practices in South-east Asia, to understand at firsthand where these women "were coming from" in a literal as well as a metaphorical sense. I saw the Hmong women in Rhode Island struggling with the Western health-care system, and I hoped that if I could understand how they conceptualized and experienced childbirth, I might be able to mediate between their worldview and that of Western bio-medicine. I wanted my research to help Western medical staff understand Hmong beliefs so that they would be more sensitive to the cross-cultural issues.

The uses of my initial study were not exactly as I had envisioned. By the time I returned home in 1988, many of the Hmong women I knew in Prov-idence had learned to speak English and were becoming educated about Western medicine. The hospitals that could afford to were hiring transla-tors, many of them Hmong, who could mediate between hospital staff and Hmong patients, so going to the hospital to give birth was not as terrifying as it had been. By the year 2000, hospitals all over the country had become sensitive to some of the Hmong health-care issues, in part due to the efforts of Hmong scholars such as Xoua Thao, Bruce Thowpaou Bliatout, Yang Dao, and Gary Yia Lee, as well as American scholars such as Peter Kunstadter, Anne Fadiman, Dwight Conquergood, Nancy Donnelly, Elizabeth Kirton, Kathleen Culhane-Pera, and others, including myself and my students. Hmong had established their own organizations to advise and educate Hmong on medical, legal, and social aspects of life in the United States.[5] Some Hmong are now lawyers, nurses, and physicians themselves and have made a point of helping other Hmong who come to them as clients or patients. Dr. Xoua Thao, who trained in the Brown/Dartmouth Medical School and practices medicine in Minnesota, where there is a large Hmong population, is just one of these. As well, Hmong children who have been educated here are able to advise their parents and families, and to explain the sometimes confusing tenets of Western biomedicine.

Despite such improvements, Hmong in the United States still face many problems in a hospital setting. Anne Fadiman's excellent book *The Spirit Catches You and You Fall Down* (1997) unravels the "misunderstanding" between Hmong culture and Western medicine that resulted so disastrously for an epileptic Hmong child in California. Fadiman's book includes specific suggestions for Western health-care professionals and notes, as do others, that an awareness of Hmong cosmology is essential for understanding Hmong responses to health care. My own study was undertaken with a similar aim—that of educating health-care workers and others in this country—but differs in that my starting point was childbirth and Hmong women's views of the world, my context was cosmology, and I conducted my research in a village in Southeast Asia.

In 1999 a Hmong graduate student in Fresno, California, sent me a letter saying that she had found my dissertation in the library and through it had "rediscovered my own background." She wanted a copy of the dissertation to help her stay connected to her traditions. I hope that this book will be of interest not only to scholars and health-care workers but to Hmong in this country, especially those who were born here, and that it will give them a sense of the village-based reality, as well as the cultural ideal, of the Hmong "way."

My research on childbirth and Hmong women has had another unanticipated use. Even as Hmong in this country acquired many mediators, Hmong in Thailand faced a new health-care crisis in the form of HIV/AIDS. In 1994 and 1995 I conducted research specifically aimed at preventing the spread of the disease and assisted Hmong in setting up education and prevention programs in villages. This later research was built on the work in this book; to be of any help, I needed to understand Hmong constructions of sexuality and gender. I have written about the results of those studies elsewhere[6]—and to discuss them in detail would need to write another book—but I feel that the issue must be mentioned here. The Epilogue serves that purpose.

And finally, my study was also motivated by purposes so much a part of anthropology that they are taken for granted: illumination of aspects of one's own culture by the study of another, "different" culture; and—beyond the uses of identification or recognition, or any use at all from such a study—pursuit of and delight in knowledge, in adding to what one knows. The Hmong culture proved to be compelling.

ACKNOWLEDGMENTS

THIS BOOK COULD not have been written without the help of many people. First I owe a great debt to my Hmong friends, assistants, and "teachers" in the United States and Thailand: to all of them I say, "Ua tsaug ntau kuv cov phooj ywg. Kuv muab phau ntaw no rau nej sawv daws." Some I must thank by name. In Providence, Rhode Island, Iab Muas (Moua) and Teeb Yaj, Pajkuam Vaj and his wife Nplias Yaj, Tsav Ntaj Thoj, his wife Xab Yaj, their son Xoua (Thao) and his wife Ntxhi Vaj gave generously of their time, believed in the value of my research, and encouraged me in my desire to go to the field. Special thanks go to Nploog Thoj and Ntxhi Vaj for assistance with translation, to Chaj Vaj for help with the line drawings, and to Padade Vwj for checking the spelling of Hmong terms. In Flower Village the Vwj family housed and fed me and, along with people in the Hawj and Mouas clans, befriended this stranger in their midst. Many people in the village taught me about the life of the Hmong and shared their food, hospitality, and knowledge about their culture and themselves. The women were especially generous with their time and their stories. I would also like to thank Mee Moua and May Kao Yang, my assistants in the field during my research on HIV/AIDS, and Prasit Leepreecha, his wife Patcharaporn, and Songwit Chuamsakul, who were instrumental in organizing the HIV/AIDS project in Thailand.

Grants from the Department of Health and Human Services, from Foreign Language and Area Studies at the Southeast Asia Summer Studies Institute, from the Watson Institute for International Studies, as well as the American Foundation for AIDS Research and the Thai-Australia Northern AIDS Prevention and Care Program all provided crucial financial support at different stages of my research, for which I am extremely grateful.

In Thailand many people offered help or friendship (or both) and made my fieldwork possible. The patience and expertise of my language teachers David Strekker and Laopov Vaj at the Southeast Asian Summer Studies Institute gave me the foundations of the Hmong language. The National Research Council of Thailand allowed me to work in a sensitive area of the country. Vishai Poshyachinda, Usanee Pengparn, and Vivavat Vannaporn and her daughter Sally gave me a home away from home whenever I was in Bangkok. Colleagues at the Tribal Research Institute in Chiang Mai were always helpful, especially director Khun Wanat Bhruksasri, who helped me find a research site, and Khun Ralana and Khun Manus Maneeprasert, who assisted me with all manner of problems, from dentistry to map making. Susan Darlington and Yoko Hayami were colleagues in the field whose talks kept me sane. In Thailand thanks for support and lasting friendship also must go to Ursula Lowenstein, Otome Hutheesing, Marjorie Muecke, Asue Choopoh and John Hobday, and Sally and Peter Kunstadter, with special thanks to Cornelia Kammerer, a colleague and friend both in the field and in the United States.

Before I ever conceived of a research project, I was fortunate to come across faculty at Brown University who not only imparted knowledge but also created an atmosphere of intellectual stimulation, especially William Beeman, Wanni Anderson and Douglas Anderson, Marida Hollos, Richard Gould, George Hicks, Phil Leis, Patrica Rubertone, David Kertzer, and Liza Bakewell. Later on, my dissertation committee—composed of Lucile Newman, Robert Jay, and Lina Fruzzetti—also provided a consistent source of knowledge, theoretical inspiration, and moral support. Their encouragement continued for the years it took me to prepare this book.

Other people who contributed comments and advice were Gary Yia Lee; Nicholas Tapp, who read an early draft of the manuscript; my dissertation writing group—Liza Bakewell, Lydia English, Susan Reed, and Donna Searles; Gayle Hanlon; and the three anonymous reviewers for the University of Washington Press. The comments and careful readings of all of these people were invaluable in the development of the book.

Lorri Hagman at the University of Washington Press believed in this book from the start. A superb editor with an eagle eye, she was on hand for advice and suggestions at every stage of the revision and rethinking process, and I count myself lucky to have had her help. Pamela Summa's editorial expertise, critical feedback, and endless questions helped test and develop the content of this book. For her unflagging energy and enthusiasm in our efforts together, and her skilled assistance in turning a rough text into a polished final draft, my thanks are immeasurable.

I apologize for any remaining mistakes in translation and for any disagreements arising from the ideas and theories presented in this book.

Finally, I would like to thank my family: my mother, Nita Stenberg MacGaffney, who had faith in me; and my children—Susan, Karen, Amy, Stephen, Deborah, Jane, and Alan Jr. Without their love and understanding I could not have spent all those years of total absorption in academic study and field research.

Last but not least, I would like to thank my husband, Alan Symonds, with all my love. He took care of the family during my several sojourns in Thailand, and often his long distance calls gave me the reassurance I needed to continue with my work despite frustration and loneliness. His support and love, his confidence and interest in my research, and his insightful, constructive criticism have been this book's (and my) greatest asset.

NOTES ON ORTHOGRAPHY

OF THE HMONG LANGUAGE

THE HMONG HAVE an oft-told tale about the destruction of an ancient written form of their language. They say that once they had a great book, filled with knowledge about life and the cycle of life, death, and rebirth. But this book was eaten by hungry cows and rats (Cooper et al., 1991:42), and their written language was lost. Other stories suggest that books were eaten by Hmong themselves when hungry (Tapp 1989b:122; Geddes 1976:20 [quoted in Tapp]). For many centuries Hmong knowledge was transmitted from one generation to the next in tales told to children around the fire at night, or in the teachings of elders, shamans, and old wives.

Today there are several written forms of Hmong using different scripts (Lemoine 1972a; Tapp 1989b:127–30). Around the end of the nineteenth century, missionary linguists created a written language so that Hmong culture could be preserved and prayers and Bible stories written down. In 1953 Linwood Barney, William Smalley, and Yves Bertrais—three missionaries in Laos—devised a way to use the Romanized Popular Alphabet (RPA) to render a written form of the Hmong language that did not need special accents, symbols, or diacritics. Their method, which has become the standard for linguists in the West, is used in this book. Hmong has many dialects;

I have used White Hmong, that spoken by the people I lived with during my fieldwork.

The Hmong language is tonal and generally monosyllabic. For a non-musical person the tones are very difficult to hear until one has listened extensively. (For example, the word for "dog" [*dev*] is difficult to discern from the word for "water" [*dej*]. For quite some time I was asking for a drink of dog because my tonal value was off.) Most words end with a vowel and then a consonant; the consonant signals the tone. The seven consonants and their tonal values are

b	high level
j	high falling
v	rising
g	breathy
m	glottal constriction/low
s	low
d	similar to an m tone but seldom used

The lack of a consonant at the end of a word signals a mid-tone. A double vowel, such as the *ee* in *neeb* (spirit) or the *oo* in Hmoob (Hmong), signals nasalization of the vowel and an ending of *ng*.

Hmong living in the West have changed the spelling of their names—and the word "Hmong," which is more precisely "Hmoob"—to make them easier for English-speaking people to read and pronounce. For example, the clan name Thoj has become Thao, Vaj has become Vang, Hawj has become Her, and Muas has become Moua. In this book I have kept the original Hmong spelling except in people's names, which follow the personal preference of the bearers of those names, and the word "Hmong."

INTRODUCTION: CONDUCTING
RESEARCH IN A HMONG VILLAGE

FROM JANUARY 1987 to May 1988, I lived in a Hmong community—which I will call Flower Village—in the mountains of northern Thailand, conducting anthropological field research. I especially wanted to discover how Hmong women understand the world, specifically how they perceive childbirth, but initially I did not make much progress. When I asked the women about aspects of Hmong life, they said that I should ask the men.

Four months into my stay, my mother died suddenly, and I went back to the United States for her funeral. On my return to the village, both men and women asked many questions about her death and funeral. They wanted to know how many cows or pigs we had sacrificed for her, and whether we had burned her body, as the Buddhists in the valley did. My answers afforded them a better understanding of what life was like for me "on the other side of the world," where, as the women said, my husband went to sleep as we woke up, and woke up as we were going to bed.

A week after my return from the United States, an old man in the village died. My observation of the consequent complete death ritual—the first I had encountered in Flower Village—impressed upon me the relationship between death and birth, how closely both are related to the spirit world, and the importance of the concept of soul. It also exemplified how culture consists of elements that form an interrelated whole.

For nine days and nights the body of the dead man lay in his house. During this time most of the villagers were in attendance. The father and children from the house where I was living spent much time at the dead man's house, as he was related to them through the mother, but because she was pregnant, the mother did not visit frequently. It is dangerous for pregnant women to spend time at a funeral; the soul of the deceased might find its way into her fetus, trying to be reborn immediately instead of making its journey to the otherworld and then waiting there to be judged and given a mandate for a new life on earth. Although there is a specific shamanic ritual (*faib thiab,* lit., "dividing the fetus") to correct this situation, it is wiser to avoid the necessity of its use.

On the day of the burial, most of the villagers walked up the hill, where a bower of tree branches hid the coffin from malign spirits. Last rituals were performed, and as the afternoon grew late (the most propitious time for a burial), a truck was heard struggling up the hill. As it came into view, we saw that it was filled with men, who were going to accompany the body to its burial place. The coffin was loaded into the back of the truck and tied securely. More men jumped into the truck and onto its sides; they had saved a place for me up front so that I would be more comfortable as the truck bounced uphill to the burial site.

"Don't go," shouted one of the women. "Hmong women don't go to the grave. Don't you go."

Men shouted back, "If you want to learn the Hmong way, you must come with us."

I did want to learn the Hmong way, but I particularly wanted to learn the Hmong *women's* way. At that point it was clear that I had a choice to make, and even though I dearly wanted to go to the gravesite, I elected to stay with the women instead.

The truck rolled off with the coffin and the fathers, brothers, and sons of the women who stood around me. We listened to the men's shouts as the truck ground its way up the hill. We watched in silence, and then turned to walk back down to the village. Nobody spoke, not even the many children who accompanied us. Finally one woman said, "You are thinking of your mother now, aren't you?" As the tears came to my eyes, several women gently touched my back.

After this experience my fieldwork became easier. When I asked the women questions, they no longer suggested that I ask the men, but tried to formulate answers themselves. If I apologized for the question because it might be embarrassing for them, they would answer, "That's all right. You ask because you don't know our ways," which was how they explained the failings of the Akha woman who had married into their village. My status had become closer to that of an "outsider" woman who marries in.

One evening, as I sat with three women outside a house grinding corn for the next day's pig feed, I began asking my companions—all of whom had infants strapped to their backs—about childbearing experiences. After much giggling, one woman wondered out loud why I wanted to know about childbirth. Was I not a wife and mother myself? Had I not experienced childbirth? I explained that there are differences between the ways women in my country give birth and the way Hmong do, and it was these differences I wanted to explore.

They were quiet and embarrassed when I described the hospitalization of women in the United States, and shocked when I explained how women remove their clothing to put on a hospital johnny for exams, and that a male doctor could be present. At one point in the conversation, the husband of one of the women appeared, and everyone fell silent or made movements to leave until he went to attend to a problem up the hill. As soon as he was gone, we continued the conversation where we had left off.

Because I myself had several children, both sons and daughters, I was able to ask questions that might have been difficult for a younger, unmarried woman to pose. Eventually my experience as a mother provided a type of shared intimacy that certainly would have been denied to a man, and also quite possibly to a childless woman. When I first arrived, if the mother and father of the household where I lived went to the valley, they called in a family elder to stay with the children even though I was willing to provide childcare. After they knew and trusted me, they often left me to care for the children alone. The children themselves were not afraid of me, and the youngest girl would sit with her arm around my shoulder in the evening when her father was telling a story. After the baby was born in the house, my own experience with infants proved quite useful. I became the baby's surrogate aunt and was given the job of keeping him quiet while his mother fed the pigs in the evenings.

I do not mean to suggest that all of the women in the village trusted me or let me know when they were ready to give birth. Although I became

FIG. *I.1* Left to right: *The author with a newborn baby, the young daughter from the author's household, and the baby's mother with her two other children. (Photo by Amanda Zafian)*

friendly with many people in the village, some never did trust me, and some simply were not interested in participating in my research. But all the women who gave birth after I had refused to accompany the men to the burial site sent for me either prior to the delivery so that I could "see" *(saib)*, or immediately afterward, when the woman and her mother-in-law would answer my numerous questions. They were always pleased with the baby clothes I had brought as gifts for just such occasions.

Women also sent for me if someone was ill and a special ritual was going to be held, or if one of the women shamans in the village was about to perform a ritual for a sick person; they knew I was interested in these events. I began to feel comfortable in the village, and that I was part of the life of the Hmong, though never completely and fully.

As might have been expected, there was no way to learn about Hmong women's experience of childbirth as something separate from and outside of the rest of their lives. Any study of childbirth requires and affects an under-standing of other major life events in the culture concerned. Anthropolog-ical research has demonstrated that birth must be studied not as an isolated domain, but as a central life-cycle experience occurring within a larger socio-cultural matrix.[1] The birthing experience became the lens through which I tried to perceive the Hmong view of the world, especially the Hmong women's view.

Although there is plenty of literature concerning birth in Southeast Asia,[2] very little of it documents the lives of the mountain dwellers of Thailand. Those who have studied the hill dwellers, such as Paul Durrenberger (1971:227–28) and Otome Klein Hutheesing (1990:94) on the Lisu, Somphob Larchrojna (1975:117–21; 1986) on the Pwo Karen, Cornelia Kammerer (1986:69) and Deborah Tooker (1988:281) on the Akha, and Yoko Hayami (1992:302–5) on the Sqaw Karen, have on occasion considered the subject of birth, but it has not been their primary focus. My review of the litera-ture uncovered scant information directly pertaining to Hmong birthing practices, and even less on Hmong women's perception of childbearing. Hugo Adolf Bernatzik ([1947] 1970:75–79), in his ethnographic comparison of the Akha and Miao (Hmong) in 1936–37, includes a very brief descrip-tion of a birth that is not consistent with my observations.[3] Possibly the dis-crepancies are due to historical change, and possibly he was misinformed; it is not clear whether his study was based on what he had been told or what he had witnessed for himself. Jacques Lemoine (1972c), in an excellent ethnography of the Green Mong in Laos, does not directly address the issue of birth but acknowledges its connection to the ancestors and the concept of reincarnation. He writes that the relationship between parents and chil-dren is important not only because children care for parents in their old age, but also because of "the idea of the reincarnation of the ancestors into the body of the newborn" (1972c:169).

In a footnote to the above quote, Lemoine acknowledges that he is less concerned with birth itself than with its religious representation. Likewise, Guy Morechand (1968:53–94) and Jean Mottin (1979:136) have written about the religious representations of birth only as they pertain to Hmong beliefs about shamanism and reincarnation. In a discussion of cosmology in his insightful study on the influence of development programs in a White Hmong village in northern Thailand, the Hmong anthropologist Gary Yia Lee presents data on funerals and wedding rituals but contends that "little of the Hmong worldview can be gleaned from birth ceremonies" (1981:88). As a Hmong man, Lee may have had little interest in the parts of the birth process that occur prior to the third-day ritual, when birth first becomes an active concern to Hmong men. The male bias in anthropology may also be one of the reasons for the omission of birth from the numerous ethnographic studies on the Hmong.[4]

My study draws on the earlier literature and adds observations from contemporary fieldwork in Thailand, showing how the birth of a child—which is also perceived as an ancestor's return from the land of darkness—is a pivotal event. I found that for the Hmong, becoming a parent gives meaning and value to the lives of both men and women.

WHO ARE THE HMONG? HISTORY, GEOGRAPHY, AND SOCIETY

How do the Hmong fit into broader historical, geographical, and social contexts?[5] The people with whom I worked are a subgroup of the Hmong, or Miao/Yao speaking people, an ethnic minority who have lived on the fringes of powerful states, primarily China, for centuries, but where they originated and much of their subsequent history is something of a mystery.[6] Part of the problem is that the Miao in China did not have a writing system of their own, so scholars have had to rely on Chinese documentary evidence to reconstruct the Hmong or Miao past. The *Shujing* (Book of documents) places the Miao in China in the third century B.C.E.(Ruey Yih-fu 1962, quoted in Schein 2000:38). Although they are documented in the Zhou (1122?–221 B.C.E.) and Qin (221–207 B.C.E.) dynasties, records on them become rare afterwards, with only a few brief mentions in the Tang and Song dynasties (618–1279 C.E.), until they reemerge in official documents in the Yuan (1271–1368) and Ming (1368–1644) dynasties.[7] This has led to confusion as to their whereabouts during the intervening centuries. The Hmong themselves, along with some scholars (Savina 1924:115–19, de Beauclair 1970:10, Mottin 1980a:14, Quincy 1988) postulate that the Miao/Hmong originated in Mongolia, migrating to Siberia and then to China. Others, including linguists (Ratliff n.d.:3), refute some of this and postulate that the Miao/Hmong originated in southern China.

The ethnonym Miao, and subsequently Meo in Laos and Thailand, also has been a source of confusion, and many explanations are given for the name. Yang Dao, a Hmong scholar, has stated that Miao is a Chinese term meaning "barbarian" (1982 :6), but in China there are still many people who are called and who call themselves Miao.[8] In the diaspora following the Vietnam War, Miao/Hmong have migrated to the United States, Australia, French Guyana, Canada, and Europe, and in these countries they call themselves Hmong.

Partly due to persecution, many Hmong moved out of southwestern China into the mountains of Laos, and into Burma (Myanmar) and Vietnam in the seventeenth century, and, in the last hundred years, into the mountains of Siam (Thailand). Although the Thai perceive the Hmong and other mountain dwellers as migrants and minorities within Thailand, for some time there *were* no Thai borders in the mountains; the Thai state was confined to lowland regions, with few links to the hill tribe villages. The Hmong lived in these villages and practiced swidden agriculture, growing dry rice and the opium poppy as well as other crops.

Swidden (slash-and-burn) agriculture was successful in the past, as Hmong had access to sufficient land to allow the soil to lie fallow until its fertility had been restored. Recent changes, such as population growth and cash cropping, have undermined the swidden system. Hmong value large families for practical and cosmological reasons, but more mouths to feed require more land. This factor, along with the takeover of land by development projects, lack of primary forest for cultivation, and the introduction of alternative market crops, has affected the traditional pattern of Hmong livelihood. More recently many Hmong communities have moved to lowland areas. Some have been forced by the government to relocate, some have joined Christian communities, and some of the youth have moved to the valleys to attend schools or universities. Others, unable to subsist by village farming, engage in construction work, cook in restaurants, and participate in other wage labor.

CLAN AND LINEAGE

Patrilineality is the framework of Hmong society, dividing it into various exogamous surname clans whose lineages are united by their traditional beliefs but are otherwise segmentary and geographically widespread (Lee 1981:16). Unlike other people in the area, such as the Kachin (Leach 1954:39–42), Hmong lineages are not ranked, and this can be traced to their cosmology. Bilateral cross-cousin marriage is the preferred or ideal arrangement but is not the rule. Polygyny and levirate, in which a man marries his (older) brother's widow, are also practiced. Clan exogamy (marrying outside of the clan) is the organizing rule for marriage, and clan membership is the basis for all significant social interaction; a married woman derives her identity from her husband's clan, rather than from her natal clan. Marriage creates harmonious new unions between clans and lineages through an intricate system of exchange of women, goods, and social relationships.

The household is the basic economic and ritual unit. Several generations may live in a single household, creating a single production unit. In times of particularly intensive agricultural activity, however, lineage and clan members exchange labor to expedite planting or harvesting. At these times other ethnic groups, such as the Karen, may be hired and paid in rice, money, or opium (Tapp 1986b:19, 30; Cooper 1984:104–7).

Hmong clans *(xeem)* are patrilineal exogamous surname groups whose geographical distribution ranges from China to Southeast Asia and, more recently, as far as Europe, Australia, and the United States. Although clan members cannot trace links genealogically, they presume affiliation through a putative common ancestor. One's clan affiliation is the source of all identification and social interaction, and a Hmong can count on clan members for assistance, especially in times of economic need or when forced to be away from the home and family. Within clans there are subclans, which share specific customary types of behavior, particularly those related to ritual, through which a person maintains his or her distinctive identity. Controversy as to the number of Hmong clans remains, but several researchers have concluded that there are at least twelve (Binney 1971:380).

Clans and subclans are further divided into lineages. A lineage (*ib cuab kwv tij,* lit., "cluster of brothers") is a group of cognates and their spouses who form around an agnatic core (Lee 1981:65). Although clan membership defines a person's Hmong identity, it is within lineages that daily interactions and a sense of identity occur. Lineage mates are able to trace their ancestral spirits back through several generations—usually four—to a known ancestor. Lineage members do not necessarily live in the same household, but they usually live in close proximity because they honor the ancestral spirits as a group. Rituals are organized and presided over by the lineage head, who is the oldest male, usually the father or grandfather. Gary Yia Lee, who studied White Hmong, also calls the lineage "one ceremonial household" since it is within this household that specific mortuary rituals take place and into which a member ideally is reborn (Lee 1981:65). One's lineage and clan define proper behavior—who helps whom in times of need and, most important, whom one can and cannot marry. All material goods, privileges, and mutual obligations are transferred from one male to another along these household, lineage, and clan lines.

The largest political unit is the village. In the village where I stayed there was a headman (Thai: *phuujajbaan*), whose main responsibility was to mediate between the Hmong villagers and the Thai officials in the valley. As a rule, there are no villagewide political meetings except to discuss this mediation. The headman's position was imposed by the Thai, who want to deal with one "top" person in a village.

The Hmong run their villages through the heads of each clan, who is usually the oldest man in the clan. The clan heads mediate between clans when necessary. These were the men I spoke with in each village for help with the HIV/AIDS education project (see Epilogue).

DIVISION OF LABOR

The Hmong division of labor mirrors its gender divisions, with designated tasks for women and men, and a few overlapping areas, such as harvesting rice, in which both sexes participate. Women are responsible for the household or domestic work, which includes cleaning, childcare, feeding pigs and other animals, food preparation and cooking, and many other similar duties. Women make cloth, sew, and embroider clothing, whereas men make baskets and work silver for jewelry and iron for tools. Men are allowed to hunt and kill animals, but women kill only chickens.

The gender-specific division of labor extends to rituals; women are excluded from the most sacred and highly valued aspects of rituals concerning the patriline. Men sacrifice animals to the ancestors, and even prepare and cook these animals. Although women can and do become shamans, they are not allowed to participate in rituals concerning the patriline; for example, they cannot call in the souls of newborns or guide the dead back to the otherworld. Women cannot "feed" the ancestors at the New Year or visit gravesites.

There are traditional divisions of labor in agricultural work as well. Only men clear the large trees to ready a field for planting, because men are considered to be physically stronger than women (Cooper 1986:177), although men and women both work at slashing and burning the fields. When rice is planted, men break the earth with a dibble stick, and women drop in the seeds. Women do most of the weeding, but both men and women harvest the rice. Sometimes men as well as women harvest the poppy, but in many villages I visited it was the women who did the backbreaking work of scoring thousands of pods and then scraping the sap off into petals for medicinal purposes, for their own use, or for sale to outsiders.

HMONG AND THE POPPY

In about the eighth century c.e. the opium poppy *(Papaver somniferum)* was first introduced into China by Arab traders. For centuries thereafter it was used primarily for medicinal purposes (Grandstaff 1979:170–79, Kammerer 1989, Tapp 1986b:19–20). In the eighteenth century the British East India Company, seeking goods to exchange with the Chinese for tea, silk, and other desirable imports, began to use opium as a barter currency. This led to the abusive use of opium on a large scale in China. Despite attempts by the Chinese government to forbid its importation, the British—for reasons of trade, and with tremendous violence—forced its acceptance. In response, the Chinese legalized the importation, cultivation, and production of the opium poppy in 1858 and imposed taxes. Eventually, Chinese poppy cultivation exceeded imports; around 1883 Hmong in China began to grow the poppy as their principle cash crop (Tapp 1986b:20) and continued to do so when they migrated to the highland areas of Southeast Asia (Grandstaff 1979:171–73, Tapp 1988:230–40). In British Burma and French Laos, colonial governments imported opium from China and India and discouraged internal growth, thereby contributing to a brisk black market in the hills as poppy cultivation continued (McCoy 1990:4–5, Tapp 1986b:20, Kammerer 1989). French taxation led to Hmong revolts, and opium production again increased (Lee 1987a). During the Vietnam war, when the Hmong were used by the United States as a "secret army" in Laos, the opium trade was endorsed by the West (Tapp 1988:230–40).

In Thailand opium was legally imported until around 1947, when the Thai government sanctioned its production in the northern highlands (Tapp

1988:233) and criminalized importation. Production did not increase notably until the end of the Second World War, and even then, less was produced in Thailand than in Laos and Burma, the other countries in the Golden Triangle. In 1949 the new Communist government attempted to put an end to opium cultivation and trade in China. Many Hmong crossed the southern borders of China into Laos, Burma, and eventually Thailand, to continue poppy cultivation and to evade Communist control (Cohen 1984:150–65). The opium poppy crop became the mainstay of the Hmong economy in Thailand and remained so although the Thai government, succumbing to external pressure, made it illegal in 1958.

In 1953 the Thai government established the Border Patrol Police (BPP) to maintain security in remote mountainous border regions. The BPP was also involved in setting up the first schools in hill tribe villages to teach the Thai language to young people. Then in 1959 the government established the National Hill Tribes Welfare Committee to help Hmong and other hill tribes change their agricultural lifestyles from slash-and-burn to sedentary cultivation, and to promote crop substitution in order to eliminate the opium poppy (Tapp 1986b:33, Lee 1987a). In 1971 a joint program in the hills established the United Nations Programme for Drug Abuse Control (UNPDAC) in Thailand. Although UNPDAC has been responsible for educational programs, road building, and health care of tribal people, its primary goal has been crop replacement—that is, the eradication of the poppy crop (McCoy 1990:412–13). The United States has invested heavily in this kind of program, and much of the funding has gone to the Thai military. What began as a means of ensuring security on the borders has continued as drug eradication and rehabilitation programs.

CHOOSING A FIELDWORK SITE

The Hmong I worked with in Rhode Island were refugees from Laos, so I wished to study Laotian Hmong, but the border of Laos had been closed to researchers by the Communist government that took power in 1975. Within the last hundred years Hmong have migrated into the northern mountainous region of Thailand, and Thai and Lao Hmong are closely related geographically, culturally, and genetically (Kunstadter 1983:15–45), but the differences between the two populations are significant. The trauma due to the loss of family members on both the Communist and U.S. sides of the "secret war" in Laos, forced migration, and refugee status has had serious effects on the lives of Laotian Hmong (see, e.g., Tapp 1986b:44, Radley 1986:65). In 1975, when Saigon fell, Communist forces overtook Cambodia and Laos, forcing thousands, including Hmong who had fought on the U.S. side, to flee to neighboring countries for safety. Many Laotian Hmong were placed in refugee camps, and eventually some were relocated to the United States.

As a minority group in Thailand, Hmong also have been exposed to economic and social pressures. Hmong are one example of a group who have been stereotyped as subversive, mainly because of their involvement on both sides of the "secret war." Some Hmong took the side of the Communist Party in Laos, and a few hundred joined the Communist Party in Thailand as well. During the late 1960s and early 1970s, the Thai army led an anti-Communist campaign in the hills, in what became known as the Red Meo War. Villages were napalmed and entire Hmong villages were moved out of the mountains and into valley resettlement areas. As Robert Hearn has shown, the extent of the Thai army's response to a few tribal insurgents was unnecessary; the real problem was not insurgents, but Hmong wrath at the attempts by Thai police to extort taxes on opium (Hearn 1974:39–44, 84–85). This led to a Hmong revolt, in turn triggering increased Thai repression.

In spite of their differences, I concluded that the cultural and environmental backgrounds of the Hmong populations in Laos and Thailand were similar enough in recent history to justify conducting my field research in Thailand. Also, the Hmong had resisted assimilation and held onto their own worldview over centuries of migration (see Fadiman 1997:13). I hoped that the traditional Hmong way of life would be more or less intact in Thailand.[9]

In Thailand there are two distinct groups of Hmong, who speak different dialects; they call themselves Green Mong (Mong Ntsuab) and White Hmong (Hmong Dawb), and although there are other groups of Hmong in Thailand, these two are the most numerous. The difference in dialects accounts for the difference in spelling, as the Green Mong do not pronounce the slightly aspirated *h* of the White Hmong.[10] These two groups have different customs and language; the White Hmong are so called because their women formerly wore white skirts, whereas the Green Mong women wore batiked skirts. I use the terms "Green" and "White" to distinguish between them. The reader should be aware that other authors frequently use the Chinese term Miao or the Thai term Meo[11] for all the Hmong groups, but some Hmong consider the terms derogatory, and I use these terms only in reference to the wider linguistic group of people. The Tribal Research Institute in Chiang Mai estimates the combined population of Green and White Hmong in Thailand to be 122,768, living in 235 villages (March 2000).

In August 1986 I received permission from the National Research Council of Thailand to spend fourteen months conducting research with the Hmong.[12] I traveled to many Hmong communities in northern Thailand before settling on the village I have given the pseudonym Flower Village. The people in Flower Village are White Hmong.

I chose Flower Village for several reasons. First, I wanted to do research in a "traditional" village that had not been affected much by outside influences such as tourism and resettlement programs. Flower Village was approximately twenty kilometers from the main road, and high up in the mountains. The road to the village was unpaved and in the rainy season difficult to negotiate on foot or by vehicle. Other than Thai teachers, official visitors, and traders, few outsiders visited. There were, however, several pickup trucks in the village, and the men made frequent trips to the valley to sell cash crops such as tomatoes and cabbages. As a result, I was able to go with them every month or so and meet with colleagues, telephone my family in the United States, and mail letters.

The size of the village was another factor in my decision. Flower Village was fairly large, consisting of fifty-eight households when I began my stay; by the time I left fourteen months later, there were sixty-four households and a total population of 487 (a small village can have as few as ten households). Yet Flower Village was small enough that I could interact with most of the inhabitants.

When I first visited the village, a funeral was in progress, and the people invited me (and the three people who had accompanied me) to visit the house where the ceremony was taking place and partake of the feast afterwards. The people in Flower Village were friendly; in other villages, people had not even emerged from their houses when I arrived. The fact that there were several pregnant women in the village also induced me to remain. Following an initial visit with the headman's oldest son, I met with the headman himself and with other family members, discussed my research goals with them, and obtained permission to stay

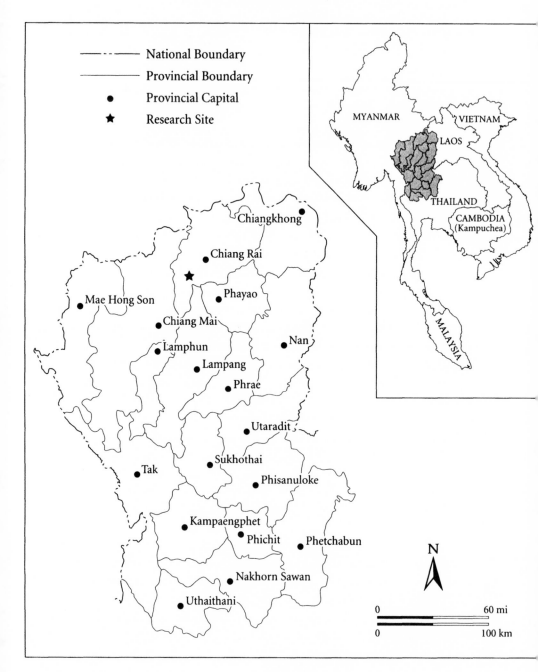

MAP 1. Northern Thailand

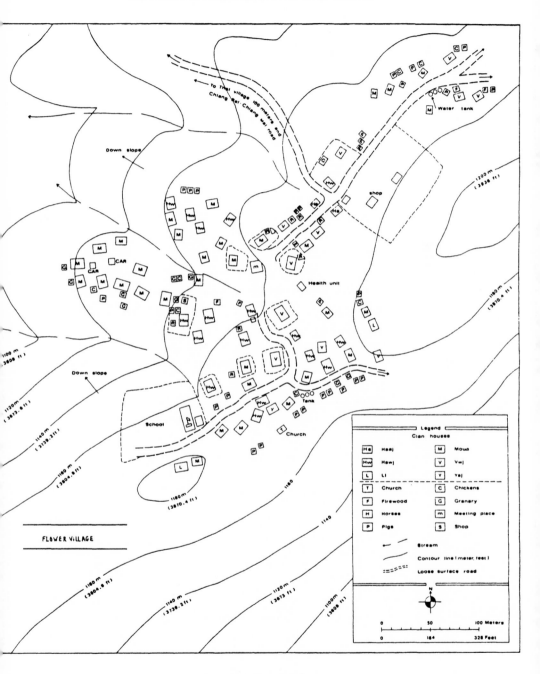

MAP 2. Flower Village

The next step was to hire a research assistant. This task presented unexpected difficulties. Although my language training at the Southeast Asian Studies Summer Institute had given me an adequate understanding of the phonology and structure of the language, my vocabulary was somewhat limited.[13] In view of the fact that I was to study women and birth, I had hoped to locate a female assistant to help with translation and continue my language training, but no Hmong women were available for the position. Concerned that the presence of a male assistant might impede the progress of my study of women, I reluctantly decided to work without an assistant.

My acquisition of language in Thailand was, I believe, hindered less by reticence on the part of the local people to teach—a problem reported by Otome Hutheesing in her ethnography of the Lisu (1990:18)—than by lack of time. Most people worked continually and did not have the time to stop, speak slowly in response to my myriad questions, and then repeat their answers until I understood them. I often stayed at home with older women and children, and I was able to enlist their help with the language. Children were particularly patient and helpful in the beginning, and eventually I was able to make myself understood and to increase my vocabulary. All of my data were collected in Hmong. In the beginning, when I could not understand many of the answers to questions I asked, I obtained the speakers' permission to tape their answers and stories. Later, when I was more proficient in the language, I translated the tapes. Although I learned to understand much of the daily conversation, my speech was never completely fluent. The villagers patiently listened to my accented Hmong and gently corrected my errors—and sometimes laughed at them. I did not understand until my last day there that I had been using the word "vagina" for "rice," asking them how many vaginas they planted.

FLOWER VILLAGE

Flower Village sits at the top of a mountain ridge, four thousand feet above sea level. Until 1984, when a new, unpaved road was built off the main road from Chiang Mai, the village was accessible by car only during the dry season. During the rainy season, from May to November, people had to walk there. Even on the new road, cars need chains on their tires to make the trip on particularly wet and muddy days.

Boarding the truck at the valley stop and riding up the mountain to Flower Village, one passes the Northern Thai, or Khonmuang, rice fields, where water buffalo stand knee deep in the mud when the fields are flooded. As the truck climbs into the hills, the soil becomes looser and thinner, and the rice fields give way to sloping swidden fields. Depending on the time of year, the fields are charred and ready for planting, or burgeoning with dry rice, maize, and vegetables. Small cross-signs *(muas phua)* of freshly cut tree branches are set in the fields as a sign of ownership; land is held in usufruct and must be marked. Many of the fields contain small field houses *(tsev teb)* where people can rest, shaded from the hot sun. During busy seasons, such as planting or harvesting, people sleep in the field houses, sometimes for weeks at a time, rather than taking the time to walk back and forth to the village. Swiddens may be as close as a half hour walk from the village, or several hours hiking distance by way of difficult slopes. Several families in Flower Village now have Toyota pickup trucks, and these travel to and from the fields filled to capacity, with people hanging off the trucks' sides.

In the cool season (December to February), the multicolored poppy fields bloom on limestone outcroppings. There are also large fields of cabbages and tomatoes, part of the government's alternative crop-growing program initiated to replace the opium poppies. Women walk to the swiddens with baskets on their backs, carrying food and tools for working the fields. When they return in the evenings, the baskets are filled with the large green leaves or pieces of the banana tree for feeding the pigs.

Individual paths, which people take to their own family swiddens, criss-cross the main tracks. The main paths are dotted with the small paper bridges and bamboo markers that serve as protection from the wild spirits of the forest.

As the road climbs higher, the valley recedes into a checkerboard of fields; the road is lined by groves of bamboo and other trees. Wild orchids peek out from the midst of the foliage, and brightly colored birds fill the air with their songs. At the crest of the ridge, Flower Village comes into view—the roofs of the wood and bamboo houses, thatched with grass or roofed in tin, a curl of smoke from the cookfires, and the crowns of the trees that surround the village.

At the top of the slope is a small store; to its left a small building houses the government Agricultural Agency. The entrance to the village itself is an extension of the roadway. A little further up the hill, off to the left, are eight

Hmong houses, and to the right another fifty-six. The village, in a forest clearing, lacks the village gates usually built by the neighboring Akha (Kammerer 1986:33, Tooker 1988:50). Hmong houses are built on the ground, not on the stilts used by the Akha or Karen. The houses at first appear haphazardly placed—none are in rows, nor are doors facing each other—but in fact they all conform to the rules of geomancy (Lee 1981:88, Lemoine 1972c:99–113, Tapp 1989b:87–95). They are built on the upward slope, with fronts facing downslope. Close to each house, small rice- and corn-storage barns are raised on stilts to prevent damage from pests. Sometimes rice is stored in sacks next to the house because there is nowhere else to put it, and one can hear rats scampering around the bags. In the evening, at various spots around the village, women and children take turns grinding corn to feed the pigs the following day.

A well-constructed modern school sits at the bottom of a small hill in the village. The school, with a Thai headmaster and Thai teachers, represents part of the government's effort to educate Hmong and other highland minority children to speak the Thai language so that they can be more easily assimilated; the new road was built at the same time as the school. Attached to the schoolhouse is housing for the young Thai teachers, who usually spend several nights a week in the village during the school year, as it is so difficult, particularly in the rainy season, to travel up and down the mountain. To ensure that such remote schools are staffed, young teachers must work in the hills before they are eligible for the more desirable teaching positions in the valley.

The village also has a small Protestant church, which ten of the sixty-four families attend, and a small clinic where a young Hmong man who was educated in the valley dispenses medicine.

Dry rice is the most important domestic crop, but many other crops are grown as well. The villagers practice what Chupinit Kesmanee (1989:80–84) terms a "mixed cropping" system: many kinds of plants are grown simultaneously in one field. Hmong men and women are extremely knowledgeable in this aspect of agriculture and know, for example, which varieties of squash or pumpkin will grow in the corn field and the precise time that each variety should be planted to reap the greatest harvest from that crop. Women, who choose and preserve the seeds after the harvest, know which are of the best quality and should be saved to plant the following year.

Of the several varieties of corn, one is used for eating; another is dried, ground, and fed to animals; and the cobs are dried and used as kindling. The corn for human consumption is not grown in great quantities, as it is not a staple food—a meal is announced with the expression "Come and eat rice" rather than "Come and eat dinner." When corn is first ripe, children eat it for a snack between meals.

Other crops include soybeans, vegetables, and fiber plants such as hemp for making clothing. Medicinal herbs are dug up in the forest, replanted, and grown in small household plots. Most people know which plants are useful for everyday herbal medicines, but there are several exceptionally knowledgeable women in the village who are paid for their expertise.

Although the opium poppy is still grown in Flower Village, the efforts of the Thai government to eradicate the crop have succeeded to the extent that its cultivation and use is no longer openly acknowledged and none of my informants were eager to discuss the subject. However, opium has been the medicine of choice for certain conditions, such as toothache and menstrual cramps, and the sap from the purple poppy flowers in particular remains an invaluable part of the folk pharmacopoeia (Lemoine 1972c:66–69, 90–93). For example, a young mother I know of who suffered a gall bladder attack in the middle of the night ingested a small amount of opium for the pain. Although opium is not generally used to treat the pain of childbirth, I was told that it is sometimes used for postpartum abdominal or breast pain.

In addition to the limited use of opium for medicinal purposes, there were thirty-eight opium addicts in Flower Village, or 7.8 percent of the population. Most of them (89 percent) were male. All of the eleven female addicts were married to men who were addicts. The fact that, with the exception of four males, the addicts were at least forty years old perhaps is due to the moral strictures sometimes placed upon frequent opium use by young children (Westermeyer 1982:72).

Unlike the cooperation one observes between families and clans when the important rice crop is harvested, the poppy harvest is a nuclear family affair, and, in some cases, a personal one. One elderly, widowed opium addict was an example of the latter. Her son and his family provided her with rice and other food, but she kept her own small poppy plot, which she tended and harvested herself.

To harvest the poppy, women use a special knife to score each pod several times and then leave the pods overnight so that the white sap can be exuded. Men often stay in the field to guard the crop against thieves at night. In the morning, the sap is scraped off the poppy and folded into the petals of the flower. It is then taken home and either processed by the men of the house or sold "raw" (unprocessed) to traders who either come to the village or are met in the city.

Many market crops are now beginning to replace the opium poppy, although it continues to be an important cash crop for some families. The cultivation of the principal substitute crops, cabbage and tomatoes, is also labor intensive, and it takes many loads of these vegetables to equal the price of a *joi* (1.6 kg) of opium. Each day, trucks travel down the mountains to Chiang Rai or to nearby Wiang Pa Pao loaded with the harvest from Flower Village.

All of these crops—rice, corn, vegetables, and poppy—are labor intensive, but it was my observation that women do more fieldwork than men. Men clear the land and burn the trees and bushes; women and children weed all the crops, especially rice, several times during the growing season. Women are also the main harvesters of opium, which is backbreaking work that must be done quickly and efficiently at the precise time that the crop is ready for harvest (Cooper et al. 1996:36–37).

I also noticed that families and clans share labor, and that men assist more in harvesting alternative crops, which they trade in the valley. Several of these crops are rotated around the year so that there is constant harvesting. Men are absent from the village more frequently than they used to be, due to the idiosyncrasies of the valley marketplace and because the village is becoming more dependent on the marketplace.

Although I observed women from Flower Village selling their embroidery work only to the occasional visiting trader, in other villages women sold both embroidery and vegetables to tourists and were able to make their own money. Women from an especially large village in Chiang Mai travel to the valley on a daily basis to sit in stalls and sell their embroidered products (E. Cohen 1989:69–82), another instance of increased dependence on the valley market.

Work in Flower Village is tied to the agricultural calendar; specific tasks such as planting or weeding change with the season.[14] Pesticides, rodent poisons, and fertilizer are used on the fields. Many people now wear protective masks, but I witnessed some who suffered from breathing problems and nausea due to the adverse effects of such chemicals.

In addition to farming, the Hmong in Flower Village raise pigs, ducks, chickens, and dogs; the latter are not eaten, as they are among the Akha (Maneeprasert 1989:152–58), but dogs are sacrificed and eaten ritually. Pigs are usually allowed to roam around the village, but particularly large ones are penned inside wooden fences. At one time cows were also kept in Flower Village, but this practice was discontinued after some of them escaped their enclosure and destroyed part of the rice crop. Now cows are purchased in the valley as needed for ritual purposes.

METHODOLOGY

My primary methods for gathering data were participant observation, formal and informal interviews, and a village survey. For the first several months, I observed household activities and daily interactions of family members and visitors. I watched to see who rose first in the morning to begin the work day, who did the housework, and who tended the children. But my most pressing concern was to develop a good relationship with my informants, especially the women, and to discover who was pregnant and how I could participate in or acquire more information about the birthing process.

As villagers grew accustomed to my presence, two to three months into my stay, I was permitted to accompany people to the fields and eventually to observe rituals. I tried to remain conscious of and to monitor my personal responses to the particular setting, whether it was a sacred ritual or a daily chore. Following the eloquent advice of Robert Jay, I was also careful not to let my self-consciousness interfere with my relationship to informants:

> The field investigating friendship requires relationship to your subjects as persons, and that must also include yourself as a person. For if you objectify your interacting self, setting it "over there," apart from your observational self, and relate to that part of you as an object (an operation often done in the name of participant observation), you will severely limit your ability to gain personal knowledge from your subjects. They will not be fooled and will keep their distance accordingly. (1969:372)

As I mentioned earlier, it took a few months for me to develop a degree of closeness and intimacy with the village women, and my refusal to go with the men to a burial helped me to earn the women's trust. Also, when they learned that I was a grandmother, it became easier for them to treat me as a mother, a grandmother, a sister, and a friend. They began to call me Niam Phiaj, or Mother Pat, a term of address for an older woman. The mother in the household in which I lived, on the other hand, was considerably younger than I, but she was always in the position of "Mother" to me, the term I used to address her once I learned that this was appropriate. She taught me how to behave in the household, outlining my role by showing me, for example, where and how to wash my clothes, where to bathe, and when to come in for dinner. When I asked "What can I do to help?" she sometimes asked me to hold the baby or sweep the floor, but if I asked permission to participate in some of the household chores, such as grinding corn for the pigs or washing dishes, I was told that I was welcome to carry out the task, but that it would not under any circumstances become "my chore." When I questioned her about this, she said, "Someday you will leave us. If we rely on you to do work, who will do it when you are not here? The children must know what needs to be done every day, and it will still need to be done after you are gone."

Guests are few, and their presence is considered temporary. The concepts of "temporary" and "permanent" have great significance in terms of one's position in the lineage; for example, women are considered temporary within the household and therefore are less integral members of their family of origin because of the practice of marrying outside the clan. My membership in the family I lived with was not determined by the extent of my participation in the labor force; I ate with them and I slept in their house, but everyone knew that it was a temporary, observing type of relationship. At the same time, the importance of my allegiance to them was strongly emphasized at all times. I became friendly with other families and individuals, and this did not appear to pose a problem, but I was given to understand that giving gifts to others was inappropriate because it meant that fewer gifts were then available for the family I lived with. Members of the family would say, "The children said you gave so-and-so a gift. Why did you give a gift to them? You don't live with them."

Children from the family I stayed with often accompanied me and reported back about what had transpired in my visits to other houses in the village. Gossiping is unacceptable in Hmong society, and I had to take considerable care not to transgress this rule. Women do not gossip with women outside their own family. If I repeated something I had heard in "my" household, it was considered a breach of manners.

In another household, that of the Hawj family, I became friendly with the young teenage daughter, which eventually led to an intimate relationship with the entire family, a large intergenerational group with whom I shared meals and conversation. Unlike the family I lived with, the Hawj family was extended: grandparents, parents, unmarried grown children, and grown children with families of their own, as well as two granddaughters (the children of a deceased son whose wife had remarried) all lived together under the same roof. I was able to observe how the Hawj family lived and was afforded an excellent opportunity to view women's daily interactions with one another (and with men) within a single household.

Women in the Hawj family also made clothing for me to wear. Clothing is of crucial importance as regards gender, and this gift of clothing allowed me to appear to have specific Hmong "feminine" characteristics for the first time. Whenever I wore Hmong clothing, the Hawj women insisted that I wear *sev* (modesty aprons) they had embroidered for me. If I wore Hmong clothing and went outside without *sev*, other women were shocked and told me quickly to go inside and put them on. They would not talk with me or answer my questions until I had done so. If I wore Western clothing, as I did occasionally, no one advised me how to dress. Western clothes marked me as a non-Hmong woman and therefore not subject to the same rules. There was a flexibility to my role as a Westerner and an outsider, and in that role I was allowed some leeway as a woman.

After a time, having gained the trust of some of the villagers, I engaged in many informal discussions with both women and men about the birthing process. My topic was a difficult one, first because birth was not discussed frequently. The Hmong place a high value on "shyness" or modesty in such matters. Second, many women were puzzled that I asked questions about childbirth at all, in light of the fact that I had children of my own. Many mothers were reluctant to talk about their experiences, and women who had not yet given birth did not seem to know what to expect. The actual experience of birthing was a private affair, and young people usually were not allowed to attend a birth; therefore they were uninformed about what the process entailed. Sexuality was also a private matter and not a suitable topic for discussion, although Hmong children learn about sexual activity and birth through sexual joking and riddles, as well as by observing animals. There were many animals around the village, and I saw children watching as a pig gave birth to a litter. But sexual love was discussed only in formal song, in a flowery, metaphorical language used just for that purpose.

The specific meanings of formal rituals—such as funerals, shamanic performances, and weddings—could be discussed only at the appropriate times, usually during or just after the ritual. Therefore a researcher had to be ready to attend such rituals at any hour of the day or night. If I wished to question a shaman on illness or cosmology, it was important that I do so immediately after a session because later, shamans often would not understand what I was referring to or simply could not think in my terms. Although many Hmong recount myths and stories, shamans are usually the most knowledgeable about these subjects. They also enjoy sharing their oral history with one another and with visitors, so they are a ready and valuable source of information. I was also able to gather information in the evenings when the father in my household, and occasionally the mother, told stories to the children.

I found that the presence of a tape recorder influenced how people spoke or presented their material. Often they would say, "It must be done the right way for Phiaj [my Hmong name]," or they would insert instructions addressed to me so that I could remember later how or why a particular action was performed, such as, "Now one level is finished. Here one step is completed." After a few months they became less conscious of me and the tape recorder, but interpretations were still often given in the form of asides by the ritual specialist and sometimes by members of the audience. (Most of these comments are not included in the texts of rituals provided in this volume.)

I transcribed some of the chants in the village with the help of young people, who corrected my mistakes. I was forbidden by the father in my house to play any funeral tapes inside the house, and he told me it was inappropriate to play them anywhere else. The death chant, "Showing the Way," which uses sacred language, was a difficult tape to translate, especially for a nonfluent speaker of Hmong. I eventually found a young Hmong scholar in Providence who did a great deal of the work. It was checked by a knowledgeable Hmong man and his son, who were my principal informants in America. Due to the inappropriateness of discussing this chant in the home, we went to a local park to complete the translation.

In my presentation of the chants, I have taken liberties with the punctuation. Hmong do not use punctuation in either transcriptions or translations; the English texts presented here thus include line divisions and punctuation not present in the Hmong originals. As Dennis Tedlock states,

> We may determine the punctuation of our text by the deciphering eye, which will seek patterns of syntax, but if we listen again we may discover that the "commas" and periods" and "question marks" of the speaking voice, as signaled by pitch contours and stresses, may not obey rules worked out by the deciphering eye. (1983:7)

I also follow the style of Tedlock (1983), Dwight Conquergood (1989), and Kenneth White (1983:7–40) in that I present the texts as ethnopoetry, in an effort to preserve the "hallmarks of orality: rhythmic repetitions and formulaic language" (Conquergood 1989:ix).

In addition to ritual chants, I collected numerous songs, stories, and myths from the Hmong in Flower Village and their visitors during the New Year celebrations. An itinerant, elderly Hmong man who occasionally came to the village to sell medicine and tell stories to the villagers also provided me with information. I made many videotapes and audiotapes of weddings, funerals, and shamanic rituals. Since my return from Thailand, I have used the videos to share and refine my ideas and observations with Hmong friends in the United States.

In addition to participant observation and informal open-ended interviews, I developed a formal interview schedule and visited each of the sixty-four houses in the village, interviewing the women of childbearing age in every household. I conducted these interviews just before I left the village, since I knew the women well by this time and they were more at ease with my questions than they would have been earlier. I used the questionnaire data to create the tables provided here.

Whenever possible in these pages, Hmong women speak for themselves, through statements recorded on site in Flower Village. Where recording was not possible, I took detailed notes and later transcribed them. Pseudonyms are used throughout except where noted.

THE AMBIGUITIES OF MY ROLE

As in any field situation, it was difficult and at times frustrating to learn Hmong ways. Soon after arriving I learned that most visitors to the village were male. The category "male" was so closely linked to the category "visitor" that I was therefore treated as a man. Usually the Thai authorities who came to Flower Village were men who were interested in obtaining information about the political realm, which was the domain primarily discussed between Thai and Hmong men. These discussions always took place in Thai, a language many Hmong women only partially understood, although they were beginning to learn Thai in the marketplace. (Hmong men have known Thai for some time, through travel and trading.) The political discourse between Thai officials and Hmong men is not one in which women share—at least not overtly, although they may participate afterward, in discussions with the men in their family. Since I was viewed as an outsider, the "other" who had come to learn about Hmong ways, both men and women assumed that I was interested in learning about what they collectively understood to be the most important part of Hmongness—male knowledge. It should be noted that I was considered unwomanly by both women and men, something that I discovered only over time. Hmong women considered me a visitor (a male category), and Hmong men did not consider me a Hmong woman; therefore both men and women treated me as a man.

Being treated as a man meant that I was privy to male-oriented knowledge and behavior, but, unfortunately, it also meant being excluded for the first few months from the world of women's knowledge. (See Edward Ardner 1975:1–19 on the male bias of anthropologists and informants, and on woman as a "muted category.") But I was interested in women's role in Hmong society, especially their experiences of birth.

In Hmong villages, women cook, feed the men and children, and then eat what is left; this is also the norm when visitors are present and after animals are sacrificed. I was always invited to eat with the men. Men eat first because they are members of the patriline, and, since many animals are sacrificed to their ancestral spirits, men must eat first. Men drink rice liquor at all rituals, but women do not, and I was always offered rice liquor. If I asked the women questions, they would always politely reply, "Ask my father" or "Ask my husband. He knows the answer," which is the proper way for a Hmong woman to answer a male visitor or a man she does not know well.

At first I ate with the men. Thinking it was impolite to refuse, I drank their liquor. I began to address my questions only to fathers and husbands as the women had requested, not realizing that women are socialized, and socialize their children, to think that men are smarter than women. Although I received important information from these men, I continued to be frustrated by the fact that Hmong women would not talk to me about childbirth, a subject in which I was extremely interested, although they would talk to me about other things, asking me questions such as "Where is your husband?" and "Where are your children?" During those early months, when a baby was born in the village, I was invited to visit only a few days after the birth, when I would, as is the custom, take the baby a gift (baby clothes) or bring some food (eggs) for the mother to eat. Women do not share the knowledge that they are pregnant with men outside the household. Since I was considered both a male and an outsider, women were not interested in sharing information with me about pregnancy or birth. The mother of the family in whose house I lived was at the end of the second trimester of her pregnancy before I became aware of her condition, and then only because her teenage daughter told me in a whisper as we were returning home one evening from grinding corn for the pig feed.

After living in the village for approximately three months, I began to accompany the women to the fields. Sometimes their husbands accompanied us, but often we went alone. The women in Flower Village routinely performed backbreaking work such as weeding and hoeing because weeding is considered women's work and usually was not done by men. When I attempted to participate, they would laugh, saying I was "too soft" or didn't have enough "strength" (zog). As a fifty-five-year old woman, I was elderly by their standards , and elderly women usually do not do fieldwork. For the same reason, they would not allow me to carry baskets back from the fields filled with firewood or vegetables for pig feed, and they laughed at the sight of me carrying buckets of water up the hill from the communal water tap.

As well as fieldwork, the women do needlework. They take pride in and achieve status by doing "flower cloth" (paj ntaub). This skill is taught to very young girls, as young as two or three, usually by their mothers or sisters. It was not unusual to see small girls sitting with their legs outstretched in front of them, embroidering small pieces of black cloth with bright silk thread. As girls mature, they begin to make clothing for themselves and sometimes for other members of their families. Women always carry pieces of needlework tucked inside their belts so that they can work on a piece in their spare time. If there is any extra time after they have eaten their lunch in the fields, young girls often sit together sewing, keeping their hands clean by wiping them with a damp cloth.

Once the harvest was brought in and there was leisure time, girls and women all over the village sat on tiny stools outside of their houses, making clothing for the New Year's celebration. Although girls sometimes were allowed to keep their needlework under their platform beds, mothers usually stored their daughters' needlework in boxes under their own sleeping platforms. A girl's needlework is considered her parents' property because they give her the time to do the sewing; some of the embroidered skirts, shirts, belts, and bags will come back to her when she marries, as part of the "things that go with women at marriage." Women also make finely embroidered burial clothing for themselves, their husbands, and their mothers- and fathers-in-law.

Since I myself do needlework, many Hmong women were interested in the needlepoint I had brought with me. They quickly learned the stitches I used and would often take the piece I was working on and do it themselves. I seemed to receive their respect for the work I was capable of doing (they praised my work to me), but I caused much amusement when I asked them to teach me Hmong-style embroidery, which is much more complicated.

They began by teaching me on the pocket of a jacket they made as a gift for my husband, who was expected to visit the village soon. It was painstaking work, and often I did it incorrectly. The women would laugh and someone would gently take the pocket from me, take out my work and redo it, often changing a color or adding a few creative swirls. They praised my diligence, just as they would a young Hmong girl who was learning to sew, and bestowed upon me the ultimate compliment: "You are becoming like a Hmong woman." When the pocket was finished, three of my women friends gave me three other pockets to complete the shirt's decoration. The jacket was shown to many people as my own effort, and the women were genuinely pleased. It was another turning point in my relationship with the women of Flower Village, when they saw me as a friend/woman rather than a visitor/man.

REFLECTIONS ON FIELD RESEARCH

Entering a village to carry out anthropological research means entering another world; the meanings people attach to their actions are not easily understood by an outsider who has not shared in the everyday language and ongoing life of the community. In a different way, Hmong women themselves experience "outsider" status.

The Hmong practice clan exogamy, and since patrilocality is the residence pattern, women often marry out of their natal village. In the past most villages were small, with only one clan living there; now some villages are larger, with many clans. Flower Village was home to seven different clans, so some girls were able to marry within their natal village, but they still needed to learn the way of a new household. Perhaps that is why Hmong women seem so tolerant of those who do not behave according to their way.

In Flower Village, there was an Akha woman married to a Hmong man. The Akha live in close proximity to the Hmong, although their language is Tibeto-Burman in origin and their ethnic self-definitions are constituted in different ways than those of the Hmong (Kammerer 1986:6). The Akha woman had lived in the village for three years and spoke fluent Hmong at the time I arrived, but she was still in the process of learning the Hmong woman's ways. She worked in the fields as Hmong women do, carrying her small son on her back. She had learned as a girl to weave and sew the patterns on clothing that signify that one is Akha; she was learning the Hmong style of embroidery. She wore Hmong clothing that she had made herself, and she cooked rice as Hmong women cook their rice. When a group of women and I were discussing childbirth customs, however, they said that the Akha woman had cried out as she gave birth to her young son but that this was appropriate since she was not a Hmong woman. In other words, although it was understood that she was learning Hmong ways, if and when she erred, it was tolerated because she had not shared the lived experience of a Hmong woman from birth. As one woman explained it,

> Hmong women are shy. We do not speak out in front of others. That does not mean that we do not know things or we cannot do things, but it means we know how to behave as good Hmong women. It is that we do not show how we feel. We do not show pain, or emotion. We do not cry when we are hurt. We do not cry out when we birth babies even though our backs and

our stomachs hurt a lot. If the Akha woman cries out, we do not think she is bad or stupid. We just think her mother did not teach her the way to behave as we Hmong.

This observation points out in their own words what it means to be a Hmong woman, at least in part. It also illustrates the bifurcation between the appearance and the reality of what Hmong women are: "That does not mean that we do not know things or we cannot do things." It is important for Hmong women to behave in a specific way so they can present a good "face" and be thought of as honorable, bringing respect to their natal families and their husbands, and not causing them shame. This statement also answered some of my original questions about the behavior of the Hmong women in the Providence clinic, outlining a portion of the behavior that is expected of a young Hmong woman.

We can infer that inasmuch as knowledge can be shared with others, one can become more or less competent in the ongoing life of a group of people by participating in that life. This is what I aspired to do as an anthropologist. Yet all of us carry our "situatedness," a context in which various actions and symbols make sense to us. An anthropologist can see people work and play, laugh and cry, and eat and drink, but the rules for engaging in these activities may be different from the rules learned in the ethnographer's own life experiences.

So it proved for me when observing childbirth in a Hmong village. Although the physiological aspects of birth are universal, the way birth is culturally constructed varies widely; it was not only the women's silence during labor or the absence of a doctor that made a Hmong birth so different from an American one, but the meaning of the whole process. Asking how the Hmong conceptualized birth led me directly to the implications such views would have for women's status and health care in the patrilineal kinship system, and proved extremely useful in my later research, although such concerns were perhaps an indication of my embeddedness in my own culture. My questions about how the Hmong perceived birth also led to an examination of the relationship of birth to reincarnation.

The Hmong believe that after death a person's soul is reborn into a new body on earth—specifically, that an ancestor's soul is reborn in a child of the same lineage. This belief profoundly affects their perception of birth and its place in the cycle of life, and thus broadened the course of my research.

What began as an investigation into birth became an exploration not only of Hmong perceptions of family, clan, and society, but also of death and the nature of the universe. I began to see Hmong women in terms of their own cosmology—to consider not just their status but their place in a cycle of life that moves continuously from birth to death to reincarnation. I began to see them as a part of their own universe, which is one where nothing can be viewed piecemeal, since everything—men and women, life and death, birth and rebirth—is interconnected, and opposing elements serve to balance and complete each other.

Calling in the Soul

HMONG COSMOLOGY:

A BALANCE OF OPPOSITES

Very little has been written on Hmong perceptions of birth, even though the Hmong view of life is cyclical and encompasses both birth and death, and a considerable amount of literature is available on death and reincarnation.[1] In his preface to a translation of a Hmong death ritual chant from northern Laos, Jacques Lemoine states that "the transition from life to death is often expressed by the Hmong as a journey . . . *to the sources of life*" (1983b:3, emphasis mine). Birth and death are not opposed; they are different stages on a continuous journey, and their difference is what makes the journey possible.

The connection among birth, death, and reincarnation is implicit, and, Lemoine suggests, is a "way of dealing with death in order to ensure the survival of the group as a whole" (1983b:3). Howard M. Radley follows up Lemoine's theme with a quote from Maurice Bloch and Jonathan Parry on the meaning of mortuary rites:

Individuality and unrepeatable time are problems [that] must be overcome if the social order is to be represented as eternal. Both are characteristically denied by the mortuary rituals which, by representing death as part of a

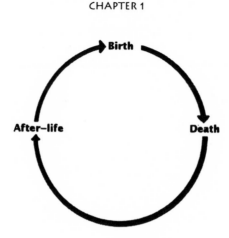

FIG. 1.1. The cycle of life

cyclical process of renewal, become one of the most important occasions
for asserting this eternal order. (Bloch and Parry 1982:15, quoted in Radley
1986:387)

The Showing the Way (Qhuab Kev) chant recited during funerals not
only refutes the finality of an individual's death but suggests that life is
not merely a fleeting period of meaningless contingency but part of an
ongoing eternal process. This conceptualization renders the reality of death
and the tearing of the social fabric comprehensible and manageable. Life
and the social order are not simply a finite aspect of the known and visible world but extend into an invisible realm of spirits, deities, and
ancestors. In pointing out these aspects of the cycle of life in Hmong
cosmological thought, Radley shows how Hmong ideas of life, death, and
continuity are interwoven with their history, politics, and economics
(1986:388).

But Radley also states that "the cycle of life, for the Mong, is completed
when a person is instructed to find their afterbirth to wear on their journey to the spirit world" (1986:388). What he seems to have missed about
Hmong cosmology, as well as the nature of a cycle, is that its distinguish-
ing feature is not completion but movement from one stage to the next in
a continuous flow. Investigations of birth, the journey *from* the sources of
life, and into the connections between the two journeys, can enrich our understanding of how Hmong perceive the cycle of life.

SOUND AND SILENCE

Childbirth is the domain of women, and it is fraught with tension, unpredictability, and danger. Yet in contrast to every other important transition in the Hmong life cycle there is no "sound" to accompany childbirth. A Hmong woman does not groan or cry out as she bears her child; she labors in silence. The wrangling and noisy revelry of weddings are absent, as are the gongs and bells of shamanic rituals, and the drums and reed pipes that accompany death. Men, so visible in all other areas of women's lives, usually do not attend the birth, although the husband arrives on the scene soon after the child is born, often in time to cut the umbilical cord with a sliver of bamboo.

On the third day after the birth, a man of the household (usually the paternal grandfather) calls in the soul and names the child, formally introducing the newborn as a social being. Significantly, that this event is accompanied by loud noise— chanting and banging the divination horns on the door— the first loud noise since the onset of labor, provides support for Rodney Needham's proposition that "there is a connection between percussion and transition" (1967:613) and that there is a prevalence of percussive sound in rites of passage. I would like to expand Needham's concept of ritual percussive sound to include any focused, humanly created sound. Richard Huntington and Peter Metcalf, in their discussion of percussion and other sounds in mortuary rituals, point out that both "great noise or extreme silence, provide, like black and white . . . opportunities for symbolic representation and heightened drama" (1979:49). The contrast in Hmong birth customs between the silence of women and the sounds of men can be viewed in these terms.

Women produce the physical body of the child; men call in its soul. In this sense, women and men hold complementary roles in the biological, social, and cosmological process of birth. Without the female's physical ability to carry and nourish her offspring with her "fat," blood, and strength, there would be no receptacle into which the soul of an ancestor could be reborn. Without the male who provides the seed, performs sacrifices to preserve the patriline, and calls in the soul of the child, there would be no continuity in the lineage, the clan, or ultimately, the Hmong people.

"Male filiation," or the male line, is, of course, a "religious and social" link rather than a natural one (Vernant 1980:136), and, as Nancy Jay says,

"All over the world social structures idealizing 'eternal' male intergenerational continuity meet a fundamental obstacle in their necessary dependence on women's reproductive powers. There are various ways to organize over and around this obstacle, to transcend it" (1992:xxv). In the case of the Hmong, the means of organization is the naming ceremony on the third day. A child who dies before the third day is not given a traditional burial, but is simply disposed of, because it is not yet considered fully human. Only after the naming ceremony, conducted by males and involving sacrifice, is the child considered a true human, a member of Hmong society.

In her cross-cultural study of sacrifice, Jay analyzes "the many vivid metaphors in which sacrifice is opposed to childbirth as birth done better, under deliberate purposeful control, and on a more exalted level than ordinary mothers do it" (1992:xxiv), and this is certainly true in the case of the Hmong naming ritual. She also extends Emile Durkheim's notion that in "ritual action people create and recreate aspects of their own society" by adding her understanding of that concept as being "always political action involving struggles for power, including power over women's reproductive capacities" (Jay 1992:xxvii).

RESEARCH ON GENDER

Over the past two decades, in response to the omission of women from the ethnographic record, feminist anthropological research has begun to challenge some of the dominant paradigms and assumptions that have shaped the discipline. Two models have emerged: universalist or sexual asymmetry and gender symmetry and sexual equality.[2] Proponents of sexual asymmetry argue that women's oppression is universal, whereas proponents of gender symmetry believe that the imposition of Western models on non-Western societies has led to inaccurate depictions of women's roles, status, and power.

A great deal has been written concerning the connections between asymmetry and female reproduction. Some theorists have suggested that because of reproduction—pregnancy, lactation, women's role as primary childcare provider, and their lack of physical strength following birth—women become economically dependent upon men. Other theorists believe that an undue emphasis on women's reproduction has inadvertently reinforced a

type of biological determinism; they reject the idea that women's reproduction causes universal gender asymmetry, suggest that motherhood is but
one of many female roles, and see the relations of reproduction determined
by relations of production (Leacock 1976:11–35; Sacks 1977:211–34). Although
both theoretical viewpoints are important, we need to look specifically at a
given society in order to understand the meanings and consequences of
reproduction. Why, as Carol Mukhopadhyay and Patricia Higgins suggest,
do we not address the reasons why men rather than women control the child-
bearers (1988:478)?

The contradictory features of the Hmong sex-gender system are worthy
of close consideration. Nancy Donnelly has pointed out that "all of the
research on Hmong women has been done by men who had little access to
the conversations of Hmong women" and that those that include women
do not give "women's view of their own experiences" (Donnelly 1994:14)
but only touch on the lives of women to clarify the ways they fit into the
world of men. Robert Cooper's work on gender in Hmong culture calcu-
lates the amount of physical labor performed by women and men and concludes that there is no "obvious pattern of exploitation of the female in the
organization and division of labour" (1983:176). However, he believes that
the ideology of male supremacy arises out of that division of labor and has
become "a major psychological distinction between the sexes" and that it
is "on the basis of that distinction that man controls woman" (1983:178).
And as Cooper makes clear, the capability of Hmong women to do physically strenuous work is made irrelevant by the psychological and cultural
constraints that prevent them from taking certain actions that they are clearly
physically capable of, such as cutting down trees with an axe and using guns
to protect their families, hunting animals, sacrificing animals, traveling
(except, increasingly, to market), and climbing on rooftops, which women
are not allowed to do because then they would be "above" men (1983:178).
In the same way, women's physical strength—symbolized in Hmong culture by the right hand—is not valued in the way that male strength is.

That Hmong society is male-dominated has been remarked upon by most
who have observed it. As Donnelly describes it, "the most immediate striking aspect of gender roles in Hmong society, described time and again by
researchers, is the apparent hierarchical relation between men and women"
(1994:29). The literature consistently reports male dominance, and most
authors emphasize the asymmetrical nature of Hmong society, in which

women occupy a structurally subordinate position. Hmong people themselves (both men and women) stress that "men are more important" and that "Hmong is maleness." The political, economic, and ritual spheres having to do with the patriline are restricted to men, and women have no public voice in these arenas. Gender roles are reinforced for Hmong children on a daily basis in the discourse of everyday life, which involves the recounting of origin stories and traditional folk tales, many of them contradictory in nature (Donnelly 1994:36).

HMONGNESS AND WOMEN AS OTHER

The Hmong lineage, spiritual rituals, and public life are male. Hmong women as well as men say that "maleness is Hmong" and believe that even if every Hmong woman died or ran away, the patriline would continue because Hmong men would be able to marry women from other groups, and those women would then become Hmong. If, however, all Hmong men were to die, Hmong society, or "Hmongness," would cease to exist. If daughters marry non-Hmong men, they too will become non-Hmong, as will their children. Only by being part of the lineage of one's father, grandfather, and great-grandfather (which is as far back as most Hmong can remember), can one "honor the ancestors."[3] Thus Hmong society is dependent upon "outside" women for survival, and in some sense all Hmong women are outsiders. They cease to belong to their natal lineage when they marry but are not truly part of their husband's lineage until death, when they join his ancestors in the land of darkness. Until then, married women use not their husband's surname but their father's, even though they have left their natal lineage.

In Flower Village there was an Akha woman who had married a Hmong man. She preferred not to speak Akha or discuss her "Akha-ness." Although she was still known as "the Akha woman," her two sons were considered Hmong and members of their father's lineage. If this woman became unhappy with her marriage and wished to leave her husband, her children would be considered Hmong, not Akha, and would remain in the village with their father and his family. The children would not be allowed to leave the family, not only because the payment of bride-price at the time of the marriage gives the father's family jural rights over the children, but also because if children leave their father's custody, the action reflects negatively

on all male lineage members. There are, of course, exceptions to these rules—
Nicholas Tapp records the instance of a Khmu' man who married a Hmong
woman, and then the Khmu' man "became Hmong" (1989b:168)—but this
was the norm described to me by Hmong men and women.[4]

Conversely, when a woman marries out of Hmong society, her child
becomes "other"—an Akha, a Lisu, or a Thai—for a child belongs to the
father's descent group. I learned of an instance in which a Hmong woman
married a Lao man and when, after several years, the man was killed, the
woman returned to her natal village with her small son. The son spoke only
Hmong, but although they lived peacefully in the community, he was still
considered Lao. He adopted the clan name of his mother, but he had no
lineage or obligations, and although he knew how to perform the rituals,
he was not allowed to do so, since that would not have been acceptable to
the lineage spirits. His lineage status was thus equivalent to a woman's. If he
had been adopted into the Hmong community, which often happens, or his
mother had remarried a Hmong man, he would have been accepted as a
Hmong, although no one would have forgotten, even a generation hence,
that he had not been born to a Hmong father.

Patrilocality is the rule of residence. Women living in a given household
are either wives who have married in or daughters who will marry out.
Women are defined and indeed define themselves in relation to the males
in whose household they reside. They are not permitted to tend to the ancestral altars of the household, nor do daughters assure the posterity of their
natal lineage. The Hmong metaphor of men as roots and women as flowers
(Tapp 1989b:158) illustrates how daughters are regarded. A Hmong man, Doua
Hang, tells us that "the important part of a Hmong family from one generation to the next is the men. . . . Women are important, but women
change. . . . Wives and daughters are like leaves and flowers, but men are the
branches and trunk of the tree, always strong and never changing" (1986:34).

Many other aspects of Hmong cosmology contain this metaphor of man
as skeleton or tree trunk, contributing to the strong/weak dichotomy and
the enduring/changing dichotomy between men and women. What is valued
is that which endures.

There is much about the patrilineal structure and ideology of Hmong
society to support such statements by Hang, Tapp, and other ethnographers.
My own work strongly corroborates these reports, finding that in the
Hmong community there is no compensatory power for women. Women

contribute to the continuance of the male hegemonic structure through special mechanisms and different roles—as daughters, wives, mothers, daughters-in-law, and mothers-in-law, and, more important, as sisters. Although women subscribe to the system of asymmetrical power by aligning themselves with the patrilineal, patrilocal, extended family in which they live, there are also areas in which women have strong voices and receive irrefutable respect from both males and females.

Hmong women's own stories demonstrate how they situate themselves, especially in relationship to their ability to give birth, in this male-oriented and male-dominated society. Some of the examples and case studies that follow support a cultural ideal as it was described to me in Flower Village. Other examples show how the ideal negates or denies an individual's lived experience; and sometimes a specific reality contradicts and may even make inroads upon the ideal.

Although it is generally accurate to say that Hmong women's roles and status are inferior and subordinate to men's, there are areas in which this is not the case: childbirth and ritual conceptions of the afterlife. These two areas, which are key to understanding Hmong cultural constructions of gender and the meanings that both women and men attach to their lives, are filled with paradox: roles are reversed, metaphors inverted, and closed boundaries crossed. But although gender roles are realigned during childbirth, female roles persist. It is in the afterlife that the souls of men and women become equal.

HMONG VIEWS OF THE COSMOS: THE LAND OF LIGHT AND THE LAND OF DARKNESS

Before examining the meaning of gender in relation to Hmong views of the afterlife, we must understand the afterlife in context of Hmong cosmology. Although an extensive examination of myth and legend is beyond the scope of this work, a look at origin myths and legends can explain how cosmology informs and organizes Hmong life.

As Anne Fadiman has noted, Hmong culture does not dissect easily into disparate parts and neatly labeled categories, as everything in it stubbornly remains connected to everything else. "Medicine *was* religion. Religion was society. Society was medicine. Even economics was mixed up in there" (Fadiman 1997:60). To complicate matters, the polarizations so dear to Western analytic thought seem absent, or at least changed beyond recognition, in the Hmong view of the universe. Opposites don't always remain in a fixed position, separate and distinct from each other; the boundaries between them are fluid. To give just two examples: Hmong consider the distinction between birth and death somewhat arbitrary (because every death represents the eventual rebirth of an ancestor), and they do not distinguish between mental and physical illness, because they consider all illness sent by spirits and a result of being out of balance.

In keeping with the way Hmong perceive the universe, this overview of cosmology includes much about how the Hmong live on earth. Like a walk on a mountain path, it is a meandering journey over uneven ground.

Hmong cosmology is interwoven with that of the dominant lowland groups with whom they have lived, particularly the Chinese, as well as with other neighboring hill dwellers in Thailand (see, e.g., Lemoine 1988:69; Tapp 1989b:131–35; Radley 1986:72–76). Also, because of the Hmong migrations and their historically diverse experiences from clan to clan, a single Hmong deity may be known by many different names and described as having many different occupations. But although the Green and White Hmong in Thailand have distinctly different traditions, and their myths and rituals may vary in both the details and the stated meanings, their underlying purpose is often similar.[5] Many ethnographers have noted that this difference within similarities is a hallmark and part of the beauty of the oral tradition. As Earl Count states, "Themes endure, though gods die and motifs change their shape" (1960:606–7).

The Hmong believe[6] that the universe consists of the land of light (*yajceeb*) and the land of darkness (*yeebceeb*). The land of light is the world of the living, and all things that dwell there are interconnected—trees, plants, water, stones, animals (including human beings), and spirits (*dab*). Wild and dangerous spirits of "the outside" live in the forest, whereas the tame, protective, and cared-for spirits of "the inside" live in the house.

THE HOME AND THE SPIRITS OF THE INSIDE

Just as the physical body of a person is a vessel for a soul, the house is the vessel for the ancestral and tame spirits. These spirits reside in every quarter of the house; they are honored with ritual offerings and in return give protection from wild spirits of the outside. Ancestral spirits live in the house pillars, and most rituals, including animal sacrifices to the ancestors, take place there. Nicholas Tapp underscores the importance of the house as a mirror or microcosm of the cosmos: "If the roof and rafters of the house represent the vault of heaven, then the earthen floor represents the world of nature. Between heaven and earth is the world of men and of social life" (1989a:63).

The Hmong home is the cosmological abode to which souls come, and from which they depart for the otherworld, and as such, its location is of paramount importance. Proximity to the homes of other patrilineal kin is a prime consideration,[7] but the house's location also must accord with the laws of geomancy to propitiate the spirits of the area.[8] If a house is built on a site where a wild spirit lives, the result will be disastrous for the people in the house.

In Flower Village a family built their home on a raised area a short distance up the hill. The first indication that not all was well with the site was that the woman in the family had a miscarriage. Then one night their small child reached for soup that was boiling on the hearth; some of the soup spilled onto her arm and burned her badly. At that point the family pulled down the house and moved farther down the hill. A member of the lineage conducted a soul-calling ceremony for the little girl who had been burned (because the accident or the spirit had frightened one of her souls away), sacrificing a chicken for the child and tying spirit strings around her wrists for protection.

The construction of a house is a village-wide social event. Families and lineage members choose a propitious day and supply rice liquor and food. Women prepare the food while men go to the forest for wood, bamboo, and grasses for the roofing. (Those who can afford it use corrugated tin for the roof, greatly reducing the amount of labor.) Both women and men prepare the ground, but only men assemble the structure. Women are not allowed to climb on roofs or anywhere else that places them higher than a man; they hand pieces of thatch or bamboo up to the men on the roof.

The first pole pounded into the ground is the center post, which connects the ancestors and the descendants (Lemoine 1972c:102), in the main room of the house. Adjacent to the main room are small bedrooms. Parents and children sleep in one room, teenagers sleep in groups in gender-specific rooms, and grandparents usually have their own sleeping room.[9] There is usually an extra platform bed for guests in the large, main room. Each house has a main entrance for family and visitors, as well as a small spirit door, which faces west and is opened at various ritual times, so that spirits may enter and depart.

After the house is built and the earthen floor tamped down, a large clay hearth—for cooking sacrificial animals and food for the pigs—is built into the side of the house. At this time the spirit door is opened and household spirits are invited to dwell in the house: the spirit of the stove *(dab ghov txos)*, the small cooking fire spirit *(dab ghov cub)*, the spirit of the loft *(dab nthab)*, and the spirit who guards the door *(dab txhiaj meej)*. Inside the house, another spirit guards the bedroom door *(dab roog)* and is responsible for the fertility of the animals. Some clans say that this spirit lives in a gourd on the bedroom wall; others say it is contained in a bouquet of leaves. My Hmong informants told me that this spirit is identified only with the fertility of animals, but, because of its location in the bedroom, it may also pertain to the fertility of humans in the household (Morechand 1968:53).

Each house also has a small altar for the spirit of wealth and prosperity *(dab xwm kab)* (fig. 1.2) on the east wall, across from the spirit door. At designated times of the year, chickens are sacrificed and their blood and feathers are pasted onto the prosperity altar along with silver and gold paper. The male heads of households care for all of these household spirits.

In July 1987 a shaman in Flower Village told me a story about the prosperity altar. "Chinese are more wealthy than we Hmong," he began, "because they met a test given by Saub."

Long ago Puj and Yawm Saub [the primary deity couple] sent a baby to the world.[10] They placed it on the junction of three paths. They sent this child because they wanted to test the people in the area. Puj and Yawm thought the Hmong would pick the child up and take it home. The child was crying. A Hmong man went by but did not pick the child up. A Lao man went by; he did not pick the child up. A Chinese man went by, and, seeing the crying child, he picked it up and carried it home. When the man reached home, the child disappeared, but Saub told the man to make an altar to the child, and as long as he honored the altar, he would be rich. Puj and Yawm Saub sent the same message to the Lao and the Hmong man saying they must

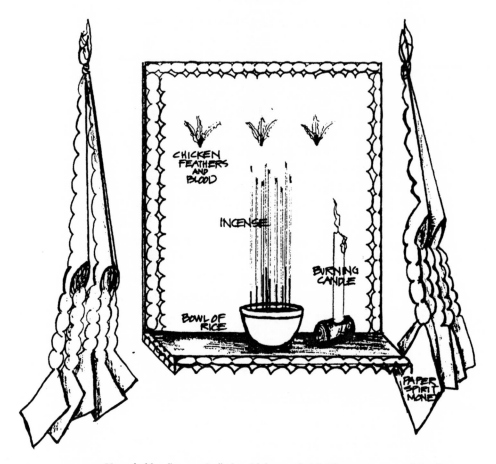

FIG. 1.2. Household or "prosperity" altar (dab xwm kab). *The components of the altar represent the spirits of wealth and possessions for a family. (Drawing by Chaj Vaj)*

also keep and honor altars, but they would never be as wealthy as the good Chinese man.

If a shaman lives in the house, there will be an additional, more elaborate altar built of special wood, covered with bamboo paper, and draped with the shaman's paraphernalia (fig. 1.3). The shaman's spirit helpers live on this altar. In a house I saw erected in Flower Village, two chickens, a rooster, and a hen were killed and their blood wiped on the two altars—the prosperity altar and the shaman's altar.[11] A "bridge" made of black hemp cloth was

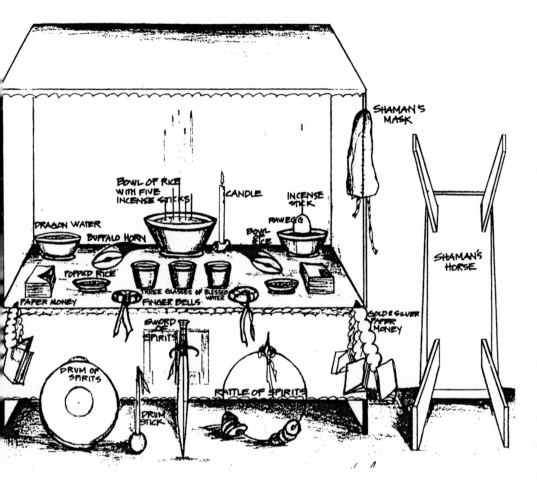

FIG. 1.3. *Shaman's altar* (lub thaj neeb). *This is where the helping spirits of a shaman dwell. The bench on the right side becomes the horse the shaman rides to find the missing soul of a sick person. His face is covered by the cloth mask, which separates him from this world. All of the accoutrements are necessary for his travels. (Drawing by Chaj Vaj)*

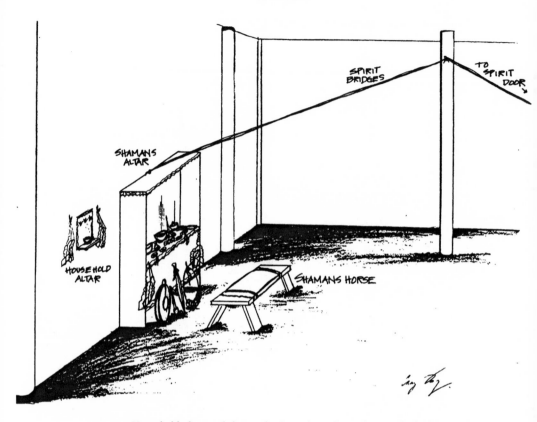

FIG. 1.4. *Household altar and shaman's altar, along the upslope wall of a house. The spirit bridge leading from the shaman's altar is the passageway used by the shaman's spirit helpers. (Drawing by Chaj Vaj)*

stretched from the shaman's altar up through the rafters to the spirit door (fig. 1.4). Hempen strings, running next to this black cloth, made the pathways by which the shaman and his spirit familiars *(dab neeb)* could come and go when he was in a trance state (fig. 1.5).

DEATH AND THE ANCESTORS

All of the beings of the living world are connected to the dark land of the gods and the ancestors—the land souls come from when they are called into the newborn child and the land souls return to at death. The same souls rein-

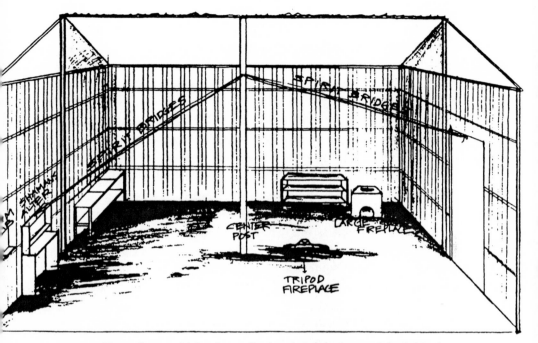

FIG. 1.5. *Hmong house, with bamboo walls. A male baby's **placenta** is buried by the center house post, and a spirit bridge stretches from the **shaman's** altar, via the center post, to the door. (Drawing by Chaj Vaj)*

carnate in a never-ending cycle of rebirth. Hmong cosmology differs from that of neighboring valley groups of Thai Buddhists in that Buddhists aim for an end to the cycle of transmigration, so that the soul will attain liberation from sentient existence through reaching nirvana, or otherworldliness (Tambiah 1970:40). The Hmong emphasis is not on becoming free of the cycle but on continuing it and assuring the perpetuation of the lineage.

The origin myths say that in the beginning of time, nobody died. This is another example of the ideal of permanence: that which does not change, age, die, or shift allegiance is superior to that which does. It is also said that when a person reached one hundred twenty years, the ideal age to have lived, he or she would change skin and get up again at the end of thirteen days (Lemoine 1997:148). Because two of the first human men killed a frog, and also because of overpopulation (see "Showing the Way" chant in appendix B, verse 178), humans were no longer allowed to live forever (Lemoine 1983b:17; Graham 1937:71–119; Morechand 1968:53–94).[12] But if at death they had collected their "skin" or "shirt" (the placenta) at their birthplace, and all rituals were performed correctly so that their souls found their way back to the land of darkness, they could return to earth again.

In the land of darkness Ntxwj Nyoog is responsible for life and death.[13] (See appendix B, verses 37–45, which tell how Ntxwj Nyoog first brought death to the earth.) In or around his house, he keeps all the things that are needed to guide a soul to the land of darkness; he is extremely wicked and cruel, and people are fearful of his powers. When the soul of a child is called on the third day after birth, or the soul of a young bride is called to the home of her new family, it is given careful instruction on how to avoid Ntxwj Nyoog. At death, however, his gate must be passed before a soul can enter the land of darkness. It is to him that the soul must appear in order to show that the correct rituals have been performed, and he is the judge who grants the papers for rebirth—or "mandate for life"—that give souls permission to be reborn and who designates what their new physical form will be.

The land of light and the land of darkness are connected by the ancestors, whom the Hmong describe as "souls still held in the memory of their descendants." These dual-gendered souls are comprised of a married couple who have died and become a single unified dyadic spirit—"motherfather, grandmothergrandfather." They must be fed and honored for as long as the living remember them. When ancestors are cared for, all will be well, but if they are neglected—if the family does not sacrifice an animal to give thanks for a good crop, or forgets to feed the ancestors after the first rice harvest—they become wrathful, bringing sickness and calamity to their descendants. The ancestors and household spirits, who are the tame spirits, must be treated with honor and respect. They must be cared for, or the result can be bad crops, illness, or even death in the household. The tame spirits also offer protection from the wild spirits of the outside.

THE FOREST AND THE SPIRITS OF THE OUTSIDE

Wild spirits live in the fields and the forest, in trees and rivers and rocks. If a person steps on one of these spirits, it can become angry and frighten away the person's "wandering" soul. One such malevolent wild spirit, Poj Ntxoog, a small hairy woman, can frighten those who come upon her, causing soul

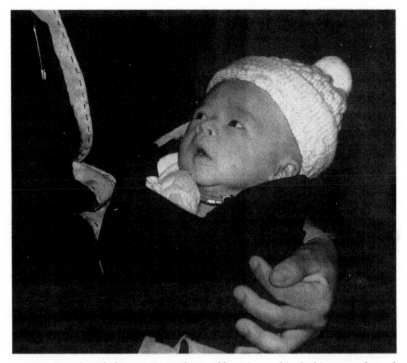

FIG. 1.6. *A newborn baby, wearing a silver necklace given to him by his paternal grandparents for protection and good wishes for his life. (Photo by Patricia Symonds)*

loss and even death if a shaman cannot get the soul back quickly enough. Poj Ntxoog can also develop a fondness for a person and steal his or her soul away. Other spirits prey on menstruating and pregnant women.

Wild spirits are not always evil or malicious. Sometimes a wild spirit, attracted to a person and meaning no harm, will entice the person's soul to leave the body and go play with the spirit in the forest, but this is still not a healthy situation for the person whose soul is lost.

In a Hmong village one sees people wearing amulets, copper and silver bracelets and necklaces that have been received during a shaman's ritual for protection from wild spirits. Many people wear white string *(khi hlua tes)*—also given during ceremonies—tied around their wrists, to ask the ancestors for blessings and protection and to tie in the souls. On the doors of houses, I often saw bamboo knives hanging from strings to protect the house from wild spirits of the outside. Small children and babies often wear cloth bracelets or silver necklaces (fig. 1.6) with herbal medi-

FIG. 1.7. A baby wearing an embroidered hat for spiritual protection. (Photo by Patricia Symonds)

cines in them, and older babies wear beautifully embroidered hats (fig. 1.7) to cover their heads and hide them from malevolent spirits. One mother in Flower Village told me that the hats are to make babies look like flowers so the spirits will ignore them. She also told me never to say that her baby, or anyone's, is beautiful, as the spirits will hear and want to steal the child's soul.

SOULS

The Hmong believe that the human body is the site for various life essences or souls, although informants in different areas and of different clans—and even the same informant at different times—provide conflicting information as to the number of souls within a human body.[14] Lemoine (1997:146) gives an excellent and detailed description of twelve souls and their vital functions in the body, dividing them into stable or sedentary souls, and unstable or elusive souls. Many of the souls, especially the unstable ones, can be frightened or stolen away, and the aim of the shaman is to restore them. The death chant from Flower Village says, "One person, three souls, and seven shadows. / Since you have gone, your body is dead, / But not your souls" (appendix B, verse 162). Although the number of souls is ambiguous and varies from account to account, Hmong themselves do not seem concerned by the discrepancies, and the theme behind the concept of souls and soul loss remains similar across groups. For the purposes of this study, I will focus on the three souls referred to in the death chant from Flower Village.

The first of these souls is called the "sun and moon soul" *(ngao nun jau li)*[15] or "shadow soul." This soul never leaves the body, and even at death stays with the bones in the grave to guard them.

The second is the "breath soul" *(nju pang fua siue),* or "satin thread." Lemoine calls it the "wandering soul" or "cow or running bull" soul and states that it "is easily frightened by spirits or noises and will bolt headlong down the path to death" (Lemoine 1997:146–47). At the body's death, this second soul makes the journey back to the land of darkness, seeking the village of the ancestors, which is much like the village it inhabited on earth. There it joins with its spouse's soul to create a unified dyadic spirit that will be fed and remembered by its descendants, and incorporated into the community of ancestors.

The third is the "returning vital soul" *(ntsuj plig si or ntsuj qaib).* It too returns to the land of darkness, but only to await the opportunity for rebirth. This is the soul that is reincarnated, or "born in living form" *(tshwm sim).* If a person's third soul is frightened away and the shaman cannot retrieve it, the person will die.

It is the third soul, the returning vital soul, that ultimately gives Hmong women a voice, as, ideally, it switches gender at each reincarnation. Inhabiting different vessels from lifetime to lifetime, the returning vital soul is alternately male or female. The patriline is thus carried on by the souls of former females who came from outside the lineage; and males, reborn as females in their next life, will leave the lineage at marriage. In the course of cycling through its alternating genders, the returning vital soul occupies different lineages and, through clan exogamy, different clans. Thus there is no clan hierarchy among the Hmong, no "better clan" to be born into, because over the course of time, spiritual essences, or souls, cycle through the whole of Hmong society. And despite the inequities between living men and women, the essences or souls of the dead are in a relation of gender equivalence to one another.

SOUL LOSS AND SHAMANS: BRIDGES, LADDERS, AND DOORS

If the souls are well balanced and harmonious in the body, a person is well. If for any reason—and there are many possible reasons—a soul leaves, the person becomes ill and may require a shaman's intercession.

Almost daily in Flower Village I heard the shamans' bells, rattles, and metal gong, which sounded like someone beating on a tin pie plate. Although there are other avenues of healing if soul loss is suspected, such as herbal medicines or a soul-calling ritual by a lineage member (as was done for the child who was burned), a shaman is consulted if the soul does not return and the person continues to be ill.

The shaman, as intermediary between spirits and humans, can cross the boundaries between the two worlds to negotiate *(ua neeb kho)* with neglected ancestors or barter with, trick, or fight wild spirits for a soul they have stolen. Jacques Lemoine states that "with the aid of his [or her] spirit helpers, the shaman will cross the hempen cloth with iron and copper girders, the spiritual bridges, seeking a solution to the problem" in the "outer space of non-ordinary reality" (1988:63).

Bridges, ladders, and doors connect the two worlds. In the beginning of time, spirits and humans came and went between the worlds as they pleased, but due to adverse actions on the part of both, this is no longer possible (see appendix B, verses 58–70). Now the land of light can be reached by ordinary people only by being born, and the land of darkness by dying. Only a shaman can cross these borders and return as the same person in the same body. By summoning the spirit helpers that live on his or her altar, the shaman can ride through space on a flying horse of "winds and clouds" (Lemoine 1988:65). What gives a shaman the ability to make this journey are the spirit helpers, who are sent by Siv Yis.

Siv Yis is a deity who was once a man, and the first shaman. He lives in a cave in the otherworld; when shamans die, their spirit helpers return to his cave, waiting there until Siv Yis sends them to call another shaman. Women can become shamans, although fewer women than men do so; in Flower Village, only three of the seventeen were women. Some of my informants said that Siv Yis's helping spirits call a woman only when no man is available. Other Hmong told me that Siv Yis makes no distinctions between men and women; he calls shamans to help fellow human beings, and the shaman's gender is irrelevant.

A person who is called by Siv Yis's helping spirits becomes very ill and may suffer from depression, lethargy, sleep disorders, or visual or audio hallucinations, which will not abate until the person accepts the call.[16] The shaman called in to diagnose will tell the sick person that he or she must either accept the responsibility of becoming a shaman or remain ill without hope of recovery. But traveling to the otherworld is dangerous, even life-threatening, as is fighting or tricking malignant spirits to regain the souls of the sick, and some who are called by Siv Yis have no desire to become a shaman. A shaman who enters a trance goes to fight; one must never walk between the altar and someone in such a state, as this could cause the shaman to lose the way and die.[17]

If a shaman loses the fight or negotiation with the spirits, the sick person will remain ill. This does not disgrace the shaman; it merely means that the illness is incurable or that the sick person's family should try another, more powerful shaman.

Shamans who have been called by Siv Yis are sometimes called black-faced shamans because they cover their face with a black cloth before going into trance (fig. 1.8). All seventeen black-faced shamans in Flower Village had become quite sick, and a few had nearly died, before accepting Siv Yis's call.

Not all healers are called by Siv Yis; those who have not been called do not go into trance, so their souls do not leave their bodies and journey to the otherworld to join their helping spirits in battle there. These healers are called "people with white faces" *(txiv neeb muag dawb),* or sometimes white-faced shamans, because they do not cover their faces with cloth (or go into trance). Kathleen Culhane-Pera informed me that she knows black-faced shamans who sometimes perform white-faced rituals (e.g., without going into trance), and that the rituals performed by both black-faced and white-faced shamans are referred to by the same names. The main difference is that the white-faced rituals take less power and skill than do the black-faced rituals (personal communication, 2002).

Some shamans simply are more powerful and experienced than others. The black-faced shamans, who have been called, are more powerful than the white-faced shamans, who have not. Of the black-faced shamans, it seems that the strongest are those who cover their faces with red cloth (although they are still called "black-faced"); but none of these lived in Flower Village, and I have never met one.

Both the white-faced and black-faced shamans learn the rituals through

FIG. 1.8. A shaman performing a soul retrieval (ua neeb) *for a sick person. His face is covered with a black mask to isolate him from this world, and he is on his "horse" to travel. (Photo by Patricia Symonds)*

apprenticeship to an experienced shaman. Apprentice shamans begin by calling souls that may have been frightened away (lineage members also can call frightened souls), as opposed to stolen, and doing rituals to ensure health rather than cure illness.

The shamanic rituals I attended in Flower Village were exciting to watch. The shaman brings his or her altar, with the helping spirits that live there, to the house of the sick person, where the lineage spirits as well can help (fig. 1.9).[18] Initially the shaman makes a diagnostic journey (*ua neeb saib,* lit., "doing the spirits in order to see") by throwing the divination horns and, if necessary, going into trance to ascertain the nature of the illness and determine how to proceed in the otherworld. This first journey is usually fairly short, and the shaman shakes only gently while in the trance state. Sometimes the shaman waits a day to see if the diagnosis was correct (for

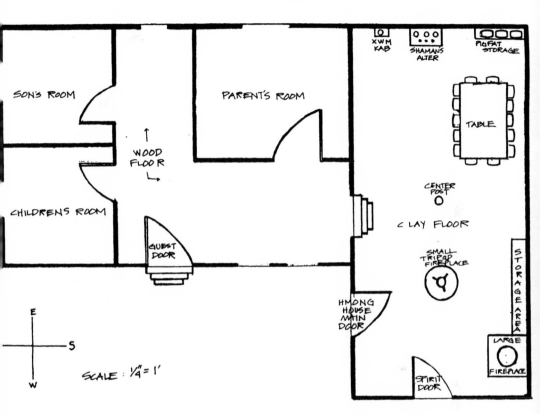

FIG. 1.9. *Floor plan of a Thai/Hmong house. The village headman has added a Thai section to a Hmong-style house. Thai visitors from the town in the valley or from the government are entertained in the Thai portion. The altar and spirit bridge is kept intact in the Hmong portion. (Drawing by Chaj Vaj)*

instance, if the spirits said the sick person only had a cold and would begin to get well without treatment), and sometimes begins the curing or healing journey *(ua neeb kho)* immediately following the diagnostic journey. The shaman wears a black face cloth tied with red string and sits astride the "winged steed," which is a wooden bench (made from a tree specially chosen in the forest) covered with cloth. An assistant bangs on the gong in a slow, steady rhythm to alert helping spirits so they will be ready to help the shaman make the journey and retrieve the soul. When entering a trance, "riding" to the otherworld, the shaman shakes rattles and finger-bells, speaking to the spirits in a language that contains phrases in old Hmong and in

Chinese, bouncing on the "horse," shaking his or her body, and stamping on the ground. This part of the ritual often lasts for a couple of hours as the shaman searches for the lost soul and then fights or negotiates to get it back. Partway through the ritual the shaman leaps onto the bench to show power; this is impressive and somewhat frightening to watch, as the shaman, whose face is covered, seems to be making the leap blindly. (To the shaman, who sees the otherworld while in trance, perhaps this leap does not seem blind at all.) But even though the human assistant has been forewarned and can brace the shaman, a shaman who misses the leap and falls can be lost in the otherworld and die. If this happens, another shaman is called in immediately to retrieve the soul of the one who fell, but I never saw a misjudgment of this leap (see Conquergood 1989:48).

The shaman, while in trance, also tells the human assistant when to burn the paper spirit money (Hmong paper marked with gold and silver) and when to have a lineage member sacrifice an animal. During all shamanic ceremonies, an animal—a chicken, pig, or dog—is sacrificed so that its soul can be exchanged for that of the person who is ill. The animal's blood is daubed onto the sick person's clothing for protection; the blood tells the spirits that the animal gave its soul, so the person's soul should be left alone. (Sacrificial pigs' jawbones are stored at the shaman's altar until New Year's, when they are burned, allowing the pigs' souls to be freed and reborn.) The sacrificed animals are cleaned and cooked, and then are eaten by the family and guests. Family members, especially spouses, usually are included in the healing ceremony. Sometimes hempen strings are tied around the sick person, the spouse, and their children, to draw their souls together for protection.

There are other reasons for soul loss besides neglecting the tame spirits of ancestors or of the household, or catching the attention of wild spirits. One can also lose one's soul *(poob plig)* if frightened by a loud noise, a fall, or an animal. In Flower Village a young girl went over to touch a horse that another Hmong had ridden into the village. The horse whinnied loudly and took a small bite out of the girl's face. She was very frightened and sickly for a few days, until her father called in a shaman who did a soul retrieval *(ua neeg)* ceremony. The child's soul had fled her body from fright and was wandering around the universe. It was believed that without the shaman's intercession, she could have died. As it was, she retained only a small scar on her cheek, which she has still.

When Hmong leave a place they have visited, such as the home of relatives in another village, with whom they have stayed for a few days, they always call out to their souls to accompany them when they leave. This is to make sure their souls do not find another place more comfortable and forget to come home. Related to this concern about migrating—or invading—souls are taboos against the participation of pregnant women in funerals, because of concern that the souls of the dead can be dangerous to the fetus or the mother, causing miscarriage or the mother's death unless a shaman intercedes.

Shamans do not ask for payment for their services; they know they will be paid. If a pig is sacrificed during a shamanic ritual, the shaman receives a front shoulder. In Flower Village I saw shamans paid in money, rice, and opium.

Hmong shamans are respected for their power, "but their talent is the power of healing" (Lemoine 1997:145). They save life or restore health by retrieving lost souls, even journeying to the land of darkness to do so, but they do not guide the souls of the dead to the land of darkness. Shamans take no part in funerary rites except in their capacity as lineage members. Also, as with the Chukchi and Koriak tribes of northeastern Siberia, the Hmong shamans have no political role.[19] Neither do they bind wounds or dispense medicine, even herbal treatments.

HERBALISTS

Herbalists are known as the "ones who give medicine" *(kws tshuaj)*. In Flower Village there were several people, mostly women, who were knowledgeable about the medicinal properties of plants in the forest or who grew herbs in their own medicine gardens. With the aid of medicinal plants and their own helping spirits (*dab tshuaj,* which also can mean "medicine altar"), they were able to diagnose and heal ailments such as headaches, menstrual irregularities, and cuts and bruises. Some of these ailments may be ascribed to soul loss; most people consult an herbalist first, going to a shaman only if the soul still does not return.

Herbalists also have knowledge of emmenagogues and abortifacients. These women learn about herbal medicines from a mother or aunt and then pass on their knowledge to the next generation; their knowledge is closely guarded. Herbalists are paid in whatever form a patient can afford; the fee is small, but some payment is necessary. I saw one herbalist paid with rice and another with opium wrapped in a poppy leaf, but if possible herbalists are paid with money.

CAUSES OF ILLNESS

Most illnesses and accidents are seen as a result of being out of balance. Although most dangerous illness is attributed to soul loss—itself a form of being out of balance—Hmong are aware of other causes of disease.[20] Blood gives strength and life, but it cannot be replaced. Losing a lot of blood can make a person sickly and pale for life, which is why the Hmong in Providence clinics did not want their blood drawn. Fat *(rog)* also gives strength, which is why people who are thin and wiry may become sick easily. Hmong often felt my skin and arms and told me I was a strong and healthy woman. They said I had fat on my body and this was why I had such good health and energy. As the months passed, they were distressed when I began to lose weight and encouraged me to eat more rice.

Some diseases are considered hereditary, and this is a subject for discussion in marriage negotiations. Hmong are especially careful to ask about leprosy, as they believe it can be passed down from generation to generation.

Other diseases come from natural causes: cold and bad weather, for instance, can put one's body out of balance and cause sickness. When I was in Flower Village in the rainy season, it became very cold at night, and the mother and father in the house made sure I had a blanket on top of my sleeping bag so that I would not catch a cold. They also made me wear a woolen hat; they told me if my head was warm I would not become sick.

Hmong are aware of and use some bio-medicine, especially antibiotics. In Thailand, itinerant "shot doctors" will inject antibiotics into anyone who asks; no prescription is necessary. Ntaj, who ran the clinic in Flower Village, once treated a woman with a huge abscess that had resulted from getting such a shot with an unsterilized needle. Ntaj, who was a son of the family with whom I lived in Flower Village, had been trained in the valley, along with other young hill tribe people, in rudimentary health care.[21] He dispensed antibiotics and cough syrup to children with colds and coughs, took temperatures, and gave antibiotics for fevers. He also treated children with severe cases of diarrhea (children often had diarrhea, but not severely enough to warrant medication). Ntaj also gave vaccinations at the school. Many of the women, however, had taken to going to the small town hospital in the valley on a specific clinic day to get their children vaccinated.

People came to Ntaj's clinic if the pesticides they used on the fields had made them ill, and he attempted to make them comfortable. He advised them to wear masks when spraying, but most people disregarded this advice or didn't use the masks consistently.

Women also came to the clinic when they had cut themselves with the huge, lethal knives they used in the fields. Ntaj would stitch the cuts and give antibiotics. One evening after the sun had gone down, it fell to me to perform this task, as Ntaj had been drinking during a ceremony. While children held up candles so that I could see what I was doing, I stitched up a young woman's finger and put it in a splint, but I balked at injecting her with antibiotics, fearing she might be allergic to them. Ntaj gave her the antibiotics the next day.[22]

Most Hmong in Flower Village were capable of giving emergency first aid. One morning a teenage boy, picking nuts from a tree outside of our home, fell and broke his arm. The man in the house set the bone, wrapped it in leaves and bark from a specific tree, and bandaged it with black cloth. Within weeks the boy's arm had healed cleanly. I saw children and even older people with broken bones that healed well and quickly after being treated in this manner. After the accident, a soul-calling ritual was held for the boy. I asked why he needed a soul calling when he had fallen out of a tree, and the answer was that he would not have fallen if he hadn't been out of balance in some way. Perhaps people would have said the same about the women who cut themselves; but if they had soul-calling rituals as well as antibiotics and stitches, I did not know it, or think to ask.

A person also can become sick from not following all the rules for Hmong life (kev cai), from being cruel, or from stealing from neighbors. Such behavior is in itself a sign of being out of balance or of having a "bad liver."

Women's bodies must be brought back into balance after they give birth. Postpartum women are in a "cold" state, so they eat only "hot" food and are protected from the wind and cold so they will not have pains in their bones when they are older. Overall, being in equilibrium—keeping a balance between opposing forces—is how health is maintained, both in the human body and in the universe.

COMPLEMENTARITY AND OPPOSITION

In most Hmong stories and in everyday life, everything—from death and life to the right and left sides of the human body—is considered in a dichotomous or complementary perspective, often a gendered one. Complementarity, which unites, is one aspect of Hmong gender contrast; opposition, which separates, is the other. This paradoxical equation is played out in numerous ways in Hmong cosmology and in daily life. All two-part objects are composed of gendered elements; so the mortar and pestle or the horns used for divination have a female and a male part. Humans and spirits are also described as being in complementary relationships or pairs, portrayed as male/female couples or as incorporating features of both sexes. Many beneficent Hmong deities, such as Saub, the father of all Hmong, are married; many other deities are unmarried but composed of two genders, such as Kab Yeeb, who guides the soul of the newborn to earth. Hmong patrilineal ancestors are invoked as a couple—motherfather—linguistically a single unit, rather than as two separate individuals. And when a person is suffering from soul loss, both the sick person and the spouse are treated, because if one member of a couple is sick, the other is sick as well.

Birth is described in two parts: the actual physiological event *(tus menyuam yug)* and the soul-calling ceremony *(hu plig)* three days later. There are also two parts to Hmong funerary rites, and birth and death themselves are complementary parts of a single whole.

Hmong conceptual paradigms follow the Chinese medical system, in which the body contains two kinds of *qi*, or life force. Cold *(yin)* is associated with the female, and hot *(yang)* with the male (Tapp 1989b:157). As Nicholas Tapp has kindly pointed out (personal communication, May 1991), the hot/cold dichotomy of the Hmong is derived from Chinese medicine rather than from Ayurvedic (which is more common in this part of Southeast Asia), and illustrates the opposition/complementarity theme so central to Hmong cosmological thought, especially as it pertains to gender.

Aspects of the physical world are also described as gendered pairs: the earth and sun are female, and the sky and moon are male. Unlike many other societies that associate the male with the right hand, which is most often considered the strongest, Hmong associate men with the left side of the body because "the right hand toils and the left hand rests" (Hertz 1960:108). So, as Robert Hertz indicates, women's significant contribution of physical labor is widely acknowledged, but it does not correspond to increased social worth.

The male principle is also associated with the "bones" of the body and the female with the "flesh" (Radley 1986:387), a dichotomy common to many South and Southeast Asian cultures (Lévi-Strauss 1969:3, 93–405; Fox 1971:219–252; Traub 1986:93). The bone metaphor is linked to the idea that men form the "skeleton of society" upon which all else is built, consistent with Hmong ideology that "men are more important," as informants uniformly report. The male principle is also associated with the direction "up," which is more valued than "down." But males are also associated with the roots of a plant rather than the flower because the roots are more durable and lasting, just as males are permanently connected to their natal families, even after death (Tapp 1989b:158–59; Hang 1986:34).

In addition to honoring husband-and-wife and mother-and-father pairs, Hmong place a high value on another gendered pair, that of brother and sister.

BROTHERS AND SISTERS

Several Hmong myths illustrate the importance of the brother/sister relationship, which is another instance of complementarity and opposition. In "The Second Origin Myth," all the people of the world come from the cut-up pieces of flesh produced by the marriage of a brother and a sister.[23]

> A long time ago, after the world was deluged with water, the only living couple on earth was a brother and a sister. Puj and Yawm Saub instructed them to marry one another and have a child together. When the offspring was born, it was not a child but a monstrous piece of flesh. Saub advised the couple to cut the flesh into many pieces, and these pieces became all of the different inhabitants of the world, including the Hmong clans. (Tapp 1989b:164–65)

Nicolas Tapp has recorded a tale in which a brother and sister compete against each other to see who can reach the dragon's pool first (1989b:154–57). The story reflects the Hmong belief in geomancy, which has as its essential principle "that it is upon the welfare of the ancestors that the fortunes of the descendants depend" (Tapp 1989b:137); thus lineage members must be buried in a location that takes full advantage of the natural mountainous areas and the flow of rivers and streams (Feuchtwang 1974:221; Freedman 1966:106; Tapp 1989b:151–59). In Tapp's story the brother wins, but his lineage suffers because his sister curses him.

The relationship between sisters and brothers has a special place in Hmong society. At the time of a young woman's wedding, her brother gives her many gifts, including clothing. The brother also brings rice or paper spirit money to his sister's funeral, and he makes sure that her husband and his family have provided everything needed for her journey to the next world. If this has not been done, he reproaches them with the traditional speech: "My sister worked all her life for you. She provided you with children and cared for you and for them. Why do you not now provide for her?" If the husband and his family cannot or will not provide the objects and rituals necessary for the burial, the brother, if he has had a good relationship with his sister, will do so.

A brother must also make sure that his sister's debts to her husband and his lineage have been paid. He asks them, "Was she a good Hmong wife? Did she provide children?" And so on. If she was not a good Hmong wife— if she did bad things or was not modest—the brother will sacrifice pigs and perform ceremonies until she is freed of her earthly obligations and can become a full ancestral member of her husband's lineage, at peace in the afterlife, and able to be reborn.[24]

A sister also performs this duty for her brother, ensuring his safe passage to the otherworld so that his soul can be reborn as a human being. A man cannot be buried until his sister and her husband arrive at his home. She too must seek assurance that all of her brother's debts have been settled and that all debts owed to him have been paid. She must be satisfied that his children have shown him sufficient respect and that the animals needed to accompany him to the land of darkness have been sacrificed. If an accident was the cause of death—an accident being a "bad death," since the deceased has not lived out the allotted time on earth—she is asked to suggest solutions and blessings. She does all of this through her husband; he speaks, she stands in the background. If a man's sister is dead or he has no sister, a man from her lineage negotiates in her place. There *must* be a symbolic stand-in for the sister.

The following examples illustrate other aspects of the role played by a man's sister. At one of the weddings I attended, a glass of rice liquor was spilt during negotiations. Because this was an ominous sign, the groom's father's sister *(phauj)* was called in to appease the spirits. She poured two more glasses of rice liquor and offered them to the spirits; then she drank one and passed the other to the groom to drink. In another instance, when a man had committed suicide by hanging himself from a tree, his sister was called in to decide whether a special ritual was needed. When in the past an inappropriate act took place between a man and his daughter-in-law in the Vaj clan, the man's sister created a taboo against fathers-in-law and daughters-in-law eating together at the same table, a taboo that is still in effect in this clan. And finally, legend has it that in the Yaj clan, one day a man ate the heart of a relative by mistake. His sister decreed that from then on, Yaj males could not eat the heart of any animal, a food taboo that is still in effect in that clan.

Although a man's sister wields considerable authority in matters having to do with her brother, it is important to note that she does not often speak for herself. It is her husband who sits with the other men during specific negotiations and speaks for his wife, although he is obliged to discuss negotiations with her before a final decision is reached (Lee 1981:291). If the sister is unmarried, a man from the lineage will speak for her.

During New Year celebrations, sisters frequently invite their brothers to visit, and sacrifice pigs in their honor when they arrive. During the next New Year celebration, a brother may return the invitation. If his sister cannot make the trip, her husband will go in her stead and a pig will be sacrificed in her honor, although she will not get to eat it. Sisters also frequently make burial clothing for their brothers, if the relationship is close. In Flower Village, sister-brother relationships usually seemed warm and caring.

A shaman in Flower Village told me this story:

A long time ago there was a Hmong brother and sister. They both married and had children. The brother had a son and the sister had a daughter. The brother's son took the sister's daughter to the field house and made love to her. She became pregnant. The sister complained to her brother, and he told her he would kill his son. [She replied,] "Don't do that, make him marry my daughter. But from now on I will have the ability to influence him all of his life." (T. Vwj 1987)[25]

This story reveals two important aspects of Hmong culture: that cross-cousin marriage is the preference, and that the father's sister can exert considerable influence, both positive and negative, on her brother's son, especially if she is also his mother-in-law. Elsewhere in the story, the mother-in-law calls the young man "son" not "son-in-law" *(vauv),* and he calls her aunt (*phauj;* specifically, paternal aunt) rather than "mother-in-law." The *phauj* can influence her nephew's marriage choices if his parents die, and through her husband, she is expected to offer her nephew advice and aid. Brothers exert little influence on their sisters' children, who are influenced instead by their father's sister or paternal aunt.

Sisters have a prominent role in Hmong society, although they cannot participate directly in discussions or negotiations of any kind. But they are approached for advice, assistance, and solutions to problems concerning their brothers and their brother's families. Thus, although this has been underreported in the literature on the Hmong to date, it is worth noting that women remain connected to their natal lineage, influencing its members in important, formally recognized, and consistent ways; their limited authority deserves further study.

GENDER AND COSMOLOGY: THE LONG VIEW

Fertility is a central organizing construct for the Hmong, partly because it provides the opportunity for rebirth. Neither women nor men are considered complete until they have had a child, a vessel for the soul of an ancestor. The ideal or culmination of one's gender image is attained in the role of mother or father, which are paired, complementary roles. Spinsterhood is feared as an incomplete or unfulfilled state of being. If a woman never marries, she is "unlucky." When she dies she is buried quickly and with little ceremony; her family hopes to prevent her unlucky soul from returning to the same circumstances and once more subjecting them to "loss of face," financial hardship, and the absence of social links with other clans. An unmarried man is also unlucky, but there are few unmarried Hmong men. I knew none.

When a married woman dies, her second soul becomes part of her husband's lineage in the land of darkness; she and her husband become one dyadic spirit, fed and remembered by their descendants. Thus, at the time of death, women do at last become ancestors; they are not entirely excluded from the patriline, and as sisters may retain a connection with their natal lineage as well. Also, since a woman's returning soul ideally reincarnates as human and as male, she will have a public voice in her next life, whereas her husband, in his next (female) incarnation, will fall silent. In the long view, intergenerationally, women carry along the patriline as they become ancestors, and as they take on male personae.

The soul itself has no gender; only the form that it takes in life makes it male or female. Cosmology defines what it is to be Hmong; and in some sense to be Hmong is to change gender from lifetime to lifetime.

MOTHERS, DAUGHTERS, AND WIVES

n March of 1988 I attended a wedding in Flower Village. Many villagers had gathered in the bride's parents' house, not only for the ceremony itself, but for the long and noisy negotiations (in this case, three days) that precede Hmong weddings. The festivities ended when the young groom and bride left to go live in his parents' household in another village. Even then, the rest of us, men and women together, continued to sit and talk. The bride's mother was melancholy. "I remember my daughter," she said. "Who will cook the rice for me now?" I had been asking many questions about the events of the last few days; now I asked, "Why does a girl always have to go to live in the home of her husband? Wouldn't it be good if she could stay at her mother's home?" One of the older men turned and said to me, "When a Hmong daughter obtains a husband, she must go to live in his house. She must be a good Hmong wife and obey her husband. She must live there because that is the way we Hmong do it. It is our way [*kev cai*]." He then told the following story, called "Why Men Rule the World":

Long, long ago there was a Hmong queen who had seven husbands. There was also a Hmong king who had seven wives. There was a struggle between these two groups of people as to who should rule the world. The queen and the king decided to go to Yawm Saub and ask him who should rule the world.

Yawm Saub said, "Each one of you will be given a test, and when it is completed, I will give you an answer to your question. You come back tomorrow," he said to the king, "and you, Queen, come back in a few days."

The next day the king went back to see Yawm Saub. "This is your test. I want you to go back to your wives, cut off their heads, and bring them to me," said Saub.

The king went back to his home. He saw his wives all sitting together in the house, breastfeeding his children. He thought about the test, and he knew he could not do as he had been told. He went back to Yawm Saub and said, "Saub, I cannot do as you ask. My wives are feeding our children milk. If I kill them and bring their heads to you, my children will have no food, and they will die." Saub nodded his head and told him to come back in a few days.

After two days, the queen arrived at the place of Yawm Saub. "This is your test. I want you to go back to your husbands, cut off their heads, and bring them to me," said Saub.

The queen went back to her husbands, cut off their heads and carried them back to Yawm Saub.

Saub called the king and queen together and said to them, "The king shall rule the world, for he knows the meaning of life."

Here, in legendary form, gender asymmetry is attributed to the superior judgment of men, who understand that the true meaning of life is its perpetuation through one's descendants. Men have the moral agency and the skills to analyze a situation carefully and then use their own judgment; they have the independence of thought and the courage to stand up to Yawm Saub. The queen's lack of judgment reveals her penchant for following instructions, even those that are counterproductive to the perpetuation of the species, and shows that women are more suited to be followers than to be leaders.

The tale was told by a man, by way of offering an explanation for patrilocal residence patterns. When I asked women about this story, most of them said they were not sure what it meant, and suggested I ask their husbands or fathers. One woman did give her interpretation: that men and women cannot live without each other, but women must do what they are told, and that was why the queen killed her husbands. An important subtext to this story is its implication that women are essential to the continuity of life, since although the queen did not hesitate to kill her husbands, the king could not kill his wives without also killing his offspring. In this interpretation, the story reveals the value of women.

The anthropological debate on gender inequality and the universality of gender-based oppression is no longer at the forefront of gender studies. To understand what, to a Westerner, appears to be an unequal relationship between Hmong men and women, we have to conceptualize our analysis within the Hmong social structure. The discourses on gender hierarchy introduce Western arguments and then place certain cultures, such as the Hmong, at the low end of the development hierarchy due to what is perceived as the low status of women. But even if we abandon the concept of and arguments around universal gender asymmetry, we are still left with the question of how to comprehend a stratified society. What measurements do we use to comprehend the meaning of gender in such a society? Does gender stratification lead to inequality? Or can we interpret the asymmetrical relation between men and women as complementarity instead?

Marilyn Strathern (1988:3–23), Chandra Mohanty (1990:1–47), and Jane Atkinson and Shelly Errington (1996:1–58) warn us against imputing a "common" meaning to our subjects' actions and thus giving the impression of worldwide parallels and common experiences. We are accountable to the subjects we study, and we should address our analysis to their own particular cultural surroundings. The anthropologist owes the society she studies a true cultural interpretation—or as true an interpretation as possible.[1]

Hmong men and women ultimately live together in the world. Neither gender can be understood fully without considering interpersonal relationships between the sexes, and the ways in which women's roles as daughters, wives, and mothers are related to men's roles as sons, husbands, and fathers.

STRATIFICATION

Hmong society is stratified by both age and gender. Elders are considered more knowledgeable than the young, and therefore control production and subsistence; they are afforded greater respect, deference, and honor. Although women are considered men's complementary opposites, males are perceived as smarter, stronger, and more capable than females.[2] This paradoxical assessment of women as both complementary and lesser is played out in legends and anecdotes on a daily basis, without concern for its contradictory qualities. Within the patrilineal family, men are responsible for the care of and communication with lineage ancestors; women are excluded from this "realm in which the highest powers of society are felt to reside" (Ortner 1974:69). In this sense all men are afforded more respect, deference, and honor than women. Although this formulation is clearly a simplification of a Hmong idea, every Hmong woman has her own experience of these general categories, which can be contextualized through individual stories.

AGE CATEGORIES AND TERMS OF REFERENCE

There are a number of age categories among the Hmong, each with its own term of reference. From birth until approximately four years of age, or until another child is born into the family, boys and girls are called "smallest children" *(tus menyuam mos)*; from approximately age four until puberty, they are called "young children" *(tus menyuam yaus)*. Although a child's given or proper name can be used until marriage, individuals are often referred to by kinship terms (e.g., "my daughter," "my son") or by their birth order (e.g., "youngest child," "middle child"). Within the family, children have pet names—or "fondness names," as Hmong call them—that describe the character or appearance of a child and are used only while the child is young. For example, a child in Flower Village who was particularly adept at climbing was called Poj Liab, or Monkey.

Unmarried females and males who have reached puberty are collectively known as "young girls and boys" *(tub hluas ntxhais hluas)*. When they begin to court, they are called "young courting girls" *(hluas nkauj)* and "young courting boys" *(hluas nraug)*. At the time of marriage, girls become "women" *(tus poj niam)* and boys become "men" *(tus txiv neej)*. After marriage, a woman is defined first according to her relationship with her husband; she is called "wife" or "woman of—" until she gives birth to her first child, when she is defined by that child and called "—'s mother." Even if she gives birth to other children, she retains the name related to her firstborn and is addressed this way by everyone in the village.

After marriage, a man retains his given name until his wife has borne several children, at which time his wife's family bestows an honorary name upon him, usually a favorite name in the family. When a man has more than one wife, the senior wife is addressed as "oldest mother," the second wife as "middle mother," and the third wife as "youngest mother." In the event that a man is wealthy enough to afford more than three wives, the first wife is known as "oldest mother" and the ensuing wives are referred to in the order in which they married—"second wife" and so on. As in other polygynous societies, the oldest wife retains the highest rank and has authority over all the others.

The elderly are known as "respected elders" *(cov txwj laus),* a term used for both sexes, although women uniformly receive less respect than men. Older women and men are addressed by everyone as "grandmother" and "grandfather." As the following examples reveal, relative chronological age, role, and gender are important markers in relationships.

One day, a woman who was busy chopping vegetables to feed the pigs asked her teenage son to fetch some water from the pipe located some distance away on a hill. His older sister was cleaning rice for the evening meal, but the boy answered his mother by saying, "Why don't you ask your daughter to fetch it? One day she'll leave, and she won't do things for you any more. I'll still be here for your lifetime." As he remained seated, his mother told the daughter to fetch the water, and the daughter did so. The son was able to deny his mother's authority, whereas the daughter was not. Although younger men are not as a rule inconsiderate or rude to older women, women—not men—are responsible for domestic chores. Also, as the son pointed out, the daughter was in some sense a temporary member of the household. She was someone who was going to leave.

In another instance, an old woman was ill. While a shaman performed a healing ritual, the daughters-in-law of the household prepared food for both the ailing woman and her husband. After the ritual and just before the elderly couple sat down together at the table, their two sons and the husband's two younger brothers (who were there for the ritual), knelt on the ground and bowed *(pe)* to them as a sign of deference and respect for the couple's age and position in the kin group. This case reveals that sons are expected to show respect to their parents and also illustrates the importance of the mother and father as the primary unit in Hmong society.

Until marriage, sons and daughters work for their parents in both the domestic and agricultural spheres. They earn no money of their own and are consequently dependent on their parents for subsistence. Sons are also dependent upon their families for the bride-price to acquire a wife. The wife-receiving group pays bride-price to the wife-giving group in exchange for sexual rights, the woman's reproductive potential, and material goods. (In Flower Village, the average bride-price was six silver bars.) Although sons and mothers participate to a limited extent in the decision-making process (with women often negotiating around the needlework the bride brings with her), fathers and other elder male lineage members always make the final decision.

When daughters marry, they need clothing and silver necklaces, as well as liquor, rice, and sacrificial animals to feed their wedding guests and offer to the ancestors. Although bride-price is paid to the daughter's household, a portion of it is returned to the newly married couple in the form of these "gifts."

GENDER STRATIFICATION

Patrilineage and clan membership mean different things for women than for men. Sons remain in the household and in the lineage of their birth. Although a daughter retains a lifelong connection with her natal family, her allegiances at the time of her marriage are transferred to her affinal family, who often live some distance from her home village. In Flower Village, which is inhabited by several different clans, there was a possibility that a girl could marry outside her clan and still remain in the village, but some Hmong villages are comprised of only a single clan.

Although cross-cousin marriage (in which the brother's daughter marries his sister's son) is preferred, and often occurs where the man has sisters, the sister often lives far from her own natal village, and there is little in the way of visiting.[3] If a family owns a truck, which was not common when I first lived in Flower Village but is more usual now, a father may visit his daughter occasionally. One of the good reasons for a girl to marry her cousin, even if he lives far away, is that a mother-in-law who is also an aunt may not be cruel, as some mothers-in-law are. But if the aunt lives in a distant village, the girl may hardly know her.

The bride-price payment, referred to as the debt owed to her parents for her milk and food ("milk and care money," *nqe mis nqe hno*), ties a woman to her husband and his lineage, giving them rights to her labor, sexuality, and reproduction. Although divorce is relatively rare, it is not unheard of; the underlying assumption is that the woman is at fault, and she must leave her children with her husband's family. The children belong to the husband's family and lineage, and children are part of a lineage's assets.

In Flower Village, a thiry-year-old divorced woman and her two-year-old daughter lived in a small room built onto the back of the woman's father's house. After returning from her husband's village, she worked her father's fields and cooked for him and her brothers. (All of her sisters were married, and her mother was dead.) After she had completed her household tasks, she and her child spent their evenings in the small, separate room, not in the main house. I asked her, "Why do you and your daughter sleep out here in this small room?" She replied,

> It is the Hmong way. When a daughter runs away from her husband, she cannot live in her father's house, or the spirits of the house will be unhappy and we would all get sick. Yes, I ran away from my husband because he had a bad liver. He smoked opium a lot and even though I cared for the house and the children and I brought in the rice, he would often hit me. It went on for several years, and I had four sons that I love. When my body became occupied again [pregnant] and he hit me, I could not live there any more. I hit him with a stone in his face. I broke his teeth and then I ran away back to my father. My husband said I was not a good Hmong wife, and he and his family kept my sons. I remember them every day. But now I have my daughter and she will stay here with me.

As this account suggests, a divorced woman occupies a marginal position, one that is beset with difficulties. No longer part of her father's lineage, she is permitted to reside on his property but is not welcomed into the home by either her father or the household spirits. This woman's four sons remained with her husband's lineage, and, despite her husband's abuse, she was considered a bad wife. Nicholas Tapp (1989b:112) has suggested that bride-price constitutes a bride's social insurance since its return cannot be demanded; if a wife decides to leave because of abuse or abandonment, her natal family still keeps her bride-price. I suggest that this is true, but only after she has given birth, since this is the point at which the marriage negotiations are considered complete. (The bride-price is for the children she will bear, as much as for her labor in the house and fields.) And then, unless the husband is perceived as being in the wrong—and even physical abuse does not put him in the wrong—she must leave her children behind if she leaves the marriage. This convention places great constraints on a woman who remarries after her husband's death as well as on a divorced woman. The Hmong practice the levirate rule: that is, a widow is usually absorbed into the late husband's family through marriage to one of her husband's younger brothers or cousins. If she wishes to return to her natal family or marry outside of the household, she must leave her children behind.

For the reasons cited above, it is unusual for a woman to leave an abusive husband. The divorced woman above later remarried. She left Flower Village with her daughter, who became part of the new husband's lineage, and the woman herself had two more sons. Although her divorce had placed her outside of society and put her in the wrong, she found a new husband and household to belong to, and seemed quite happy when I saw her again.

If a woman is extremely distraught, she may give vent to her feelings (expressing them loudly) within the home and occasionally outside it as a form of social control. Very few women, however, seek to undermine male authority in the presence of others. Women want to be thought of as good daughters and wives, an image that brings them, their parents, and their husbands respect. Also, women fear the very real threat of disciplinary action from the men they live with.

I do not mean to suggest that Hmong men have no respect for their wives. Although their ideology stresses male dominance, these ideals do not prevent husbands from discussing economic or political issues with their wives. Although final decisions rest firmly with the men, wives do appear to exercise some influence over their husbands.

On many occasions, women and men told me what constitutes the ideal Hmong woman and man. The following are typical answers to the question "I have been told that I wasn't a good Hmong woman because I didn't wear my *sev*. What qualities besides wearing the *sev* make a good Hmong woman?" Paj Niam, a thirty-six-year-old mother of seven, answered,

> First, a good Hmong woman must wear the right clothing. If she does not wear her *sev*, she is shameful and not shy. She must be energetic and vigorous [*nquag nquag*], not lazy. She must want to get the rice planted and harvested so that her family will not be hungry. She must work hard in the field

and in the home and make sure that her children do that too. She must want to see her husband respected by people in the house and village. By doing everything the right way, she can bring honor and respect to her husband and children and to her parents[-in-law]. She must want at least as many children as her mother or mother-in-law does, and she must teach them to be good Hmong girls and boys. She must respect her husband and her mother [-in-law] and father[-in-law] and all other elderly people. She must be polite. She must know how to entertain guests when they visit the house. She must not be greedy. She must know how to care for the animals and how to sew well for her daughters and sons. She must be able to teach her daughters how to embroider and make clothing.

Paj, her 16-year old daughter, added, "I think she must also have long hair and be clean and pretty. She must know how to sing love songs [*kwv txhiaj*]."

To the question "What do you think makes a good Hmong man?" the mother replied,

A good Hmong man is also energetic and vigorous but not so much as a woman. He must be strong so that he can cut down the big trees in the field. He must care for his wife and children. His family must know the Hmong way and have no health problems. He must not have a bad liver [*siab phem*][4] and must not hit his wife or children unless they deserve it. He must not be lazy and leave the work for his wife and children. He must love and care for his parents and know the rituals needed to feed them after they die. If his wife or children get sick, he must go and find someone to help them. He must care for his wife for one month after she has a baby. He must feed her chicken and be sure she rests and gets back her strength.

To this, the daughter added, "He must come from a family that has money and perhaps a truck. He must be smart and handsome, and he should know how to sing love songs."

A number of Hmong cultural values are revealed in the definitions presented above. Of particular interest are the different emphases of the mother and daughter. The mother is concerned with a future husband's character, specifically with his ability to provide for his family, whereas her daughter is most concerned with a man's physical appearance, his ability to sing love songs, his intelligence, and whether he comes from a family in good standing; the daughter's list is a mixture of practicality and vanity. It should be noted that the daughter was also teasing her mother over her serious and conservative list of virtues. Unlike her mother, she giggled as she gave her answers.

The Hmong believe that all human beings—women and men—should work hard. Since men are supposed to be stronger, they do the heavy work of felling trees to prepare the fields, but women also work hard at farming, as well as feeding their family and caring for the children. In this context, women are expected to be more "energetic and vigorous" than men. Men must also know the "Hmong way" (the rituals and traditions of the clan and lineage) to honor the ancestors properly. Women are responsible for the care of their parents-in-law. Men must possess worldly knowledge and be able to make informed decisions. Women are expected to listen, be polite, and gain respect for themselves and their families. These ideals are transmitted from generation to generation, with women—specifically mothers, grandmothers, and older sisters—primarily responsible for socializing children to become good Hmong. Behavioral norms are inculcated through proverbs, folklore, oral history, riddles, and jokes. As has been pointed out (see Fadiman 1997:21), Hmong love their children very much, but when children shirk their tasks, they are scolded and sometimes hit. When punished, Hmong children cry in a stylized sing-song fashion, often for extended periods of time.

A girl spends her childhood with female relatives who are responsible for her socialization until marriage. Boys are left in the care of women and spend their time in and around the home until the age of six, when they begin to spend more time with their fathers and brothers (both real and classificatory) and other young boys.

To fit into any society, an individual follows the rules for behavior. As Ralph Linton has shown, status and role are "models for organizing the attitudes and behavior of the individual so that these will be congruent with those of the other individuals participating in the expression of the pattern" (1973:188). Although there are ways to manipulate the system—not all women or men fit the ideal Hmong pattern—a significant amount of social control is exerted on both sexes, and both strive to fulfill their assigned roles.

CHAPTER 2

WOMEN AS DAUGHTERS

In a Hmong family, the first question about a newborn child is "Boy or girl?"
Just as the Native American Navajos bury a daughter's placenta under the
loom to ensure that she will become a skilled weaver, the Hmong bury a
daughter's placenta under the bed to ensure that she will be the mother of
many children.

When Mae, a twenty-seven-year-old Hmong woman, gave birth to her
seventh child, who was also her third daughter, I asked, "How does it feel
when you give birth to a daughter?" Her answer revealed how the outsider
status of daughters affects the mother-daughter relationship even from the
moment of birth:

> They are both lovely. I love my children so much. I feel better when I have a
> son. When you give birth to a son, you feel stronger. We need sons to care
> for us in our old age, to feed us when we die. They stay home with us. When
> you have a son, nobody complains. Everybody is proud—your husband, your
> mother[-in-law], your father[-in-law], all of the household, all of the village.
> A son will marry and bring in a daughter-in-law. You don't love her as you
> love your own daughter, but you will love the babies he gives her.
>
> But they are all lovely. We need to have a daughter, too, but we feel different.
> Girls help their mother. Daughters stay close to the mother. Maybe mother
> and daughter-in-law are not so close. Maybe when you die or when you are
> sick and dirty, no one will care for you, but if you have a daughter, she will
> wash you when nobody else will. I love to do special things for my daughter.
> I want to make her skirts or shirts; then people will look and see that I am a
> good mother. They will admire my work, and when I teach her to do needle-
> work, people will know I have taught her well. But daughters go away to other
> families, and it is very painful when they go far away.

The birth of a son not only brings a woman more respect from her husband and in-laws, but gives her a sense of security; sons care for their mothers in their old age and even in the afterlife. A mother knows that eventually
she will "lose" a daughter. In this way the social status of Hmong women
greatly influences their family relationships, possibly undermining the
mother-daughter bond from the very moment of birth. On the other hand,
the poignance in the knowledge of future loss may make for a more intense

bond in the relatively shorter time that a mother and daughter have together. In some way a mother may even value the daughter all the more because she is going to leave. Despite the ideal of "Hmong is maleness," the gender division in Hmong society leaves plenty of room for ambiguities. Sons have more power and are responsible for their parents' well-being in old age and in the afterlife; but individuals love and value each other for many reasons, not all of them practical.

Both women and men both appear to derive a great deal of pleasure from the company of infants and children. Infants are held constantly—in people's arms or in specially designed backpacks. Although women and small girls are primarily responsible for the care of children and babies, men often hold their children, although it is unusual for a man to bathe or feed an infant. When an infant cries, usually the mother breastfeeds until the baby falls asleep. Then she straps the baby onto her back or hands her/him to another member of the household so that she can finish her chores. Children breastfeed on demand, and young children sleep in the same bed as their parents. Mothers take their infants to the fields in a backpack; while the mother is working, daughters as young as age four care for the infant in the small field house. As mothers-in-law grow older, they may stay at home and care for small children.

By age two or three a child usually has been weaned, although this depends upon how quickly the mother becomes pregnant again. After the age of four, daughters begin to help with household chores. They may sweep, carry small pots of water from the village tap, or wash clothing there. Boys, on the other hand, often stay in the village with other small boys, climbing trees or trying to catch or shoot birds with slingshots.

At approximately six years of age, children begin to attend school. The school in Flower Village, which has been in operation only since 1984, is administered by the Thai Department of Education and runs from grades one through six. Children are taught the Thai language, mathematics, and social studies. They go to school when they are not needed at home or in the fields, and most of them seem to enjoy it. Even at school, girls often continue to do childcare: it is not unusual to see young girls with infants strapped on their backs, sitting at their desks diligently writing a Thai assignment.

At approximately the same time as they begin school, girls begin to learn to make "flower cloth" (paj ntaub). These pieces of cloth are thickly embroidered with thread and/or reverse appliqué, and are used to decorate clothing. Some girls love to sew and take to it quickly, enjoying the praise they receive from their mother and older sisters, whereas others need to be chided to practice and scolded until they learn. These pieces of needlework are used by girls for everyday wear; as they grow older, especially when they reach puberty and begin courting, they also make special pieces to be worn at New Year celebrations. Mothers also make flower cloth for their sons and daughters, and later for their son's children.

I rarely saw daughters sitting around the house or standing around talking in the village. Girls are encouraged to be industrious at all times, both in the fields and in the home, and if they complete their subsistence labor, they are expected to work on their embroidery in whatever spare time they have.

FLOWER CLOTH

In the past men built looms, and women spun hemp *(maj)*, wove cloth, and made it into clothing. Although much of the cloth and thread are now bought in the valley, the embroidered flower cloth that decorates clothing is still a defining mark of ethnic identity. As Jane Schneider and Annette Weiner have shown, "in the form of clothing and adornment, or . . . for exchange and heirloom conservation, cloth helps social groups to reproduce themselves and to achieve autonomy or advantage in interactions with others" (1989:1).

Hmong textile art is not only part of the bride's dowry and a significant subject for marriage negotiations; it visually identifies a person as Hmong. The clothing Hmong wear—batiked cloth skirts for Green Mong women and closely pleated white skirts for (some) White Hmong women—gives these groups their names and identity. In fact, all of the highland tribes wear distinctive clothing that signals their ethnic identity. Despite the many geographic variations in Hmong clothing, one can spot a Hmong person by traditional clothing styles and colors, and by the patterns in the flower cloth that decorates the clothing.

Flower cloth is also a defining craft for Hmong women. A girl's needlework skills in the embroidery stitches, cross stitches, appliqué, and reverse appliqué that go into the making of the environmental motifs (e.g., trees, flowers, elephants' feet, and pumpkin seeds) and geometric designs of flower cloth reflect her patience and perseverance as well as her talent. As girls grow older and become more experienced needlewomen, they are expected to know how to make intricate and colorful patterns with hidden stitches. These patterns are passed on from mothers, grandmothers, and aunts, and every Hmong girl is expected to use her own talent and creativity to improve upon traditional patterns or create new ones. When a girl reaches marriageable age, her needlework is closely inspected by many people, some of them prospective in-laws. The Hmong believe that one can determine a great deal about a girl's character and abilities from her flower cloth, because it requires patience, creativity, and industriousness—all the virtues of a good Hmong woman. Small, even stitches indicate that a girl is good at organizing her life; her ability to reuse thread she has pulled from pieces of old cloth portends the skills of a good manager. If a girl has completed many impressive pieces, she earns a reputation for industriousness, and if her needlework is clean (not covered with the red soil of the area), it is predicted that she will raise clean and well-behaved children, and be a good housekeeper. If she is creative in her patterns and stitches, then she will be creative in the ways that she cares for and manages her family. On the other hand, if the small embroidered collar on the back of a her shirt is not considered good work by the women who examine it, they will say, "That woman has one shirt collar done very badly, and she should not be a woman."

Flower cloth is worn on everyday clothing—even when working in the fields, women wear jackets with colorful pieces sewn on as a collar, whereas men's jackets are decorated with embroidered front panels and pockets. I was struck by the interest women showed in every new pattern they saw; when Hmong visitors came into the village, the women examined their flower cloth eagerly, so they could copy the patterns later in their own work. Although some women in Flower Village said they chose patterns and colors for their beauty, several said that specific patterns were symbolic as well. The snail-shell design *(qwj)* represents family growth, and the elephant's foot pattern promotes wealth. Some flower cloth patterns are supposed to protect the wearer from wild spirits in the forest. Crosses or geometric figures are often sewn on the backs of children's shirts to ward off wild spirits. Sometimes crosses are sewn on a sick person's shirt to help her or him recover and then stay healthy and balanced.

Although all of the work-a-day clothing is decorated with flower cloth, the finest and most important pieces are made for New Year celebrations, weddings, and the liminal periods of birth and death. A newborn child is vulnerable to wild spirits, so baby carriers are embroidered richly, and, as mentioned earlier, mothers make flower hats for their children so the wild spirits will think the child is a flower.

Flower cloth also aids the spirits of the dead when they make the perilous journey to the land of darkness. Children of the dead person usually lay pieces of flower cloth (made over the years and saved for the funeral) under the head of the corpse, and clothe the corpse in garments decorated with especially fine flower cloth so the soul can travel safely. A piece of flower cloth made (often long ago) by a woman of the family (usually the dead person's mother, who herself probably is already dead and thus an ancestor) is often placed in the coffin as well, to make it easier for the ancestors to recognize the spirit when it reaches the land of darkness. Both the flower cloth in the coffin and the placenta that the spirit will retrieve from its birthplace assure that the soul will find its own ancestors and be with them through time.

At the New Year everyone dresses in their finest clothing, which is covered with flower cloth; old, plain clothing does not bode well for the coming year. New Year is also the time of courtship, an important time for marriageable girls to display their embroidery skills, and they wear embroidered jackets and *sev*, and carry small embroidered bags hung with bells and coins for luck.

SEV (MODESTY APRONS)

Very small girls, like their brothers, run around naked; but at four years of age or so, daughters are taught the codes of conduct and instructed to wear clothing appropriate to their gender. This includes a shirt that usually has an embroidered or appliquéd collar, black trousers, and the *sev*, the two apronlike pieces of cloth that hang from a girl's belt in front and in back, covering even the faint outline of her buttocks and genital area. Trousers alone are considered too suggestive to be truly modest, and even when Hmong women wear skirts they wear *sev* as well. If a young girl leaves the house without putting on her *sev*, she is admonished by anyone who sees her to return home and get them. By the time a girl reaches adolescence, she would be ashamed to be seen without her *sev*, having been socialized to understand that it is shameful for females to go about with their genitalia and buttocks "uncovered."

As I mentioned earlier, when Hmong women made clothing for me to

FIG. 2.1. *A little girl wearing* sev *(modesty aprons).*
Girls are taught early to wear this article of
clothing, which covers them front and back.
(Photo by Patricia Symonds)

wear in the village, they insisted that I always wear my *sev;* to do otherwise, they said, would cause me to be shamefaced *(txaj muag)*. When questioned further about the significance of the *sev,* the women said things like "We cover ourselves because we would be embarrassed to have anyone see us. We are shy and we would be ashamed" and "We just do it. It is the Hmong way" or "Women do not look good without them." One man told me, "It would be dangerous for women to go without *sev,* dangerous for them and for men too." My subsequent efforts at explication were met with puzzlement; it appeared to be knowledge they could not or would not analyze further. Over time, I was able to relate their attitude toward *sev* to other aspects of Hmong life.

Until they become toilet trained, at about age three or four, very small children go about naked from the waist down, although occasionally a small girl may wear *sev* (fig. 2.1). I frequently saw mothers fondling their small sons' genitals; I never observed similar fondling of daughters during any of my village stays. At about the time children begin to learn to use outdoor toilets, they don sex-appropriate clothing, which is trousers and shirts, with the addi-

FIG. 2.2. Young girls dressed for the day. All are wearing unembroidered sev, *as they are not yet ready for marriage. (Photo by Patricia Symonds)*

tion of *sev* for girls. The small girl's *sev* are plain, made from black cloth with a blue stripe down the center (fig. 2.2). Sometimes mothers dress their small daughters in embroidered *sev* at New Year when everyone wears their finest clothing. After girls learn to embroider and do reverse appliqué, they make their own *sev*, which are put away and saved until they begin to court.

New Year is when courting rituals take place. Young men travel to the various villages that their kin have recommended, to discover for themselves whether any of the girls living there meet their approval. Boys and girls play games and sing love songs, and, eventually, if both of their families agree, make love matches (Lemoine 1972c:163–71; Lee 1981:40–42). The boys' clothing is made by mothers and sisters, and the girls' clothing is made by the girls themselves and their mothers. They wear heavily embroidered shirts, small bags, and turbanlike hats, all decorated with silver coins, and *sev* that often take as long as a year to complete. These *sev* are covered with needlework on both the front and back panels, and the belt that holds the panels in place is also beautifully worked (fig. 2.3). After marriage, women still wear *sev*, but these are plain, as they were in childhood (fig. 2.4). Only on special occasions, such as a visit to another village, do married women wear embroidered *sev*.

FIG. 2.3. *Ready for the New Year's celebration, these young adolescent girls wear beautiful embroidered sev. (Photo by Patricia Symonds)*

FIG. 2.4. *Married women and young girls. (Photo by Patricia Symonds)*

Even elderly women wear *sev;* when a woman dies she is buried in her finery, and once again wears the embroidered *sev*. Even divorced women and spinsters wear embroidered *sev* for New Year celebrations.

Sev signify femaleness, the age cycle, and sexuality. As Lila Abu-Lughod portrays the practice of wearing the veil among Awlad 'Ali Bedouin women, the wearing of the *sev* for Hmong women constitutes the most visible act of modest deference (1987:157). Women do not have to be coerced into wearing *sev;* through social conditioning they accept the necessity. Although men will feel shamed if women in their family go out without *sev,* it is the women who enforce the practice and instruct their young daughters to conform to this and other social norms (as they do in many cultures, as we know from feminist analyses of how women enforce norms such as female circumcision and footbinding).

Before they reach the age of puberty, daughters learn that sexuality is secretive; it is not discussed in the home by anyone except to say that one must keep the genital area covered. During the New Year's courting rituals, however, *sev* are transformed into symbols of a young woman's fecundity. Although girls wear them to hide genitalia, *sev* are also the most decorative of clothing, accentuating that area of the body they are purported to cover. In Abu-Lughod's terms, *sev* symbolizes shame because their purpose is to cover and hide; but they also symbolizes a woman's fertility, and celebrate it.

At the time of courtship, when the expression of a woman's sexuality becomes socially desirable, the beautifully decorated *sev* (substituted for the unadorned one she wore as a child) serves the second of its dual functions: it signals that a women is ready for marriage and motherhood. Girls do not participate in courting games until they have started menses. The term for menstruation is *coj khaubncaws*—literally, "to wear to send a message."

COURTSHIP

During the New Year, courting girls and boys sing love songs to each other. These songs *(kwv tshiaj plees)* reveal feelings and emotions they cannot express in everyday speech, feelings that would be considered inappropriately intimate or assertive out of this context. For years prior to these courtship meetings, girls and boys have been instructed in the ways to speak or not to speak with the other sex—to be "shy" and "avoid shame."[5] Kisrin Narayan's

(1986:47–75) analysis of the songs of unmarried girls in Northwest India shows how girls may express emotions in these songs that they would not otherwise state so directly. She particularly notes the sadness girls feel at the prospect of leaving their girlhood friends when they marry. The same sorrow is expressed by Hmong girls in their courting songs. Their friends are almost always kin who are classified as sisters, which means they can discuss family problems with each other, something they cannot do with people outside of their clan. It is particularly difficult for girls to leave these childhood confidantes if they marry outside of the natal village. Sometimes they are able to marry within the natal village, as in Flower Village, where there are several different clans. But more often they must leave everyone behind.

Just before the New Year in 1987, while we were sitting alone together in the small field house, I asked a sixteen-year-old girl I was close to, "You've made beautiful flower cloth to wear for New Year, Yim. Are you happy the day has come to wear it?" She replied,

Yes, I am happy, but I am shy too. I hope at New Year a boyfriend will come to the village and we will throw the ball to each other across the way. Maybe I will like him and he will like me, but maybe I will like him and he will not like me. Then I will be sad and think of him a lot. Maybe I will sing a song and let him know, or let my father know, and they will try to arrange for us to marry. I am sixteen, and it is time for me to find a boyfriend. If I do not find one, people will wonder why not. My parents will think I am choosy and do not want to leave.

Sometimes I am afraid. I want to marry, and I want to stay here. I will miss my grandmother, and I will miss my sisters. We work together in the field and talk when we are angry or sad or we want to know about things . . . how boyfriends and girlfriends get together. Sometimes I am afraid that I am not pretty or I do not work hard enough, and no one will want me. I am very scared that my new mother[-in-law] will not like me and I will be sad and lonely for my home. But sometimes I am more afraid that I will not find a boyfriend who will want to marry me and I will be alone forever and live with my mother and father.

Her answer reflects young women's ambivalence about marriage. To be a good Hmong woman, a girl must marry; becoming a spinster, dependent upon her natal family all of her life, is a socially undesirable outcome. But marriage entails leaving her family and friends and, in many cases, going to live among strangers.

The degree of skill and grace with which girls sing love songs is highly valued. The songs are not formalized but improvised and sung in a distinctive stylistic form. These love songs are melancholy—telling of unrequited love, or requited love that means leaving home—and poetic, and families are proud when their daughters sing well. The father of a deaf girl in Flower Village asked if I could help him find a cure for her. When we went to a physician in Chiang Mai and the doctor asked the father what the girl's problem was, he answered, "She cannot sing. Can you help her to sing?"

Love songs provide a forum for communicating ideas that are unacceptable in other social contexts. They are also a yardstick for measuring a girl's attractiveness, and a boy's too. The songs use the "flowery language" *(paj lug)* with which courting girls and boys attract each other.

Like the heavily decorated *sev* and flower cloth, love songs and "flowery language" signal sexual availability. After marriage, women are forbidden to sing love songs without the express permission of their husbands,[6] but because Hmong society is polygynous, singing is not taboo for married men. The prohibition against women's singing even extends to the special songs sung while weaving. Married women informally teach these songs to girls while they are working in the fields together, but not in the presence of males. The only time married women are permitted to sing in public is during a funeral, and then they must sing a keening song about how the dead will be missed (see chap. 4).[7]

But at New Year girls sing to attract husbands. The boys come into a village, dressed in their finery. They line up in a row opposite the row of girls to play the game of *pov pob,* which involves tossing a homemade cloth ball back and forth. A boy throws the ball to a girl he likes, and if she returns his interest, she deliberately drops the ball. Then he takes something belonging to her as a token to be returned when they meet again. The air is charged with expectation, and many villagers stay to watch the ball throwing, for it is great fun. People notice what each girl is wearing, to see what a good needlewoman she is. The colors at New Year are wonderful to see, and many girls carry umbrellas to protect their skin from sunburn. Pigs and chickens are sacrificed to the ancestors, and are cooked and eaten by the villagers. The courting couples then wander off to get to know each other.

Later in the evening, a boy will go to the house of a girl who has shown interest and tap on the wall of her bedroom. (It is said that in earlier times, and in other villages perhaps, the boy would play a Jew's harp [*ncas*] quietly outside her bedroom instead of tapping on the wall.) When she hears the tap, she slips outside and goes with him, usually to the field house, to experiment sexually. In the privacy of the fields, the couple sing to each other.

Living as they do in small open houses, no one in the girl's family is unaware of what is happening; even so, the couple are as quiet and surreptitious as possible, and no one in the household discusses it—to do so would be improper. Although her social life has been restricted until this time, a young, shy, and easily shamed daughter is given the privacy and freedom to experience her sexuality with a boy who attracts her. Young couples are free to engage in sexual activity without harassment, although courtship is governed by a number of rules. For instance, the boy may not go into the girl's bed; that would be an offense to her family and would shame them in the community, offend the lineage spirits, and possibly bring illness upon the household. And no one would consider a sexual liaison with a person from the same clan; the first question a young couple ask each other at the New Year is "What Hmong are you?" If both are from the same clan, they will address each other as brother or sister. The taboo against marrying within the clan is so strong that I never heard of it happening.

Elders make the ultimate decision about marriage, but a daughter does have some influence over the choice of her future husband. In Flower Village I heard of only one case in which parents refused to give their daughter permission to marry the boy she had chosen. The daughter had fallen in love with a boy who lived in the village, but his family was very poor *(txom txom nyem)* because his father was an opium addict; the family had to work hard to feed themselves and take care of the father. Her family did not want her to marry into such difficult circumstances, and they would have preferred a groom who could pay the bride-price. One morning she left for the fields as if to work, but went off by herself and swallowed opium, which killed her. The whole village mourned her loss—she was extremely pretty and good-natured—and her family was devastated. Later the boy went off to a village in the north, where he met and married another girl. Although the Hmong practice is to live virilocally after marriage, the young man moved in with his wife's family, working for them to pay off her bride-price.

If a couple want to marry and have run into family problems, such as an overly high bride-price or trouble between the clans, sometimes the boy and his male relatives will "kidnap" the bride while she is working in the fields. They take her to the boy's home, where she stays for three days; at that point the couple must marry. When this is done without the bride's consent, the union can be a sad one.

If a girl becomes pregnant as a result of one of these sexual liaisons during the New Year's courting, she usually marries the father of the child. If marriage is not an option—if the families do not get along or the boy changes his mind—then his family pays a fine to her family and the child is absorbed into her clan. If the girl marries someone else later, her child goes with her.

During my stay in Flower Village, a girl told me the story of an acquaintance, Mim, who had become pregnant before marriage, and the problems it caused:

> Mim is going to have a baby. It happened to her at the New Year. Txoov came to visit, but Mim did not want to go out with him to the field. She told her parents that he came to the house when she was asleep and she did not know what happened until she awoke and he was in her bed. Now he has another girlfriend in another village. She is also having a baby. He and his parents think she is prettier than Mim, and he is going to marry her. Mim is very sad and cries a lot, but his parents must pay Mim's parents silver bars. They have offered two, but they must pay more.

Mim and her parents were consequently the subject of gossip in the village, which caused them a great deal of embarrassment. The infant was born in a small room behind the parents' house, and the child, a daughter, stayed with Mim's parents, but Mim left Flower Village to live and work in town. Leaving the village has only recently been considered an option for girls, and it is still seldom done. Txoov, the father of her child, married the other pregnant young woman, who lived with him in a village nearby.

The concepts of shame and shyness, or modesty, are integral to Hmong life; they are particularly relevant to sex roles but also affect other behavioral codes, such as obedience to elders, industriousness, and conformity. A Hmong, male or female, who isn't modest and deferential to elders is shamed. However, as seems to be the case in many asymmetrical societies, a double standard is apparent in Mim's story. If Txoov truly had sex with

Mim in her parents' house, he had shown disrespect for their lineage spirits; but most people assumed that Mim was lying about this detail to save face. No one thought less of Txoov, but Mim was considered immodest, and was embarrassed and ashamed. As to the question of whether he forced Mim to have sex with him, I doubt that most Hmong would consider that a possibility. If a Hmong man wants sex, his wife does not refuse. Part of married life for a woman is always being willing. If a Hmong man raped another man's wife, however, he would be ostracized and so would his family; they would no longer be considered Hmong. Robert Cooper, Suav Ntxais, and Kiab Lis write that

> Hmong customary law copes with the problem of rape by introducing preventive measures from the earliest stages of socialisation, and by the institutionalisation of the rapist-victim relationship into a socially acceptable form: marriage. Where this preferred system is not possible, compensation is provided for the injured party and the rapist suffers punishment and social disapprobation, sometimes to the point of ostracism, which effectively removes a rapist from meaningful participation in Hmong society while reinforcing norms and values central to prevention. (1998:1)

At New Year's courting, if a boy shows interest, a girl usually gives in, perhaps partly because this is a time when her sexual curiosity is sanctioned by society. But she does have the choice of catching the ball instead of dropping it, thereby letting the boy know that she is not interested in him. Mim was embarrassed because Txoov found someone else more attractive. It made sense that Mim would try to explain away what had happened by saying that he had crept into her bed before she knew what was happening; I doubt that even her friend thought that Mim's story was true. If what a Westerner would perceive as rape had occurred, a girl who did not get pregnant probably would keep quiet about the incident; she would be embarrassed. Also, if a girl has made problems for a man, usually no other man wants her.

An example of this occurred in California, when Hmong refugees first arrived in the United States. A Hmong girl was walking home from school when some Hmong boys drove by in a car; one of them wanted to perform a bride capture. They tried to drag the girl into the car, but she fought them and got away. She was running down the street when a policeman drove by, saw her distress, and took her to the station. The incident ended up in court, and the boy went to jail for attempted rape. The Hmong community was furious with the girl's family and said that Hmong could have taken care of this in their own way, bringing the case before Hmong elders and letting them set things right instead of going to an American court. The last I heard, she was still unmarried (Goldstein 1986:135–44).

In Mim's and Txoov's case, things did not end so badly. Txoov's parents had to pay Mim's parents four silver bars because Mim was pregnant. Mim moved to town, where she met and married a Thai man, and her child joined her. Her new husband also paid her family four silver bars in the wedding negotiations.

MARRIAGE: OBTAINING A WIFE OR HUSBAND

Yves Bertrais (1978) has described five different ways for Hmong to marry:

1. Arranged marriage: this is the cross-cousin marriage, arranged by the parents, and good for both families because they know each other.
2. Mutual consent: the young man and woman request their parents' permission to marry, and negotiations are favorably concluded.
3. Elopement: the couple run away together and sleep in the young man's house.
4. Bride capture: a man and his male relatives "grab" the young woman in the fields or, as in the case below, take her from her house. Usually she has given some sign that she wants this.
5. Forced marriage: the young woman is pregnant.

In all of the forms of marriage, negotiations take place, even, as we have seen in Mim's case, when there is no marriage but there is a child.

Following the New Year's courting rituals, male lineage members begin marriage negotiations in earnest. The phrase used to describe the marriage process is "buying/getting a wife" *(yuav pojniam)*. I was surprised to hear girls use the same term for marriage—"buying/getting a husband" *(yuav txiv)*. Despite the implications of these terms, marriage is not thought of as "buying" a woman (or a man) but rather as a series of exchanges between wife-givers and wife-takers leading to an alliance between clans. Bride-price is only one aspect of the exchange. The exchange is not formally complete until the bride gives birth to a child, at which point the contract is fulfilled and the alliance sealed.

The birth of a child is an exchange in a very practical sense, since it is the child, especially a son, who will continue the lineage, feed the ancestors, and eventually procreate again, producing bodies that allow the souls of dead lineage members to be reborn. These exchanges are obligatory. If bride-price is not paid, the groom's family forfeits jural rights to the children. If a woman doesn't conceive, the groom may return her to her family, who then return the bride-price. For Hmong, the need is not only for the immediate marriage and all that it entails, but for the connections that may be formed from it, allowing other marriages between the families. Because the Hmong follow a preferential cross-cousin marriage rule, those who are the wife-givers this time may become the wife-takers next time.

Traditionally, marriages occur in the first phase of the waxing moon, a propitious time that bodes well for the future of the couple and their offspring. (A waning moon is unlucky for marriage.) I will not attempt a full description here of the long and noisy ritual negotiations that occur when a man and his family negotiate for his future wife, but will briefly describe a representative wedding I attended in Flower Village in March 1988. (See Bertrais 1978 for a complete description of the Hmong marriage ceremony.)

MARRIAGE NEGOTIATIONS

The particular rites described here involved the Muas and Hawj clans. All of the negotiations were conducted at the home of the girl, Mai. Prior to these negotiations, the boy, Ntaj, and some of his "brothers" (what Westerners would call cousins) came to Flower Village early one evening. Mai and Ntaj had participated in the courting game (throwing the ball and dropping it) and then met on a couple of occasions afterward. As far as I know, her parents had not realized that the two were going to run away together.

Ntaj and his "brothers" went to Mai's house one night and knocked quietly on the outside wall of her bedroom, calling her to come outside. When she emerged, the young men took hold of her arms, quickly escorted her out of the village, and hurried to the home of Ntaj's parents, in a nearby village. Mai did not cry out or fight to be left alone. The young couple spent three days and two nights at Ntaj's home, but if his natal village had been farther away, they would have stayed with one of his close clan members nearby.

Although Ntaj "took" Mai from her home, it seemed that Mai was well aware of his intentions and wished to marry him, so their marriage had elements of elopement as well as bride capture. In bride capture, which is an acceptable method of marriage, the young men come to the young woman's house at night or simply meet her in the fields and take her away. I saw this occur in the fields one day, when a couple of young men came and took a young woman away with them. She did not look happy about the event, but she went with them. Once a woman has left, she has to stay in the man's house for three days, after which it is taken for granted that the couple will marry. Unlike Mai, this young woman did not seem pleased about her marriage, but when she came back to visit a year later, she had a small son and looked very happy.

During the three days Mai spent at Ntaj's home, the couple spent most of the time in Ntaj's bedroom, but many members of the village, especially women and children, came by to see Mai and comment on her dress and appearance. The male elders of the family and the clan sat around discussing the history of the relationship between Mai and Ntaj's families and speculating upon what price Mai's family would accept for her "milk and care money." This is the money the wife-takers pay to the wife-givers for the young woman's upbringing; the higher the price, the more status the girl has. A high price shows that she is pretty and works hard, and has all the virtues prized by Hmong.[8]

As the third day drew to a close, the young couple prepared to return to the home of Mai's parents. But before Mai left, Ntaj's grandfather, as the eldest male member of the household, stood in front of the spirit door, opposite the small prosperity altar, and performed a soul-calling ritual for her.

First Ntaj's grandfather set a little stool just inside the threshold of the spirit door. On the stool, he placed a small bowl containing uncooked rice, an uncooked egg, and a stick of incense. His son brought in one hen and one rooster, tied their legs together, and placed them on the stool. The grandfather picked up his divination horns and banged them against the door jamb as he began the soul-calling chant, "Hu Plig":

Today is a good day and tonight is a good occasion.
I will call the soul of Mai.
She will come to have a partner and have a long life.

She will live a thousand years with no sickness.
She will come to have life until her hair is white and long to her knees.

Even though she may be wandering in Ntxwj Nyoog's sour vegetable
    fields,
We will call Mai back to this side to live a thousand years without
    illness or laziness.
Come to have a husband and partner.
Come to live a thousand years without sickness, a hundred years
    without illness.

Come to be the elder of others, a thousand years without sickness,
A hundred years without illness and laziness.
Do not be sad along the road.
Do not be sad along the orphan road.
The house spirits will go to protect you
And help pull you to this side of a family
To have a partner.

Come to live a pure life.
A thousand years with no sickness,
A hundred years without illness.
Come to live strong as a rock and strong as a tree.
Come to live a pure life for thousands of years.

Come to have a mother and father.
Come to have many children.
Come to stay a thousand years without illness
And hundreds of years without sickness.

Yaj Kuam will open the road and lead you back into the house.
The house spirit will go and catch the arms and legs
So that you will come to this side of the family.

So come and have a family.
So come and have a partner.
Come to live well and pure,
Thousands of years without sickness,
Hundreds of years without illness.
Come to live permanent as the rock.
Come to be the elder of others.

Come to live pure and well, live white and pure.
Yaj Kuam will open the way into the garden and to the house.
Come to live thousands of years without illness,
Hundreds of years without sickness.
Come into the garden and the house.
Come to live until your hair is white.
Come to live thousands of years without sickness,
Hundreds of years without illness.
Come to have a mother and a father.

Then the grandfather banged the divination horns against the door jamb again and tossed them onto the floor. The horns fell into a propitious pattern, and he signaled to the family that all was well. Ntaj's brother took the chickens from the stool, slit their necks, and caught the blood in a bowl. (The blood would be mixed into soup.) He plucked the chickens and gave them to his wife. She boiled them and gave the pot back to him. Then Ntaj's brother took the pot to the spirit door, at which time the soul-calling ceremony was repeated, as above. After the second soul-calling, Ntaj's brother took the chickens from the water and cut them up. The grandfather examined their feet and heads to make sure that the future life of and Mai and Ntaj looked to be a happy one. (Hmong have ways of moving the bones slightly to make sure they auger well for the young couple.) The breasts and legs were saved to feed the elders, and the rest was made into soup. Everyone present, including myself, then sat down to eat a festive meal.

At the end of the meal, the groom knelt to his father and the other elders in respect and gave thanks for the food and the efforts everyone had made on his behalf. While the male elders began discussing the amount of money they were willing to give Ntaj for a wife, the young couple hurried off to Mai's father's house. They were accompanied by Ntaj's father, brother, sister (who served as Mai's chaperone), and two go-betweens *(mej koob)*, one of them carrying a black umbrella tied with a checkered ribbon from Mai's turban.

Meanwhile Ntaj's father had sent a message to Mai's parents, who had contacted their own go-betweens—two men who would represent them at the negotiation table. When Mai and Ntaj's party returned to her parents' house, they were met at the spirit door by these two men, who offered them rice liquor. Polite toasts were exchanged, and wedding songs were sung; then Mai and Ntaj's party was invited into the house. As they entered, one of the visiting go-betweens handed the umbrella to one of Mai's family's go-betweens, who hung it over a rafter near the small prosperity altar (figs. 2.5, 2.6). The closed umbrella remained there throughout the three days of negotiations that followed.

A long table had been set up in the main room and branches placed on the floor to either side of it. Small bamboo cups, made especially for this occasion, were set out with several bottles of rice liquor, and bowls filled with pieces of cooked pig fat, which is a delicacy. The men from the visiting clan (except for Ntaj) and from Mai's clan sat down together at the table. They drank rice liquor and ate pig fat as the negotiations commenced. The amount of bride-price and the goods the bride would bring *(nyiaj phij cuam)* were discussed at length, as were problems that had arisen between the two clans in the past. If these problems could not be settled amicably, the young man and his retinue would have to take their unopened umbrella and leave without a bride. Several pigs were sacrificed during the three-day negotiation period, and the visitors were fed many special meat and rice dishes.

The go-betweens, male lineage members, and other men who had been invited to participate in the negotiations made many loud and noisy toasts, expressing the wish that the young couple would have many children for the family and the patriline. Ntaj and his brother bowed frequently to the elders in a show of gratitude and deference, and the men sang many songs about how and why these rituals were being performed. Eventually Ntaj was invited to join in the toasts, and he soon became very drunk. Mai assisted him to her bedroom, where he fell asleep. That night they slept in the same bed in Mai's room. Ntaj's sister and brother stayed in the room as well, acting as chaperones. Sexual intercourse is prohibited in a woman's father's house since the household spirits do not approve and will "bite" the young couple, causing difficulties for them in the future; also, it is wrong to con-

FIG. 2.5. Presenting an umbrella at the door. When a young couple marry, the family of the groom brings along an umbrella to the bride's home, where it is hung on the wall until just before they leave for the groom's home (after negotiations). It is then opened, and the spirits from her natal household go into the umbrella. When it is closed and carried to his home and opened there, her spirits become part of his household. (Photo by Patricia Symonds)

ceive a child in the house of the woman's father, where the spirits of his ancestors live, and where she is the reincarnated soul of an ancestor, and about to change her lineage. Ideally, children are conceived in the house of their own lineage.

Early the next morning, negotiations continued, and eventually six bars of silver were agreed upon for the bride-price.[9] Two silver bars were for "milk

FIG. 2.6. *Relatives of a bride and groom negotiating the bride price and discussing family and clan ties and roles. The umbrella hanging on the wall (to the left of the central vertical support) contains the family spirits of the bride; it will be taken to the groom's house and opened there to incorporate her into his family. (Photo by Patricia Symonds)*

and care," to compensate Mai's mother and father for her upbringing. Two silver bars were paid for the "shirt" *(nqe tsho)*—the birth shirt *(lub tsho tu menyuam)*, or placenta—the bride would produce when she bore a child. In other words, payment was made for the rights to her fertility and her children. These two silver bars are saved by the wife-givers and used later to acquire the "shirt" of another young woman for their son.

Throughout the negotiations, the term "shirt" was used as a euphemism for money. The wife-giver's go-between said, for example, "Mother and Father want a big shirt," to prepare the wife-takers for the idea that a considerable amount of money would be requested. After much negotiation, Ntaj's go-betweens replied, "If you give us a wife and take a small shirt, then when you come to our lineage *(caj ceg*, lit., "roots and branches") for a wife in the future, we will take a small shirt." Finally two silver bars were offered for "the mouth of an animal" *(ncauj tsiag)*, to ensure that a cow would be sacrificed for the bride's parents upon their deaths. Of the six silver bars, some of the money was returned to the young couple, to be saved until Mai's death to help buy a sacrificial cow for her. Five of Mai's family members were honored with additional gifts of money (*ntaus nco,* lit., "hit with remembrance") to signify their importance to Mai. The people remembered were Mai's father's older brother; Mai's father's younger brother; Mai's father's older sister (in this case the money was given to her husband), which linked the clan this sister had married into, the Yaj, to the newly married couple; Mai's oldest brother; and Mai's sister's husband, linking Mai and Ntaj to yet another clan, the Thoj. If Mai's sister had been unmarried, the family would have chosen to remember a husband of a married classificatory sister instead. Mai's parents, through their go-betweens, said, "We live in a different place than you are going to, but other Muas will live there. Through the people we remember here, they will pass the word and our daughter will be cared for." They also said, "We give you the top of the rope [the bride], but we hold on to the bottom" (Hauv hlua peb muab rau nej, qab hlua peb tseem tuav rawv), meaning that they will always be connected to her.

As the negotiations drew to a close on the third day, Mai's mother brought two boxes to the negotiating table. The go-betweens opened the boxes and examined the contents—clothing embroidered by Mai and her mother. Then Mai's mother offered several of the embroidered shirts and *sev* for Mai to take with her. When the visiting go-betweens asked for more, she began to cry, saying,

> I have loved this daughter for a long time. I taught her to sew and now she is leaving. I want her to have more, but I have five other daughters, and they must also have some of this flower cloth when they leave. I have five other daughters, and I love them, too. I must save some of the clothing for them when they marry. I am getting older, and I cannot do so much sewing any more. I am not so fast, and my eyes cannot see so well.

Eventually, four jackets, a white hemp skirt, four *sev,* and several blankets and pillows were settled upon. In addition, Mai's parents gave her a silver necklace to pass on to her own eldest daughter. Mai's brothers also gave her a silver bar; although this bar was for both members of the young couple, it was recognized as Mai's property. Male cousins, classificatory brothers of the groom, also gave their new sister gifts of clothing. Several of the pieces were *sev*, embroidered by the cousin's wives, for Mai to wear at the New Year and on special occasions or to give to her own daughters. She will also wear the embroidered *sev* in her coffin.

On the third day, negotiations were completed to the satisfaction of all the parties involved, and the guests and the couple prepared to return to their village. One of the go-betweens from Mai's side of the family took the umbrella from the rafter, opened it, and hung it in front of the household altar. Ntaj and his brother stood in front of the altar and kowtowed while a male from Mai's natal lineage called out the names of her ancestors, married couple after married couple. People quieted down for this part of the ceremony; the mother of the bride was especially solemn.

Afterward Mai's mother wrapped up in a cloth a knife used for field work. She placed the knife in Mai's back–carrying basket and handed the basket to her daughter. She gave Mai the haunch of a large pig that had been killed earlier in the day to feed guests, as a gift Mai could give her in-laws so they would eat well when she arrived at her new home. She gave Mai a cooked chicken for the couple to eat on the way, since what one eats during the marriage rituals is symbolic of the food that one will always eat. Meat is a prestige food, a sign of wealth; eating meat during the marriage means that one will eat well for the rest of one's life. For this reason, the bride is forbidden to eat any vegetables or rice during the ceremony.

Mai's family's go-betweens sang a farewell song and passed the umbrella, now closed, to Ntaj's go-betweens. Ntaj's group, led by the new wife and husband, left the house via the spirit door. The groom's party had come to the village by truck, so when the ceremonies were concluded they all climbed inside to leave. The bride was the last to get in. Mai and her mother stood crying quietly together. As Mai turned to go, her mother said, "Go well. Listen to your husband well. Do good work in the fields, have many children, and come to visit me soon." Significantly, she did not use the familiar form of the word "come" (*los*, "to come home") but the more formal *tuaj*, which is used for visitors, not family. Mai had become part of her husband's brotherhood (*kwv tij*), and her mother was no longer her *niam* (mother) but her *niam tais* (lit., "maternal grandmother").

A Hmong marriage is far more than a union between two people; it is one of a series of unions between clans and lineages. Marriage not only facilitates new alliances and family networks but repairs old alliances through the resolution of past disagreements. In Mai and Ntaj's case, there were no problems that had to be settled between the two clans, but issues sometimes arise concerning divorce of women, women who had not been treated well, or disagreements about land use. Also, each clan always wants to know about the health of the people in the other clan, specifically if there has been any leprosy in the lineage or household. But these questions are always brought up with diplomatic indirection.

The inclusion in the ceremony of the villagers, who are all invited to share in the food and drink, illustrates that aside from strengthening clan relationships, these ceremonies fulfill obligations to other villagers. It is important to note that daughters indirectly produce these networks; also, through their marriages they bring in the bride-price that will buy future daughters-in-law to carry on the family and lineage. A daughter keeps her father's clan name until her death; only then does she become a full-fledged member of her husband's clan.

In the marriage ceremony, the umbrella is an important symbol. It is brought into the daughter's family's house empty and hung on the rafter until negotiations are complete, then opened at the household altar during the naming of her ancestors. When she leaves with her new husband, all the good things she has contributed to the natal household—including good spirits who entered the earthly realm at her birth—are caught up and closed into the umbrella to be taken along to her new home. After her first three days in her new husband's home, the umbrella is opened and hung from a rafter for a month.

Although no woman wants to become a spinster, a woman usually feels a great sense of loss when she is wed. I asked one thirty-year-old married woman, "How did you feel when you were marrying your husband and you knew that you would leave and go away to another village?" She replied,

All my life I had given to my family—to my parents and to my sister and brothers. When we brought in the rice it was for us to eat. When I worked to scrape the [poppy] pods, it was for my father to smoke. If someone was sick in the house, they could use it for medicine.

All my life, my mother had given to me. I had obeyed my mother and my father. I had watched my mother do flower cloth. I cared for my small brothers and sisters, and they cared for me. When it was time for my sister to marry, she married a man in the same village as my parents. I came here to this village because my boyfriend visited us at New Year and we liked each other. I was happy to find a husband, but I was afraid, too. I had to change to bringing in rice for another family that I did not love and who did not love me. I had not seen his house, and my grandmother long ago told me that you can see a dove fly, but that does not mean you have seen his nest [*pom nquab ya, tsis pom nquab zes*].

I cried when I left. My mother and my grandmother cried, too. I wondered for a long time about my family. I was sure they could not do all the things I had done. When I had my first child, my mother and my father came to visit. They had a new baby, too. But I did not care any more. I had my own small son, and all my giving now would go to him. I went back to my parent's village when my father died. My other sisters had married away from the village, too, and we had not seen each other for many years. It was nice to sit and talk.

Marriage for Hmong women is a time of loss and a time of gain. Mothers, and often fathers too, are saddened when their daughter's allegiance shifts from her natal to her affinal family, and this is especially true when a daughter moves to a distant village. Even if she marries a man from her natal village, she no longer belongs to her natal family. She must adapt to the ways and customs of her husband's family, and most especially to her mother-in-law.

But a daughter's departure from the natal family is the beginning of new relationships between wife-givers and wife-takers, as every marriage creates new sets of affinally related groups, setting up a mechanism to perpetuate and enlarge the consanguine group. It is not surprising that the most conspicuous features of the alliances are ceremonial gifts and functions, for as the word "affine" (from the Latin *ad finis,* "border") suggests, two groups make an exchange, or series of exchanges, across the border that divides affines from consanguines.

The marriage ritual and the exchanges that accompany it assure participants that a couple's personal duty to continue the male patriline will be fulfilled. Although marriage involves loss for the bride, she stands to gain personally through the eventual status that children, particularly sons, will confer upon her. Also, it is the only way for her to be reborn as a person. The divorced woman mentioned earlier wanted to be reborn as a chicken or a pig because that was the best she could hope for. She wanted to come back quickly and have many offspring.

DAUGHTERS-IN-LAW AND MOTHERS-IN-LAW

When a Hmong woman marries, she moves into the house of her in-laws. As Margery Wolf says of Chinese brides, "Marriage is not conceived of as a man taking a wife, but as a family calling in a daughter-in-law, and every bride is well aware that . . . it is her mother-in-law's face she must watch" (1972:142).

In Flower Village, women often discussed how difficult it was when they first arrived in their new home, and how lonely they felt. One woman who had been married for three years described her experience:

> When I first came here, I felt sorry for myself. I was sorry that I am a girl. If I had been born a boy I would have stayed with my family. I felt sad because I had to leave my family. To become a daughter-in-law is not easy. You have to take care of yourself. In your own house you can be excused for making mistakes. But as a daughter-in-law you are not excused. You must be first up in the morning, without anyone calling. In my home my mother would call, "Yaj Mim, sawv" ["Get up, Yaj Mim"]. But Mother-in-law does not call. If you are not up first, she will be angry and call you lazy. She will make your husband angry too. So you try to do things her way. You are not excused. If you do not cook, you do not eat.

Aside from her daily interaction with her mother-in-law, a daughter-in-law—if her husband has married brothers—must learn to live with their wives. Competition between sisters-in-law can be fierce. The newest member of the family does not know her mother-in-law's ways: how her mother likes rice cooked or how to make pig mash or where she should sit at the table. Her sister-in-law will already know the ways of the household, and if she has children, she has a decisive advantage over the new bride and can push off her own work onto the younger woman. In the beginning a newcomer often is too intimidated to question such situations, but as she becomes accustomed to the household and her place within it, friction may ensue. Competition over the household's often-limited resources may escalate after the newcomer gives birth for the first time, especially if the grandmother favors one grandchild over another.

However, intrafamilial tension does not always occur. In fact, I rarely saw sisters-in-law treat each other cruelly. Most often they liked each other and were supportive in times of need and crisis, caring for each other's children if one of them was preoccupied with domestic chores or fieldwork. One mother-in-law in Flower Village talked about how she trained her own daughters-in-law to coexist peacefully in her household:

I remember how when I first came to my mother's [mother-in-law's] house, I was afraid and lonely. Mother did not like the way I steamed the rice, but she showed me her way, and I learned. She did not like the way I greeted guests in the house, but she showed me her way, and I learned. My own mother had taught me the ways of our clan, but they were different. My own mother had told me I would have to learn to live in the house of a new mother. She might not love me, and I might not love her, but I would have to obey her because she gave my husband life.

When my own sons married and their wives came to live in this house, I had to teach them the way we did our work. I had to watch carefully to see if these new daughters liked each other. I had to be able to settle small quarrels between them and to make them share the workload. I still worked in the field with them, but soon, after I showed them the way, they could go alone, and after the children were born, I could stay home with them. If they disobeyed me, I would tell my sons, and they would be sure to make these new daughters listen to me in the future.

But I see my daughters now; they have grown children, and they like each other, but they quarrel when one boy uses the money to go to the valley to school. Each one wants her son to go to school, but as we are poor, only one can go. I know how this is. I did not like one sister-in-law when I was younger, and I was glad when she and her children moved to another house.[10] Now I am getting older, and my daughters care for me. I still look after the children, but when you are old you do not cook. My daughters always say, "Come to eat rice, Mother." This is important when you are old.

The relationships between the women in a household can be mutually supportive, or competitive and antagonistic. If the latter is true, the women are chastised by their husbands, whose mother has complained of their wives' behavior. Not much social pressure is exerted from outside the household, of the kind Wolf reports for Chinese women (1972:42–52); Hmong frown on gossip, and family difficulties tend to be kept within the household. The Hmong have a saying that means "Keep troubles within the family" (*Nthuav koj tiab npog koj quav*, lit., "Cover your shit with your skirt"). Most women follow this injunction, but if conditions become unbearable, they may sit outside another household where women are sewing and begin crying in front of them. These other women may then be moved to influence their husbands to intervene in the situation. But since women who become involved in gossip are themselves criticized, they usually confine themselves to comforting the crying woman, without taking the matter any further.

Another strategy employed when household problems cannot be resolved internally involves a woman standing outside her own home and shouting at her husband or mother-in-law. When this happens, other natal clan members usually intervene, and discussions take place. The family can be pressured to treat the wife better, or the woman may be reprimanded and told that she must not quarrel so much. There is yet another strategy that a woman may employ if life within the household becomes difficult: she can run away. This does not mean that she goes far, especially if she has children, but she may go to the small field house and stay there for a day or two until her husband goes in search of her and brings her home. As we have seen, in rare cases the woman returns to her natal home, divorcing her husband. If she does so she will most likely have to leave her children behind. Within the marriage, a woman's final means of protest is to ingest opium, which frequently results in death. If she takes opium and does not die, she has made a powerful statement to the community that she is being severely mistreated by her mother-in-law or husband, and although the other villagers say little to the family, the woman's kin often intervene in such a desperate situation and thereby improve her lot.

Women rarely take collective action in response to abuse or unfair decisions, although within the household and lineage they frequently develop friendships with one another. These friendships are strong and close, but they do not appear to create female solidarity of the kind Mary Moran observed among Liberian women (1990).

After the first child has been born to a new daughter-in-law, her life becomes somewhat easier. She has fulfilled her most important role for the family by providing continuity for the patriline, especially if the child is a son. Even if the child is a daughter, the new wife has given an ancestor—as her mother-in-law will one day be—a chance to be reborn. Her allegiance is now fully with her child and her husband, and she begins to experience the respect of her new "mother" and other household members, men as well as women. Because every birth is a rebirth (e.g., a grandparent dies and a grandchild is born), there is no real death in the Western sense, for, as Pierre Bourdieu states, "In a universe in which a man's social existence requires that he be linked to his ancestors through his ascendants and be 'cited' by and 'resurrected' by his descendants, the death of an outsider is the only absolute form of death" (1977:154). For the Hmong, it is the person who has no sons, and therefore no descendants, who is the outsider. This concept makes childbirth, the work of women, an important and indispensable part of Hmong life.

HMONG WOMEN IN CONTEXT

Hmong women explicitly accord less prestige to themselves than to men. They believe that men have better judgment than women and that men are both more intelligent and more capable. For that reason, men have the power to make formal and final decisions in most areas of Hmong social life, but women have limited power over other woman who are lower in rank, especially younger women. In addition, as we have seen in chapter 1, sisters have considerable influence over both men and women in matters involving their brothers; although sisters always speak through their husbands and remain in the background, it is their judgment that is asked for.

Hmong women's sexuality is both valued and feared. Female genitalia must be covered by *sev,* not because they are believed to be polluting but because they are alluring, attractive, and dangerous to men. When I returned to the United States from Flower Village, I discussed my findings on *sev* and sexuality with Hmong women living in the United States, one of whom summarized Hmong prohibitions for woman as stemming from the belief that "if Hmong men do not put women down, the women will be powerful and play around, maybe go out with other men, run away with the silver. That is women's way and men's fears." In other words, Hmong women are viewed as "naturally" sexual and their sexuality is feared. At the same time, *sev* draw attention to and celebrate a woman's sexuality, without which the patriline could not continue. As we saw in Mim's story, the double standard places a woman who may have been raped (and who became pregnant but did not marry the young man) in the position of "blame" and "shame."

Hmong women are excluded from participation in the highly valued rituals pertaining to the realm of the ancestors, but at death they become ancestors themselves, and part of their spiritual being, the second soul, goes to the ancestral village in the land of darkness, but their third soul ideally will return to earth as male. In this way women return to their husband's family and lineage in male form, to participate in all that has been denied to them as women.

A Hmong woman's power is located in the realm of reproduction. She provides the vessels to which souls of the lineage can return and continue the cycle of life. After a Hmong woman has lived her life as a wife and mother, one of the vessels produced by her descendants will be hers. If all goes well, she may be fortunate enough to return as a male.

BIRTH: THE JOURNEY

TO THE LAND OF LIGHT

D uring my first stay in Flower Village, twenty-six babies were born. About six months into my stay, women began to trust me enough to invite me to births. I then attended six births, usually because I was friendly with either the young woman herself or her mother-in-law. They would let me know when the woman was about to give birth—sometimes early on in the labor—and allow me to come to the house. I waited either in the main room where other people went about their business or in the small bedroom where the woman labored, sometimes with her mother-in-law in attendance. As the roofs are thatch and the walls bamboo, I could hear what was to be heard—very little, in most cases—even from the main room. Birth is a very private affair, and it was something of a privilege for an outsider such as myself to be invited to witness such moments.

When I say women are alone in labor, I am speaking of their ideal of birth, not of what always happens. Especially if a woman goes into labor during the day, she is likely to have company during labor and delivery; at night the mother-in-law is usually there in case she is needed. I was told, but did not observe, that sometimes a husband is present.

In the case study below, Ntxawm went into labor in the fields. I was there and accompanied her and her sister-in-law back to the village, so I was in attendance throughout her childbearing. This was a normal birth, in that Ntxawm had no difficulties during labor or delivery and the child was healthy.

NTXAWM'S LABOR AND DELIVERY

Ntxawm was a young, newly married woman. In the hours before she gave birth to her first child, she and her (husband's) family had been harvesting the annual rice crop, men and women working together in the fields. The rice harvest is a stressful time because rice is the principal staple food for the coming year. The family had been in the field for several days, sleeping out in their small field house in order to spend as much time as possible bringing in the crop.

Each morning at sunrise the women gathered firewood to cook the morning rice. On this particular morning, as she bent over to cut the first sheaf of rice, Ntxawm felt a pain in her lower back. It was not the usual pain one gets from leaning over to cut rice plants; she suspected it might be the onset of labor. Her husband and the other men had left early in the truck to pick and sell tomatoes in the valley, a trip that would take several hours. Ntxawm went to her mother-in-law and said, "Mother, my back hurts and I have a sick stomach." The phrase she used for "sick stomach" was *mob plab*, a euphemism for labor pains. The Hmong use this phrase, instead of being explicit, to keep from alerting malevolent spirits who might harm the newborn or the mother, and also out of modesty. Ntxawm's mother-in-law, who would spend the rest of the day working in the fields, immediately sent Ntxawm and Ntxhi (a daughter-in-law who already had a child) back to the village.

The two young women walked the seven kilometers back to the village. Ntxawm carried a basket of empty rice containers on her back. When they reached the village they bathed at the village water pipe and then sat down to talk and sew until it was time to do the afternoon chores. No one mentioned Ntxawm's sick stomach, nor would anyone have been able to tell that she was in labor by looking at her.

As night fell, people began returning from the day's work in the field. All the rice had been cut and was drying; the following day, if there was no threat of rain, the threshing of the rice would begin. As Ntxawm's father-in-law drove back from the valley, other people climbed aboard his truck, dusty and tired, and hung on to the sides while the truck jogged and bumped its way back up the hill to the village.

Ntxawm fed the pigs, helped her mother-in-law Mai prepare the evening meal, and, after eating, got ready for bed along with everyone else in the family. Ntxhi brought in firewood for the morning fire, and Ntxawm washed and cleaned the rice as usual, removing chaff and mouse droppings, leaving some rice to soak overnight so it would be ready to steam in the morning.

Ntxawm and her husband Ntaj had a very small room to themselves; their bamboo platform bed took up most of the space. Ntxawm asked Ntaj to cut down some big banana leaves, which she placed on the floor in the corner of their room. She set a small wooden stool on the leaves. Then she lay down in bed, and her husband left to go sleep on a small platform bed in the main room. Ntxawm's contractions were still far apart, and she was able to doze off.

Around midnight the contractions became stronger. Ntxawm took off her Chinese-style trousers and wrapped a sarong around her waist; she kept the rest of her clothing on. The rest of the household, tired from the hard day's work, slept soundly. Ntxawm sat on the low stool, tensing with each contraction. She did not cry out in pain or even moan; to do so would shame herself and her family. If the emerging child heard its mother cry out, the child might think the world was an unhappy place and refuse to be born; and her cries would alert the wild or malevolent spirits that a new child is arriving.

At approximately 1:00 A.M., Ntxawm pushed the stool away, gave a strong push, and the baby slid out onto banana leaves that had been placed under her. The baby's cries awakened Ntaj first and then Mai, who came into the room to help. Mai quickly tied a white-and-red plaited hemp cord, which she had made for the occasion, around the baby's neck. The white cord "ties in" the two souls now in the child's body, and the red one protects the child during the first three days of life, before the baby's naming and the coming of the third soul.

Mai also tied a white thread around the child's umbilical cord in two places—the first about two inches from the belly and the second two inches from the first. Using her embroidery scissors, which she had passed through

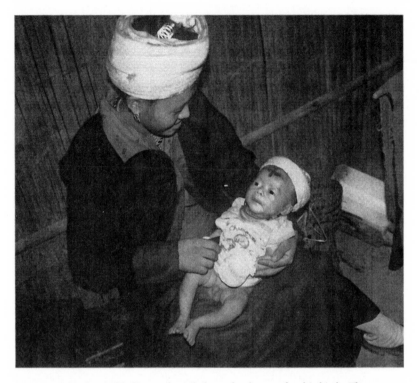

FIG. 3.1. A mother holds her newborn baby, a few hours after his birth. The cross on the baby's forehead as well as the necklace offer protection from evil spirits. (Photo by Patricia Symonds)

the ashes in the fireplace to sterilize them, she cut the umbilical cord. She then wrapped the baby boy tightly in a clean piece of old black cloth and laid him on the bed before attending to Ntxawm, who delivered the placenta in the same squatting position.

Ntxawm cleaned herself while her mother-in-law gave the child his first bath, heating the water in a pan on a tripod over the fire. Mai rolled up the legs of her trousers, sat, and stretched out her legs, placing the child along the length of her legs with his head toward her body. Using an old piece of black cloth, she rinsed his head and washed his face, paying particular attention to his eyes. She cleaned off all the white vernix, or "fat" *(xwv xyem)*, which covers a child's body at birth, rewrapped him tightly in a new piece of black cloth, and handed him to his mother, who, by then, was lying by the fire.

BURYING THE BIRTH SHIRT

Meanwhile Ntaj had been digging a hole next to the main house post *(ncej dab)*, where the household lineage spirits reside. There he buried the infant's birth shirt, or placenta. This is always done with great care because the child's health may suffer if insects or animals eat any of it. In the Showing the Way chant (see chap. 4), the soul is instructed at death to return to its father's house to regain the birth shirt for the journey to the land of darkness.

Ntaj had built a fire in the main room and spread a blanket on the ground next to it. Ntxawm lay down on the blanket with her baby next to her, and watched as her husband collected the effluvium from the birthing process. He went outside to wash her bloody sarong in a wash basin. He dug a small hole in the ground, poured the blood into it, and covered it carefully with dirt, a task that falls to the father. The blood has to be buried with care, since if the spirits find it they would desire more, and could make both mother and child sick.

Mai boiled water, beat an egg and some pepper into it, and gave it to Ntxawm so she might regain her strength and produce good milk for the child. Ntxawm placed a tiny piece of the yolk on her baby's tongue, a traditional sign of welcome for the child, as eggs are nourishing and a symbol of life. Then Ntxawm fell asleep for a few hours while her husband stayed awake to keep the fire burning.

POSTPARTUM DIET AND PROSCRIPTIONS

The mother and child must be kept warm for a month after the birth, especially during the first three days. A postpartum mother is in a "cold" state and her body must be returned to balance. With the exception of an occasional papaya for producing good strong milk, she cannot eat any fruit or vegetables, which are "cold" foods that can congeal the blood; if her blood flow is impeded now, she is at risk for a multitude of sicknesses in old age. (This is why postpartum Hmong women at the hospital in Rhode Island refused to drink fruit juice or cold water, and ate only freshly cooked rice.)

Ntxawm did not drink cold water or eat the rice cooked for the family, since the everyday rice is made in the morning and has cooled by midday, to be served cold at both midday and evening meals. Instead, Ntxawm's husband or her mother-in-law cooked fresh hot rice for her at every meal. Every day her husband killed one of the family's chickens for her, or bought one for her in the valley or from another Hmong family in the village. The chicken was boiled with special green herbs and freshly cracked white pepper to remove any residues of stale blood from her body, to keep her strong, and to cleanse her uterus (*lub tsev tus menyuam,* lit., "the house of the child") for her next pregnancy. Chicken fat and blood are supposed to replace the fat and blood that nourished the child in utero, and to assure a several years' supply of breast milk for the child.

For thirty days Ntxawm stayed at home to rest with her son, eating the special postpartum diet to regain her strength and speed her body's return to balance. Throughout this period she was not permitted to visit the houses of other families, because she was in a "new" *(tshiab)* state, which might harm people in other households, and then her family would be required to pay damages. If her family refused to pay these damages, her soul would have to return as a slave to work off the debt in the household of those who had been harmed. To warn others of her condition, her husband wove pieces of bamboo into a taboo sign and set it up outside of the house (fig. 3.2). The sign also warned anyone who was ill that there was a newborn in the house and that they should not enter. Pregnant women also are forbidden to visit such a household, since they might diminish a new mother's milk supply. Those who may enter the house during this time must remove their shoes and leave their bags outside, both to show respect and to make sure that no wild spirits are brought into the house, where they might prey upon the mother and the newborn child.

For thirty days Ntxawm bathed in warm water, although before, typically she had washed only in cold water. She refrained from washing her hair for a full month, since this too could cause illness.

Other proscriptions were also observed. Hmong women do not breast-feed their children immediately after birth. Traditionally, they wait a day or two until they begin to produce milk, believing that the yellow colostrum available in the breast immediately after childbirth is unhealthy.[1] Ntxawm washed the colostrum away, and it, like the other effluvia, was buried so that no animal could ingest it and make the child ill. When the baby cried during the first two days, and Ntxawm or her mother-in-law thought he was hungry, another lactating woman from the lineage nursed him. The

FIG. 3.2. *Taboo sign made of bamboo (caiv). This sign is placed outside to signal the presence of a newborn in a house. Lactating women and sick people may not enter. (Photo by Patricia Symonds)*

breast milk of lactating mothers is regarded as a very powerful medicine, dangerous if used incorrectly, and a number of taboos attach to it as a consequence; for instance, lactating women who have recently given birth are not permitted to cook, because the milk might accidentally become mixed with the family food.

For the first three days following the birth—the most dangerous period for a newborn because the third soul does not yet inhabit the body—Ntxawm and her nameless baby lay in front of the fire.

THE NAMING RITUAL: CALLING IN THE SOUL (HU PLIG)

Traditionally, the child's paternal grandfather names the baby. He selects a name from the pool of ancestors, especially those who were lucky and/or respected, so that the baby may embody the positive traits of that forebear. After careful deliberation, the grandfather chooses a name that he believes will suit the child, a name that the child will "like." If the name is wrong,

FIG. 3.3. Calling in the soul. Several days after a baby's birth, an older man in the household calls in the newborn's soul by banging on the door jamb with split buffalo horns. A chicken has been sacrificed so that its soul can go off to assist the new soul in its journey from the land of darkness to the land of light. (Photo by Patricia Symonds)

the child will cry a great deal and/or be thin and sickly, and the grandfather will have to choose another name. Only after a child has received a name is she or he considered a true human being and a true Hmong.

The naming ritual occurs on the child's third day of life. On this day, at the first sign of light, just as the rooster began to crow, Ntxawm's father-in-law opened the small spirit door directly across from the family altar. This spirit door is opened only for ritual purposes, such as when the ancestors are honored or when the family thanks them for favors or for their assistance. On this particular day, the door was opened to coax the newborn child's soul *(tus plig)* to return to earth, the land of light. As mentioned before, the third soul is the returning or vital soul that reincarnates and that was once an ancestor. (The Hmong are not sure which ancestor, although often they will remark that a child has character traits of someone who is dead.)

The grandfather placed a bowl of uncooked rice, topped with a raw egg and a stick of lit incense, on a small stool just inside the spirit door (see fig. 3.3). He set two small cups of rice liquor beside the bowl. A rooster and a hen (sometimes this is a single chicken, but of the opposite sex of the infant) were brought into the house, sacrificed, and placed in the bowl. The grandfather burned bamboo paper spirit money as an offering to the spirit parents, Niamtxiv Kab Yeeb, who would accompany and guide the child's third soul from the land of darkness. Then the grandfather took his buffalo or goat horn, which is cut into two pieces to form a pair, male (Father Kuam) and female (Mother Kuam) *(yaj kuam yeeb kuam),* tapped them on the side of the door, and threw them to the ground, repeating this until they landed in a propitious pattern. At this time, he began the soul-calling chant. The English translation below (see appendix A for the Hmong version) includes the name of this particular baby boy, Qig, in the place for the newborn's name.

CALLING IN THE SOUL:
THE JOURNEY TO THE LAND OF LIGHT

Today is a good day to receive, tonight is a good night to call.
I call this child Qig—his twelve reindeer souls[2]
Which may have stood wavering on the mountains and on the sides
     of the mountains
To get up.
Come, get up.
There are chickens and eggs on the doorstep to guide the hands,
And there are eggs on the doorstep to guide the feet.
I call Qig to get up and to return to have a mother and father,
To have a place to live and to sleep,
To be a brother to the hearth pole.[3]
Get up and return.

Come and be a brother [sister] to the back door.
Get up and return.
Do not wish to be on the road.
Do not wish to be on the pathways.
Do not wish to be on the mountainside.
There are chickens and eggs and the smoke from the incense
On the doorstep waiting to guide in the feet.
There are chickens and eggs and smoke from the incense
On the doorstep waiting to receive.
I call Qig—his twelve reindeer souls.

Come and have a mother and a father.

Get up and be a brother to the hearth pole

And be a brother to the center house post.

Get up and return.

Do not wander on the road.

Do not wander on the mountainsides.

Do not wander around the back yard.

There are chickens and eggs on the doorstep waiting for twelve reindeer
    souls.

Come and stand in the backyard,

And get up and come into the house.

The chicken and eggs inside the door are waiting to guide the feet

And to continuously call Qig's twelve reindeer souls.

Qig's twelve bamboo souls.[4]

Come and be in the house.

Come and be reunited with the family.

There are chickens to help lift, and there are eggs to carry.

There are chickens and eggs to protect.

There are roosters with claws

Who will stretch out their claws to protect and to help grab

Qig and his twelve reindeer souls.

So get up and come and have a mother and a father

And a bed to sleep in and a place to live.

Get up and return.

Do not wander onto the road.

Do not wander onto the way.

I call Qig's twelve reindeer souls.

Do not wander onto the mingling roads.

Do not linger on the crossroads.

There are roosters who have claws that will be shades for protection.

Their shadow[s] shall cover Qig's twelve reindeer souls

To have a mother and a father.

The claws will protect Qig's twelve reindeer souls

So that he can have a father and a mother.

Come and live straight like grass and strong like a mountain.

Come and live to be one hundred twenty years old and be an elder.
Get up and return.

Today is a good day to receive
And tonight is a good night to call.
Today is a good day to cross over.
Tonight is a good night to return.

I call Qig's twelve reindeer souls,
Which may have wandered onto Ntxwj Nyoog's mingling roads
And Ntxwj Nyoog's crossed roads.
We have chickens to help wake up,
And an egg to help bring all the souls.
The chicken and the egg together.
The hen will lift up the soul
And use its wings to guide you.
The rooster will use his claw to defend you.
So get up and return.

Even if Qig's souls have wandered onto the other side of the sky,
There is incense smoke to guide them.
There is incense smoke to guide.
There is a hen to guide you with her wing,
And the rooster with his claw to guard and protect the twelve souls
And to guide them from the other side of the sky.
So come and have a mother.
So get up and come.
There are hens with wings to protect you.
There are roosters with claws to protect you.
There is food and paper money.
There is a rooster who will grab the paper of longevity
From the other side of the world.
So come and have a father and a mother.
Have a bed to sleep in and a place to live.
Get up and return.
Miss Incense Smoke will follow and will come to gather
Qig's twelve souls.

Get up and return.

Do not wander onto the other side of the sky.

Get up and follow your footsteps to your home

I call Qig's twelve souls the spirits of chickens, ducks, and birds.

Get up and return to this side of the sky.

Get up and return.

Do not wander onto the clouded roads.

Do not wander on the windy roads.

Do not wander onto the merchants' roads.[5]

Get up and return.

The chickens and eggs are on the doorstep,

And they are continuously calling.

Get up and return.

Come home and take the chickens and the eggs.

There are chickens and eggs on the doorstep to guide the feet,

And they will never stop calling.

I call Qig's twelve souls.

Get up and return into the house to have a mother and a father.

Have a bed to sleep and a place to live.

Have a hearth and warmth.

Be a brother to the hearth.

Be a brother to the burning wood and to the hearth.

Come and be straight like the weeds

And be strong like a mountain.

Get up and return to live as clear as the water

And as clean as rice.

Come live for a thousand years

And grow up to be an old and wise man.

Come.

I am calling you to get up and return.

We have a hen to guide you with her wings.

We have a rooster who will defend you with his claws.

Come into the yard and into the house.

Come be a brother to the hearth and the log.

Come to the sleeping place,

Even though you might have gone to the other side of the horizon.

If you see the smoke from the incense and the paper money,
They are calling you constantly to come.
Do not wander onto the forked roads.
Do not wander onto the mountain top.

Do not wander into the backyard.
Do not wander into the front yard.
Get up and return from the corner of the gate and the house.
Get up and come and have a father and a mother.
Everybody opens the door wide.
Mother and father of this world,
Get ready to open wide the door to the yard and the house.
Mother and father of this world,
Get ready to open wide the gate to the yard and the house.
Open it wide.

[At this point the grandfather bangs the buffalo horns on the door jamb.]

Open the pathway wide to the house.
Mother and father of this world,
Get ready to open wide the gate to the yard and the house.
Mother Kuam [female half of the buffalo horn],
Open the door wide because Father Kuam [male half]
Is going to guide the twelve souls into the house.
Mother Kuam is opening the door with chickens and eggs
And calling constantly at the doorway.
There are chickens and a mother and a father
And everyone to open the gate and the door to welcome
Qig's twelve reindeer souls into the house.
Do not wander into the mountains.
I call Qig's souls.
Do not wander into the outside corners of the house.
Father Kuam opens the door wide
For Qig's souls to come into the house.

Mother Kuam protects and guides the souls into the gate.
Father Kuam opens the way wide.

Mother Kuam protects and guides it by having the hen open her wings.
Father Kuam protects and guides the souls by using his claws.
Father Kuam opens wide the road.
Mother Kuam opens wide the ways to welcome them into the house.
To have a mother and a father
And a sleeping place and a place to live.
(Translated from Hmong with the assistance of N. Vaj)

At the end of the chant, Qig's grandfather said,

Come little one, Qig, twelve reindeer souls, spirits of money, silver, and gold,
mother and father. Spirits of money, gold, silver. Mother and father, be wings
to guide and claws to protect—go and tie up the twelve reindeer souls to come
and have a mother and a father, to have a bed to sleep in and a place to live,
to be a brother to the hearth and be a brother to the center house post. There
will be wings and claws to protect and guide. Let the tongues of the chickens
curve inward. Let the bone heads of the chicken be as white, clean, and clear
as a grain of rice, and the four compartments in their skull be even and clean.[6]

At this point in the ritual, the grandfather placed two eggs in a pan of
boiling water and waved burning incense sticks over the bodies of the two
live chickens. He also set fire to the spirit money, and smoke and incense
enveloped all the witnesses. He addressed the spirits of silver and gold a final
time, saying, "Thank you for bringing us a new child. You are free now to
go back to the otherworld."

The chickens were taken to be slaughtered and cooked for the feast. The
spirit door was closed, and Ntxawm and her husband ate the two cooked
eggs. The grandfather tied hempen threads around the wrists of the child,
his parents, and the other witnesses. This thread-tying ritual *(khi hlua tes)*
is to bind people's souls more firmly to their bodies and strengthen or
reaffirm connections among family and lineage members. When the food
was ready, the entire household sat down to a meal of chicken and freshly
made rice. At the conclusion of this first meal, the new father extended an
invitation to other lineage and clan members to come back to the house at
a later date for a feast to honor the birth of the child. At this later feast the
visitors would tie hempen strings around the baby's wrist to signify that they

are welcoming the new child to life as a social human being, a Hmong, and offering their good wishes for the child's future.[7]

PRIVACY, THE BIRTH SHIRT, AND THE POSTPARTUM DIET

This case study illustrates several important facets of the birth process, the first of which is that privacy is important: the mother gives birth alone. Although solitary labor was not the rule in Flower Village, it was the ideal. In the case of the first-time deliveries in my sample, solitary labor occurred only 27 percent of the time (see table 3.1), but women who already had a child tended to labor alone more often. They may have felt less frightened of childbearing and more able to fulfill the ideal. In general, if a woman wanted to be alone, she was; but she did not have to be alone if she needed assistance or support. In first-time deliveries 51 percent of the women were assisted by a mother-in-law, and 13 percent by a husband. Mothers-in-law cut the umbilical cord 60 percent of the time, and husbands 26 percent. Although a woman's husband was not typically present for the child's birth, he was responsible for burying the placenta (84 percent) and cleaning and removing the birth detritus (70 percent); shame is attached to the neglect of this duty. Only 19 percent of the time did mothers-in-law attend to these tasks, and then only under unusual circumstances, such as when husband was away from the village.

TABLE 3.1

People Assisting with Childbirth in Flower Village

	Delivery	Cutting of Umbilical Chord	Burial of Placenta	Cleanup of Effluvia
Mother-in-law	51%	60%	8%	19%
Husband	13%	26%	84%	70%
Self	27%	7%	5%	1%
Nurse at Hospital	4%	3%	2%	2%
Sister-in-law	2%	1%	1%	4%
Other Wife	3%	3%	0%	4%

In many societies the disposal of the placenta is ritualized, and many cultures share the Hmong belief that a person is connected to the placenta for life. In some Southeast Asian cultures the placenta is thought to be the child's twin; in others, it is believed to have sympathetic magical powers (Hart et al. 1965:34–40).

For the Hmong, several important symbolic associations surround the placenta and its disposal. The amniotic sac, in which a fetus develops, is considered analogous to the shell of a chicken's egg and is buried along with the placenta. The placenta is attached to the mother via the umbilical cord *(txoj hlab ntawv)*, which the Hmong call the "lifeline" or "encircling paper" in an interesting parallel with the "mandate for life," which is the paper the soul must collect from Ntxwj Nyoog before returning to the earth.

The amniotic sac, the placenta, and the small piece of the umbilical cord that remains after the cord is cut are known collectively as the birth shirt. A boy's birth shirt is buried beneath the main post of the house since it is the connecting link to the ancestral spirits, and a son will be responsible for the spiritual duties of the lineage. A daughter's shirt is buried under her parents' bed; she will leave the lineage and has no connection to the central house post.

Like the birth effluvia, the birth shirt is buried with care—wrapped in leaves, placed flat in a hole with the umbilical cord on top of it, and then completely covered with soil so that animals cannot eat it, which might cause the infant to vomit food or contract skin diseases or other ailments. At this time, a woman who has not yet borne a son may ask the deity Kab Yeeb to send her a boy child at the time of her next confinement; when her husband buries the placenta, he must turn it inside out and promise to sacrifice a pig if the requested son arrives.

A post-parturient woman is fed a diet high in protein and fat, and these meals are prepared by her husband. The women in Flower Village frequently related the following origin tale about how men and women struck a bargain in the ancient past about who would give birth. Women never told it when men were around, but when I was back in the United States, a Hmong man told me this same story in front of his wife. It is unusual in that it reverses the sex roles:

A long time ago Hmong men used to give birth to the babies of the lineage.
It was difficult and painful for men to do, as they only had a small hole for

the child to come out of. This caused them to labor for seven days and seven nights. One day a man delivered a child as small as a grasshopper. The man killed and ate a cow in order to replenish his strength, and then, because he was too lazy to carry the infant on his back, he tied it to his shin. Then he went off to the field to join his wife, who was already working there. As he walked along, he came upon a chicken. The chicken saw the baby and pecked it off the man's shin and ate it. The man started to cry and continued to do so until he reached the field where his wife was working. "Why are you crying?" his wife asked. "Because the chicken ate my baby after I labored painfully for seven days and seven nights," he answered. "Stop crying," said his wife. "From now on why don't I have the babies? The hole I have is bigger and if I open my legs the child could be as big as a small stool we sit on. Then the chicken will not be able to eat it. But if I do this, you must kill me a chicken to eat every day for a month after I give birth, and I must stay at home eating chicken that you have prepared for me, regaining my blood and strength." The man agreed, and from then on women gave birth and men killed chickens for them to eat and cared for them for a month after the birth of each child.

(Translated from Hmong with the help of N. Vaj)

As this story illustrates, the Hmong believe that although women are more suited to giving birth, men were once able to do so, if not very skillfully. It also reveals that giving birth is an important task, and one that changes the physical and the spiritual state of women. Because childbirth depletes a woman's body of blood and strength, she must eat well or risk illnesses later in life.

Of particular interest, because it is in striking contrast to everyday Hmong life, is the idea that all the decision-making concerning birth appears to rest squarely in the hands of women and that husbands must cook their wives' meals, a reversal of the ordinary household roles in which men make decisions and women cook and wait on them. During this month-long period, women not only eat first, but they eat meat, a prestige food because of its expense and scarcity. In addition, a mother is given special privileges in that she rests, is kept warm and comfortable, and is not allowed to work in the fields.

The aforementioned concept of hot and cold foods and body temperatures, and the belief in women's postpartum vulnerability, has been documented for most of Southeast Asia.[8] Several authors report that the Southeast

Asian understanding of hot and cold foods is derived from Indian Ayurvedic humeral traditions, but I agree with Nicholas Tapp that for the Hmong, the influence is traditional Chinese medicine. In the Chinese system the human body is composed of two opposing vital forces—cold (yin) and hot (yang)—that must be in equilibrium for optimum health. In giving birth a woman is depleted of heat and must therefore eat only those foods that increase heat, while avoiding cold foods such as fruit juice. Throughout South and Southeast Asia, chicken is considered a heat-building food par excellence, which is why the woman in the story specifically requested a chicken a day. Although the Hmong make sure that a postpartum woman is kept physically warm, they do not follow the tradition of lying throughout the month by the fire, called "mother-roasting," that is common throughout Southeast Asia.[9]

This case study of birth also portrays the value of breast milk. The Hmong do not eat dairy products even when they keep cattle, but breast milk is highly regarded as the food that sustains life in newborns and young children. One of the debts for which wife-takers must pay is breast milk. The story "Why Men Rule the World," presented in chapter 2, vividly recognizes women's physical contribution to the continuity of life in its depiction of a king who cannot behead his breastfeeding wives.

The first soul inhabits the infant as soon as its bones begin to grow in the uterus. The second soul is brought by the wind at the moment the child takes its first breath. When a woman begins labor, the third soul, which is waiting in the land of darkness, learns that it is time for its rebirth; it goes and waits at the gates of the ancestral village to obtain the "mandate for life," the paper that will allow it to return to earth (Thao 1984:323–30). But this third soul does not enter the body until the naming ceremony, and if an infant dies before the third soul has been called in, the body is disposed of in the forest without ceremony since it was not a full human being, or Hmong person. In much the same way that the Showing the Way chant guides the soul to the land of the dead, the soul-calling chant guides the soul to the land of the living.

Men are responsible for guiding the soul; through chants and animal sacrifice they ensure that the soul returns to this earth. In this sense, males are ultimately responsible for the creation of the social individual when the third soul is called. Although the child is nourished by and grows inside of a woman's body for ten moons, it cannot properly be said to belong to the mother. The uterus, called the "house of the child" or "house for the child" is merely the vessel or "basket" in which the seed grows (see Chindarsi 1976:63).

BECOMING A WOMAN

In Flower Village the onset of menses fell between the ages of fifteen and sixteen for 77 percent of the women (see table 3.2). This was also the approximate age at which 60 percent of the young women married, and at which 47 percent gave birth for the first time, showing that the timing of these three major life events is closely correlated. The onset of menses *(coj khaubncaws)* is therefore a time of major transition for a young girl, and is referred to as "being/doing a woman" *(ua poj niam)*. Although there is no formal ritual recognition of menses and it is seldom discussed, it signals the end of childhood; a girl is no longer referred to as a child *(tus menyuam)* but as a young courting girl *(hluas nkauj)*. Also at approximately the age of fifteen, boys are called young courting boy *(hluas nraug)*.

TABLE 3.2

Age at First Menarche, First Marriage, and First Childbirth
for Women in Flower Village

Age	First Menses	First Marriage	First Child
<15	20%	4%	0%
15–16	77%	60%	47%
17–18	3%	21%	34%
19–20	0%	11%	8%
>20	0%	4%	11%

SOURCE: Survey of 108 women.

The Hmong do not consider menstrual blood polluting and place few restrictions on a menstruating woman. A girl's first menstrual blood is considered a very powerful substance and sometimes is collected and dried as medicine for those who are gravely ill. Like pregnant women, menstruating women are in a state of coldness and must keep physically warm and eat only warming foods, but no one waits on them. Their state of disequilibrium makes them vulnerable to physical illness as well as to malevolent spirits, in particular those along pathways and near streams and other bodies of water.

The following myth, related by a Hmong shaman in Flower Village, explains women's vulnerability during menstruation and pregnancy:

Long ago Siv Yis looked down from his cave above and saw three very wicked brothers killing people—cutting off their heads and eating their bodies. He decided to do something about it and went down to where they lived to meet them. He introduced himself and chatted for a while and asked where they lived. He was told they lived in a cave nearby and that he was welcome to spend the night. He refused but made plans to meet them the next day.

"Would you like me to bring along a beautiful girl?" he asked.

The three brothers were delighted. On his return to his cave, Siv Yis formulated a strategy for dealing with the wicked brothers. At the appointed time the next day he changed himself into a beautiful girl with beautiful clothes. He then appeared at the appointed place.

"Where is Siv Yis?" the wicked brothers asked in surprise.

"He cannot come today. Tomorrow, if possible, he will come. He said if any one of you think I am beautiful and if you wish, one of you can marry me," she said.

The wicked brothers talked together and decided that she was indeed very beautiful and that the oldest brother would marry her. They took her home to the cave and their parents, who were most happy to have a daughter-in-law to help in the house and to produce children for their lineage.

The young woman said to her future husband, "Bring me a very large pig and place several large pans around the cave, and I will cook for a party for our wedding." The brothers brought into the cave a very large pig, which they sacrificed and butchered and put in the pots they had arranged around the cave. The daughter-in-law waited until there was a lot of fat in each pan and then upset it in the cave and set fire to it all. The wicked brothers and their parents were burned to death. The daughter-in-law escaped quickly to the outside and prepared to return home. Then she noticed the youngest brother had hidden outside of the cave and escaped the flames.

"Why did you kill all of my family?" he stormed.

The daughter-in-law quickly turned back into Siv Yis and answered, "You and your brothers are wicked. You kill and eat people. You, too, should be killed, but you have been saved, and I cannot kill you now, but you will live forever in a hole in the earth."

The young wicked brother answered, "I will not kill and eat people anymore, but if young menstruating girls and pregnant women walk over the holes in the ground in which I live or over springs or lakes that I visit, I will enter into them and cause them trouble."[10]

(Translated from Hmong with the assistance of N. Vaj)

When a young woman has severe cramps or other menstrual problems, midcycle spotting, or complications during pregnancy, the trouble is blamed on the surviving wicked brother of the story. The Hmong characterize menstrual blood as "shiny" and say that it gives off a strong light that attracts the wicked brother. A fetus is even shinier; although ordinary people cannot see the light from the fetus, the wicked brother can, and if a pregnant woman steps over one of the holes where he lives, or over a body of water where he is visiting, he sends a beam of his own light into the woman. A struggle between the fetus and wicked brother then ensues and causes spotting or bleeding. One of the indications that this has occurred is when a woman dreams that she is visited by a strange and unusually loving male.

If a young or pregnant woman has this dream, she must tell her father-in-law or her husband immediately, since there is only a short period of time during which she can be helped. A shaman must travel to the otherworld for her, to ascertain whether her dream is indeed the work of the surviving wicked brother. The woman sits behind the shaman on a small stool while powdered dried corn is flung around the house and set aflame. This scares away the wicked brother, who sees the burning corn as a sign that Siv Yis is preparing to burn him to death. The light that links him to the fetus or the menstruating woman is thus severed, and the wicked brother can no longer cause miscarriage or menstrual pain.

Nicholas Tapp (1989b:148) presents an interesting case linking the wicked brother story to geomancy. He suggests that competition over land is fundamental to the geomantic system, which is used for the burial of the dead and the siting of new houses or villages. He relates the case of a Hmong shaman who was said to have explained several miscarriages and stillbirths in another village as the workings of a malevolent spirit who, because of the alignment of the encircling mountains, was inhabiting a nearby spring. The shaman suggested that the village be moved to a safer place, and the villagers followed his directive. The shaman was then able to cultivate the land they had vacated, which was particularly suitable for growing opium. The shaman, Tapp suggests, was using the "geomantic idiom" to gain access to land and thus increase his own power and prosperity. I suggest that both the villagers and the shaman were familiar with the legend of the wicked brothers, and that therefore the villagers were willing to leave their land to avoid future problems with births. (Tapp also suggests that shared cosmological and geomantic knowledge enabled the shaman to take the land.)

CONCEPTION

The Hmong believe that conception occurs when the seed *(tus qab)* of a man fertilizes the egg *(lub qe)* of a woman. Another name for the seed is *tus kab menyuam*—literally, "worm" or "insect." The seed is produced in the testicle (*noob qes,* or "seed egg") during intercourse. The egg is produced inside the uterus at about the time a woman menstruates. Thus a woman's most fruitful time is just before or during her menses. The planting metaphor, analogizing rain and menstruation, is used in a Hmong saying about conception: "It is better to plant the seed when it is raining or about to do so." The Hmong also say that a menstruating woman is "blooming" and consequently more apt to conceive, or more "open" to conception. If the egg is stronger than the seed, the egg will eat the seed and it will die; then the egg will leave the body and the woman will not conceive. Only if the egg and the seed are of equal strength can the seed be planted inside the egg to create an infant. The child is sustained in the uterus by its mother's blood and fat. Once the seed, which possesses all of the human attributes provided by the man, is planted in the egg and begins to grow, the placenta, or birth shirt, begins to take shape around the developing body.

Hmong fetal development theory posits that the child first forms its eyes, then its head and neck, bones, internal organs, and stomach. At three months the sex of the child can be determined according to whether conception occurred during a month when a male or a female egg was produced and whether the husband slept on the right or left side of his wife. If a child is born with the amniotic sack over its face, it will be an exceptional person who will have luck and good fortune.

Because the Hmong have seen and studied premature fetuses, they are aware of the various stages of fetal development. In Flower Village when I asked people if they knew about the inside of the body, usually they looked at me as if I were asking a silly question. One day one of the women took me over to where a man was cutting up a pig after a sacrifice. "Phiaj, we know about the inside of animals' bodies because we cut them up often. We know about the house for babies because we see them inside the animal often with babies in them. So, we don't know how the inside of a person looks, but we know we breathe and have a heart and a place where babies grow—" (here she could not keep from laughing) "and where they come out."

CARE DURING PREGNANCY

Families take great interest in observing how long it takes for a new wife to become pregnant, although it is not unusual for a woman to become pregnant before her marriage, during the New Year's celebration. Many weddings occur in the months following the courtship period.

It is common for newlyweds to spend their evenings in the small field house rather than in the busy household, which gives them a chance to get to know one other. Quite often they have grown up in different villages, and as only males visit back and forth, they probably do not know each other. In addition, it is a difficult time for the bride since her new family may not know her. Her in-laws observe her to see if she has been trained properly, whether she works hard and is humble. If complimented on her sewing skills, a good Hmong woman should deny that it is skilled work and state instead that it is poorly done, engaging in culturally sanctioned self-deprecation. The in-laws also watch for signs, such as paying attention to her mother-in-law, that the bride is willing to become part of her new family. Mothers-in-law also keep a vigilant eye on their daughters-in-law for any increase in their consumption of sour food—the first sign of pregnancy. If a woman becomes pregnant, and her pregnancy is progressing normally, a shaman performs a ritual promising that the family will sacrifice an animal to the ancestors for the birth of a healthy child.

Even though the Hmong believe that pregnancy makes women more vulnerable to spirits, they consider pregnancy a normal physical condition, and pregnant women continue to do most of their daily chores, although they are expected to ask for help with heavy lifting or extensive reaching. Although postpartum women must eat "hot" food, there are no dietary prescriptions or proscriptions during pregnancy. Pregnant women eat whatever they desire, because if they do not, the child will be scarred or marked in some fashion. For instance, if a pregnant woman has an urge to eat chicken and there is no chicken available, the child's ears may be notched or chickenlike as a result. Similar beliefs concerning pregnancy and food cravings are found in other Southeast Asian cultures; in parts of the Philippines it is believed that "left unsatisfied, such cravings may cause miscarriages" (Hart et al. 1965:34–40), and in Malaysia, people believe unsatisfied cravings may cause problems for the fetus (Laderman 1987:90–91).

At approximately the seventh month of pregnancy, a ritual called "doing the spirits" *(ua neeb)* is performed to ensure the child's and mother's safety during the actual birthing process. At this time, a shaman reiterates the earlier promise that the family will sacrifice an animal to the ancestors if a healthy child is born. Two joined paper dolls are placed on the floor in front of the pregnant woman, who sits on a small stool. The shaman cuts apart the paper dolls and burns them to signify the successful separation of the mother and child, since if the child is very strong and the mother tired and weak from the birth, the child may steal the mother's soul and cause her death. This ceremony may also be performed during a difficult labor, to untangle the child's and the mother's souls (see Loo's case below).

As mentioned earlier, pregnant women are advised to be cautious around water and to avoid crossing rivers or streams. They must also take care not to step over the rope that is used to leash or tie animals (such as pigs or horses) for fear of twisting the umbilical cord and causing complications during the birth. Pregnant women do not reach above their heads for the same reason, and they do not cut cloth in their bedrooms, for fear that the child will be born with a harelip. Pregnant women are not allowed to walk far by themselves in the woods or gardens, because something (such as an animal or a wild spirit) might frighten them, resulting in soul loss and physical sickness. If a woman is having a difficult pregnancy, her family may call in a woman who is an herbalist to prescribe herbal remedies *(tshuaj ntsuab)* or root teas *(tshuaj qhauv).*

LABOR AND DELIVERY

Women often are working in the fields when labor begins. On occasion they will go to the small field house to have their baby, but most attempt to reach their home in the village, where the household spirits will protect them. A woman I knew named Yim did not quite make it.

YIM'S LABOR AND DELIVERY

At the time of the rice harvest, Yim was twenty years old and expecting her fourth child. The whole family was in the fields, hurrying to bring in the rice before the weather changed, when, at about midday, Yim's back began to ache. Her mother-in-law advised her to return home quickly. Yim packed her sewing and her reaping knife, put her basket on her back, and set off toward the village. The field was about a mile from home, and Yim hurried, wanting to be under her own roof, where the household spirits would protect her, instead of outside and at the mercy of wild spirits. She was about halfway home when her contractions became so severe she had to stop. Between each contraction she moved on; but about a quarter of a mile from the village, she lay down by the roadside and pushed out the baby girl. She lay there for a while, and then cut the cord with her big knife. She delivered the placenta, wrapped it in a large leaf, and placed it in her back basket. Then she wrapped the baby girl in her own coat and struggled on to the village. As she came into the village—what a sight!—several women in the clan hurried to help her wash and get to bed, and one of the older women buried the placenta under the bed. When the family returned in the late afternoon, they were quite startled to find the baby already born. Yim's husband killed a chicken, and Yim's mother-in-law gave her an egg to eat and chicken broth with herbs to drink. Despite the dramatic delivery, both Yim and her baby girl were healthy. On the third day the family did a soul-calling ceremony, calling on the ancestors for protection for Yim and the child, and tying strings around Yim's and the baby's wrists.

If labor becomes difficult, as it did in Loo's case, the family may call on a shaman for help, or even go to the hospital in the valley.

LOO'S LABOR AND DELIVERY

Loo went into labor early one Tuesday evening after everyone had finished work in the fields, eaten dinner, and cleaned up for the night. Loo was fifteen years old, and this was her first child. She bathed as usual at the village tap and then changed her trousers for a sarong. I was called in so that I would know a baby was coming. Everyone, tired from the day's work, settled down to rest for the night; I was given a place in a room with some of the teenage girls in the family. When morning came, the family, except for Loo's mother-in-law, went off to bring in the crop; Loo and I sat together outside the house to wait, working on our flower cloth so that we wouldn't seem lazy, while Loo's mother-in-law chopped up pig feed, fed the pigs and the chickens, and swept the house. I could tell that Loo's contractions were coming quite close together when she became quiet and placed her flower cloth on her lap. She ate nothing that day and drank only small sips of water.

In the early evening the family returned, and Loo lay down on the bed in the little room she and her husband shared. She was very uncomfortable and tossed and turned. At about 10:00 P.M. the father of the family called in a shaman. He talked to the family, and a very big rooster was brought in and waved over Loo's head. The rooster was sacrificed and cooked; then the shaman and family elders looked at its throat and feet in order to diagnose Loo's problem. Had the spirits entered her body or were they after the baby's soul? They decided to conduct a ritual so that the shaman could go to the otherworld and retrieve the straying or stolen souls. Another large chicken was brought in, and the shaman again waved it over Loo's head. Its feet were tied together, and it was placed on the floor near the end of Loo's bed. Paper was cut in the shape of two individuals, and the shaman snipped them apart, to separate the mother's and the baby's souls. The shaman then placed his mask on his face and began to journey. The gong and finger bells could be heard all over the village. The shaman journeyed for about an hour and a half, but Loo became more and more uncomfortable as the night wore on. By 5:00 A.M. everyone was worried; Loo was exhausted. The family decided to take her down the mountain in the truck to the Thai hospital. One of the household members was a white-faced shaman; he put on a tall white hat made of cloth and paper, took up the gong, and accompanied Loo, her husband, and her parents-in-law to the truck. He jumped up and down all the way to the truck, and banged on the gong to frighten away any spirits that might be lurking in the vicinity. The rooster was waved over Loo's head again and placed in the truck with them all, and they set off.

One hour later the truck returned to the village. Halfway down the mountain Loo had delivered a fine little boy, so she never went to the hospital after all. The rooster was killed and cooked and fed to Loo. Loo recovered, and she and the baby were healthy.

MISCARRIAGE AND STILLBIRTH

If her baby dies at birth, a woman attempts to become pregnant very soon thereafter, since the loss of the child is also the loss of a place for an ancestral soul. If the soul arrives and is displeased with the family or the body it finds, or if a debt remained owing at a funeral ceremony, the soul may return to the land of the ancestors to wait for a body that suits it better. When a woman has several miscarriages or stillbirths, it is assumed that she has done something unacceptable to the returning soul—she may not be a good Hmong woman, or she may have displeased a wild spirit—and that the soul keeps coming and leaving to punish her. Or it may be that the soul itself is too critical, and there is nothing wrong with the child's body or the woman. In such a case, the husband's sister will come in and mark the dead infant's face with the blood of a sacrificed animal to give notice to this particular soul that the family is aware of what it is doing, in an effort to make the soul desist. A ritual will be held for the mother as well. In Flower Village I was told that a child who had a red birthmark was a returning soul who had been one of these overly critical spirits.

MIDWIVES

Although Hmong midwives are not formally trained, they are extremely knowledgeable about pregnancy and birth. They know how to turn breech babies in utero, something that many Western gynecologists will not attempt (for fear of twisting the umbilical cord around the baby's neck). Although there are very few midwives, they are widely known and respected. I learned of the midwife I interviewed when I was in the city of Chiang Mai, which is a long distance—about seventy kilometers—from the village where she lived.

When I visited this woman, I asked her how she had come to know so much about the birth process. She explained that she had given birth to only one child, a son, when she was a young woman; it was a difficult birth, and both she and her child almost died. After she had been in labor for several days, she began to hemorrhage; her mother-in-law became frightened and sent the husband and the father-in-law to fetch a midwife who was known to be highly skilled. When the midwife arrived and examined the woman, she found that the child was in a breech position; she rotated the child in the birth canal, and the mother delivered a healthy son. Afterward, the midwife told her and her family that she would be unable to have any more children. She gave the young mother medicinal herbs to cook with her chicken and to steep in water to drink at frequent intervals. The woman regained her strength; and when her son was grown, she sought out the midwife and asked to be trained herself.

Because of the scarcity of midwives, women who have given birth usually assist young mothers who want or need help. If problems occur during labor and birth, a shaman may be called in, as happened in Loo's case, to "see" what is creating the trouble and try to help the woman in labor.

INFERTILITY

A barren woman is known as one who has a "dry egg" *(lub qe quav),* and her life is a difficult one. She is considered unfortunate, unlucky, and unfulfilled in this life and—perhaps even more important—in the next life as well. I once heard a childless woman say, "When I reach 120 years old [a Hmong euphemism for death] and I return to this world, I want to return as a pig or chicken so that I can have many children."

When a woman cannot conceive, she first consults with herbalists from her own village; if their remedies prove unsuccessful, she may seek out women from other villages who possess special knowledge of fertility-enhancing herbs. Since women are considered responsible for a couple's inability to conceive, it is incumbent upon the woman to seek help, but husbands may consult shamans who perform a diagnostic ritual invoking the aid of Niamtxiv Kab Yeeb, the spirit couple who aid fertility.[11] If the couple remains childless after having availed themselves of fertility rituals and herbal medicine, they may adopt children or the man may take a second wife.

A woman in Flower Village who had been married for several years was unable to become pregnant despite all the rituals and herbal medicine. Then her husband died in an accident. The Hmong practice levirate, so the young widow was married to her deceased husband's younger brother. Soon she became pregnant and gave birth to a healthy child. The explanation offered for this was that the rituals and the herbal medicine finally had worked; however, several women told me in confidence that they believe that infertility can result when the seed of the man is not strong enough.

The dominant ideology, supported and voiced by women, conflicts with the underlying subdominant voice of women. The responses women gave in the presence of men clearly differed from those they gave when they were alone with me or in very informal situations with other women. For example, when asked what would happen if there were no men around to perform soul-calling rituals, women replied that they were capable of doing it themselves. When I returned to the United States, I heard of two instances, one in Laos and one in the United States, in which the men of the family had died, and the grandmother did indeed call in the soul of the newborn child. Men, on the other hand, stated that women do not have the knowledge to perform such rituals.

BIRTH CONTROL

Thus far, the Thai government's efforts to encourage valley people to use birth control have met with a great deal of success, but the government has not done as well with minority highland groups such as the Hmong.[12] Researchers have suggested that these groups continue to have many children because they need a lot of children to work in the fields, or because large families are a mark of status. Although these points are valid, the ideological and cosmological components that control women's reproduction have not been explored.

Hmong women are reluctant to use any form of abortion or birth prevention, in part because preventing conception might deny a soul its opportunity for rebirth. In Flower Village, 82 percent of the women who had been pregnant had never used birth control. Although Hmong women know about emmenagogues and abortifacients, they are seldom used. Even after a woman has had several children and believes that her family is complete, or that she would like to space the births of additional children at greater intervals, she is under considerable constraint by lineage members not to practice birth control of any kind.

When I asked women in the village, in the presence of their mothers-in-law, whether they practiced birth control, I was almost always told no. If I visited these women later, when they were alone or with other women, they sometimes confided that they were trying one or another method. Most of those using birth control used Depo-Provera™, a hormone shot given every three months. The rest used birth control pills. (On family planning, see Epilogue.)

A factor that further complicates fertility regulation is that Hmong women traditionally marry when they are quite young and continue to give birth until they are middle-aged. Because of their long reproductive life, it is not at all unusual for a mother-in-law to be pregnant at the same time as her daughter-in-law. The Hmong believe that a woman must give birth to more children than did her own mother or mother-in-law if she is to fulfill her destiny. If she does not, she will not have paid all of her earthly debts (Kunstadter et al. 1990:6). (Nowadays this particular stricture is not taken as seriously as it once was.)

In addition to risking her family's disapproval, every woman must deal with the personal consequences of deciding to limit her reproduction. Many women state that birth control pills or injections leave them feeling weak; they have a poor appetite and cannot work in the fields. Instead they must stay home and rest just as they do during the postpartum period. In addition, they feel depressed and are afflicted with a difficult liver *(ntxhov siab)*.

Byron Good's study of women in Iran shows that chronic situational stress becomes embodied in "complaints of the heart," the organ that is for Iranians the central physiological organ as well as the organ of emotional functioning (Good 1977:36). He also finds that although cases of heart distress are common in both genders, they appear more frequently in women, especially in those who use contraception. According to Good, the role of women in Iranian social life centers around their reproductive capacities; loss or negation of this role can cause considerable emotional and physiological trauma. He also posits that the conflict between the social pressure to have large families and the economic difficulties of doing so creates additional stress.

Similar issues affect Hmong women. This comparison is not meant to suggest that Hmong women do not experience actual physical side effects from Depo-Provera, the contraceptive pill, or other methods of birth control but to acknowledge the effects of social pressure to produce children. The depression these women feel manifests in the form of complaints of liver distress, the physical organ that is an idiom for the expression of emotion. Hmong women experience the added fear that if they refuse to have more children for the lineage, their husbands will take junior wives. There are times when a man's taking a second or later wife is necessary and even desirable for a senior wife, but it is not the solution that most women prefer.

Heirs are necessary to ensure one's well being in the afterlife as well as in this life, and only sons can care for the family altar and the ancestors. If a married couple is childless, there will be no one to care for them in old age or after death, no one to remember them and feed them when they have become ancestors in the land of darkness. If a couple has only daughters, a son-in-law may join his wife's household, but this solution is not looked on favorably. In the event that a married couple is childless or has only daughters, a second wife may be able to have the sons who will feed the entire household, including the senior wife, upon her death.[13] Women who do not have sons may encourage their husbands to take junior wives, because they too need descendants to feed them after death and provide bodies in which they may be reincarnated.

In spite of the importance of sons, great value is also placed on having an equal number of sons and daughters. The bride-price a family receives in exchange for its daughters can be used for a future daughter-in-law who will continue the lineage through the children she has. In this way, both sons and daughters ensure the continuity of the lineage—sons by fathering lineage members and feeding the ancestors, and daughters by bringing in bride-price.

WESTERN HEALTHCARE FOR WOMEN AND CHILDREN

I have calculated the infant mortality rate in Flower Village at 11.4 infant deaths per one thousand live births, based upon the year that I was there, when three infants died out of the 26 born. Although this calculation is based on a relatively small sample size, it does indicate a significant healthcare problem.[14]

In the household where I lived, my host's son Ntaj was a community health worker, trained to run the dispensary in a special program offered by the

Ministry of Public Health in 1981, in an attempt to "provide comprehensive health and family planning services" for hill tribes in northern Thailand. Supported by the United Nations Family Planning Agency (UNFPA), the program's primary objective was to "establish a low-cost health care delivery model that could overcome the language, cultural, and topographic barriers associated with working in hill tribe communities."

Individuals from indigenous hill tribe communities were trained to provide services similar to those offered by "midwives and/or sanitarians stationed at the lowland health facilities." Each of the Community Health Workers (CHWs) was assigned a cluster of villages in her/his area and maintained health records on patients, reported to the District Health Office, and attended ongoing training sessions. This program continues to improve as organizers learn from their early mistakes. Ntaj frequently visited his village cluster to provide emergency pediatric care and give inoculations.

In 1987 Ntaj's "clinic" was simply a little cabinet in the corner of the household. People came to the house to consult him throughout the day and evening. Late one night, a man brought his child who had been severely burned, and banged on the door until someone woke and let him in. After this incident, Ntaj and his father felt that such emergencies were too disruptive to the household; a few months later Ntaj and several village men built a small shed next to the house to serve as the clinic and dispensary.

The clinic was furnished with a platform bed and a cupboard for medications and other supplies. On the walls were posters describing fetal development and birth. Village children examined these posters with interest, but I seldom saw women looking at them, even though they were written in Thai. One explanation for this may be that the Hmong are not accustomed to reading or viewing drawings, diagrams, or illustrations—I once observed the mother in my household looking at a picture book upside down. When educational initiatives are undertaken, posters or books may not be the most effective means of reaching the intended population. (On the use of posters in HIV/AIDS education, see Epilogue.)

Ntaj was also able to dispense birth control pills, but the few women who asked for them were usually members of his own clan. Because they are "shy," women from other clans do not as a general rule go to the CHW for birth control, prenatal care, or assistance during delivery; to save face, they do not visit one another's homes or expect non-clanspeople to visit them during pregnancy.

I observed only two cases where the cultural reluctance and modesty around pregnancy were disregarded. In the first case, a woman who had had a miscarriage continued to hemorrhage even after a shaman had performed a ritual. Finally Ntaj was called in, and he took the woman to the hospital in the valley, where she was admitted for a stay of several weeks. Without hospital assistance, she probably would have died. In the second case, a woman gave birth after a greatly protracted and arduous labor; the child survived, although it was born with birth injuries. The mother, however, did not deliver the placenta, and this, I was told by Hmong women, could result in the mother's death. After a short period of deliberation, the woman's husband conferred with Ntaj, who immediately borrowed his father's truck and drove the woman and her child down the mountain to the hospital in the valley. This woman's survival was also quite likely the result of Ntaj's quick response to the situation.

In most cases pregnancy and birthing are considered women's business rather than health issues; it is only when problems are beyond their own expertise and that of knowledgeable community women and herbalists that Hmong women will enlist the aid of the shaman or the CHW, or go to a hospital. The same was true of the Hmong women in Providence, Rhode Island, where I first observed these situations.

EARNING A PLACE

Giving birth, especially to a first child, is a major rite of passage for a young woman. She has fulfilled her most important role in life by proving that she is fertile; she links the ancestors with future generations of Hmong and has earned herself a place within her new household. Giving birth produces a visible change in a young woman's behavior. She is no longer a lonely young bride but a mother, a woman in the truest sense of the word.

CHAPTER 4

DEATH: THE JOURNEY

TO THE LAND OF DARKNESS

O n the third day of life, the vital soul journeys from the land of darkness to the land of light, guided by the soul-calling chant. At death another chant guides the souls back to the land of darkness (Lemoine 1983b:6–8), to join the ancestors and await rebirth.

Several researchers have viewed mortuary rituals as the most elaborate and important of Hmong rituals, and the Showing the Way chant, which guides the souls to the ancestors, is often cited as a key to Hmong cosmology. Although accounts of mortuary rituals in different locations and among different groups of Miao/Hmong vary in nuances, the journey to the land of darkness is a constant among them all.[1] Jacques Lemoine's work (1972b, 1983a) on mortuary rituals focused on the Green Mong in Laos, whose practices share many similarities with those of the White Hmong in Thailand.[2]

Lemoine concludes that for the Hmong, death is the journey of the soul, which lives on after the body dies and travels to another existence. The purpose of the soul's journey is to reach the village and then the house of its ancestors. There, the soul locates the sources of life, at which point it may reincarnate, ideally, through the body of a Hmong woman (1983a:6–7). In this way the returning vital soul (which I have called the third soul) perpetuates the clan, the lineage, and the family. I found that, for the White Hmong, two souls make the journey to the land of darkness—the second soul to join with the ancestors, and the third soul to reincarnate—whereas the first soul stays with the bones in the grave.

For the Hmong, the death of an older, married person who has died of natural causes sets into motion a series of rituals to ensure the safe journey of the souls from this world to the next. Hmong death rituals are concerned with the individual's position in the community, and the continuity and cohesiveness of the community. Robert Hertz's study on funerary practices of the Malayo-Polynesian people, which was carried out under the direction of Emile Durkheim, began with the premise that mortuary rituals were undertaken in the belief that the dead person was not only a biological individual but also a "social being, grafted upon the physical individual whose destruction is tantamount to a sacrilege against the social order" (1960:77). The anthropological generalization that mortuary rituals are a means of transcending individual deaths to maintain the continuity and solidarity of the social order appears to be accurate for the Hmong (Hertz 1960:77; Malinowski 1948:52–53; Radcliffe-Brown 1964:285). Funerals are a means by which the fragmentation of the social group, and the grief created by the loss of one of its members, can be healed.

In addition, the concept of death as necessary to the continuation of life (through the rebirth of the individual soul in a different body) illuminates Hmong beliefs about the meaning of life itself. Their concept of death and rebirth gives the Hmong a way to contend with the contingencies of life and death, and provides them with the assurance of continuity.

During my stay in Flower Village, I attended three funerals. At two of these I was able to attend only part of the ceremony, but I witnessed the funeral of one elderly man in its entirety, except for those times when I left to get some sleep.

The full sequence of mortuary events is divided into two complementary parts. In the rituals described below, the first part lasted for the recommended period of thirteen days, commencing in the house of the deceased with the Showing the Way chant. The dead man was taken from the house and buried on the tenth day. For three more days after the burial, men of the dead man's household, especially his eldest son, fed the ancestors and the deceased. Finally, on the thirteenth day, the Xi Plig ceremony to free the first soul was held at the dead man's old home, in silence, with only the household in attendance. (Other clans perform these ceremonies in different ways; I will be report here what I saw in the Muas clan.)

The second part of the ritual was the Freeing of the Soul ceremony (Tso Plig). Whereas the Xi Plig frees or releases the first soul, which will stay at the grave, the Tso Plig refers to the third, or returning vital soul, which has gone to the land of darkness. In this case the Tso Plig was not held on the thirteenth day after the actual biological death, which would have been the ideal time for it, but six months later, because of the expense of both rituals. Until this ceremony occurs, the soul is considered to be dangerously proximate and uncontrollable, so people attempt to free the soul quickly, especially in the case of a bad death, such as a suicide. But although this is the ideal, at the three funerals I attended in Flower Village, the second ritual was held weeks or months after the first. In the case of the two bad deaths (a suicide and an accident) that occurred while I was there, the second ritual did follow immediately after the first. The second ritual was also held immediately afterward at a Hmong funeral I attended in Minnesota, but in that case the family was wealthy enough to afford two expensive, consecutive rituals.

These two parts, elaborated upon and described by Hertz as the pattern of "double obsequies," represent a major symbolic theme characteristic of many Southeast Asian societies—that is, the disaggregation of the individual from the social group, and the subsequent regrouping by sending off the soul, which reasserts the solidarity and continuity of the social group. For the deceased this rite of passage comprises the disconnection with past status and role, a liminal period, and finally an incorporation into a new position. For the survivors the same issues apply. Their roles as parents, spouses, and so on transmute and disconnect at this time. After a liminal period of bereavement, these individuals are reincorporated into new roles within the social group (Van Gennep 1960:46–65; Turner 1967:93–103).

Ntxhi Vang writes that, for the Hmong, "all the elements and activities in a funeral service serve to strengthen and unify the living relatives as well as to seal off the separation [of the living from the dead]" (1985:4). The Hmong call the ritual processes that follow a death the "way of illness and death" *(kev mob kev tuag)*. The following funerary ritual, for a respected, older Hmong man, occurred in October 1987 in Flower Village. His was a "good death" because he had lived a long life and had many children. Also, he had died in his home, the ideal place from which a lineage spirit can depart.

Because of his advanced age, many people came to pay their respects and/or to repay or collect debts, and the ritual chanting about his life was long and descriptive.

The series of rituals ensures that the souls of the deceased will reach the land of darkness (or, in the case of the first soul, the grave) safely. This journey, through which the souls of the dead person are so carefully guided, is only the embarkation. Although Radley states that "the cycle of life for the Mong is completed when the person is instructed to find his afterbirth" (1986:388), I was told that it was only after the souls have joined their own group of ancestors in the land of the darkness that the souls can rest. At that time, Ntxwj Nyoog and Nyuj Vaj Tuam Teem review the third soul and give it the "certificate" or "mandate for life" *(ntawv niaj ntawv xyoo)*.[3] This "paper for every year" entitles the returning vital soul to embark on the next stage of the journey—that is, to be reborn. A person who becomes acutely ill when visiting another household is quickly moved to the house of her/his own lineage if possible. Only those who share a particular household's lineage spirits *(dab qhuas)* may die in the lineage house, where the central house post connects the land of human life to the land of the spirits, and more particularly, to the ancestral mass that will be the source of rebirth.

THE FUNERAL: PART 1

After Tooj had been sick for many days, his wives, sons, daughters-in-law, and his brothers and their wives called in several shamans, as is usually done for someone who is very ill. The shamans, including the most noted shaman in the area, conducted several sessions, but Tooj faded and died. As soon as Tooj stopped breathing *(tu siav)*, his son went outside and fired a gun three times to inform villagers of the death, to warn the good spirits that the dead man's souls would soon be embarking on a journey to join them, and to scare off any malevolent spirits lurking in the area. Inside the house, the eldest son and daughter-in-law of the household washed the body and dressed Tooj in "fine new clothing" *(tu zam)*. Hmong are afraid of the dead, and because of this they sometimes do not want to wash the corpse, but they generally do so; otherwise the deceased will not give them good fortune when, as an ancestor, he or she is in a position to bestow it. After they washed the corpse, they emptied the pot of water under his bed and placed the washing cloth under a container for storing clothing.[4] Both actions are supposed to ensure the good fortune of the household.

Tooj's body was dressed in a pair of black trousers, an intricately embroidered shirt with an unusually large embroidered collar *(dab tsho)*, and a wide belt of red cloth. The elaborate flower cloth would show the ancestors how highly esteemed and loved Tooj had been. As well, it would enable the souls of women already dead (such as Tooj's mother and grandmother) to recognize Tooj's second soul when it reached the village of the ancestors.[5] A dead woman, seeing that the soul of the newly dead wore flower cloth that she had embroidered, would know the soul as kindred. A black turban was set on Tooj's head, and a pair of woven hemp shoes, purchased from a Chinese trader, were placed next to Tooj's feet. If a household cannot afford to buy these, they use homemade shoes.

Tooj's silver necklace and a twisted silver and copper bracelet were removed, and his clothing was searched to be sure that it was free of bone or metal buttons, so that his souls could completely shed the body. (Gold teeth are also removed, and Tooj's wooden coffin was put together with bamboo nails instead of metal ones.) Since metal does not decay, it may impede the soul on its journey to the land of darkness or on its return to this world (Tapp 1989b:135), and then the unhappy soul can become malevolent, making the dead man's children or grandchildren ill or bringing the household bad fortune; or the unhappy soul might be malformed at rebirth.

Tooj's body was laid on the ground on the upslope side of the house, the auspicious side, with his head facing west. One of his brothers, a shaman who also lived in the house, had his altar on the upslope wall. He covered this altar completely with bamboo paper to prevent his spirit familiars, who reside on the altar, from taking offense at the odor of the dead body. Shamans, who only heal the sick and save lives, have nothing to do with death (except in the instance of protecting the household from the effects of a bad death), nor do their helping spirits, at least not in the sense of guiding the souls of the dead.

Tooj's sons, brothers, and other lineage members who were hosts *(xyom cuab)* of the funeral visited neighbors to offer them rice liquor, a sign of courtesy and respect, and invite them to the funeral. Tooj's male relatives also contacted the man who would chant the Showing the Way ceremony *(tus txiv Qhuab Kev)*. I call him the "chanter" to distinguish him from the father of words *(tus txiv xaiv)*, even though the latter also chants in singsong fashion, on the last night before burial, the life story of and messages from the dead in funeral songs. But the man who performs the Showing the Way chant is the soul's guide to the land of darkness. Most Hmong songs, from love songs to funeral songs, are improvised around set themes, but the Showing the Way chant is recited—or "sung"—as it was learned. Until the 1950s the Hmong had no written language, so the Showing the Way chant has been passed down orally for generations.

As soon as Tooj's relatives apprised the chanter of the death, the man left expediently for Tooj's house; it is important to begin the Showing the Way chant as soon as possible after a death so the soul doesn't wander around, get lost, and cause trouble for the living. Tooj's male relatives then enlisted the services of the men who played the reed pipes *(tus txiv qeej)* and the men who played the drum *(tus txiv nruas)*, as well as an "important man" *(tus kav xwm)* from Tooj's clan to run the funeral. This man, the funeral manager, hires men to cook the meat from the sacrificed animals, haul the water, gather the firewood, and cut the wood for the coffin. He also makes sure that parts of the sacrificed animals are distributed as payment. Tooj's relatives also contacted a "man who feeds the people" *(tus tshwj kab),* who makes sure that visitors from other villages and guests are fed (see also Chindarsi 1976:90–91). Finally, Tooj's male kin enlisted the services of the father of words. Ideally he should be from the deceased's lineage, but since the men who possess the special talent necessary for this role are in short supply, this was not possible at Tooj's funeral. The father of words is responsible for mediating the discussion of debts and obligations, as well as for providing the funeral songs that follow the Showing the Way chant. These improvised songs tell of the deceased's life, and in this case the songs were many and their duration long, as befitted Tooj's age and status. In circumstances such as this, the father of words may assign someone else to chant (and he did— there were two fathers of words at Tooj's funeral), but he himself must stay in the room to ensure that the songs are sung correctly.

Some of these people—the chanter, who recites the Showing the Way chant and guides the souls of the dead to the land of darkness; the reed-pipe players, who play the "Song of the Expiring of Life"; the drummers, whose percussion guides the souls to the land of darkness; and the father of words, who acts as a messenger for the dead in order to condole the living—are at risk by the very nature of their roles. Their proximity to the dead makes them vulnerable to death. They are in danger from the wild and malign spirits who are attracted by death, from the souls of the newly dead who have not yet been changed into ancestors, from the spirits of the land of darkness, and even from the ancestors. The spirits of the land of darkness are inimical to the living.

Tooj's kin also found a woman to cook the rice *(tus niam fam txam)* for the thirteen days of funeral rituals. An older, widowed woman was summoned for this time-consuming job, as she had more time and fewer responsibilities than a woman with a family. This older woman delegated tasks, such as pounding rice and grinding corn, to other women. Tooj's household needed all this outside help because for the next thirteen days all customary activities, including work in the fields, were proscribed for them. During this time the women of his household did no work at all, beyond guarding the dead man before his burial.

THE FIRST DAY: SHOWING THE WAY

In Tooj's house, the members of his household sat watching quietly as women swept the packed earthen floors. The drummer stretched dried cowhide (from a cow sacrificed at an earlier ritual, whose hide had been saved for a special occasion) over a wooden water carrier to make his drum. Men had propped a tree sapling at about a forty-five-degree angle against the central house post, and the drummer balanced his finished drum and a reed pipe *(qeej)* at the juncture of the sapling and the house post (see fig. 4.1.). Several men came into the house carrying paper spirit money tied to tree branches, which they propped against the wall near the altar. After paying their last respects to the deceased, the men sat down on the stools lining the opposite wall.

The chanter asked for a chicken, some rice liquor, and a boiled egg. He also requested a split gourd, a short length of bamboo, some red cloth, a crossbow, and a small paper umbrella. One of Tooj's brothers went to fetch these things, while Tooj's son went outside and fired three shots into the air to announce that the body was now washed and ready. Then the chanter sat on a small stool next to Tooj's head and began to chant quietly.

The Showing the Way chant took four or five hours to recite in full. (See appendix B for the full English translation, and appendix C for a full transcription in Hmong.) The chant guided the souls[6] of the dead man to the land of darkness, showing him how to get past various obstacles and how

FIG. 4.1. Preparing for a funeral. A drum and reed pipes are placed upon the house-post. Paper money is being cut so that the dead person will have it on the journey to the land of darkness. The reed pipes will be taken down and played by one of the men. The drum will be beaten on the post. (Photo by Patricia Symonds)

to answer and behave when anyone spoke to him along the way. But first it taught the dead man and the listening mourners about the origins of life: how the world began, how sickness and death came to the earth, and how people acquired all the things they needed for the journey to the land of darkness—which happen to be the same things people need to live in the land of light.

The chanter began,

It seems like the world is turning
And the light is breaking through every valley.
The sky is created to last.

The human body of Tub Nraug Laj [the name given to a dead man]
 is created to stay.
There is light on earth.
The sky is created to stay.
The human body will be created.

It seems like you are truly dead.
The body is lying down.
Is it truly dead or are you just pretending?
If you are just pretending,
Then get up to chase the chickens and the pigs around the house.
If you are truly dead,
Then turn your ears to listen.
Txawj Nkiag [the chanter][7] will chant the death song for you to hear.

You dress up and go until you reach the slope.
The elder looks and sees that it is you.
You dress up and go until you arrive over there.
The younger looks and sees that it is like you.
Now that you are truly dead,
Turn your ears to listen.
Close your eyes,
And Txawj Nkiag will sing a death song for you to hear.

At this point the chanter turned to me and said, "Now one level is finished." He poured some wine from the bottle near his feet into three small bamboo cups. Then he poured the wine onto the ground next to the dead man's head, thereby giving the wine to Tooj's souls. The chanter explained how the water to wash the deceased had been obtained and warmed, and how and why Tooj had been washed and dressed.

The chanter then explained the origins of rice wine, which is used to sustain the traveling souls of the dead:

It is like at this moment
Long time ago.
There Txawj Nkiag had arrived.

The dead son had dropped in.
There was yeast for making wine.
Wine was not available.
Then there was a question:
Where is the yeast for making wine?

It was answered:
The yeast was at the foot of Ntxwj Nyoog's cliff.
There was a question:
Where was the wine?
It is like Nkauj Iab and Nraug Oo [the primal couple] saying
That the wine was at the foot of Ntxwj Nyoog's cliff.
They took the yeast in.
.　.　.　.　.　.　.

Place the yeast on a bamboo tray for one day and two mornings.
Then the wine will be tasty, as good as honey.
It will be the wine that shows the way for the dead son.
It is like taking the yeast
And spreading it on the bamboo mat.
One day, two mornings.
The wine will be tasty, as good as honey.
It will be the wine showing the path for the dead son.

The chanter said to me, "Seems like now one level is finished." He filled the three cups with wine and poured them out onto the ground next to the dead man's head again, saying that the dead man must drink so that he could go on to meet the ancestors. Rice wine offers sustenance to the souls of the dead, and also protection from hostile spirits.

There is no hemp seed.
.　.　.　.　.　.　.

Where was the hemp seed?
Where would the hemp seed be available?
A long time ago, the dragon made the sun shine for three months.

The dragon blew [the wind] for three months.
The hemp seeds here on earth were all dead.

Now here is the answer:
There were hemp seeds at Ntxwj Nyoog's rocky mountain,
And hemp seeds were available at his cliff.
There was no servant.
It was Nkauj Iab and Nraug Oo who sent
Niam Kag and Nkauj Quag[8] to bring back hemp seeds
From Ntxwj Nyoog's cliff.

Having brought back the hemp seeds,
They spread the seeds on the earth for thirty days.
In thirty days the hemp seeds would be sprouting all over the field,
Spreading the hemp seeds over the valley,
And they would be shooting up all over the valley.

Now it is one moon, thirty days.
Nkauj Iab and Nraug Oo took a basket and went to cut some hemp.
Use one hank of hemp to make clothing for the dead son to wear.
Use three hanks of hemp to make a pair of shoes for the dead son
    to use
When he steps on Ntxwj Nyoog's green caterpillar mountain.
. . . .

Now use the hemp seeds to make clothing for you to wrap around
    your body.
You have a new outfit when you arrive at the mountain slope.
Use the hemp seeds to make clothing to wrap around you
When you are going to meet your grandmother.

Then the chanter said to me, "Now one level is finished."

You arrive at Ntxwj Nyoog's caterpillar mountain and cold caterpillar valley.
The caterpillars are jumping, as big as pigs.
Your hand reaches out to put on your hempen shoes,
So that you have a way to get to your ancestors.

The chant went on to say how difficult it was for the first hen to lay eggs: she took thirteen days to lay thirteen eggs. Only three eggs hatched and became chickens. Two were stolen, and one survived. It became the rooster that had been sacrificed to accompany the dead man's soul to the ancestors:

> The rooster is crowing.
> The noise of the rooster's crowing
> Is reaching far back into the otherworld.
> It is the dead son's chicken to show the way.
> The sound of the rooster's crowing is reaching the otherworld.
> It becomes the dead son's chicken to show the way.

The chanter said to me, "Now one level is finished. Here one step is complete." He picked up the dead rooster from the plate near his feet. He cut out the liver and handed it and the rooster to a man standing nearby. The man took the rooster to the fireplace, plucked its feathers, and singed its body. He placed the liver on a stick and seared it over the flame. Then he returned the rooster and the liver to the chanter, who placed both next to the dead man's head. The chanter filled three bamboo cups with rice liquor and said,

> We give three cups of wine for you to drink
> Before giving you your chicken to show the way to the ancestors.
> Now we are giving you your chicken's liver
> So that you will know the way to the ancestors.

> Eat, you eat alone.
> Drink, you drink alone.
> . . . .
> Die, you die alone.
> Though you cannot eat, put it in your gourd.
> Though you cannot drink, pour it in a bamboo container.
> Though you cannot eat, endure to carry on.
> Though you cannot drink, forbear to carry on.
> Take them to your ancestors.
> Go looking for your grandfather and his brothers
> In the dead son's world.

The rooster was placed in the gourd, the liver on top of it, and the three cups of rice liquor in a larger bamboo container. All were set next to Tooj's head.

Then the chanter told how death came, how once there was no sickness on the earth, and nobody died.[9] But human beings wanted to die. They killed a tiger and a gibbon and performed a noisy ritual for them, alerting Ntxwj Nyoog in the otherworld. He sent down a fly and a bee to see what the noise was, and they returned and told him that the humans had begun to kill. Then,

> Ntxwj Nyoog released the seed of sickness down to earth.
> Now the seed of dying has been planted on the land.
> For seven years, Ntxwj Nyoog released the seed of sickness down
>   to earth.
> The earth has been silent ever since.
>
> .   .   .   .
>
> Ntxwj Nyoog opened the sky gate to look,
> Opened the earth gate to see.
> There the sickness seeds of Ntxwj Nyoog
> Were hanging in the middle of the sky,
> And the seeds of death were not reaching to earth.
> Ntxwj Nyoog took his copper scissors
> To cut the string that held the seeds of sickness,
> Using the metal scissors to cut the string
> And send the seeds of death down to earth.
>
> The seeds of sickness were hanging on a hemp branch.
> The seeds of death were hanging on a tree branch.
> While people were farming,
> They picked up the seeds of sickness and death.
> When they picked them up,
> They stuck the evil seeds in their pockets.
>
> Unlike other people, Tub Nraug Laj [the dead man],
> You did not know how to pick up the seeds.

When picking them up,
You stuck them in your liver.
As for other people,
They knew how to pick up the evil seeds.
When picking them up,
They stuck them into their pockets.
You, Tub Nraug Laj,
Did not know how to pick them up.
When picking them up,
You stuck the evil seeds into your heart.

The chanter went on to say that during the deceased's final illness, his brothers and his sons had called several shamans to go to the land of the spirits to plead for an extension of his life. Their efforts were to no avail, not even those of a noted living shaman named Tooj Nchai Siv Yis.

You are wailing with the sickness.
The young son arrived in the valley.
The sickness of Tub Nraug Laj is not healed.
You are wailing with Ntxwj Nyoog's sickness seeds,
And you are feeling no better.
Now the oldest son asks,
"Who is the best shaman in the world?
Who is the expert?"

It is Tooj Nchai Siv Yis who is the best shaman on earth.
Tooj Nchai Siv Yis is the expert.
Now your brother's left hand is holding the incense.
His right hand is holding the paper money
And calling to Tooj Nchai Siv Yis,
And he has arrived.
He has laid down his shamanic equipment.

He is in his trance,
And the shaman rattles are ringing and sounding on the slope.
However, this is the year that Tub Nraug Laj will disappear [die].

The chanter fell silent and poured three cups of liquor. He poured them out next to the dead man's head, telling him to drink. Then he told the dead man of the days when humans were smarter than spirits.

Humans had great knowledge
And used spirits to trade for something to drink.
Then humans used almost every spirit to trade
For something to eat.
There were only two spirits left
To go and ask for wisdom from Puj Saub,
To go to Puj Saub's country to ask for knowledge,
For Puj Saub to point the way,
And for Yawm Saub to teach the name.

Puj and Yawm Saub told the spirits how to become invisible to humans so that they would be safe; it was only this trickery that saved the spirits. But dogs tricked the spirits; thus dogs can see spirits to this day, and give warning at their approach.

Now the spirits can trick human beings to walk on the upper road.
The spirits will take human beings to sell for something to eat.
Now the spirits trick human beings to walk on the lower road.
The spirits will take human beings to trade them for something to wear.

Here the chanter turned to me and said, "Now one level is finished. One step is completed." Once again he poured out three cups of rice liquor for the dead man.

The chanter told of how the earth had dried, and bamboo disappeared from the land. But the seeds of bamboo were found in Ntxwj Nyoog's garden and brought back to earth.

Now the bamboo shoots are fully grown.
One of them belongs to Nas Kos [a rodent].
One belongs to the Chinese man,
Who takes it away to make a winnowing tray.
When Txawj Nkiag arrives,
There is only one left.

He cuts it and makes it even at both ends.
He splits it in the middle.

He splits it into two pieces.
Txawj Nkiag [the chanter] uses it for your pointer
To show the way.

.   .   .   .   .

He splits it into two pieces
To be your pointer to show you the way.
Grandmother Saub will use your pointer to teach you language.
She will use the pointer to teach you the way.

"Here one level is finished," the chanter told me. "One step is complete."
One of the men in the house handed the chanter a piece of bamboo about
seven inches long, which the chanter then cut in two, suiting actions to words.
The two split pieces of bamboo *(cwj ntawg)* are a divination tool; the dead
cannot speak, but with the help of Grandmother Saub, their spirit com-
municates through the bamboo, letting the chanter know if they understand
his instructions. Whenever the chanter throws the bamboo pieces, or pointers, the souls of the dead can tell him whether they understood his directions or not. If the bamboo pointers give a negative answer, the chanter will
give the dead a few more words of explanation, and throw the bamboo again,
continuing in this way until the bamboo falls to signify the positive answer,
meaning that the souls have understood and are ready to proceed.

The chanter turned to some of the young men in the house and asked
them to go into the forest and cut down a tree to make the coffin. The young
men took machetes from the wall of the house and departed.

Now there is light all over the earth.
It was a long time ago that the earth was created.
Now your body is created to live.
Now there is only one tree left of all the seeds.
There are no servants to help.

Txawj Nkiag asked the villagers to pick up their axes.
Three of them marched into the woods.

They cut down one tree
And slid it into the field.

They slid it down to the flat land,
Took it to make a striped dragon horse for the dead son.
Using one axe,
Cut a piece of log and slid it to the field,
Used it to make a horse.

For the dead son to ride into the otherworld.
It is a striped horse for the dead son to ride.

The chanter told me another level was finished. He then gave an account of how seeds for domestic crops were lost. At the urging of the primal couple, Nkauj Iab and Nraug Oo, mice went to Ntxwj Nyoog's mountain cliff, found the seeds, and sneaked back to earth with them; because of this, people had rice to eat, and to offer to the dead, and now they had rice to give Tooj. (In other words, all people—and all dead people, and this particular dead person—have rice to eat because the mice brought back the seeds.) The chanter offered rice liquor and three spoonfuls of rice to the dead man, and told the dead man to offer some to the ancestors in the otherworld.

Then the chanter told of the creation of the earth and of human beings (*noob neej,* lit., "seeds of men"). This included the story of Lady Sun and Lord Moon:

Now, a long time ago,
Puj Saub created human beings to live,
And created everything on earth.
Saub created the sky to cover above,
Created the earth below,
Created thirty suns and thirty moons.
Suns ruled for thirty days.
Moons ruled for thirty nights.
Then who on earth had the ability?
Which couple had the knowledge?

There is a saying that the peacock and the quail
Have the ability and the knowledge.

It was the peacock's copper bow that had thirty arrows.
The bow shot the suns, and twenty-nine of them fell down.
Twenty-nine moons were shot down too.
Then there was only one sun and one moon left.
Lady Sun was afraid
And hid on the other side of the sky.

The earth was in darkness for seven years.
Lord Moon had hidden on the other side of the earth.

In this long story, several animals are told how to call Lady Sun and Lord Moon out of hiding.[10] But all the animals fail until the rooster, with his powerful voice, is called upon:

When the rooster crowed three times in the north,
Lady Sun came out.
When the cock crowed three times in the south,
Lord Moon came out.
Then there was light on earth for seven years.
Lady Sun allows people to plant the earth and eat,
To be fertile and nurture.
Lady Sun nurtures,
And Lord Moon clothes the two of them together.

The chanter offered liquor and rice to the dead man again. In the above section, the souls were taught how the world began and how people obtained all the things needed for the journey to the land of darkness. In the next section, the chanter tells Tooj what to do as his souls begin the journey.

Now you dress up in your new clothes
And will be on your way.
.   .   .   .

The spirits of the doors extend their hands to block the road.
They stretch their hands to grab your arms.
You are the animal of our people on earth.
You are the crops of our people on earth.
You are dressing up.
Where are you going?

When asked, you will answer
That it was because you got sick on earth.
You will say,
"So, now I come."
Then the spirits of the door will ask you,

. . . .

"Why did you not seek help from the shaman?
Why did you not talk to your parents and brothers
To ask the shaman to heal you?"
Then you will answer,
"The shaman did nine trances and it did not help.
Eight kinds of medicine did not heal my sickness."

. . . .

Even your brothers sought help from the shaman.
Your sickness, nevertheless, was not cured.

. . . .

Now you put on your new outfit and go along.
When you arrive at the spirit of the back wall altar,
The *xwm kab* spirits will extend their arms to you.
They will stretch their fingers to grab your arms, saying,
"It is the earth that is good for planting crops.
It is the land that is good for making clothing.
So, why are you going?"
You will answer,
"There is a lot of illness on earth.
The cruel Ntxwj Nyoog released the sickness on my arms,
And the death seeds fell on my hands."

. . . .

You say a word of thanks to the *xwm kab* spirits
So that you can go on your way to meet your ancestors.

The chanter listed all the spirits of the Hmong household: those of the fireplace, side door, and front door, all of whom needed to be told why the dead man was leaving. They had to be thanked for their protection during Tooj's lifetime, so that he would be free to leave. The chanter then offered more liquor and rice to the dead man.

Txawj Nkiag will send you to the slope.
He will send you, Tub Nraug Laj, to meet your grandmother.
He will send you, dead son, to the valley to meet your grandfather.

The chanter said to me, "Now one level is finished. Here one step is complete." Then he continued,

You have put on good outfits to go.
Then you will climb to get your "mandate for life" paper.
Then you can descend to be reborn on earth.
You will wander around the plain.
You go climb Nyuj Vaj Tuam Teem's silver ladder.

. . . .

You must remember this in your heart.
You must remember this in your liver.

You must remember to go and get your "mandate for life" paper from
    Nyuj Vaj Tuam Teem.
Come back to be reborn on earth,
So that you will have a good life.

. . . .

You must remember to get your paper.
Should you get a cow paper,
You would be afraid that a human being would use you to plow.
If you should get a horse paper,
You would be afraid that another would ride you.

Should you get a pig paper,
You would be afraid that you would be sacrificed.
Should you get a dog paper,
You would be afraid that others would beat you.
Should you get a bird or insect paper,
You would be afraid of the rain and the sunlight.

The chanter continued to advise the dead man which papers to avoid so that the great spirit would give him the "mandate for life," the paper that would allow him to be reborn as a human being. The chanter said it would take thirteen days to climb Nyuj Vaj Tuam Teem's silver ladder between the worlds, one step for each day of the ritual. Nyuj Vaj Tuam Teem himself is at the top of this ladder, where he tells the souls of the dead that they can go on to the ancestors.[11] The chanter told the dead man to remember what he was hearing so that on each of the thirteen days to come, he could follow the instructions exactly as they had been given. Then the chanter poured three cups of wine onto the ground for Tooj, telling him that in the next section of the Showing the Way chant he would take the deceased to find his fine clothing so that he could continue on his journey. The chanter took the bamboo divination pointers and threw them on the ground near the dead man's head, saying that if Tooj had understood the previous sections, they would now go on.

The pointers fell in the affirmative position, so the chanter guided Tooj back to all of the places where he had lived on earth, so that Tooj could thank the spirits of those places. Finally they went to his natal village for Tooj's birth shirt.

One person, three souls, and seven shadows.
Since you have gone, your body is dead
But not your souls.
One of your souls will go to put on the rebirth shirt.

You will go to get your rebirth shirt
From the village in which you were born.
In order to get there,
You must go from village to village
Until you reach the place where you were born.

. . . .

Since you have wasted part of their forest
And used some of their firewood,
As you pass their territory,
You will use your paper money to pay and give thanks to them.
Use your incense and paper money to pay your tolls
So that the guards will let you through to your ancestors.

The chanter took some spirit money made from bamboo paper, cut it into small patterns (like a paper doily), and burned it. He lit incense sticks at the head of the corpse, saying,

Your mother and father and your brothers and sisters
Give you paper money.
You will take it with you.
You will use it to pay your tolls.

. . . .

If you come to a big river, remember these words,
Now that you are going to obtain your rebirth shirt from your birth
    village.
When you arrive at the river and the river is very wide,
Even if you go to the upper part of the river,
You could not cross it.
Even if you go to the lower part of the river,
You could not cross it.

You must take your money and your incense
And pay the fare of the spirit boat.
Then the spirits will take you to the other side
So that you will have your way to go.
The spirits will send you across to the other slope
So that you will have a road to march on.

The chanter burned more paper spirit money and lit more incense. He said,

Now that you have given thanks to the spirits of the land,
You will go to obtain your rebirth shirt to put on.

If you are a woman, your rebirth shirt is at the bedpost.
If you are a man, your rebirth shirt is at the main pole.
You must come to look for your rebirth shirt to wear.
You must search around the fire for your shirt.

You must look around from the side door to the front door.
You must look around the poles.
You will then find your rebirth shirt
So that you will have it to put on and wear.
Then Txawj Nkiag will take you to be reborn on earth.

Three more cups of rice liquor were poured in the bamboo cups and then out on the ground for the dead man.

Now we give you three drinks of wine.
Then you will jump on your path and look for your ancestors.

Now you are a human being on earth.
One body, three souls, and seven shadows.
Your body and your shadows are all dead.
One of your souls will put on new outfits
And go to look for your ancestors.
. . . .

When you get there, Nyuj Vaj Tuam Teem will ask you,
"Since you are a human being on earth, why have you come?
They say that earth is a good place to find food and clothing."
You will answer,
"If the leaves do not fall, the forest will not grow.
If no one dies, there will be no place on earth to plow.
If the leaves do not fall, the forest will not be clear.
If no one is sick and dies, there will not be a place on earth to dwell."

So, now you have put on your new outfits and come.

The chanter told the dead man that he must not be distracted by anyone along the way. Should people who are "peeling onions" ask for his help in an effort to detain him, he must tell them that his "fingers are sore." Here the chanter tied red thread onto the dead man's fingers as a symbol of blood. Next, the dead man would come to a mountain swarming with poisonous caterpillars; he must put on his shoes. The chanter placed the shoes on the dead man's feet. He directed the bamboo pointers at the dead man and then threw them on the ground to be sure that his directions had been understood.

The next section of the chant described how the dead man would meet a dragon and a tiger along the way. When they roared, the dead man should throw a ball of hemp into their open mouths. The chanter placed two balls of hemp in the dead man's hands. Eventually the dead man would reach a body of water. He would be asked to drink the water, but he must say that his mouth was bleeding and refuse to drink. The chanter covered the dead man's mouth with a red cloth, again to symbolize blood. He placed a small paper umbrella in the man's hand, telling him he would need it for protection from the elements on the journey.

> Now you have put on fine clothing to go.
> You will take your chicken with you.
> Your chicken will be in front of you, and you will follow your chicken.
> When there is a sunny day, you will hide under your chicken's wing.
> On a rainy day, you will hide under your chicken's tail.

> When your chicken combs his wings, fix your shirt.
> When your chicken combs his legs, fix your leggings.
> When your chicken combs his tail, fix your shoes.
> When your chicken combs his head, fix your turban.
> When your chicken combs his waist, fix your belt.

The chanter told the dead man how to recognize his own ancestors. This was extremely important, as his soul must be reborn into the same lineage.[12] If the souls don't reach their own ancestors, they can get lost and become wandering spirits, caught too near the land of light, who cannot rest and who cause trouble for the household and the lineage.

> When you arrive at the cold sky and dark land,
> The sunny sky and dried land, the dried world,

If their rooster crows and your rooster answers,
Those are not your ancestors' coffins.

.   .   .   .

If your rooster crows and their rooster answers,
Those are your ancestors' coffins.

.   .   .   .

Should their rooster crow and your rooster answer,
It means they will trick you into jumping off the rocky mountain.

.   .   .   .

When you arrive and see the happy faces who are waiting for you in the south,
They are not your ancestors;
They are the ones who would take you to trade for food and clothing.

.   .   .   .

When you arrive and see the unhappy faces who extend their arms to you,
Jump into their laps,

.   .   .   .

For they are your grandmother and grandfather.

.   .   .   .

Your living threads are broken.
Now that you have come to the world of cold and darkness,
You will not return home.

The chanter told the dead man that this was as far as he could accompany him on his journey. He asked the dead man to tell the ancestors that the chanter had returned to the world of the living long ago, so it was no use for them to come looking for him; they could not find him even if they tried. (The chanter has to leave the dead man quickly at this point—at the foot of the silver ladder between the worlds—as the ancestors can drag the chanter over the boundary between this world and the next. Chanting is a dangerous profession.) The chanter threw the bamboo pointers onto the ground to see if his instructions had been noted. He poured three cups of liquor onto the ground for the dead man, picked up the bamboo pointers in his hand, and said,

Txawj Nkiag will send you to this point only.
Take three cups of wine for you to drink.
Then you will let one soul go back to the land of the living.
Now reply when I throw the horns.

He threw the pointers on the ground again. Both landed in the affirmative position, so he continued,

Txawj Nkiag sends you to this point only.
Put on your hempen shoes and go to the other side.
Txawj Nkiag is not going to that side,
Because Txawj Nkiag does not have any hempen shoes.

You will close your eyes and ears and head
To stay with your grandmother and grandfather.
On a new day,
You will change your bodily form
And become a beautiful butterfly.

As soon as he had finished speaking, the chanter hurried out of the house, with tears in his eyes. He fled because he was afraid of Tooj's ancestors and Tooj's own unsettled souls.

The chant was finished. For a long, painful moment there was nothing but silence. It was broken when the people from the household went over to the dead man and stroked his body, crying softly as they did so. No one is supposed to weep until the Showing the Way chant is over and the dead person's souls have been led to the land of darkness. The tears of the living may distract or seduce the souls of the dead into staying near the land of light.

The land of darkness, through which the souls journey, is rocky, steep, and barren. The souls of the dead can look down through the rocks and see the land of light, in all its color, liveliness, and variety. They are attracted to the land of light, but they do not belong there, and can do harm simply by remaining too near their old home. So the newly dead must be told where they belong, and must be guided there. If the dead person's kin and friends hold back their tears, the souls are more likely to reach their destination.

But now that Tooj's souls were on their way, the people of the household wept softly. The drummer and reed pipers began to play "The Song of the Expiring of Life," the pipers dancing around the house post, to help guide Tooj's souls. The six tones of the reed pipe are similar to spoken Hmong, which is a tonal language, and many people—though not everyone—could understand the "words" in the piper's music. As the main piper asked questions, the drummer answered with a specific pattern of beats (Vang 1992). The reed pipe is played only at funerals and at the New Year (the death of the old year). At funerals the pipers dance and move about because, as guides for the dead souls, they are on that journey with the dead and come close to the land of darkness. They dance to elude the spirits who would harm them.

The men who had gone out to the forest returned with bamboo planks they had tied together with rope to make a platform. This is the "striped dragon horse," which takes the spirit on its journey. It was suspended about a foot off the ground by ropes of white cloth, next to the wall on the upslope side of the house. The men of the house placed the dead man's body into a plain wooden coffin, which they lifted carefully onto the "horse" while the pipes and drum played the song for raising the body onto the horse (tsa nees). The men arranged Tooj's wide embroidered collar under his head. They put the chicken in the gourd and provisions for the journey at his head, and his crossbow on his chest. They burned incense sticks at his head and foot, both in respect and to conceal the odor of decay. Then they shut the lid of the coffin.

The drum and pipes played as people arrived with incense sticks, rice, and paper spirit money tied to tree branches. After a while the pipe and drum fell silent. A man of the household sacrificed a pig and set its front shoulder and leg on top of the drum as an offering to Tooj. A man from outside the lineage cooked the rest of the pig for the visitors and household. Some people left after eating, and others arrived to offer their respects, while village children came into the house to see what was happening.

During the next nine days and nights the women who had been closest to Tooj in life, by blood ties as well as lineage, would take turns keeping watch over his body to make sure that no one slipped a piece of metal into his clothes or the coffin. Although I never heard of anyone tampering with a corpse, Hmong assured me that it is always possible that someone jealous of the lineage would try to harm them in this way. At the Hmong funerals I attended, including one in the United States, women guarded the body.

Tooj's eldest sister had the chief responsibility for guarding him, but his wives and daughters-in-law, who lived in the house, as well as his sisters-in-law and his daughter, who all lived in the village, kept watch until his sisters arrived on the eighth day, and then the women all took turns.

When a woman dies, her brother's wife has the primary responsibility for guarding her body. In both cases, the sister/brother relationship determines who has the main responsibility for guarding the dead, but the guardians are women. Adult daughters guard the corpse of their natal mother as well as of their father, and so do a dead woman's natal sisters. That these women's lineages are sure to be different from the dead person's does not matter; it is their relationship to the dead person, not to the patriline, that determines which women guard the corpse. In death, when the souls are on their way to the village of the ancestors (of a particular lineage), blood ties take precedence over lineage.

Occasionally a man will guard the body of his child or brother, but usually men are busy in their role as lineage members and hosts of the funeral, and it is up to women to guard the body.

THE SECOND TO EIGHTH DAYS:
FEEDING THE SOULS ON THEIR JOURNEY AND RECEIVING GUESTS

For the next seven days, the drum and the reed pipes were played before each meal—in the mornings, at noon, and in the evening—when rice and a sacrificed pig were set out for household members and visitors to eat. Before people ate, Tooj's eldest son offered the food *(laig dab)*, along with liquor and incense sticks, to the dead man. Sometimes the eldest son tipped the food, as well as the rice liquor, onto the ground by Tooj's coffin; dogs ate it later. But most of the food sacrificed for the dead was eaten by the living— the funeral guests and Tooj's household. Women from outside the lineage cooked the rice, and men in the lineage sacrificed a pig for every day of the nine days of this part of the funeral.

Sometimes during the day, people—usually women—sang sorrowful songs *(nkauj tuag)* to the dead man. Women of the household took turns sleeping and keeping constant watch over the body, making sure no one placed metal in the coffin. Even a silver needle could harm Tooj and bring misfortune to everyone in the lineage. Men gambled and played cards inside

FIG. 4.2. A large offering of part of a pig at the start of a funeral ritual. Such offerings are brought to the deceased's family by visitors from outside the village. Such visitors may be related or may be nonrelatives who had great respect for the dead person. (Photo by Patricia Symonds)

the house all day and night, and Thai men from the nearby village played cards outside the house. I was told that the card games were to entertain the soul of the dead man (the first soul, which stays with the body, and with the bones in the grave) as well as the visitors from other villages.

The smell of putrefaction became worse as the days passed, and villagers walked around with cloths over their noses and frequently spat on the ground to get rid of the taste in their mouths. Friends and neighbors came to stay until the burial. Many brought parts of pigs to share. Four oxen were purchased from the Thai in the valley and tethered outside the house. On the day of the burial, they would be sacrificed to feed Tooj and the ancestors as well as the people attending the funeral.

Meanwhile, knowledgeable men from the clan went up the hill to choose a good site for a grave. This was done with a great deal of discussion and attention to the principles of geomancy; the task took about four hours.

The arrival of the deceased's affines on the afternoon of the eighth day was an important event; Tooj could not be buried until his eldest sister was present. The affines brought rice, liquor, incense, a great deal of spirit money so Tooj could pay the tolls on his journey, parts of pigs to help feed Tooj and the funeral guests, and money to help defray expenses. A large tree branch bearing bunches of spirit money was mounted on the main house post next to the drum. The funeral manager attached small paper boats to the money, into which lacelike designs were cut. These "male" and "female" boats would help Tooj to take the spirit boat across the river (see appendix B, verse 168). A great deal of paper money was hung over the coffin, and the reed pipe and drum were played off and on throughout the day while the two reed-pipe players danced around the main house post. As people arrived, they bowed to the people of the household. Occasionally the dead man's sons bowed in return.

Women began to keen, rubbing the coffin and weeping profusely. Women from the lineage and affines keen loudly, but so does any woman who has known and liked the dead person. Like the flower songs at the New Year, the funeral keening is a singsong chant improvised around traditional themes—women do not simply wail, they speak to the dead. Women within the lineage say how much they will miss the dead person; women from outside ask the dead person to take messages to their own ancestors, for instance, "Tell my grandmother I love her."

Men can keen also, but usually they just cry softly, and keen for a few minutes only when the women have invited them to do so. I was told by the Hmong that the reason women keen more than men do is that they have much "smaller livers" than men, meaning that they are more emotional and cry more easily. Although it is rare, it is not unheard of for older men who are especially "clever" to join in and keen, telling the story of the dead man's life. I heard of a grandfather who was so good at telling these stories that he keened at many funerals, and if he accidentally kicked a rock or a tree, he would keen his apology (for hurting the spirit that dwelt there) on the spot.

As everyone keens in unison, and they are accompanied by the pipes and drum, the noise can be ear-splitting. When the first women began to tire, others took their places. Throughout the keening, Tooj's first wife sang mournfully:

Husband, you have left us behind forever,

And there will not be anyone to love the children when they are crying.

There will not be anyone to love us.

Husband, you go to work in the field.

If only you had gone to visit relatives as usual.

Are you missing me?

Husband, there is nothing for us to eat now.

Oh, heaven and my parents.

There is nothing left for us now,

And the children will have nothing to eat.

Is there anyone who will give us anything?

Are you going to help the poor mother and children

Who live without any love?

We will be crying until the house falls apart.

Now there is no one who comes from anywhere to help repair the house.

Is there anyone going to look for a place for your poor wife and children
    to live?

Since we have no husband, as others do,

We will see only others eat and dress correctly.

Where will you go to live now?

Can we follow you to where you are?

Husband, now we do not have anything like other people have.

Do you know that?

Come back and take us to live with you.

Do you hear what we are saying?

You left the house behind for me to look after.

If mother and father do not love us,

We do not have relatives from anywhere.

Do you remember that I am still here?

Husband, I will be missing you until the day I die.

Until then I will not forget you or my parents.

Now we wait only for the parents to love us.

You have gone to rest in peace

And left me behind to suffer in the sunny and rainy days.

Do you love me?

If my parents do not love me, then there is nobody else.

Where did you go?

All the children are crying without anyone to love them.

Do you remember that there is nobody to love us?

How will I live?

Do you hear me?

Whom did you go to live with?

Do you know there is no one to love your wife and children?

Send back a message to tell your poor wife and children where you are.[13]

The women's keening, accompanied by the drum and reed pipes, rose until it was quite shrill, and painful to hear. This continued for an hour and a half, and at times I wanted to cover my ears. When silence fell most people left the house to rest, and returned the next day. Tooj's sisters, wives, sisters-in-law, daughters-in-law, and daughter took turns staying up through the night to guard the body.

When a woman dies, her husband sings a mourning song, but it is usually brief, as his brothers and other male kin will interrupt him, saying, "Don't be sad. You can get another wife." It is true that a widow stands to lose much more than a widower by remarrying. If she marries anyone other than one of her dead husband's younger brothers, she will have to leave her children behind when she goes to live with her new husband.

THE NINTH DAY: SETTLING DEBTS

All through the ninth day and into the evening, people arrived in the village from near and far. At dusk everyone gathered in the house of the dead man. Two pipers danced and played to the beat of the drum. The house was extremely crowded and hot, and the air was thick with the smell of decaying flesh even though the coffin was closed. In some villages I visited, Hmong don't use coffins for burial, and the corpse lies decomposing on the "horse" for nine days.

Men sat along the upslope walls smoking, laughing, and talking. Women, many with babies on their backs, and children stood along the other walls. The talking and music continued for several hours. Outside the house, men shot off guns to signal people to come, and to scare away the malevolent spirits attracted by death.

Then the music died down, and a man from Tooj's lineage sacrificed a small pig and placed it raw on a tray of rice in the center of a low table in the middle of the room. Along with the pig and rice were two bottles of rice liquor, several small bamboo cups, and some spoons. The father of words acted as the mediator, and the dead man's sons, brothers, brothers-in-law, and son-in-law sat around the table, the latter two categories of affines representing the dead man's sisters and daughter, while the women listened and followed the proceedings from the side of the room.

The dead man's oldest living sister's presence was essential, assuring that any debts that Tooj's children owed him would be paid, thus allowing them peace and prosperity, as well as contributing to Tooj's welfare in the land of darkness. Tooj's eldest sister paid close attention to the discussions between the men. When her opinion was necessary, her husband left the table and asked her how she wished things to be done. She would tell him, he would return to the table and continue conferring until a consensus was reached.

The father of words began by asking people to step forward if they owed Tooj anything or if he owed them anything. Then the father of words asked a series of questions, so that people would have an idea of what Tooj's debts and obligations in the land of light had been, and whether or not Tooj had fulfilled them. Were his harvests good? Did he provide well for his wife and children? Was he respected by his lineage and clan members? Was he on good terms with his affines? Was his son's bride-price paid in full? Was he a wise leader of his family? In times of trouble did he make good decisions? Throughout his life did he feed the ancestors? Did he use the correct methods of geomancy for burying his parents?

Such questions not only clarify the nature of a person's obligations in life; when answered in the affirmative, they increase the listeners' respect for the dead. As the questions show, men are responsible for monetary debts, such as the son's bride-price, or money for pigs, and there is a material component to their obligations to their wives and children as well. That Tooj had been able to provide well for his family on a material level showed that he had met his spiritual obligations, that the ancestors were pleased with his care of them and had sent him good fortune. In other words, Tooj's good fortune was proof that he had lived as a good Hmong. He had provided for the ancestors, and they, in turn, had taken care of him. A man who is dogged by ill fortune has neglected the ancestors, perhaps inadvertently, by not feeding them, or by not feeding them enough. (But if he has the bad luck to be childless, then the assumption is that his wife is at fault.)

The debts and obligations of a woman are somewhat different from those of a man. At one woman's funeral that I attended, her brother participated in the negotiations. His task was to verify that his sister had provided children for the lineage she had married into and had been a good Hmong wife and mother, and he asked the questions. The question "Was she a good wife and mother?" was concerned not only with whether she had children, although that was the crucial piece, but with whether she had raised them to be good Hmong, had clothed and fed her family, had made flower cloth for her in-laws, and was modest and respectful, never arguing or disagreeing with her husband (at least not in public) and never gossiping outside the home. If she had been considered deficient as a wife and mother, her brother would have paid recompense to her husband's family to ensure that her obligations were discharged before she went to the land of the ancestors; only in this way could she be reborn as a whole human being. In most cases, however, rather than paying recompense, the brother is more concerned that his sister's husband's lineage has done everything correctly for her funeral, sacrificing enough animals and burning enough spirit money so that she can be reborn.

If a dead person's debts remain owing, the soul cannot be freed to be reborn.[14] Or there may be an "offensive" reincarnation; for example, a woman in that soul's lineage may experience multiple stillbirths or have many infants who die before their third day of life (Lemoine 1983a). If something remains unpaid to the dead, the debtor is at risk and can be harmed.

During the debt negotiations at Tooj's funeral, the music stopped and all the men consumed a great deal of rice, pork, and liquor, which is offered as a sign of friendship and respect. The father of words invited men to come to the table, eat, and discuss their obligations to or debts outstanding from the dead man. Also, all of the people who had helped in the funeral were assured that they would receive compensation in money, meat, or both. For instance, the main piper was paid with half of a pig, as was the father of words. In addition, people who had taught these men to perform were called up to the table and paid off with parts of a pig.

The sons and brothers-in-law consulted their wives if there were questions. Although the eldest sister is the most important one, Tooj's other sisters could certainly express their opinions—through their husbands—and be listened to. At one point Tooj's eldest sister was consulted when his daughter-in-law did not wish to burn a great deal of paper money for Tooj.

His sister asked the daughter-in-law's brother to come in to hear the complaint against her and try to persuade her to be more generous. As we have seen, cross-cousin marriage is the preference for Hmong, and in this case Tooj's eldest sister was the daughter-in-law's birth mother, and the brother asked to intercede was the eldest sister's son. Despite this, Tooj's sister did not speak directly to her children; she spoke through her husband (their father). Only men "publicly" discuss these issues. It was in Tooj's sister's interest that no obligations were outstanding, so that her brother could go freely; at the same time she wanted to protect the linkages between the two clans through marriage.

The negotiations continued into the night, with several arguments on each side as to the validity of claims, which the father of words mediated. Late in the evening, after everyone was satisfied, the drummer and reed-pipe players took up their instruments once more. There were two men from outside the village who sang the funeral songs—the father of words and the man who assisted him. The songs told of the life of the dead man, and since Tooj had lived a long life, the songs lasted all night, which was why it took two fathers of words, taking turns, to chant them. These improvised songs told how Tooj had cared and provided for his family, paid the bride-price for his sons, fed and provided for the ancestors, and so on. At the end of the songs the primary father of words gave Tooj's final instructions to his household: they should be good to one another; they should help each other every day, and in times of difficulty; they should never forget to feed the ancestors; and they should call in a shaman if anyone lost a soul. Tooj wished his descendants a long life, that they would live to be 120 years old with long white hair. He predicted that they would all have many children, who would be talented and successful.[15]

The father of words is paid generously because he gives the dead man's message and blessing, the sacred words, to the household. He ends the sacred words by telling Tooj to let the ancestors know that he is nowhere near the land of darkness so they needn't try to grab him, they will never find him. The father of words sends the same message as the chanter. Even though the father of words may be from the same lineage as the dead, he is not safe from the ancestors, or even from the dead person whose message he brings.

As the chanting drew to a close, all of the paper money, gifts from all the people who knew and respected Tooj, was burned. This money would help the dead man pay his way to the land of the ancestors. The village women and children left to go sleep, while many men stayed in the house to gamble, and close female relatives guarded the coffin.

THE TENTH DAY: THE BURIAL

The next morning the men of the household served the women who had guarded the coffin a morning meal of rice and pork. As in weddings, when the bride eats no vegetables, these women ate no vegetable dishes, and, as occurs after childbirth, the women were served by men and ate first.

Afterward men cut two large bamboo poles to carry the coffin and took them to the dead man's house. The eldest son gave rice, pork, and liquor to the dead man. Two men took turns beating the drum, and two men played the pipes. The musicians fell silent as Tooj's sons gathered the rope for the coffin lid and opened the coffin one last time. The eldest son wrapped a plug of opium in a leaf and put it in his father's hand, in case he needed to smoke on his journey. Tooj's eldest sister examined the body and the coffin to make sure it was free of metal.

The lid was set back on the coffin and tied tightly. The two bamboo poles were strapped to the coffin, which was suspended between them, while the drum and reed pipes played loudly and mournfully. Two men took down the drum and the tree sapling it had rested on and carried them out the spirit door and up the hill. As men made ready to take the coffin out of the house, two men from another clan ran around outside, banging on the walls with large sticks to roust any evil spirits from around the house so they would not bother the dead man as he left his home. The people inside fled the house, frightened of the wild spirits who might be lurking near the body. With the primary reed-pipe player leading the way, the procession exited through the spirit door. The piper was followed by the chanter, who carried the dead man's crossbow, a wooden spoon and bowl, a bottle of rice liquor, and a plastic bag containing a small basket, a dead chicken, some rice, and paper money. Then several men carried the coffin through the spirit door, followed by most of the people in the village.[16] The procession wound up the hill until it reached a small area that had been cleared earlier by some of the village men, where two more pipers joined the crowd.[17] Sometimes the chanter threw the bamboo pointers to the ground to make sure the dead man's first soul was following the body to the grave.

A platform had been built in the clearing to hold the coffin; the four oxen to be sacrificed were waiting there. The eldest sister's husband would sacrifice one in his wife's name, the son-in-law would kill one in the name of Tooj's daughter, and Tooj's sons would sacrifice the other two. Each married son must kill an ox for his father; he owes this, as his father paid the bride-price for the son's wife. Although a married daughter is no longer part of her father's lineage, she tries to have an ox—which has been purchased with money that was given to the son-in-law at his marriage to the dead man's daughter—killed for him at his death. This part of the bride-wealth is a debt owed to the dead man.

The platform itself had been hidden by a bower of tree branches so that evil spirits would not be able to find the dead man. The pipers walked around the bower, clockwise nine times and then counter-clockwise nine times, followed by the men carrying the coffin. (The coffin was extremely heavy, and men relieved each other in this task.) Then the coffin was placed inside the hidden bower; the crossbow and other accouterments were set at the foot on a small platform. Women stood over the coffin, fanning away the flies. Hemp strings were tied from the four oxen to the coffin, to connect the spirits of the oxen and the souls of the dead man. The clearing became quiet, and people watched as the chanter offered the dead man food and liquor. Then he threw the pointers, and they showed that the dead man had accepted the food. The chanter then attached the bamboo divination pointers to the threads that connected the oxen to the coffin.

The dead man's sons gave water and rice to each of the four oxen. They threw water on their heads and slapped them with a small tree branch. They bowed to each ox and thanked it for its life and its assistance in accompanying their father to the land of darkness. Then they threw water over all of the watching people. (Water is a blessing, and it purifies; this is why shamans spit water—called "lustrous water"—spraying it through their teeth around a sick person.) Men struck the oxen on their heads with mallets and killed them. The eldest sister's husband killed the first ox, and then Tooj's two sons killed their oxen, and finally Tooj's daughter's husband killed an ox. The hempen threads that had connected the coffin and the oxen snapped as the oxen fell. The chanter examined the bamboo pointers to see if the ancestors had accepted the oxen, while the drummer beat his drum, and the four pipers danced around the coffin and the dead oxen. Men placed tree branches under the oxen, slit the oxen's throats, and caught the blood in buckets. Women related to the dead man keened over the coffin and brushed away the flies on its lid. Most of the villagers stood at the edge of the clearing. They spat often and held their noses because of the odor.

As we stood watching, a truck came up the hill. The coffin was loaded onto the truck, and many men accompanied it on up to the burial place. Elders in the clan had decided on the best time for burial, as well as the place, the day before. The women did not go, nor did I. Women, the Hmong said, are more easily frightened than men; if women went, they might lose their souls and become sick. The women went back down to the village with the children, and the village women did their usual work, feeding pigs and cooking.

When the men returned from the burial, they butchered the dead oxen where they lay, which took several hours. The men cooked portions of the oxen, eating, drinking, and gambling while they skinned the remaining oxen and divided the meat. The hides would be dried and used to make basket straps and perhaps another drum. The funeral manager made sure that everyone who had assisted in any way was given specific parts of the animals.[18] Most of the villagers received at least one piece of meat; in the late afternoon women went up the hill with their back-baskets to collect a share.

Although other ethnographic reports (Radley 1986:373; Tapp 1989a:85) describe purification ceremonies after a Hmong funeral, I saw very little of this. On their return to the village, Tooj's male relatives washed their hands and feet at the communal water tap—that was all. Upon my return to the United States, I asked several knowledgeable Hmong about pollution during the Hmong funeral ceremony. They informed me that the reed-pipe players absorbed much of the pollution as they breathed in the air while they played their instruments. Proof of this, they said, was the bad smell these men made when they passed gas.

The day after the burial, many of the visitors left for their own villages.

THE ELEVENTH TO THE THIRTEENTH DAY:
FEEDING THE DEAD AND RELEASING THE FIRST SOUL (XI PLIG)

For the next three days, the men of Tooj's household—his brothers and sons— went to the grave to offer rice, a chicken, and rice liquor to the dead man and the ancestors, as well as a hard-boiled egg split into three parts, one part for each day. (I cannot describe this part of the ritual, as I did not attend.)

On the thirteenth day after Tooj's death, the Xi Plig ceremony was held, to release the first soul. The men of the household invited the dead man's first soul, the one that "stays at the grave with the bones," to visit its home on earth for the last time. The Xi Plig is a private affair; it is between the dead person and the people closest to him or her, the household and affines. Although I was not there, I was told that the men made a hole in the grave and, speaking through the hole, invited Tooj to come home for a final meal. Then the men returned to the house and offered Tooj's soul rice, a cooked chicken, and liquor.

Tooj's jacket had been draped over a bamboo structure and set on a tray to represent his first soul. The men of the household offered food and liquor to this "spirit shirt," and then the eldest son threw the bamboo pointers to make sure Tooj's soul had indeed visited the house and eaten. When the pointers landed in the affirmative position, indicating that the soul had eaten, the eldest son told Tooj's first soul to return to the grave. It was no longer part of the family and must never come back to the house. It must stay at the grave with the bones. The eldest son threw the pointers again and saw that the first soul had returned to the grave. Then the pointers were burned, ending the thirteen-day ritual. The last few visitors departed. Tooj's household could now return to their usual tasks.

Some clans do many more rituals at this time (Radley 1986:360; Tapp 1989a:53–54). Others do these rituals differently. A Hmong from the Xiong clan told me that his clan does not give the first soul a final meal in the home at the Xi Plig, but says to it, at the grave, "Now you must find your own food."

THE FUNERAL: PART 2

The second part of Tooj's funeral took place six months later, in March 1988. Although it is not a second burial, as Hertz's (1960:53–76) double obsequies theory suggests, the bereavement period is not complete until the soul is set free with the Tso Plig. Until then, villagers are fearful that the soul will be restless and harm the living, causing sickness or a poor harvest. As well, the soul of the dead may entice other souls to follow, causing more deaths.

The soul freed by the Tso Plig is the one that will be reborn in the body of a new child, which I have called the third soul or returning vital soul.

The first soul, as we have seen, stays in the grave with the bones. The fate of the second soul has been difficult to determine, but from discussions with people in Flower Village and Hmong in the United States, I have concluded that it stays in the land of darkness as part of the ancestral mass. This is the soul that can come back in the summertime as a butterfly or a moth; it is the part of a person that is ritually fed and cared for by the descendants (see appendix B, verse 206; Lemoine 1983b:40).

The concept that a person is composed of a body, seven shadows, and three souls, as indicated in verse 162 of the Showing the Way chant, is not an easy one to discuss with Hmong (Tapp 1989b:166n5), because to speak of death may invite spirits to visit and steal one's soul. In addition, requests for an explication of the meaning of the rituals that guide the souls on the journey from life to death and back to life again are often met with confusion and puzzlement. Attempting to understand the meaning the ritual has for the actors themselves can lead to frustration, until one remembers that this meaning is not accessible to a researcher in the way it is to the actor. As Nancy Jay put it,

> There are two kinds of situatedness, that of the sacrificer and that of the interpreter. The one is unattainable and the other inescapable. The task is to build some kind of bridge between the two to hold the worlds together, to make what they do intelligible for us. (1992:19)

FREEING THE SOUL: TSO PLIG

Some months later, the news had spread that the Freeing the Soul ritual was about to take place, and Tooj's relatives and friends had gathered at his house. Although the ritual is similar in many ways to the first part of the funeral, it lasts only a day or two, fewer visitors from outside the village attend (friends and some affines came to Tooj's Tso Plig ceremony, although none were required to attend at this time), and the main actors are different. Two drummers and two pipers (not four) were present at this Tso Plig but neither the man who performed the Showing the Way chant nor the father of words. Instead, the eldest son did all the chanting/singing. It is crucial that he remember the names of the ancestors and speak their names correctly, or people in the lineage can get sick and can even go blind. Despite the enor-

FIG. 4.3. *Releasing the soul of the dead to be reborn. At this ritual usually performed a year after the funeral ritual, the dead man is represented by a shirt on a tray. (Photo by Patricia Symonds)*

mity and seriousness of this, the ceremony for freeing the soul is for the living and is usually quite a festive affair, with much eating, drinking, and laughter. Even Hmong women drink rice wine at the Tso Plig.

The spirit shirt from the Xi Plig had been set up the night before. On the rice-winnowing tray, a bamboo structure was covered with a jacket that had belonged to the dead man. A bamboo cup, three rice cakes (*lub ncuav*), a bowl with rice and a boiled egg, and two small pieces of opium had been placed inside the jacket. Red soybeans and corn were set on the tray as food for Tooj and the ancestors.

At 8:30 A.M. the drums and reed pipes began to play. The eldest son, who was now the head of the household, picked up the tray with the spirit shirt ("Tooj") on it, and followed the two pipers outside. Behind him came a man carrying one of Tooj's crossbows; they were followed by Tooj's immediate relatives, and many villagers. They proceeded to the edge of the village. Rice liquor had been poured into cups made from the hollow stems of bamboo.

Lineage members offered the liquor to both men and women, and everyone took a cup. This was the only time I saw Hmong women drink liquor. A lineage member shot off the crossbow, and then everyone followed the reed pipers back to the house.

The eldest son set down the tray with the spirit shirt on a small table on the downslope side of the house; he placed a bamboo cup of rice liquor next to the tray. The drummer beat his drum, which was once again propped against the house post, and the reed pipers played, instructing Tooj's soul. The eldest son picked up the spirit shirt and circled the house post nine times before setting the tray back down in the same place. Women of the family squatted around the tray, and, taking hold of Tooj's jacket (the spirit shirt), started to keen. People from nearby villages came by to pay their respects, bowing to the spirit shirt as they entered the house. They brought liquor, rice, incense, spirit money, and pigs, which they gave to the household to defray expenses. As the women continued to keen, men drank, talked, smoked opium, and laughed.

The women fell silent when the eldest son, who stood facing the tray, began to chant, improvising the song. He told the soul of the dead man to be free, to bring his descendants good fortune, and to remember his "mandate-for-life" paper so that he could be born again and have a good life. Although this was an important speech—if the son gets it wrong, people in the lineage can go blind—only a few people listened to it, and overall there was an atmosphere of gaiety. People sat in groups talking and sharing cigarettes, while outside a tape deck blared modern Hmong songs from America. The eldest son paused and poured some liquor into a bamboo cup and offered it to the spirit shirt, then poured the liquor into the bowl of rice and egg. The son poured more liquor and offered it to the pipers, who drank it. Then the eldest son picked up the tray and, with the pipers leading the way, walked around the house, setting the tray down this time on the eastern slope of the house. Women came again to keen over the dead man, the drum and reed pipes played, and the noise level rose in intensity and volume.

Male kin sat around a table near the tray, drinking whiskey and talking. Men of the household dragged in a large sow, squealing, to the tray. They thanked the sow for its soul, which would go to Tooj and the ancestors to honor the dead man and show appreciation for his life on earth, and then they cut the sow's throat. The pipe and drum played loudly. A new pointer had been made from a buffalo horn cut in two, and the horns were thrown to see if the ancestors had accepted the pig's soul. They had. Some pig's blood, a symbol of its soul that would accompany Tooj, was dabbed on a banana leaf, and the leaf tied up and slipped into the right sleeve of the spirit shirt. Then a smaller pig—a boar—was brought in. The buffalo horns were banged on a large stone and then on the back of the boar. A second piper joined the first, as a lineage member sacrificed the boar. The visitors cut paper money into triangles and boats to hang on branches over the tray. Men in the lineage cooked the pigs, and there was enough for everyone in the village to eat. For the rest of the day, people sat around talking, eating, and drinking rice liquor.

As night fell, the drum and pipes began again. Tooj's sons unfastened the paper money and burned it in front of the tray, and the eldest son told Tooj to use it on his journey. The drummer went outdoors and dismantled his drum. The pipers led Tooj's son—who carried the tray with the spirit shirt—and the villagers to the edge of a mountain. The night was pitch black, with only the flicker of torches and flashlights to show the way. By this point everyone had drunk a great deal of rice wine; they were merry and laughing. I was grateful that a few of the young women, who had taken it upon themselves to watch out for me, stayed close to help me follow the procession over the uneven ground. The tray was set down and the eldest son threw the buffalo horns to ascertain if the soul was following instructions. Each time the horns came up in a negative position there was much laughter as more liquor was poured down the eldest son's throat. When the horns finally came up positive, the tray and everything on it, except for the rice cakes that would go to a sick man in the village,[19] was rolled down the mountain amid shouts, laughter, and applause from the crowd, including the dead man's relatives.

BAD DEATHS

In marked contrast to the rituals held for Tooj—the public mourning of the thirteen-day ritual, and the ebullience of the Tso Plig—the funeral rituals for a bad death are private, and there is no relief from their sadness. Throughout Southeast Asia many different ethnic groups make a distinction between natural and unnatural—or "good" and "bad"—deaths.[20] Thomas Kirsch, one of the first scholars to study the hill tribes, writes that many of these people and many other southeast Asians as well defined bad deaths as those caused by suicide, drowning, childbirth, attack by wild animals, or other "violent accidents" (Kirsch 1973:15). Such deaths were seen as being due to "supernatural displeasure" (Mills, 1922:160, quoted in Kirsch), and in some hill tribes "the personal effects, house, crops, animals, and even cash of a person dying in such a way were either destroyed or abandoned" (Kirsch 1973:15), the family preferring to face financial ruin rather than risk supernatural repercussions (Mills 1926:283, quoted in Kirsch). Howard Kaufman, in his study of a community in Thailand, notes that in the case of a bad death, the body is cremated quickly to keep the evil spirits that in some measure caused the death, and that lingered around the corpse, from doing further harm (1960:158). Nicola Tannenbaum (1995: 150–51), in her study of the Shan of Thailand, tells the story of a man killed by the police: his family quickly cremated his body in the hill field where he had been killed, and then abandoned the field (which had been theirs) to avoid further contact with his spirit, which they feared would be especially vengeful and dangerous. Because the man had died unprepared for death, he was "likely to attempt to carry out plans made while living, putting those that live at risk." This idea of a vengeful or unsatisfied spirit who causes trouble for the living because it died badly and remains in distress in the otherworld is also common throughout Southeast Asia.

The Hmong also believe in the negative effects of the spirit of a person who died badly, the necessity of quickly disposing of the body, and separating the family and household from the spirit of the dead. Although Hmong believe that wild and dangerous spirits are attracted by death, I do not know if they believe that bad deaths are caused by these spirits, or if bad deaths attract more malign spirits than do good deaths. The extra precautions in such cases seem to concern danger from the spirit of the person who died.

THE CASE OF XIA

While I was in Flower Village, a young woman I will call Xia killed herself by eating opium because her parents wouldn't allow her to marry the young man she loved, who was the son of an opium addict and very poor. Xia had been a pretty, good-natured, and very well-liked young woman. She was fifteen years old when she died. The entire village was upset by her death, which could not be seen as other than tragic, and her parents were heart-broken. Suicide is a very bad death, and Xia had been young and childless as well. She had not lived out her allotted span, she had no descendants to feed her, and the deities in the land of darkness would punish her for killing herself; they would not allow her to be reborn again quickly, or as a human being at all.

Despite this, the Showing the Way chant was performed at Xia's funeral. (I was told that the only time this chant is not performed is for soldiers in wartime, when no one knows where the bodies of the dead lie.) Xia's grand-father was a shaman, and he performed a "doing for the spirits" ritual to see how her spirit was faring in the otherworld. When he found her, he said Xia's spirit was crying without cease. Xia could easily become a lost, wan-dering spirit, unable to reach the ancestors or the land of light, hungry and lonely, causing trouble for the lineage through malevolence, or simply through her own distress, because she was out of balance and was not where she belonged. The family sacrificed a huge pig to send to her for food, and also to exchange the pig's soul for hers so that she could be cleansed from the suicide act, and her soul freed to be reborn—not as a human being, but at least as something animate in the land of light. My informant said that the other purpose of this ritual was "to build a fence around the household" and protect them from Xia's spirit. (Although Xia had been good-natured in life, she had killed herself because she wasn't allowed to marry the boy she loved, and she was suffering after death as well. That she would be angry and spiteful seemed quite possible.)

Xia's father's eldest sister was in attendance at the funeral. She told Xia that she must·not eat any more of that "bad medicine," meaning the raw opium she had eaten and died from, and that she must take with her all of the bad feelings she had had and not curse the family, which could cause one of her sisters to commit suicide too.

The first part of Xia's funeral was only a few days long, and there were no outside guests; thirteen days later the Tso Plig was held, to separate Xia's dangerous and unhappy souls from the rest of the household as quickly as possible. There was no Xi Plig ceremony, to feed and then release the first soul that stays at the grave. As far as I know, there was no discussion of debt or obligations, as Xia had died unmarried, and there had been no bride-price or other exchanges between clans.

I did not attend this funeral, or the one for the other bad death that occurred in the village while I was there; they were for household members and affines only. I could find out very little about these two funerals; no one wanted to talk about them, and it would have been very bad manners, as well as bad luck, for me to persist in asking. As I have mentioned, Hmong look down on "gossip" about other clans, and they certainly do not want to talk about a bad death, as such talk can draw down misfortune. A bad death in another village was no matter for gossip either.

THE CASE OF AN UNNAMED GIRL

Near Flower Village there was a Hmong village close to the main road that was frequented by tourists and Thai people. A Thai woman visited this village and persuaded three of the Hmong girls to go away to Bangkok with her. She promised them good, high-paying jobs as waitresses.

The village headman warned the girls not to go with the Thai woman, but they went anyway. Two of the young women returned immediately, as soon as they discovered that the jobs were for sex work. The third girl, both of whose parents were opium addicts, stayed in Bangkok because the Thai woman promised her a lot of money if she would be a prostitute. The Hmong girl sent money home to her family by way of her brother every month. Her brother was glad to get the money and bought himself a motorcycle.

About a year later the girl tested positive for HIV and was forced to leave the brothel. When she came back to the village, her brother was angry because he could no longer make the monthly payments on his motorcycle and had to return it. He told her that no one would want to marry her, she was good for nothing, and she had disgraced the family. Her parents, who had bought opium with the money she sent, weren't pleased at her return either.

The girl went out to the field, took rat poison, and died. As with Xia's death, the funeral was short, the girl was buried swiftly, and no outsiders were invited. This girl had relatives in Flower Village, and they attended the funeral, which was so brief they were back the same day. They refused to let me accompany them, but in their comments about this unnamed girl they seemed to suggest that killing herself was a way to escape a long slow death from AIDS and a very difficult life, and to get reborn into a better life. Later on, other Hmong I met in connection with the HIV/AIDS project said the same thing about the disease—that suicide would give the AIDS sufferer a chance at a new, healthy body. But I never heard of a man committing suicide for such a reason. But as shown with Xia's suicide (p. 154), the souls of those who commit suicide are forced to wander around the world and may not be reborn as a human being.

REVERSALS AND DUALITIES

Within the Showing the Way chant and throughout the funeral rituals that follow, there are many reversals of symbol, meaning, and role. Fixed boundaries become fluid, metaphors invert, and meanings unravel and re-form: to cross the boundary between life and death is to change. Thus a plank made from bamboo and rope in one world becomes a striped dragon-horse in the other, wine poured out onto the ground becomes sustenance for traveling souls, and a dead person becomes an ancestor.

The transformation of the dead from dangerous entities into benevolent ancestors is achieved by feeding the dead, who need food and drink just as the living do, and by guiding their souls to the village of ancestors in the land of darkness with reed pipes, drum, and the Showing the Way chant. The chant not only offers guidance and instruction to the souls of the newly dead but effects a series of transformations for those who hear it. It achieves this through powerfully wielded metaphors that move back and forth between the symbolic and the material realm, encompassing the primal past, the future, and the present moment.

To take just one example, in the origin story of the first rooster, "The sound of the rooster's crowing is reaching the otherworld" and "becomes the dead son's chicken to show the way." The first rooster is a symbol for all roosters, every rooster that will be or ever has been, reaching back into "the otherworld"—which is a time (the beginning of life) as well as a place (the land of darkness)—and forward into the present, where it has become the particular rooster that was sacrificed to accompany a particular dead person. The symbolic, first rooster has become the rooster that the chanter holds in his hand. The symbol is made concrete; the metaphor is visible and tangible.

At the same time, that which has been made material is about to or already has become disembodied. The rooster must die for its spirit to go with the dead person, the rice wine must be spilled upon the ground, and the dead person must alter to return to the land of darkness and be reborn.

The series of transformations accomplished in these few lines—and this is only one example, for the chant is full of them—sets up a context in which death is another transformation, and not the final one. Later in the chant this metaphysical context is made explicit when the placenta, or birth shirt, is called the "rebirth shirt," and the chanter says he will guide the dead, not to the land of darkness, but "to be reborn."

Within the chant and throughout the funeral, the expected and familiar are turned on their heads to be replaced by perceptions that may be opposing, or only slightly different. Like events in a dream, there is an odd logic to these reversals, even when they go unexplained; the complementarity and need for balance in Hmong society show up here as a kind of duality or doubleness. This doubleness extends to the number of oxen sacrificed, which must be even, not odd, and the number of pipers (two or four, never one or three) and drummers (two, who spell each other). In the Showing the Way chant many phrases are repeated but are expressed differently the second time around, and verbs often are given in sets of two—the bamboo is "cut" and "split," the souls must "endure" and "forbear" to carry on, and so on—as if to stress that nothing is singular, simple, or one-dimensional but that there are two parts (at least) to everything.

THE SHOWING THE WAY CHANT

The Showing the Way chant abounds with reversals and dualities; to dip into the chant at any point is to come across them. (I will discuss only a few examples here.) These reversals and dualities set up a feeling of movement and connection between opposing forces or states of being. As in the example about the first rooster, the movement is from there to here and back again. The way the metaphors are used creates or invokes the metaphysical realm—the cycle of life—that they describe.

The Hmong death chant begins with the origins of all the items that souls need to journey to the land of darkness. These items so necessary to the dead are also the essentials of life. In a curious reversal, the chant seems to imply that food and clothing were given to the first people so they could make the journey to the land of darkness, as if living in the land of light were of less importance—or as if the two worlds, or states of being, were linked by common threads.[21]

As well, most of these necessities for life and death came from Ntxwj Nyoog's mountain, cliff, or garden in the land of darkness—the yeast for rice wine, the seeds for rice (the staple food of the Hmong), the seeds for all of the other domestic crops, the bamboo that allows communication between the dead and the living, the hemp for shoes and clothing. The beneficence of the earth, then, comes from the garden of Ntxwj Nyoog, the fearsome deity that the soul of a young bride is cautioned to avoid when she changes her household and her lineage at marriage. This "wicked" deity,[22] who preys upon traveling souls, nevertheless supplied these same souls with most of the things they needed to reach their ancestors—even the hempen shoes that allow them to pass his own poisonous caterpillars in safety. In a peculiar, behind-the-scenes way, Ntxwj Nyoog appears to be a deity of agriculture as well as of death. In one of the many instances of doubleness in the chant, the deity who sent the seeds of death to the world also provided, or allowed the retrieval of, the seeds of life.

Although deities are prone to doubleness, the role of the spirits is the ground for a whole series of reversals. The point is made and reiterated that humans and spirits are hostile toward one another, "selling" each other for food, drink, and clothing, and this is of a piece with Hmong fears of wild spirits.[23] The story of the war between humans and spirits, however, is told from the point of view of the spirits, and in it the spirits have sustained the greatest losses; indeed, they are nearly extinct from the predations of humans. They are saved by the "benevolent" deities, Puj and Yawm Saub, who make them invisible so they can trick humans. Thus the grandparent deities responsible for human fertility also ensure that the humans' natural enemies will survive and continue to prey upon them. It seems an almost ecological conclusion to the story, but very ungrandparentlike, and certainly not favoring humanity.

Later in the chant, when the dead person reaches the spirit boat, it is spirits who, for a fee, help him cross the river and set him on the right road. In this instance the spirits are helpful to the human soul; and the human, instead of harming or fearing the spirits of the land, pays them and thanks them.

Meanwhile the tame spirits of the household, who have protected the dead person in life, now must have the new situation explained to them, more than once; at both the Xi Plig and the Tso Plig they have to be thanked profusely and cajoled into letting the dead person's souls go, like overprotective parents whose desire to help becomes harmful when a child needs to grow up. The image of the household spirits stretching out long arms to catch and hold the souls of the deceased is quite eerie and unsettling, both in the chant and in the death ceremonies.

In yet another reversal of what might be expected, it is the female deity Grandmother Saub (and indirectly, Ntxwj Nyoog, who grows the bamboo in his garden) who gives the dead the ability to communicate through a length of bamboo split in two (the pointers the chanter throws to make sure the dead have understood his instructions). In life women are silent; in death the soul cannot speak. But it is a female deity who releases the souls of the dead from total silence. And it is living women who give a voice to sorrow.

GENDER REVERSALS IN FUNERAL RITUALS

As soon as the Showing the Way chant is finished, and the souls of the newly dead stand at the foot of the silver ladder between the worlds, women begin to keen. In childbirth women are silent, but at death women express their pain—the pain of loss. In weeping and in words, they bid the souls goodbye.

Men are not silent at funerals, but they are nearly so about their grief. Although the Hmong themselves say that this is because women have smaller livers and cannot contain their grief, which may be construed as a sign of women's weakness, the fact remains that in this instance of voicing grief, women have a power of expression that men are denied in most cases. As we have seen, a husband's mourning song for his dead wife will most likely be cut short by his brothers, who advise him to remarry instead of mourn. The instances of men who keen for any length of time are so rare that those who do so are regarded as exceptionally "clever," and all of them are elderly, so they needn't fear a loss of status.

At the last meal before the deceased is buried, the women who have guarded the coffin eat first, and the men of the household serve them. This and the thirty days after childbirth are the only times when women eat first and men wait on them. But there is no story or explanation that I have been able to find about how or why this situation came to be. When I asked the Hmong, they said only that this was their way.

Women are allowed to drink rice liquor at the Tso Plig, and at no other time. As rice liquor is supposed to protect the souls of the dead, perhaps it also protects the living who mourn. Or perhaps, since the Tso Plig is the most festive of the funeral rituals, the camaraderie fostered by drinking many cups of rice wine is another way to mend the hole in the collective left by death. I have been told that the drinking at the Tso Plig is a way of toasting the dead person, of saying farewell, of praising and honoring their life. But once again, I could find no story or reason behind this custom that reverses tradition.

Men also haul water and gather firewood throughout the first part of a funeral, tasks that normally fall to women. Since women are hired to cook the rice and other food, excepting the sacrificed meat (which men always cook), I wondered why women weren't hired for these jobs as well.

It seems to me—a Westerner, a woman, and an outsider—that Hmong women have some kind of intense power around death. They do nothing of their usual work for thirteen days, not even flower cloth, while men are busy acting as hosts of the funeral. Men feed the ancestors and, for one meal, men also feed the women who keen and guard the coffin. In the soul-calling ritual at birth, sound in the form of chanting and percussion is associated with rites of passage and with power; and at death it is mostly women who make this sound, in the singsong ululation that typifies keening. Last but not least, women guard the dead. The Hmong are afraid of the corpse, of the unsettled souls of the newly dead and the wild spirits the dead body attracts, but for nine days women guard it, and keep it from being harmed. These are not just the women in the dead person's lineage, who might be expected to be less at risk from proximity to the ancestors of that lineage, but any woman with a blood tie to the dead person, including married-out sisters and daughters. Where did women get the power to guard this dangerous entity, the unburied dead?

I have asked Hmong men and women, and received no satisfactory answer. Hmong seem as disinterested in the questions of women's power around death as they are in the "meaning" of origin stories. "It is our way," they say, as though the meaning were self-evident or unimportant. One woman said, "The women guard the body because the men are doing everything else," as if I were being a little stupid. But why the men were doing "everything else," including what is usually women's work, even to serving the women a meal, she did not say.

CLOTHING THE SOUL

The power that women clearly have is that they provide the birth shirt for the newborn child, which is also the rebirth shirt for the returning vital soul of the dead. The body of the child clothes the soul physically for its sojourn in the land of light; the rebirth shirt clothes it spiritually, on the journey to the land of darkness and, if all goes well, back again to the land of light. Through their bodies women connect the two worlds, creating the body of the child and the birth shirts that make the journeys possible.

Women also connect the two worlds through the work of their hands. With flower cloth, they make another form of clothing that, like the birth/rebirth shirt, is both physical and spiritual. Unlike the body, the flower cloth that clothes the dead person is able to cross the boundary between life and death. In the land of darkness, a dead mother or grandmother can see and recognize her own needlework. When she discerns the flower cloth that she made in the land of light, she knows the soul for kindred. Perhaps this is why, in the death chant, the chanter says he will send the soul to meet first its grandmother and then its grandfather. Although at a child's birth, men greet the soul that will make the child a true Hmong (during the soul-calling ritual), it seems that the souls of married-in women, or the female half of the ancestral mass, recognize and greet the soul at death. On their journey to the land of darkness, the souls of the newly dead are guided and fed by men, and strung between two groups of women; they are guarded and mourned by women at the beginning of their journey, and greeted by those who once were women at its end.

THE CYCLE OF LIFE

Maurice Bloch and Jonathan Parry have pointed out that what people use and value in funeral rituals are the resources that their culture sees as most essential to the social order (1982:7). One of the more striking aspects of Hmong funerals is the value placed not only on what sustains life—the crops that provide food, drink, and clothing—but on life itself. Life is not seen as something to transcend or endure in the hope of nirvana or a heavenly reward. The reward for a life well lived and for funeral rituals correctly performed is the return of the soul of the dead person to the land of light, which is filled with beauty. As we saw in Xia's case, even to come back as a stone or a tree is better than not to come back at all. Life is the great blessing.

At the same time, Hmong value the land of darkness, which, together with the land of light, makes the universe whole. The land of darkness is fearsome, and the spirits of the dead inimical to the living, but the connection between the two states of being is inherent, part of their very fabric. As the Showing the Way chant makes clear, everything that living people need came from, or came back from, the land of darkness, including their souls. The land of darkness is not the end of life, or not only the end of life, but the source of life.

Victor Turner's (1967:93–103) seminal work with the Ndembu found that liminal stages of life-cycle rites were characterized by reversals. But these reversals presaged chaos: roles had no structure, social and gender codes were discounted, and the result was a lapse or break in meaning that lasted until the liminal phase was over, and order restored. For the Hmong, reversals are not precursors of anarchy, and liminal phases do not disrupt the meaning of the universe. Indeed, both are part of the continually shifting balance that *maintains* the universe. To follow the soul's journey is to be made aware that things change—even to approach the threshold of the land of darkness is to see the shape of things waver and shift, like reflections in water—but balance is maintained, not by holding still, but by movement along a continuum from here to there and back again.

Just as the first rooster became the rooster in the chanter's hand, and then the spirit rooster that went with Tooj, so Tooj became "the dead son." He was transformed from an individual to a symbol, from one dead man to all of the dead Hmong, throughout time. The chant says, "If the leaves do not fall, the forest will not grow." As others died to make room for him, Tooj died to make room for other Hmong. He was one of a vast number of leaves—all of which will fall. But the chant and the rituals offer consolation in their imagery, which is of the turning wheel of the seasons. The imagery of the Hmong death rituals promises that, in a new form, the soul may return.

CHAPTER 5

REFLECTIONS ON POWER,

GENDER, AND THE CYCLE OF LIFE

For the Hmong, parenthood is the path to fulfillment in this world and the means toward peace as an ancestor in the afterlife. It is the reproductive power of women and the subsequent existence of children—both daughters, whose bride-price makes it possible for their brothers to marry and have their own children, and sons, who feed the ancestors—that assures the continuation of the lineage and the immortality of the individual's soul.

But, as in many other societies, the understanding that women are essential to the continuity of life coexists with their lower social status. The actual labor and delivery of a child express a dominant theme in Hmong society: women's role is to be private and silent, men's is to be public and vocal. As we have seen, women are quiet and acquiescent to the male voice in the public domain. In the private sphere of the home, older women exert some influence and power, but this is over younger women, not over men—at least not overtly. Even when a woman's judgment is deferred to in public, as in the case of the eldest sister at her brother's funeral, it is her husband who speaks.

Although some scholars have argued (Ortner 1974:75) that giving birth is seen as part of nature instead of culture and is therefore devalued, Cornelia

Ann Kammerer states that this is not so for the Akha of northern Thailand (1986:357). Nor is it true of the Hmong. For the Hmong the creation of life is highly valued; it is an act both natural and cultural, in which neither quality is opposed to the other. Women contribute the substance of life, the vessel for the reincarnated soul of an ancestor, and men call that soul into the newborn's body.

WOMEN'S POWER

Because the sexual asymmetry of Hmong culture has been so frequently remarked upon, I would like to reiterate some of the areas of Hmong life in which power is associated with women. In some of these areas the power is obvious, in others, so taken for granted as to be nearly invisible.

REPRODUCTION WITHIN MARRIAGE

Hmong women's primary source of power in the patriline is their fertility, and they have a long reproductive life because they marry in their teens and traditionally have been reluctant to use contraceptives (although this is slowly changing after years of Thai government efforts to encourage the use of birth control). Hmong have many reasons for valuing fecundity, and love of children is one of them. Also, Hmong need children to till the fields and to perform religious rites, especially the funerary rites that guarantee safe passage into the land of darkness; and they have a history of high child-mortality rates due to natural causes, as well as generational losses such as those during the Vietnam War. Other reasons that contraception is avoided are that only the birth of a first child is believed to seal the marital union (Symonds 1991:135), that only sons perpetuate the patrilineal kinship system, that every new birth is believed to provide another body for an ancestor's soul to be reborn into, that women have difficulty requesting that their husbands use birth control, and that in spite of years of Thai government family planning, women are still enjoined by their families to have as many children as possible. Hmong women's social powerlessness in these arenas arises from cultural norms that encourage them to exhibit deference to male authority and that discourage women from behaving assertively.

COURTSHIP AND SEXUAL FREEDOM

Although young girls are taught to cover themselves with *sev,* to speak to males only in certain ways, to exhibit "shyness," and so on, at the time of menses the expression of a young woman's sexuality becomes socially desirable and she wears an embroidered *sev* rather than the plain *sev* worn by girls and married women. The New Year's courting ritual, with its love songs and "courting ball game," is a time when sexual experimentation is condoned unless the suitor is from the same clan. Young women need not feel shame or fear punishment for engaging in sex with as many partners as they like unless they become pregnant and remain unwed. Virginity does not appear to be highly prized and in fact seems to be unusual by late adolescence.

Opinions vary as to the degree of shame attached to pregnancy when no marriage is forthcoming. For example, Robert Cooper says that "if there is no marriage, the girl is partly compensated for the cost and trouble of the pregnancy by a fine levied against the genitor (if known)... the girl is not hindered in finding a marriage partner, and . . . there is no jealousy of a partner's pre-marital sex life" (Cooper 1983:185), but in my observation considerable shame was attached to that state. If the girl becomes pregnant and remains unmarried, the child is accepted into her own clan. In the case that I witnessed, a great deal of gossip created embarrassment for the young woman's family (see chap. 2). So a degree of sexual freedom is permitted in Hmong culture and there is considerably less pressure to maintain one's virginity than in other Asian groups, but the risk of pregnancy if no marriage follows impinges upon that freedom.

PROTEST WITHIN MARRIAGE, AND DIVORCE

Hmong women's lack of social power means that they have little control over their husband's behavior and few options if they leave the marriage, although "institutionalized protest" affords women some leverage, and the "threat of the forfeiture of bride price" provides some protection against mistreatment (Cooper 1983:181).

Although final decisions rest firmly with the husband, wives do appear to exercise some influence over their husbands. Very few women seek to undermine the authority of men in the presence of others, "but if things become unbearable, an unhappy wife may sing of her grievances openly in front of her husband's family, in the form of the spontaneous *lus taum* 'story-telling song'" (Cooper 1983:181) or go sit outside another household where women are sewing, and begin crying in front of them in the hopes that they will give comfort or influence their husbands to intervene.

Another strategy for an unhappy wife is to run away from home, but this is usually only as far as the field house, and only until her husband goes and brings her home. A final means of protest is the threat of suicide, or an actual attempted suicide, often by swallowing opium. In this case, and if the woman lives, her kin often intervene and the entire community seeks to ensure that her lot is improved, showing that social norms are enforced by a larger network of kin and that "a woman's welfare is not completely delegated to her husband upon marriage," as it might be in Western countries (Cooper 1983:181).

A woman may also return to her natal home. As Cooper notes, turning to her natal family is considered "the first step in the initiation of divorce by a female, although it is rare for this action to actually lead to divorce, unless it is wished for by the husband" (1983:181). In most cases, the threat of forfeiture of bride-price (which may condemn a man to a life of bachelorhood unless he is wealthy enough to afford another bride-price) "acts to maintain marriage but not to subject women. . . . Bridewealth maintains the disparity in the sexual status quo, but prevents a man abusing his 'property'" (Cooper 1983:181).

But if a woman leaves her husband, she also must leave her children—at least her male children—behind. Children belong to the husband's family and lineage; they are part of the lineage's assets. As we have seen, the life of a divorced woman is marginal at best, as she belongs to no lineage, but there is nothing to prevent her from remarrying and taking her daughter with her to become part of a new lineage.

BREAST MILK AND MENSTRUAL BLOOD

In Hmong culture there is an undisputed belief in the power of breast milk, not only as the food that sustains life in newborns and young children but as a powerful medicine. Hmong informants in America report that shamans still ask for it because "it is considered to be very pure and good and has the power of life" (May Kao Yang, personal communication, March 2001). One breastfeeding Hmong woman reported that a shaman had requested some breast milk to "toss over his shoulder because it was good medicine." She also reported that "the use of breast milk in healing rituals performed with a shaman's familiars is supposed to be the most powerful of medicines if a person is very sick or chronically ill" (ibid.). Breast milk is regarded as such a powerful medicine that it is dangerous if used incorrectly, and a number of taboos attach to it as a consequence; for instance, lactating women who have recently given birth are not permitted to cook, for fear that the milk might become mixed with the family food.

Like breast milk, the first menstrual blood of a young woman is considered a very powerful substance and is sometimes collected and dried to be used as medicine for those who are gravely ill. The association of these substances with healing indicates the degree of awe surrounding women's reproductive powers. Women's sexuality in general is associated with power and danger, and women are required to cover their genitalia with *sev,* not because they are considered polluting but because of their power of sexual attraction.

THE POSTPARTUM PERIOD

Pregnancy and more especially birth and the post-birth period are considered a liminal time, during which a woman has both great power and great vulnerability to evil spirits. For thirty days after a woman has given birth she is considered especially vulnerable and especially dangerous. During this time women stay at home, with a bamboo taboo sign outside the door. The anthropological literature reveals that cross-culturally these kinds of transitional periods (e.g., initiation, vision quests, and so on) are often associated with the acquisition of spiritual power (Turner 1969:94–96). Birth and the postpartum period are a time when both the woman and her child are between worlds and, like all transitional persons, must be separated from society at large (ibid.:94–96, 102–6) because of the danger to themselves and others. The woven piece of bamboo that is placed outside the door of a new mother is one of the clearest indications that reproductive power is feared.

During the postpartum period, the woman rests and her husband cooks for her, giving her meat (chicken), the prestige food. This reversal of sex roles is explained in the traditional story describing how it was decided which of the sexes would give birth (see chap. 3). Here again, an origin myth gives contradictory meanings to gender differences, with the discourse asserting that males were once physically capable of giving birth but opted to transfer that power to females, who then negotiated certain privileges and a period of role reversal.

THE ROLE OF THE SISTER

Anthropological researchers have recorded several origin myths illustrating the importance of the brother/sister relationship in Hmong society. In one such myth all the Hmong clans are descended from a brother and sister who were the only people left on earth after a flood (see chap. 1).

At a woman's wedding, her brother gives her special gifts; at her funeral he also must bring gifts and make sure that she is given a proper burial and that her debts have been paid. A man's eldest sister must do the same at his funeral in order to ensure his safe passage to the land of darkness. He cannot be buried until his sister and her husband have arrived at his home. She oversees the discussion of her brother's debts and obligations, she guards his body, and, before burial, she checks to be sure no one has slipped metal into the coffin, which would harm her brother's soul and all the lineage. (At a woman's death her brother's wife assumes primary responsibility for guarding the body.)

A sister also has the power to make decisions and to designate ritual actions related to her brother's well being. If her brother's wife has many stillbirths, the sister will mark the dead baby's forehead with blood as a warning to the critical spirit that is refusing to inhabit a baby's body. If her brother has died a bad death, she will recommend strategies for alleviating harm to his spirit and the lineage, and give blessings; and in the case of a bad death in her brother's family, she may intercede and speak to the unhappy spirit of the dead to keep it from cursing those in the lineage. The spiritual power of the sister extends to establishing decrees and taboos for her brother's clan, as happened in the Vaj clan, where an elder sister decreed that fathers-in-law and daughters-in-law cannot eat at the same table, and the Yaj clan, where a an elder sister said that males cannot eat the heart of any animal.

The sister also has some authority over her brother's son, especially if, in the event of cross-cousin marriage, she is also his mother-in-law, or if his parents are dead. Through her husband she can give her nephew help and advice, even on whom he should marry.

Thus sisters retain a powerful connection to their natal lineage through their importance and authority in matters regarding their brothers, and this in some measure diminishes their "outsider" status in the patriline.

BRIDEWEALTH AND REBIRTH

Westerners perceive bride-price as the commodification of women, but to Hmong it has many levels of meaning besides the financial one. Although the phrase used to describe the marriage process is to "buy" or "get" a wife, marriage is not thought of as "buying" a woman but rather as a series of exchanges between wife-givers and wife-takers to form an alliance between clans. In the United States, some Hmong use the term "nurturing charge" instead of "bride-price" to avoid giving the impression that Hmong women are bought and sold (Fadiman 1997:189), but the terms used in the marriage negotiations continue to be those of the marketplace. As Cooper points out,

> Whilst a Hmong has an idea of buying a wife for himself or his son, he does not in the same way consider that he sells his daughter. These different perspectives on the marriage contract the different interpretations of "bride-price" and "bride-wealth" that separate formalist and substantivist schools of economic anthropology: both interpretations are equally relevant in the Hmong context. (1983:180)

Bride-price is divided into two parts: the "milk and care money" that compensates the mother and father for the care and upbringing of the young woman, and the "money owed for the shirt," which is payment for the birth shirt, or placenta, of the child (children) the young wife is expected to produce—in other words, for her fertility. But a Hmong woman's fertility seems to encompass rebirth as well as birth; that the bride-price is for the "shirt" suggests as much.

At death, a Hmong person must retrieve the birth shirt to wear on the return trip to the land of the ancestors (Lemoine 1983b:28, 63; Tapp 1989a:81–82). The placenta, then, is not only essential for a child's development in the womb but as spiritual clothing for the journey back to the land of darkness. When a child is born, the birth shirt is buried—not because it is trash, but because it must be saved and available for the soul to retrieve at death. In this "shirt," the third soul can make its way to the land of darkness and eventually be reborn. In this way the burial of the placenta is a ritual creation, representing the individual's birth, death, and rebirth, and the buried placenta is the transitional object around which the liminal states of birth, death, and rebirth revolve.

In their creation of the child's body, women clothe the soul in a physical garment for its sojourn in the land of light, even as they provide the spiritual garment—the birth/rebirth shirt—for the journey to the land of darkness and back again. The bride-price is for both sets of clothing, or both journeys. That Hmong say the bride-price is for "the shirt" instead of for "children" is a clue, or perhaps a stipulation, that this exchange is about rebirth as well. Men guide the soul, and women clothe it, even after death.

FLOWER CLOTH AND IDENTITY

In theory, the bride-price payment ties a woman to her husband and his lineage for her lifetime, and includes the rights to her labor, sexuality, children (especially male children), and the goods that she brings. Chief among these goods are the pieces of clothing (bags, belts, *sev*, shirts, and skirts) that are richly embroidered with geometric designs and stylized depictions of the natural world—her flower cloth.

A girl's flower cloth belongs to her parents because they give her the time to sew, and her needlework is an important part of the "things that go with women at marriage." Although flower cloth was not traditionally sold in the marketplace, it often is today, which gives women some economic advantage. But the worth of flower cloth goes beyond its monetary value.

To protect against soul theft, flower cloth decorates the clothes of those in vulnerable situations. The embroidery on a baby's flowerlike hat deflects the interest of wild spirits and protects the growing infant. Crosses embroidered on shirts guard children, the sick, and those who travel through the forests from wild spirits.

Flower cloth can attract as well as protect. The flower cloth that decorates the New Year's clothing—especially the special *sev* that may take a year to embroider—attracts young men and women to each other. It shows off a young woman's skill with the needle as well as her other charms, and, in the case of a young man, the beauty of the flower cloth that decorates his clothing shows how highly his mother and sisters value him. The sumptuousness of the flower cloth that everyone wears at New Year also attracts good fortune.

All ceremonial clothing is decorated lavishly with flower cloth, not just at New Year, but whenever a person is assuming a new social identity. A bride and groom wear flower cloth, and so does a corpse. In this sense, flower cloth defines one's identity, heralding a new state of being, and is spiritual clothing, mirroring the state of the soul. But even work clothes are decorated with some bit of flower cloth, attached as a collar or pocket, for instance, and it is a marker of identity here, as well.

First, flower cloth defines the woman who made it as a good Hmong if she is a skilled needlewoman, or a bad one if she is unskilled, who "should not be called a woman." Flower cloth also defines the Hmong wearing it by clan and subgroup, signifying who this Hmong is, where he or she belongs in the world. Hmong have been categorized and named based on the how their women decorate clothing—the Green Mong use batik, the White Hmong used to wear white skirts, and so on. For the Hmong themselves, clan and subgroup are important in tracing kinship relations in the larger world. When two Hmong meet, their first question is, "What Hmong are you?" This alerts them to whom they can and cannot marry, but also, once they have found a clan or blood tie, they can refer to and treat each other as kin.

Finally, flower cloth defines where the soul belongs at death, broadcasting the soul's identity in the land of darkness. The corpse is dressed in fine new clothes thickly decorated with flower cloth that has been made and set aside for just this purpose. If all "goes well," mothers and grandmothers die before their children and will be waiting in the village of the ancestors. Seeing the flower cloth they once embroidered makes it possible for the ancestors who had been women in life to recognize and welcome another soul from their lineage.

SPIRITUALITY, FUNERAL RITUALS, AND THE LAND OF DARKNESS

As shamans or herbalists, women are in direct contact with the spiritual realm; they have their own helping spirits and the power of healing. But in their role as women in their fathers' and then their husbands' houses, it seems at first glance that women have no spiritual role in Hmong life. Men perform all the rituals concerning the ancestors, including calling the soul into the body of the newborn at birth and guiding the souls to the grave and the land of darkness at death. But although men bridge the two worlds through the use of sound— chanting, the music of the reed pipes, and percussion— women do so through their bodies and the skill in their hands, and through their mourning songs.

As we have seen, the bride-price is for the "shirt," the soul's spiritual clothing—and its ability to be reborn—as well as for its physical vessel, the body of a child. The flower cloth that women make, like the birth/rebirth shirt, is another form of clothing that is spiritual as well as physical, in that it protects and defines the wearer and can be worn by the soul when the body has died.

Although Hmong women are excluded from participation in most of the highly valued rituals pertaining to contact with the realm of the ancestors, as sisters they can establish decrees for their natal lineage, even when they have left it, and they *must* be on hand at their brother's funeral, which argues a high degree of spiritual authority, although in a limited arena. As well, women keen at death. Their tears and funeral songs are an essential part of the funeral; they *must* keen, and for some while. (As we have seen, men keen also, but much less; the primary responsibility for keening, as for guarding the body, falls on women.) Men from the lineage greet the soul at birth, but women tied to the dead person by blood and friendship as well as lineage bid the soul farewell at death (and, as part of the ancestral mass, may be the first to greet the soul in the land of darkness).

During the dangerously liminal states of birth and death, when souls are in transit between the worlds, women watch over the body. For the three days before the naming and soul-calling, a woman lies next to the fire holding her newborn child; for the nine days and nights before burial, women guard the body of the newly dead. This seems to argue a profound spiritual power, or strength, although Hmong themselves make little of it.

As wives, women become part of the ancestral pair after death, when their second soul joins with their spouse's to become a single dyadic spirit. Thus the second soul of a woman is revered in death as equal to that of her husband, whereas the third soul, or returning vital soul, ideally switches gender at each incarnation, becoming alternately male or female from lifetime to lifetime. Thus the patriline is continued by the souls of those who have been female, and came from outside the lineage. In the land of darkness, the souls of women and men are of equal status, and gender is a garment that is changed from one life to the next.

To be a good Hmong woman in the land of light, one must work hard in the fields, feed the pigs, cook food, create exquisite embroidery, marry, bear many children in silence, keen over the dead, and guard the body before burial. The reward is equality in the land of the ancestors and the opportunity to be reborn in the body of a man in the next incarnation. If anthropologists limit their analyses solely to what they themselves see rather than to what the informants see, they will conclude that the Hmong patriline is carried on by males. If Hmong perceptions are attended to, they will see that the patriline is continued by women as well.

POWER VS. STATUS

As we have seen, in these arenas—reproduction, sexual freedom during courtship, the role of the sister, protest within marriage, divorce, bride-price, flower cloth, funeral rites, and cosmological beliefs—Hmong women do have power and even some freedom in an otherwise male-dominated society. But power does not always translate into status, and even when it does, a wife's status will be less than her husband's until both are dead. Although women's power seems, in some instances, to be very great, it is only in the land of darkness—as souls—that their status is equal to men's.

As I hope this book has shown, Hmong women have ways of working around this lack of status. In a very strictly gender-stratified culture such as that of the Hmong, the ways are few but the means are there. Some—such as the power of fertility and the acknowledged power in the role of the sister—are codified into the tradition, and others are carved out on an individual basis.

A woman with an abusive husband may wail to the neighbors or the household until someone intercedes on her behalf; she may attempt to kill herself; or she may fight back, run away, divorce, and remarry, if she is willing to leave her sons behind. A woman who cannot have children may still gain respect as an herbalist, a shaman, or a midwife; or, if her husband can afford it, she may encourage him to take a second wife, in the hopes that the second wife will have sons who will call her "mother" and feed her when she is an ancestor in the land of darkness.

Within the context of an exogamous, patrilineal family structure, women's behavior has been severely circumscribed, but as traditional codes of conduct weaken, prohibitions on women's behavior—regarding their ability to travel to markets and cities, to make their own money, to become educated, to use birth control, to attend public meetings, and so on—are also beginning to weaken, however gradually. As Hmong women encounter and absorb Western freedoms, they, like Western women, both benefit and suffer from the changes brought about as traditional protections are discarded or lost and new freedoms are obtained.

EPILOGUE: HIV/AIDS

AND THE HMONG IN THAILAND

For over a century the Hmong have lived in the northern mountains of Thailand, on the periphery of the dominant Thai political and economic sectors in the lowlands. Although they have never been completely isolated, in the 1950s the Hmong, like other highlanders, experienced the incursion of various outside influences—including pressure to integrate with the Thai state, and Thai as well as global pressure to cease opium poppy cultivation—that have necessitated changes in traditional patterns of Hmong livelihood. Hmong also have experienced considerable social ostracism in Thai society, where hill tribes—and especially Hmong—are viewed as insurgents, drug producers and smugglers, destroyers of the environment through slash-and-burn agriculture, and illegal immigrants. The Thai majority regard Hmong as backward and unhygienic (Kammerer 1994b:12).

Along with economic upheaval, Hmong cultural traditions are undergoing rapid changes. As a history of geographic marginalization intersects with increasing contact with contemporary culture in the form of Western media, highland tourism, and Hmong migration to the cities in search of seasonal labor, Hmong have lost some of their cultural autonomy. This in turn has led some people to intravenous heroin and amphetamine use (as opposed to smoking opium), consumption of alcohol in other than ritual contexts, and visits to the brothels in valley towns, all of which increased their vulnerability to HIV/AIDS as the epidemic exploded in Thailand. As a disempowered minority group, Hmong are placed at further risk because of their poverty, economic degradation, and social marginalization, and Hmong women even more so because of gender stratification and the culturally sanctioned sexual behavior of Hmong men. Yet even while their culture places women at risk, the loss of cultural autonomy has eroded women's traditional protections and prohibitions. Any evaluation of Hmong women's vulnerability to HIV/AIDS has to consider these various contradictory aspects of their lives.

GENDER STRATIFICATION

As Christopher Elias and Lori Heise have shown, women (other than sex workers) are often overlooked as a high-risk population and do not believe themselves to be at risk because they do not engage in high-risk behaviors, yet they are placed at risk by partners/husbands who engage in unprotected sex with prostitutes, who have had clandestine homosexual encounters (homosexuality is not even considered a possibility for a Hmong, probably because of the Hmong ideal of complementary opposites), or who have used intravenous drugs (Elias and Heise 1993:17). As compared with other hill tribe women, Hmong women's participation in the commercial sex industry is relatively low, although their numbers are increasing. Because prostitution has been identified as "the most important risk for the acquisition of AIDS" (Beyrer 1998:19), Hmong women are currently protected by various aspects of their culture. The relative wealth of the Hmong also may explain in part their ability to resist offers of this kind of employment for their daughters. Other factors may include certain aspects of traditional Hmong culture, such as bride-price, gender stratification, cosmological beliefs about reincarnation, and social control through the mechanisms of "shame," "name," and "blame."

But although women may be protected from AIDS by certain traditional values and social structures of Hmong society, including those that limit their freedom to travel to cities (where they might be tempted to enter the sex trade), they are also disempowered and placed at risk by cultural norms that include polygamy (which includes unprotected sex as well as sometimes multiple partners during the New Year's celebration), early marriage/intercourse (sexual activity before genital maturation has been shown to increase risk)(Elias and Heise 1993:15), and unprotected sex within marriage. Hmong codes of conduct (Symonds 1998:24) punish transgressive behaviors by women (e.g., engaging in prostitution, leaving a marriage, and so on) more harshly than they punish men, and women who acquire HIV/AIDS experience a dual stigma for both sexual transgression and contagion. So severe is the social stigma that in several cases, suicide has resulted (see chap. 4).

Hmong women's culturally encouraged deference to authority, especially male authority, and obedience to social codes must also be taken into consideration, especially as it intersects with their relative powerlessness to dissuade their husbands from engaging in unprotected sex with prostitutes, to persuade their husbands to use condoms, to refuse sexual intercourse with husbands who may have been exposed to an STD or the HIV virus, or to divorce husbands who will not comply.

Although Lisu (another minority group in Thailand) wives reportedly have refused sex with husbands who have contracted STDs, even to the point of leaving these men, in the more patriarchal culture of the Hmong, instances of female protest are rare, and instances of successful protest even more so (Kammerer et al. 1995:12). Hmong codes of "shyness" may prevent Hmong women from even speaking to their husbands about the use of condoms or the dangers of visiting prostitutes. As a result, their ability to protect their sexual health is severely impaired.

Because Hmong women's social power is contingent upon their ability to conceive, the adoption of safer sex practices within marriage is not easily negotiated. The use of barrier methods such as condoms, for example, is met with resistance for many reasons, among them that the Thai government and missionaries have tended to emphasize population control over STD protection, and have neglected to inform women about and teach them how to use barrier methods such as condoms or diaphragms. Other reasons include the Hmong desire for large families—for children to till the fields, carry on the patriline, care for the ancestors, and provide bodies for the ancestors' souls to be reborn into.

Gender stratification is also implicated in Hmong women's inability to participate in public discourse or to understand the information conveyed by the media, because of their lack of education in the Thai language. When women and men in Flower Village were questioned about the cause of AIDS, only twenty-five of the fifty-five women had heard of AIDS, and none knew about HIV, whereas forty-three of the forty-seven men and *all* of the local schoolchildren had heard of the disease. Until our Hmong-language AIDS Education Project was well underway in 1994, many women expressed complete indifference to it, as if AIDS affected men only (Symonds 1998:18).

EDUCATION AND NATURAL PATHWAYS OF KNOWLEDGE ABOUT SEX

As a decade of research has shown, education that uses natural pathways[1] to teach about the spread of HIV/AIDS is crucial to the control of the AIDS epidemic, and finding ways to facilitate woman-controlled prevention is a vital subset of that effort. The very idea of woman-controlled prevention is problematic among the hill tribes of northern Thailand. A long history of family planning by the Royal Thai government and missionary groups did little to encourage female empowerment in this arena, and a great deal of cultural work has yet to be done so that Hmong women will be willing and able to negotiate safer sex and use female-controlled methods such as microbicides when they become available.[2]

Education about HIV/AIDS requires that Hmong and other hill tribes' views of sexuality be understood so that culturally appropriate channels of information and culturally sensitive information can be transmitted. As in most cultures, ideas about sexuality are contradictory and complex, but Hmong "shyness" (both male and female) creates even greater reluctance to discuss such matters. This work of identifying cultural and linguistic obstacles could have been begun by the Thai state and others in the early years of their family planning efforts—but it was not.

Here again, women's lack of voice or place in the public arena means that they are not always well educated about social issues such as HIV/AIDS prevention. Gossip and folk wisdom often substitute for scientifically accurate information and lead to misconceptions such as that AIDS affects only men and can be contracted only from prostitutes, that it can be contracted from breathing the same air as an infected person or from sleeping in the same bed, that pigs have been deliberately infected with the HIV virus, and so on.

Sexual information is usually transmitted in the form of jokes, gossip, and anecdotes, so it is important that official channels of HIV/AIDS prevention information be as similar as possible to informal channels, or natural pathways of knowledge, rather than in Western forms such as public service announcements or formal, public, mixed-gender meetings. Women do not usually discuss sexual activity in mixed groups, so it is important that this information be exchanged in culturally appropriate ways, from woman to woman and from elder to younger, whenever possible. (In some instances, however, Hmong were surprisingly receptive to mixed-gender meetings; see below.)

FAMILY PLANNING

Hmong men's resistance to the use of condoms with their wives/partners appears to be related to Hmong pronatalism and the various cosmological and cultural issues attached to fertility, although some inroads have been made by family planning programs over the years. Cornelia Kammerer and others have outlined many of the complex issues that attach to hill-tribe condom use, such as its associations with prostitution in Thai culture (Kammerer 1994:7) and the history of family planning efforts that emphasized population control at the expense of STD protection. Throughout the world, negotiation of the desire to conceive and to secure protection from STDs has proved a complicated issue, one that is not always handled sensitively by governmental and other agencies, whose perspective may be skewed by the urgency of the AIDS epidemic or focused on their own priorities.

The symbolic association of condoms with sex workers is not, of course, confined to Thai culture. As Christopher Elias and Lori Heise have noted, the use of condoms is historically an "emotionally loaded" issue in which a woman's request that her partner use protection may be interpreted as a desire to be promiscuous or as evidence that she mistrusts his faithfulness, either of which can place a woman at risk for physical violence (Elias and Heise 1993:27–32). Thus, although women may influence men to use condoms, women do not control the use of condoms, and the distinction is an important one (Elias and Heise 1993:26). The Thai government's tendency, before the onset of HIV/AIDS, to prioritize "effective" birth control over and against protection from STDs also has influenced Hmong attitudes toward birth control, as evidenced by the choices made by Hmong women who, like other women in developing countries, have been strongly encouraged to use methods such as sterilization, the pill, Depo-Provera™, and Norplant™—without condoms. Here too, Hmong ethnoepidemiology comes into play because STDs/AIDS are viewed as "outside" diseases, meaning outside the Hmong scope of expertise because of their origin outside of Hmong territory/culture/ethnic group (see Kammerer et al. 1995:7). Hmong experience some difficulty constructing a cultural response to the disease, and many fears and much confusion attach to it (Symonds 1998:37), even though traditional Hmong views have evolved to accommodate new diseases, and Hmong have included Western biomedicine in their repertoire of treatment.

Historically, Thai family planning methods have not encouraged the use of barrier methods because they require a greater degree of agency on the part of women, which is considered too difficult and time-consuming to secure. This desire to bypass women's agency with so-called female-centered methods (Elias and Heise 1993:12) and "selective application of the culture concept" has been well documented (Kammerer 1994:8), but it has finally reached an impasse now that the connection between a medical history of STDs and enhanced risk of HIV/AIDS infection has been established. The question of women's agency is critical to the issue of HIV/AIDS prevention. We now know that if women's social, sexual, and economic empowerment continue to be neglected, the spread of AIDS will go on unimpeded. This makes the cost of excluding women very high.

In Hmong culture, as in many other patriarchal cultures, a double standard that gives men sexual license and restricts women's knowledge and power has created dangerous social conditions, ripe for the spread of the AIDS virus through heterosexual contact. The close association of women's sexuality with maternity and the corresponding practice of outreaching women through natal clinics and/or midwives means that, with the exception of sex workers, unmarried women and childless married women have never been targeted for sex education. Similarly, male-centered contraception was never given priority, leaving women solely responsible for contraception through the so-called woman-centered methods (Kammerer 1994:12).

THE AIDS EDUCATION PROJECT, 1993–95

During my initial stay in 1987–88, there were no known instances of HIV/AIDS in Flower Village. By 1991, when I returned to Thailand, the disease had become a major problem in the country, and highland dwellers had become infected. To make matters worse, most of the health education and prevention advice was in Thai, a language many hill dwellers did not speak or understand. The posters in the village health clinics were equally useless, since many Hmong were not literate in any language. In one village, Hmong assumed that since the posters were in Thai, only Thai or people who interacted with Thai could contract the disease.

In 1993, along with anthropologists Cornelia Kammerer and Otome Klein Hutheesing, and sociologist Ralana Maneeprasert, who had conducted research on the Akha, Lisu, and Green Mong respectively, I returned to Thailand to conduct research on the hill dwellers' knowledge of HIV/AIDS and on issues related to gender and sexuality. We spent three months in the summer of 1993 in the villages, focusing on four related topics: ideas about the body and sexuality, and actual sexual practices; vectors of potential transmission; the extent and depth of understanding about HIV/AIDS; and indigenous social structures and ideational factors influencing this understanding.

I was able to obtain research funds to hire two Hmong research assistants: Mee Moua, a graduate student at the University of Texas, and May Kao Yang, an undergraduate at Brown University. Although Hmong were patient with me and willing to answer my questions, these two assistants were better able to frame the questions in a culturally acceptable way; they were a great asset to the project. (As Laotian Hmong who had migrated to the United States when quite young, they also were surprised at the way Hmong villagers lived.)

In 1994–95 I continued the work begun in 1993, this time with Dr. Vichai Poshyachinda and his assistant Usanee Pengparn, who had accomplished a great deal in Hmong healthcare—particularly relating to drug use and rehabilitation—and who ran a health clinic in a Hmong village in the mountains. Together we hired and trained young educated Hmong to go into the mountain villages to teach people how to prevent HIV infection.

The main aims of these research projects were to gain data and insights; to use these insights and, working in collaboration with Hmong assistants, to develop prevention education and materials that would be culturally and linguistically appropriate; to use these educational materials and methods in the villages; and to test the effectiveness of our efforts.

The process of teaching Hmong—especially Hmong women—to negotiate HIV/AIDS prophylaxis was complicated by sociocultural issues such as

- Hmong women's monolingualism and lack of formal education
- Women's social powerlessness to investigate or demand the use of condoms or other means of protection from infection due to cultural norms that discourage women from behaving assertively in the sexual arena; and the cultural acceptability of polygamy, early intercourse, and the sexual partnering at New Year, which increase the risk of contracting HIV/AIDS
- The conceptual difficulty of understanding biomedical concepts of latency, transmission, or causation; as well as difficulty recognizing symptoms, especially when the appearance of good health is present (Symonds 1998:17)
- Cultural identification of female sex workers rather than male partners as "disease vectors" (Kammerer 1994:11)

Recognizing that the HIV/AIDS epidemic among the Hmong was already underway and that education must encompass not only prevention but care, I began by investigating local responses to those individuals known to be HIV seropositive, and examining Hmong interactions with health care providers and institutions. In 1994, using what I had learned in 1993, it seemed to me that any prevention education must be sensitive to social and cultural issues and that it was imperative that the Hmong language, instead of Thai, be used in the educational process.

With a committee of six Hmong (three men and three women), we interviewed educated Hmong who were interested in spending time in northern villages. We chose six people—three teams consisting of a woman and a man each—and then Dr. Poshyachinda and I trained them. The teams spent about a month in each village, which were in several different provinces. I also visited villages with members of the committee. We showed a home video about Hmong families and marriages in the United States, and although it was not specifically about HIV/AIDS, it did address some issues concerning sexuality. The video never failed to draw a crowd, even though such gatherings are unusual outside of clan gatherings or New Year celebrations. The villagers invariably were interested in seeing how Hmong fared in other parts of the world.

Once we had attracted a crowd, we could invite people to an education session afterward, where we used flip charts as visual aids to explain HIV/AIDS to people who were not literate in any language (usually this was older women, as women in their twenties had been to the Thai schools in the villages; however, even literate Hmong were interested in the flip charts) and handed out condoms. Many people understood that condoms could protect them from AIDS, but Hmong were shy about asking for them. The women team leaders gave them surreptitiously to the village women, who hid them in the belts of their *sev*. Of course there was no way to evaluate how many of these condoms were used for protection and in what circumstances. Unfortunately, microbicides are not clinically ready for use, nor would they be accepted culturally in some circumstances. A great deal of international research is being conducted on their projected use; in my opinion, the sooner they can be used, the better.

Sometimes we visited women more informally in their homes and spoke with them. As Hmong women don't really get together as a group, it was easier to visit them in their homes or, as the teams did, to work with them in the fields and talk with them there. When visiting homes, we often ended up speaking with whole families, men and women together. This came as a surprise; we had not thought it would be acceptable to discuss such a subject in a mixed-gender group, although our initial education sessions had been in such groups. Frequently the daughters-in-law stayed in the background while we spoke, but they were obviously listening to the discussion.

One of our problems was that our Hmong teams were educated, and therefore young, but in Hmong society authority comes from elders. Because it is not considered respectful, young people do not usually educate elders in Hmong, thus some awkwardness arose. To address this issue, we met with village leaders as well as the Hmong committee who had interviewed and hired the teams in Chiang Mai. Village leaders explained to the villagers why we were passing out this information, and they conducted a soul-calling ritual for us to ensure that the spirits would help us in our AIDS project.

Another issue that surfaced was that some clans do not want to be taught by a person from another clan; they were suspicious that this would raise the other clan's status at the expense of their own. Once again, the village leaders intervened to help us.

We also attempted to teach harm-reduction techniques with needle exchange to prevent IV drug users from sharing used needles, but this was not met with much enthusiasm or help. Since our project, however, many Hmong have tried to educate people about the risk of contracting HIV through unsterilized needles and even have attempted to get rid of the heroin problem in their villages. Also, enough people have died from HIV transmitted through needles that villagers have become aware of the risks and are more careful. But the same political and economic issues that brought about heroin use are still in effect, and change does not occur overnight.

During the planting and reaping seasons, it was particularly difficult to teach people, as they were too busy to take time out to listen, or too tired to join in the evening discussions. Early in the project I saw many children using condoms as balloons, and, as I have mentioned, many women seemed to think the disease was confined to men.

Another difficulty, and one that continues to surface and must be addressed, is how to explain that a person can be infected with HIV and show no symptoms of ill health. Since Hmong perceive disease by its symptoms— when one is really ill, one cannot get out of bed to work—they are struggling to understand how a person who appears healthy can be infected.

As well, the way the disease is transmitted remains unclear to many people. Villagers are still frightened of those with AIDS and are not comfortable visiting them. A man died of AIDS in one of the villages where we were working. Before he died, people from the village, who were distantly related to him, went to visit him and his family, but because he was sneezing and they were afraid the mucus would infect them, many of them refused to enter the house.

Some people wanted to know what a person with HIV looked like, so the teams brought Hmong with HIV into the village to speak about their experiences. Most Hmong were fearful of encountering such people and did not invite them into their homes. At one village, however, a woman whose husband had died from AIDS, and who was HIV positive herself, visited with her small daughter to speak to the people about her experiences. At the end of the meeting, a family invited her and the child into their home to eat. But afterward the family threw their guests' dishes over the mountainside into the bush.

One day I visited a village in the far north where a man had just died from AIDS. The crowd there was curious and nervous about the effects of this man's disease on others, and many contemplated the reason behind his death. How did he get AIDS? Was it because he shared needles to inject drugs? He wasn't a young man and did not go down to the valley frequently. Only the man's immediate family, his sons and daughters-in-law and his two wives, sat inside the house where his body lay. Usually extended family, friends, and neighbors gather near the body to reminisce about the life of the dead person, to make sure all debts are paid, and then to share food together (see chap. 4). Because this man died from AIDS, visitors stood at the threshold, peered through the door, and refused to enter. They handed paper spirit money, pieces of meat, and other offerings to the family, but held cloths over their mouths and noses, and spat on the ground as they moved away from the door. When a person dies, the body can be kept at the home for as many as nine days, and the house and the air around the village become permeated with the smell of the body's corruption. People then spit to rid themselves of the "taste" of death. Yet this man had been dead for only a day. People told me they spat because they were afraid to swallow the "bug" that had killed him.

I had come to the funeral with one of my informants from Flower Village. His sister was one of the dead man's wives. He himself is an eminent shaman, and I had consulted him when planning the prevention education for HIV/AIDS. I asked him, "Why would you not enter the house of the dead man? You and I have often spoken about how one acquires HIV."

He answered quickly, saying,

Now we know how AIDS comes to a person, and we know that you and your teams are concerned with prevention of this disease, but for Hmong, knowing that a Thai woman can give one sickness, and yes, even kill one is one thing. But when buying a Thai woman for twenty baht in the valley makes a young man, or sometimes an older man, feel he has something good, how can he stop? Knowing that using the same needles as someone else can kill you is one thing. You showed us pictures of a man cleaning his syringe and needles before he passed it on to his friend or relative, but when you want white opium [heroin] and this is your chance to get it, how can you stop? You and your teams have taught us about HIV/AIDS, but touching, eating, and shitting in the same place as a sick person is still suspect for us. We are

afraid to visit people who we think have this sickness or who die of the disease that the outside has brought us. We believe what you and your teams
are teaching, but we worry much more each day whether the rice will grow,
if the land will be ours, and if our children will be healthy.

This interaction, and others, reinforced my belief in peer education and
empowerment, which are easy to talk about but difficult to encourage. That
Hmong are a disempowered minority in Thailand exacerbates their problems. But during our project, as the months went by, people began to listen and ask for information, and to take the condoms we left behind in a
basket for them. They also requested that the teams spend more than one
month in the villages. It was not a bad beginning, but it was only a beginning. The education on sexuality and efforts to control intravenous drug
use continues in Hmong villages.

For all the reasons given above, the highlanders in Thailand are extremely
vulnerable to HIV/AIDS. Although their political, economic, and minority
status need to be addressed to lessen this vulnerability, there is also a need
to identify linguistic and cultural obstacles to HIV/AIDS prevention. Only
then can prevention be taught in a culturally appropriate and culturally sensitive manner. If this cultural work is to be effective, it must involve a two-
pronged approach so that both short-term and long-term Hmong-led
strategies for women's empowerment are put into place. The prospect for
newer and safer forms of woman-centered contraception, especially through
the use of microbicides, which do not require male cooperation, will be a
bright one if and only if the cultural and institutional obstacles outlined
below can be overcome.

In the long term, it is imperative that the following be done:

Women's self-esteem must be fostered, and here the issue of agency is crucial. Women's compliance or lack of agency is often regarded as an obstacle to sweeping social changes, such as in "contraceptive failure" with barrier
methods (Kammerer 1994:12).

Women's social vulnerability must also be addressed. With sufficient economic and political empowerment, Hmong women will be able to with-
stand the pressures of social ostracism and will have the ability to support
themselves if rejected by their families for perceived transgressions, such as
seeking divorce.

Gender-specific education efforts must be undertaken. Women must be addressed in a culturally appropriate manner by other Hmong women whenever possible. Emphasis should be placed on women's sexual health and on "effectiveness" by women's own standards, not by social policy standards. As Cornelia Kammerer states, sex education should be "female-controlled as opposed to female-centered" (1994:12). Hmong women will neither use microbicides, when they become available, nor other barrier methods until they have a history of controlling their own sexual health.

"HU PLIG"

(CALLING IN THE SOUL)

HMONG TEXT

1. Hnub no yog zoo hnub tos hmo no ces tsuas yos zoo hmo Kuv hu os tus me Qig no ces kaum ob tug nyuj cab kaum ob tug nyuj kaus los seev li yees lawm qab roob es saub yees lawm qab ntsa lawm los cia li sawv tsees los rau muaj qaib muaj qe nqua li nrho ces nyob rooj vag thaiv tes hu muaj qe nyob lawm rooj loog thaiv taw toj tsuas hu me Qig no cia li sawv tsees hlo los los tau niam mus tau txiv los tau txaj tau chaw yuav los nrog lawm neej cub ua kwv tij es sawv tsees los

2. nrog lawm neej tag ua kwv luag tos cia li sawv tsees los rau tsis saub lawm yas kev tsis seev lawm yas ncua tsis saub lawm nraum toj ces tsis seev lawm nraum li pes muaj qaib muaj li qe muaj pa xyab pa li ntawv ncho li rhawv nyob rooj vag thaiv taw hu muaj qaib muaj qe muaj pa kyab pa li ntawv ncho li nrho nyob lawm rooj loog thaiv taw tos tsuas hu me Qig no ces nws kaum ob tug lawm nyuj cab kawm ob tug los lawm nyuj kaus los tau niam mus tau txiv los tau txaj tau chaw los nrog neej cub ua kwv tij es sawv tsees los nrog ncej tag ua kwv luag tos cia li sawv tsees rov hlo los rau tsis saub lawm yas kev tsis seev lawm yas ncua tsis saub nraum toj os tsis seev lawm nraum li pes tsis saub lawm qab vag mus

See chapter 3 for a complete English translation of this chant

tsib taug tsuas mua qaib muaj qe nyob lawm rooj vag rooj loog ces tsuas hu nqee
li laws tsaus hu me Qig no kaum ob tug nyuj cab kaum ob tug

3. nyuj kaus tsuas yuav los li saws rau hauv vaj es sawv tsees los rau hauv tsev es
tsuas muaj qaib muaj lis qe es ncho li nro nyob lawm rooj vag roog looj thaiv
taw tos xi lis nqia ces tsuas hu me Qig no kaum ob tus nyuj cab kaum ob tug
nyuj kaus os kaum ob tug ntsuj xyoob kaum ob tug ntsuj lis ntoo cia li sawv tsees
los txoos lis niab rau hauv vaj es sawv tsees los txoos li zaws rau hauv tsev ces
muaj qaib mus nrog tsa muaj qe mus nrog nqa tsuas muaj qaib muaj qe mus ua
daj teg kav lis ntua lau qaib ua lawm daj taws mus kav li zuag me Qig no ces nws
kaum ob tug nyuj cab kaum ob lug nyuj kaus sawv tsees los tau niam tau txiv
los tau txaj tau chaw

4. Cia li sawv tsees los rau tsis saub lawm yas kev tsis seev lawm yas ncua tsuas hu
me Qig no ces kaum ob tug nyuj cab kaum ob tug lawm nyuj kaus tsis seev lawm
kev khaub lig tsis saub lawm kev sib tshua muaj nkauj qaib mus ua daj teg tav
lis ntua os muaj lawm lau qaib mus ua daj taws roos lis nkaus es tsuas koos lis
ntua me Qig no kaum ob tug nyuj cab los tau niam tsuas ua lawm daj taw mus
kav li nkaus es me Qig no kaum ob tug nyuj kaus los tau txiv es los nyob ntseg
lij ntsheeb txoos txooj nqeeb ces los nyob ntseg li ntshua xws txooj tsuas yuav
los nyob txhiab nyeej puas pes vaj nyeej txhiab pov los nyob xeeb luag txwj xeeb
luag laus ua cia li sawv tsees los rau

5. Hnub no tsuas zoo hnub os hmo no ces tsuas yog zoo hmo hu os hnub no yog
zoo hnub rais hmo no ces tsuas yog zoo hmo rov os tsuas hu me Qig no kaum
ob tug lawm nyuj cab kaum ob lug lawm nyuj kaus seev lis yees lawm Ntxwj
Nyoog kev khaub lig seev yees lawm Ntxwj Nyoog kev sib tshuam tsuas muaj
qaib mus ua daj tes kav li ntua muaj lau qaib mus ua daj taw koos lis zus os loj
rau hauv vaj es kav lis nkaus los rau hauv tsev cia li sawv tsees los rau tsuas hu
me Qig no kaum ob tug lawm nyuj cab kaum ob tug lawm nyuj kaus seev li yees

6. lawm ntug niaj ntug tim ub os seev lis yees lawm ntug niaj ntug tim ib muaj nkauj
pa xyab ncho lis tsawv ces hu os muaj lawm nkauj pa ntawv ncho lis ho thaiv tes
hu lau qaib ua daj tes mus kav lis ntau mes Qig no kaum ob tug nyuj cab ntug
niaj ntug tim ub los tau niam muaj lawm nkauj qaib ua daj taws mus koos lis
zus me Qig no ces kaum ob tug lawm nyuj kaus ntug niaj ntug tim ib qauv noj
qauv haus ntawv nyiaj ntawv xyoo los tau niam tau txiv es los tau txaj tau chaw

cia li sawv tsees los rau nkauj pa xyab soj qab taug lw mus nqa nkauj pa ntawv
soj qab taug lw mus nrog rub cia li sawv tsees los tsis saub mus lawm ntug niaj
ntug tim ub tsis seev lawm ntug niaj ntug tim i cia li sawv tsees rais lis hlo los
rau hauv tsev es sawv tsees rais hlos los rau hauv vaj es tsuas hu me Qig no nyuj
cab nyuj kaus ntsuj qaib ntsuj os ntsuj pag ntsuj nyoog es tsis seev mus lawm
ntug niaj ntug tim ub tsis seev lawm ntug niaj ntug tim i cia li sawv tsees los tsis
saub lawm kev ywj huab los mus ywj cua tsis seev mus

7. lawm kev ywj lag mus ywj luam cia li sawv tsees los rau coj qaib coj qe ncho li
tsawv nyob rooj vag hu tsis tseg cia li sawv tsees los rau hauv tsev es coj qaib coj
qe ntshu lis nrho ces nyob rooj vag rooj loog thaiv taw hu tsis so os me Qig no
ces kaum ob tug lawm nyuj cab kaum ob tug lawm nyuj kaus sawv tsees los rais
lis hlo los rau hauv vaj es sawv tsees rais hlo los rau hauv tsev es los tau niam tau
txiv los tau txaj tau hauv yuav los tau cub mus tau taws los nrog neej cub mus
ua kwv tij es nrog lawm neej tawg ua kwv luag yuav los nyob ntseg lis ntsheeb
xws txooj nqeeb los nyob ntseg lis ntshua xws lawm txooj tsuas sawv tsees los
nyob ntshiab lis dej huv lis txhuv los nyob txhiab nyeej puam pem vaj nyeej mus
txhiab pov los nyob xeeb luag txwj xeeb luag laus ua cia li sawv tsees los rau nkauj
qaib ces ua daj teg mus tav lis ntua nraug qaib ces ua daj taws mus kav lis zog
Qig no kaum ob tug nyuj cab kaum ob tug nyuj kaus os ntug niaj ntug tim ub
ntug niaj ntug tim i los rau haus vaj los rau haus tsev los tau niam tau txiv los
tau txaj tau chaw los nrog neej cub es ua kwv tij los nrog neej tag ua kwv luag
tsis seev lawm yas kev mus yas ncua tsis saub nraum toj nraum pes

8. tsis seev lawm qab vag mus tsib taug cia li sawv tsees los rau tsis seev lawm taw
vaj tsis seev lawm taw loog cia li sawv tsees los niam txiv txhiaj meej pem yim
xeeb ces qhib rooj vag rooj loog qhib kom zoo niam txiv txhiaj meej pem xeeb
rooj vaj rooj loog qhib dav ces yaj los rau hauv tsev es niam txiv txhiaj fab civ
feem ces qhib rooj vag rooj ces yaj kuam qhib kev lug los rau hauv yuav pov lis
nkaus me Qig no kaum ob ob tug nyuj kaus los rau hauv tsev ces lug los tsuas
muaj qaib muaj qe nyob rooj vag rooj loog hu tsis tseg cia li sawv tsees los niam
txiv txhiaj meej pem xeeb qhib rooj vag rooj loog qhib kab yaj kuam qhib kev
lis lug los rau hauv tsev es tsis saub nraum rooj tsuas hu me Qig no nyuj cab
nyuj kaus tsis seev nraum ntsa yaj kuam qhib kev li lug los rau hauv tsev ces

9. yeeb kuam li yuav pov li nkau los rau hauv vaj es yaj kuam qhib kev lug los ces
yeeb kuam pov li nkaus nkauj qaib ua daj teg mus kav nraug qaib ua daj taw mus

191

koos kav lis ntau me Qig no kaum ob tug nyuj cab kaum ob tug lawm nyuj kaus
tsuas ua daj teg daj taw mus koos ces yaj kuam qhib kev lug los yeeb kuam pov
li nkaus los rau hauv tsev los tau niam tau txiv los tau tij tau viv los tau txaj tau
chaw(hais lus) los os me Qig no kaum ob tug nyuj cab kaum ob tug nyuj kaus
plig nyiaj plig kub plig niam plig txiv ua daj teg mus kav li ntua ua daj taw mus
kas lis nkaus roos li nkaus os mus khiv nws kaum ob tug nyuj cab kaum ob tug
nyuj kaus los tau niam los mis tau txiv los tau txaj los tau chaw, los tau cub los
tau tawg los nrog neej cub ua kwv tij los nrog ncej tawg ua kwv luag os neb ua
daj teg mus kav lis kaus daj taw mus kav lis nkaus mas tseev kom ncauj nplaig
nkhaus lis nkoos tuajnruab nrog os oh taub hau dawb li paug kaj lis liag huv li
si txhav tau plaub txub plaub sib luag ne

"SHOWING THE WAY"

(QHUAB KEV)

ENGLISH TRANSLATION

1. From here on,
   It is the Showing the Way chant—Qhuab Kev.
   It is about the Hmong traditional custom.
   When there is a dead person,
   An elder [usually an old man who knows how to chant and another who
      knows how to play the reed pipes] would be asked to come and do the
      chant.
   It is a chant that will send away the dead person
   So that the dead will go to meet his/her grandparents
   So that he/she will arrive at the world of the dead.

2. It seems like the world is turning
   And the light is breaking through every valley.
   The sky is created to last.
   The human body of Tub Nraug Laj is created to stay.
   There is light on earth.
   The sky is created to stay.
   The human body will be created.

3. It seems like you are truly dead.

   The body is lying down.

   Is it truly dead or are you just pretending?

   If you are just pretending,

   Then get up to chase the chickens and pigs around the house.

   If you are truly dead,

   Then turn your ears to listen.

   Txawj Nkiag [the chanter] will chant the death song for you to hear.

4. You dress up and go until you reach the slope.

   The elder looks and sees that it is you.

   You dress up and go until you arrive over there.

   The younger looks and sees that it is like you.

   Now that you are truly dead,

   Turn your ears to listen.

   Close your eyes,

   And Txawj Nkiag will sing a death song for you to hear.

   [End of one level]

5. So, long time ago,

   Where did the earth spring from?

   It sprang from Ntxwj Nyoog's rocky garden.

   Where did the root of the earth spring from?

   It sprang from Ntxwj Nyoog's garden.

6. Who sees where the water of the water root is?

   It is the old Chinese woman [or foreigner] who sees where
      the water is.

   It is the old Chinese woman who sees the house.

   Which couple sees where the house of the water root is?

   Now the Chinese woman pours a bowl of water into the pan.

   The water is boiling.

7. Then pour a bowl of water into the metal pan.

   The pan is boiling, and the cold water is warming.

   In the forest it will be the water to wash the dead son's face.

   Mix the cold water with the warm water.

Wash the face of the dead son.
Wipe out the water from the face and head down to earth,
So that your brothers and sisters will see you clearly.

8. Now is a good time to mix the cold water with the warm water.
Wash the dead son's face.
Wipe out the water from the face and head, down to the plain.
Your brothers and sisters will truly see you.
[End of one level]

9. Here, we will give you water so you can wash.
We will send you to meet your grandmother and grandfather.
It is like using the original water [*dej ntxheb*] to wash the dead son's
     face clear.

10. Heading back to earth,
After washing the dead son's face.
The dead son will ride a horse to Lwm Yeeb [the world of the dead].
It is like the dead son's face is clear
And heading down to the plain.
It is as if now the dead son will ride a horse
Back to Yeeb Nrag [the land of the dead].

11. It is like at this moment
Long time ago.
There Txawj Nkiag had arrived.
The dead son had dropped in.
There was yeast for making wine [*poov xab*].
Wine [*poov cawv*] was not available.
Then there was a question:
Where is the yeast for making wine?

12. It was answered:
The yeast was at the foot of Ntxwj Nyoog's cliff.
There was a question:
Where was the wine?
It is like Nkauj Iab and Nraug Oo's saying

That the wine was at the foot of Ntxwj Nyoog's cliff.

They took the yeast in.

13. Now, let Nkauj Li Kwm go and take the yeast from Ntwxj Nyoog's cliff

And take the wine from the foot of his cliff.

Now Nkauj Mim goes to take back the wine from the foot of his cliff.

14. Place the yeast on the bamboo tray for one day and two mornings.

Then the wine will be tasty, as good as honey [*zib ntab*].

It will be the wine that shows the way for the dead son.

It is like taking the yeast

And spreading it on the bamboo mat.

One day, two mornings.

The wine will be tasty, as good as honey [*zib mes*].

It will be the wine showing the path for the dead son.

[End of one level]

15. Now Txawj Nkiag has come down.

The brave son has arrived and will place the yeast over there.

It will be the wine pointing the way for the dead son.

He will place the yeast at the cliff.

It will be the wine for the dead son.

16. Now using the yeast to be the principle [*txuj*, principle or way of doing things],

Now using the yeast to be the method,

A long time ago the yeast became wine,

Showing the way for the dead son to meet his ancestors.

[End of one level]

17. Take three cups of wine for you to drink.

Then you will be taken to meet your ancestors,

Now that Txawj Nkiag has come down

And the brave son has arrived.

There is no hemp seed.

18. Then there was a question asked:
    Where was the hemp seed?
    Where would the hemp seed be available?
    A long time ago, the dragon [zaj] made the sun shine for three months.
    The dragon blew [the wind] for three months.
    The hemp seeds here on earth were all dead.

19. Now here is the answer:
    There were hemp seeds at Ntxwj Nyoog's rocky mountain,
    And hemp seeds were available at his cliff.
    There was no servant.
    It was Nkauj Iab and Nraug Oo who sent
    Niam Kag and Nkauj Quag to bring back hemp seeds
    From Ntxwj Nyoog's cliff.

20. Having brought back the hemp seeds,
    They spread the seeds on the earth for a thirty days.
    In thirty days the hemp seeds would be sprouting all over the field,
    Spreading the hemp seeds over the valley,
    And they would be shooting up all over the valley.

21. Now it is one moon, thirty days.
    Nkauj Iab and Nraug Oo took a basket and went to cut some hemp.
    Use one hank of hemp to make clothing for the dead son to wear
        [wrap].
    Use three hanks of hemp to make a pair of shoes for the dead son
        to use
    When he steps on Ntxwj Nyoog's green caterpillar mountain.
    No braiding on the heel.
    Give them to the dead son to use when stepping on Ntxwj Nyoog's
        caterpillar mountain.

22. Now use the hemp seeds to make clothing for you to wrap around
        your body.
    You have a new outfit when you arrive at the mountain slope.
    Use the hemp seeds to make clothing to wrap around you
    When you are going to meet your grandmother.

23. Wrap one hank [of hemp] around the dead son.
    The dead son puts on a new outfit and arrives over the deep
        valley.
    Use the hemp seeds to wrap the dead son
    When he is heading to meet his partner.
    [End of one level]

24. You arrive at Ntxwj Nyoog's caterpillar mountain and cold caterpillar
        valley.
    The caterpillars are jumping, as big as deer.
    Your hand reaches out to put on your hempen shoes,
    So that you have a way to get to your ancestors.

25. You arrive at Nyxwj Nyoog's caterpillar mountain and cold caterpillar
        valley.
    The caterpillars are jumping, as big as pigs.
    Your hand reaches out to put on your hempen shoes,
    So that you have a way to get to your ancestors.

26. Now it is a hen that is crying at the foot of the mountain.
    A rooster is crowing in the valley.
    The hen is crying for seven years without a chick.
    The rooster is crowing for seven years without a chick.

27. Now the hen is crying to lay an egg.
    The hen is crying the whole day.
    In one day, lays one egg.
    In two days, lays two eggs.
    In three days, lays three eggs.
    In four days, lays four eggs.
    In five days, lays five eggs.
    In six days, lays six eggs.
    In seven days, lays seven eggs.
    In eight days, lays eight eggs.
    In nine days, lays nine eggs.
    In ten days, lays ten eggs.

28. In one complete cycle of thirteen days, lays thirteen eggs.
    Now the hen is crying to cover her eggs.
    The hen covers her eggs for a month, thirty days.
    Then the eggs are hatched
    And there are only three chicks.
    The chicks are crying behind the house.
    An eagle is soaring with a cruel heart.
    The eagle is soaring down to snatch away one chick.

29. The hen leads her chicks
    Crying and scratching for insects or worms at the front of the house.
    It is the cold-hearted wildcat
    That comes and carries away another chick.
    Now there is only one chick left.
    The chick is growing into a full-size chicken.
    The chicken is causing trouble on the house platform.
    The elders and youngsters are cursing
    That it is the dead son's chicken to show the way.

30. The chicken is growing to be a full-size chicken.
    The chicken is causing trouble around the house.
    The elders and the youngsters are cursing
    That it is the dead son's chicken to point to the path.
    Now we will let the rooster change form to be your chicken.
    If the red chicken is to change form,
    It will change its feathers at the open fire.
    The chicken that is good for the dead son to use
    Is covering the bowl.

31. Now it seems as if the chicken
    Will be plucked of its feathers on the fireplace,
    And it will become a chicken to cover your plate.
    The rooster is crowing.
    The noise of the rooster's crowing
    Is reaching far back into the otherworld.
    It is the dead son's chicken to show the way.

The sound of the rooster's crowing is reaching the otherworld.

It becomes the dead son's chicken to show the way.

[End of one level]

32. We give three cups of wine for you to drink

Before giving you your chicken to show the way to the ancestors.

Now we are giving you your chicken's liver

So that you will know the way to the ancestors.

33. Eat, you eat alone.

Drink, you drink alone.

Disappear [die], you die alone.

Die, you die alone.

Though you cannot eat, pour it in your gourd.

Though you cannot drink, pour it in a bamboo container.

Though you cannot eat, endure to carry on.

Though you cannot drink, forbear to carry on.

Take them to your ancestors.

Go looking for your grandfather and his brothers

In the dead son's world.

34. Long time ago,

There was no sickness and dying on earth.

35. It was the cruel-hearted Ntxwj Nyoog

Who released illness and dying onto the earth.

So now there is illness and dying,

And you have died.

There were Chinese clothes that were very expensive.

Your brothers made one piece of cloth for you.

There were the Chinese clothes that were very expensive.

Your brothers made one piece for you.

Your brothers used one piece of Chinese cloth

To cover the dead son's mouth.

36. What lives in Ntxhiav?

It was a long time ago

That the strange birds lived to kick or scratch Ntxhiav.
Your brothers would use one piece of cloth
To cover the dead son's teeth.

37. What kind of earth are we living on today?
    A long time ago,
    There was no illness on earth.
    There was no laziness on the earth.
    It is human beings on the earth made this happen.
    It is our people on the land who wanted to die.
    Humans took in a dead tiger and made a funeral,
    As a symbol or death sign for human beings.

38. Making a funeral for a gibbon as a symbol of death,
    Using cow skin to make a drum to bang on,
    Using hemp stalks to make reed pipes to blow,
    Hitting nine times, sounding in nine tones.
    Then the sounds of the tones and the drum were vibrating.
    They reached to Ntxwj Nyoog's green world.
    Hitting nine times, sounding nine tones,
    The sound vibrated to Ntxwj Nyoog's yellow world.

39. Ntxwj Nyoog opened the sky gate and looked down to see.
    He opened the earth gate to look and see.
    It seemed that the human beings wanted to die.
    People on the land wanted to die.
    Ntxwj Nyoog sent a large green fly [mos ntsuab] to [survey/spy on]
        the earth.
    He sent a large bee [mos muv] to gather knowledge on the land.

40. When the fly and the bee returned to Ntxwj Nyoog's world
    He asked,
    "What were all those noises on the earth that reached my sky gate?"
    The fly replied, "It was the people on earth who want to die."

41. The earth people killed a tiger on the road.
    They killed a gibbon on the path.

201

They brought in the tiger
And made a funeral for it as a symbol of crying.
They brought in a gibbon
And made a funeral for it as a sign of wailing.
Using the cow skin to make a drum to hit,
Using the hemp stalks to make reed pipes to blow.

42. Hitting the drum nine times, sounding nine tones.
    That is why the sound is shaking Ntxwj Nyoog's garden
    And reaching Ntxwj Nyoog's sky gate.
    Hitting nine times, sounding nine tones.
    That is why the sound is reaching Ntxwj Nyoog's sky garden.

43. Ntxwj Nyoog released the seed of sickness down to earth.
    Now the seed of dying has been planted on the land.
    For seven years, Ntxwj Nyoog released the seed of sickness down to earth.
    The earth has been silent ever since.
    Ntxwj Nyoog released the seed of death unto the land for seven years.
    The land had then been silenced.

44. Ntxwj Nyoog opened the sky gate to look,
    Opened the earth gate to see.
    There the sickness seeds of Ntxwj Nyoog
    Were hanging in the middle of the sky,
    And the seeds of death were not reaching to earth.
    Ntxwj Nyoog took his copper scissors
    To cut the string that held the seeds of sickness,
    Using the metal scissors to cut the string
    And send the seeds of death down to earth.

45. The seeds of sickness were hanging on a hemp branch.
    The seeds of death were hanging on a tree branch.
    While people were farming,
    They picked up the seeds of sickness and of death.
    When they picked them up,
    They stuck the evil seeds in their pockets [ngaws tiab].

46. Unlike other people, Tub Nraug Laj,
    You did not know how to pick up the seeds.
    When picking them up,
    You stuck them in your liver.
    As for other people,
    They knew how to pick up the evil seeds.
    When picking them up,
    They stuck them into their pockets.
    You, Tub Nraug Laj,
    Did not know how to pick them up.
    When picking them up,
    You stuck the evil seeds into your heart.

47. While you were farming,
    The evil seeds fell into your stomach.
    While you were toiling in the fields,
    The evil seeds fell into your body.
    So then the evil seeds caused you illness in your liver.

48. The fever was initiated inside your body.
    You lay down when you arrived home from farming.
    With the oncoming of your illness, you kept lying still.
    Your brothers then made a plan in the household
    And decided who would be the best shaman to heal you.
    Your brothers consulted each other at the side door
    To determine who the best shaman would be.
    Txiv Muam Mab was the expert in shamanism.
    There is a saying that Txiv Muam Mab is the shaman expert.

49. Your brothers' left hands held the incense.
    Their right hands held the paper money calling Txiv Muam Mab.
    Txiv Muam Mab said this year you came not in good time.
    He said that the striped horse will be needed.
    Txiv Muam Suav says this year, son, you do not come at a good
        time.
    Here comes Nraug Laj's horse.

50. There the older son comes back and arrives at the slope.
    There he heard that Tub Nraug Laj is wailing with Ntxwj Nyoog's sickness
       seed.
    The younger son comes back and arrives in the valley.
    There Tub Nraug Laj is moaning with Ntxwj Nyoog's sickness seed.

51. There the older son's heart is not happy.
    The younger son is not happy about it.
    The older son asks, "Who is a good shaman?
    Who is an expert in shamanism?"
    Your brother's left hand holds the incense sticks.
    His right hand holds the paper money
    And calls the shaman Txiv Muam Mab.

52. Txiv Muam Mab says that every year you do not call your relative.
    I, Txiv Muam Mab, live far away.
    This year you call me to do the shaman ritual.
    The soul of Tub Nraug Laj is lying in the coffin.
    Txiv Muam Suav says that, younger son,
    Every year you do not call the shaman.
    Txiv Muam Suav lives far away this year,
    When you call on me to do the shaman ritual.
    The soul of Tub Nraug Laj is lying in the grave.
    The heart of the older son is breaking;
    He is returning.
    The heart of the young son is breaking;
    He is returning.
    The older son is arriving at the plain.
    It is Tub Nraug Laj;
    Your sickness is aggravated.

53. You are wailing with the sickness.
    The young son arrived in the valley.
    The sickness of Tub Nraug Laj is not healed.
    You are wailing with Ntwxj Nyoog's sickness seeds,
    And you are feeling no better.
    Now the oldest son asks,

"Who is the best shaman in the world?
Who is the expert?"

54. It is Tooj Nchai Siv Yis who is the best shaman on earth.
Tooj Nchai Siv Yis is the expert.
Now your brother's left hand is holding the incense.
His right hand is holding the paper money
And calling to Tooj Nchai Siv Yis,
And he has arrived.
He has laid down his shamanic equipment.

55. He is in his trance,
And the shaman rattles are ringing and sounding on the slope.
However, this is the year that Tub Nraug Laj will disappear [die].
Tooj Nchai Siv Yis sets up his equipment and goes into his trance.
The rattles are ringing into the forest.
This is the year that Tub Nraug Laj will die with Ntxwm Nyoog's
sickness.

56. What is wrong with the world today?
What is happening?
It was a long time ago
That there was no sickness on earth and no illness on the land.

57. There was no disappearing on the earth.
Nobody died on the land.
A long time ago,
Human flesh was made of copper.
Bones were made of metal.
Nowadays flesh is made of honey and wax.
Bones are made up of the layers of the hemp plant.
It was a long time ago
That human beings had wide knowledge
And humans sold spirits for something to eat.

58. Humans had great knowledge
And used spirits to trade for something to drink.

Then humans used almost every spirit to trade
For something to eat.
There were only two spirits left
To go and ask for wisdom from Puj Saub,
To go to Puj Saub's country to ask for knowledge,
For Puj Saub to point the way,
And for Yawm Saub to teach the name.

59. Puj Saub teaches that
It is like the spirit takes away.
Puj Saub teaches words that give humans great knowledge.
Human beings fool the spirits
And take them away to sell for something to eat.
Human beings have lots of wisdom
And fool the spirits and take them away to sell for something to drink.
Now there are only two of the spirits.
So you go to Ntxwj Nyoog's mountain.

60. There, take three handfuls of Ntxwj Nyoog's ash and bran,
And descend to earth [*yab ceeb*].
Go to stay with the one who scatters the ash.
Stay close with the spirit that scatters the bran.
Now the spirits return.
They ascend to Ntxwj Nyoog's big rocky mountain.
There they pick up three handfuls of Ntxwj Nyoog's ash.
The spirits ascend to Ntxwj Nyoog's sharp rocky mountain.
There they pick up three handfuls of powdered bran.

61. The spirits came back to earth and said,
"Human beings, it was a long time ago.
You had great knowledge and you took us to sell for something to eat.
You had great wisdom and took us to sell for something to drink.
Now you come closer to us so that we can scatter ash to you.
Step close to us so we can scatter powdered bran to you."

62. The human beings said,
"You spirits, scatter your ash to us first."

The spirits said,
"Because you have greater knowledge,
You scatter your ashes first."
When the human beings scattered their ashes to the spirits,
They hid behind the front door.
Then the spirits scattered their ashes on the human beings' eyes.
So human beings' eyes are blurred,
And they can no longer see spirits.
When the human beings scattered their ashes on the spirits,
They hid behind the wall.
Then the ghosts scattered their ashes on human beings' eyes.
Human beings' eyes can no longer see ghosts.

63. Now the spirits can see human beings.
Human beings' cannot see spirits.
The spirits said to the dogs who were barking from the garden,
"Step a little closer, so we can scatter the ashes on you.
Step a little closer, so we can scatter bran.
It was a long time ago
That human beings had great knowledge and sold us for something
     to eat."

64. "It was human beings who had much wisdom
And sold us for something to drink.
The human beings fooled us here and everywhere.
They sold almost every single one of us for something to eat.
Human beings tricked every one of us spirits here and everywhere.
They traded almost every clan of us for something to drink.

65. "Now there are only two of us left.
Step a little closer so that we can scatter you with ash.
Come a little closer so that we can scatter you with bran."
The dogs said,
"Spirits, you have hands, so you scatter your ashes on us first."
The spirits said,
"If that is so, come a little closer,
So that we all can scatter ashes on one another."

207

The spirits scattered three handfuls to the dogs.
The dogs hid behind the door
So that the ash would not destroy their eyes.

66. The spirits scattered three handfuls of ash to the dogs.
The dogs hid behind the wall,
And nothing harmed their eyes.
The spirits then asked,
"Can you dogs see us anymore?"
Now the dogs are barking in the garden.
The spirits then asked,
"Why are you barking in the garden?"
The dogs answered,
"Because you took away all the human beings and stepped on them."

67. Now the dogs are barking down on earth.
The spirits asked,
"Why are you barking down on earth?"
The dogs answered,
"Because you take away our human beings and ascend to Ntwxj Nyoog's
    stony gate."

68. Now dogs can see spirits,
And spirits cannot see dogs.
Now human beings step closer
And scatter three handfuls of ashes to the spirits.
The spirits hide behind the wall.
The spirits scatter three handfuls to the human beings
And destroy their eyes.

69. It was when the human beings scattered three handfuls of ash
    to the spirits.
The spirits hid behind the door.
The spirits scattered their ash to the human beings
And destroyed their eyes.
That is why now spirits can see human beings,
And human beings can no longer see spirits.

Now the spirits trick human beings in the otherworld
And sell human beings for something to eat.
The spirits trick human beings in the otherworld
And sell human beings from every clan.

70. Now the spirits can trick human beings to walk on the upper road.
The spirits will take human beings to sell for something to eat.
Now the spirits trick human beings to walk on the lower road.
The spirits will take human beings to trade them for something
   to wear.
[End of one level]

71. It seems like the world is turning.
The light is breaking through every valley.
It was a long time ago that the world was turning
And Tub Laj, your own body was created.
Now there is light in the sky and on land.
It was a long time ago that the world was created.
Then your body was created to stay.
It was a long time ago that the dragon made the light shine
   for three months.

72. The dragon blew the wind for three months.
Here on earth, the sky dried for three years.
The land dried for seven years.
Every bamboo seed died.
All the tree seeds died.
The earth was cleared, having nothing for seven years.
The land was cleared for seven years.

73. Nkauj Iab and Nraug Oo said,
"Where could there be any bamboo seeds?
Where could there be any tree seeds?"
Nkauj Iab and Nraug Oo said,
"Ah, there are bamboo seeds at Ntxwj Nyoog's chicken
   coop.
There are tree seeds at Ntxwj Nyoog's pigsty."

74. Now there were no servants around
    Who could be sent to take the bamboo seeds.
    Which couple would go to bring back the tree seeds?

75. Nkauj Iab and Nraug Oo said,
    "Nkauj Tseeg Lis Tseev goes to bring back the bamboo seeds
    From Ntxwj Nyoog's chicken coop.
    Let Puj Tseeg Lis Tseev go to take the tree seeds
    From Ntxwj Nyoog's pigsty."

76. Puj Tseeg Lis Tseev flew away
    And met Ntxwj Nyoog's auxiliary spirits.
    They said,
    "Every other year you did not travel.

77. "So why are you going this year?"
    Puj Tseeg Lis Tseev answered,
    "Because the sun has been shining on earth for three months,
    The dragon blew the wind for seven years,
    And the field was cleared for seven years."

78. Now Nkauj Iab and Nraug Oo,
    Let me come to bring back the bamboo seeds
    From Ntxwj Nyoog's chicken coop.
    Go to take the tree seeds
    From Ntxwj Nyoog's pigsty.
    Are there any bamboo seeds?
    Are there any tree seeds left?
    Then Ntxwj Nyoog's auxiliary spirits said,
    "There is only one string of bamboo seeds left.
    Only one string of tree seeds left."

79. Puj Tseeg Lis Tseev flew to Ntxwj Nyoog's pigsty.
    There it took one string of bamboo seeds.
    It carried the seeds in its beak.
    Then it took one string of tree seeds.
    It carried it with its feet.

80. Puj Tseeg Lis Tseev flew back.
    When it arrived on earth,
    Nkauj Ia and Nraug Oo said,
    "Puj Tseeg Lis Tseev, spread the bamboo seeds
        on the mountain over there,
    And spread the tree seeds in the valley."
    Puj Tseeg Lis Tseeg flew and spread the seeds
        on the mountain
    And spread the seeds in the valley.

81. Then in thirty days,
    The bamboo seeds were sprouting.
    The tree seeds were branching.
    Three bamboo shoots came out.
    Three trees sprouted.

82. Now the bamboo shoots are fully grown.
    One of them belongs to Nas Kos [a rodent].
    One belongs to the Chinese man,
    Who takes it away to make a winnowing tray.
    When Txawj Nkiag [the chanter] arrives,
    There is only one left.
    He cuts it and makes it even at both ends.
    He splits it in the middle.

83. He splits it into two pieces.
    Txawj Nkiag uses it for your pointer [cwj]
    To show the way.
    Now the seeds are fully grown.
    One is for the rodent to cut with its teeth.
    One belongs to the Chinese.
    They cut it to make hai[?].

84. Now there is one that belongs to the Hmong.
    They cut it to make a large water storage tank.
    There is only one piece left when Txawj Nkiag arrives.
    He cuts it into four sharp angles.

211

85. He splits it into two pieces
    To be your pointer to show you the way.
    Grandmother Saub will use your pointer to teach you language.
    She will use the pointer to teach you the way.
    [End of one level]

86. Now there is light all over the earth.
    It was a long time ago that the earth was created.
    Now your body is created to live.

87. Now there is light all over the earth.
    It was a long time ago that the earth was created.
    Now your body is created to live.
    Now there is only one tree left of all the seeds.
    There are no servants to help.

88. Txawj Nkiag asked the villagers to pick up their axes.
    Three of them marched into the woods.
    They cut down one tree
    And slid it into the field.

89. They slid it down to the flat land,
    Took it to make a striped dragon horse for the dead son.
    Using one axe,
    Cut a piece of log and slid it to the field,
    Used it to make a horse [*nees txaij nees kuas eeb*].

90. For the dead son to ride into the otherworld.
    It is a striped horse for the dead son to ride.
    [End of one level]

91. Now the wise son arrives, and so does Txawj Nkiag.
    There are no seeds for domestic food crops.
    Then there was a question:
    Where will there be seeds for food?
    Where can one obtain them?

92. Txawj Nkiag answered,
    "Where are the seeds?
    The seeds are at Ntxwj Nyoog's rocky mountain.
    The seeds are available at Ntxwj Nyoog's rocky valley."

93. Who will go to collect the seeds?
    There are no servants,
    So who can we send to bring seeds
    From Ntxwj Nyoog's rocky valley?

94. Let the mouse go and collect the seeds.
    Along the way the mouse saw Ntxwj Nyoog's helpers.
    They said,
    "Where are you going?
    You have not been anywhere for a while."

95. The mouse answered,
    "I have not gone anywhere recently,
    Since there was no business to do.
    This year Txawj Nkiag and the wise men have arrived,
    And there are no seeds on earth for food.

96. "So Nkauj Iab and Nraug Oo asked me to come
    And take some crop seeds from Ntxwj Nyoog's rocky mountain."
    Ntxwj Nyoog's helpers said,
    "There is only one string of crop seeds left."

97. Then the mouse took back the string of seeds.
    All along the road the mouse spread the seeds.
    One month—thirty days—later, the crops are growing all over
        the fields.

98. They spread the seeds all over the valley.
    One month—thirty days—later, the crops fill the valley.
    In five months thirty days, the crops are fully grown.
    In five months, they are fully grown.

213

99. Now there are nine people making cups
    And eight people making plates.
    Using the crop seeds to make food offerings for the dead son.
    There are nine people making plates
    And eight people making cups.

100. Spreading the crop seeds on the slope.
    When they are ripe,
    Bringing in the crops to make food offerings for the dead son.
    Spreading the crop seeds on the mountain.
    Bring the crops in
    To offer three spoonfuls for the dead son at the deep valley,
    So that the dead son will have a way to meet with his ancestors.
    [End of one level]

101. The road guides will lead you,
    So do not be sad.
    You can take your things now and go.
    When offering food for the dead body,
    Say this to it.

102. Now the dew is dropping from the leaves.
    The hay is everywhere.
    The dew is dropping the human seeds of Ci Txuj and Tuj Nplug
    Down to the heart of the earth.

103. Now there is grass and hay all over the slope.
    It was a long time ago
    That people knew how to die and how to come back.
    Now Ci Txuj and Tuj Nplug created human beings on earth.
    They know how to die but do not know how to return.

104. Now there are falling leaves and dry hay all over the slope.
    The people on earth are dying together each day.
    Now the dew is dropping from the leaves.
    There is hay everywhere.
    The seeds of human beings are dropping on the earth.

105. A long time ago
     People knew how to die and how to return.
     Now Ci Txuj and Tuj Nplug,
     The two of them are cruel hearted.
     The falling leaves and the dry hay take away the dead people,
     And they do not return.
     Now if anybody dies,
     They pick up the road of falling leaves and dry hay.

106. Take three cups of wine for you.
     Drink it and go to see your ancestors.
     Eat all alone.
     Drink all alone.
     If you cannot eat, put it in the gourd.
     If you cannot drink, pour it in your bamboo container.
     Even if you cannot eat and drink, take it to your ancestors.

107. You will serve each spoonful to your ancestors in the dark world.
     Serve each spoonful to your ancestors in the shining and drying world.
     They will rise up and eat and then go to look for new life on earth.
     They would then again live a good life for a long time.

108. Now, a long time ago,
     Puj Saub created human beings [*noob neej*] to live,
     And created everything on earth.
     Saub created the sky to cover above,
     Created the earth below,
     Created thirty suns and thirty moons.
     Suns ruled for thirty days.
     Moons ruled for thirty nights.
     Then who on earth had the ability?
     Which couple had the knowledge?
     There is a saying that the peacock and the quail
     Have the ability and the knowledge.

109. It was the peacock's copper bow that had thirty arrows.
     The bow shot the suns, and twenty-nine of them fell down.

Twenty-nine moons were shot down too.

Then there was only one sun and one moon left.

Lady Sun was afraid

And hid on the other side of the sky.

110. The earth was in darkness for seven years.

Lord Moon had hidden on the other side of the earth.

There was darkness for seven years.

Tuj Nplug and Ci Txuj were sent from earth

To consult Grandmother and Grandfather Saub.

They said,

"When you go back to earth

Tell the bull to call Lady Sun,

And she will come."

111. "The two of you ask the horse to call Lord Moon,

And he will come out."

The sun said,

"Twenty-nine suns died.

Twenty-nine moons died, too.

So the sun and the moon would not come out to give light."

When Ci Txuj and Tuj Nplug returned,

They asked the bull to call Lady Sun.

Lady Sun said,

"The bull has a loud voice."

112. Then the horse called Lord Moon.

The moon said,

"The horse has a wild voice."

Lady Sun stayed hidden and did not come out.

Lord Moon also stayed hidden and did not come out.

The world was in darkness for seven years.

113. Then Ci Txuj and Tuj Nplug asked for advice from the
grandparents.

Grandmother showed the road,

And Grandfather showed the way.

114. The grandparents said,
     "Ci Txuj and Tuj Nplug,
     If you want the sun and the moon to come again,
     When you go back,
     Ask Nkauj Mog to call Lady Sun three times at the north end of the
         earth.
     She will come.
     Ask Nkauj Mim to call the moon three times at the south end of the
         earth,
     And he will come.

115. When they returned,
     They asked Nkauj Mog and Nkauj Mim
     To call the sun and moon three times.
     But the sun and moon kept hiding.

116. The earth was in darkness for seven years.
     Ci Tuj and Tuj Nplug went back to the grandparents.
     They said,
     "If you want the sun to come out,
     When you go back,
     Ask the rooster who shares the same liver [has the same philosophy]
         as Saub to call the sun.
     Then the sun will come out.

117. Let the rooster who shares the same heart with Saub call
         the moon.
     Then it will come out.
     When they returned,
     They asked the rooster to crow three times.

118. When the rooster crowed three times in the north,
     Lady Sun came out.
     When the cock crowed three times in the south,
     Lord Moon came out.
     Then there was light on the earth for seven years.
     Lady Sun allows people to plant the earth and eat,

To be fertile and nurture [*ua noj ua hnav,* to be fertile, to live].
Lady Sun nurtures,
And Lord Moon clothes the two of them together.

119. The moon gives light
So people can make clothing for seven years.
Now there is light in the sky and on earth for seven years.
A long time ago, when the sun came out,
It came from the land in the north.
Lady Sun came from the north.

120. It was the moon that was hidden behind the earth.
The earth was in darkness for seven years.
The moon was hidden behind the end of the world for seven years.
The sky was dark for seven years.
There was silence on earth.
The earth was in darkness for seven years.
The earth remained silent.
The people on the earth had no way to do their work.

121. Now the sun comes out
To rule all four corners of the earth.
One rule is for people to work for their living.
One rule is for the dead son to go and meet his grandmother.
The sun rules one side
And leaves it for the people on earth to work for their living.
It rules the other
So that the dead son can go to meet his grandfather.
[End of one level]

122. There was light,
And the sky was created to stay.
This year, Tub Nraug Laj,
Your body was created.
There was light on earth,
And your body was created to stay.

123. Now you dress up in your new clothes
     And will be on your way.
     It is the earth that is good for planting crops.
     It is the land that is good for making clothes.
     Then you will dress up and go.
     The spirits of the doors extend their hands to block
          the road.
     They stretch their hands to grab your arms.
     You are the animal of our people on earth.
     You are the crops of our people on earth.
     You are dressing up.
     Where are you going?

124. When asked, you will answer
     That it was because you got sick on earth.
     You will say,
     "So, now I come."
     Then the spirits of the door will ask you,
     "You are the animal of our people on earth.
     You are the crops of our people on earth.
     There is much sickness on earth.
     Why did you not seek help from the shaman?
     Why did you not talk with your parents and brothers
     To ask the shaman to heal you?"
     Then you will answer,
     "The shaman did nine trances, and it did not help.
     Eight kinds of medicine did not heal my sickness."

125. Now you will say,
     "The left hand is holding the end pole of the house."
     Your hands are lying on your stomach.
     The left hand is holding the waist [*lauj nas nplawm ntawm tes*].
     Even your brothers sought help from the shaman.
     Your sickness, nevertheless, was not cured.
     Though they sought help from the Chinese expert.
     Your sickness was not healed.

126. The bells of Siv Yis are ringing,
   Following your sickness.
   This year, however, is the year you will die.
   The bells of Siv Yis are ringing,
   Following your sickness.
   This year is the year you will die.

127. Now the left hand [*lauj nas*] is kicking the black stone.
   Lauj nas is smoothing the thread with the stone.
   It seems there is a lot of fine clothing.
   Then you put on your new outfits to go.
   You will speak to the spirits of wealth,
   So that you have the way to meet your ancestors.
   [End of one level]

128. Now you put on your new outfit and go along.
   When you arrive at the spirit of the back wall altar [*txiv dab xwm kab los yej*],
   The *xwm kab* spirits will extend their arms to you.
   They will stretch their fingers to grab your arms, saying,
   "It is the earth that is good for planting crops.
   It is the land that is good for making clothing.
   So, why are you going?"
   You will answer,
   "There is a lot of illness on earth.
   The cruel Ntxwj Nyoog released the sickness on my arms,
   And the death seeds fell on my hands."

129. Your hands are holding the bamboo because your body is weakening.
   Your hands are holding the metal because your chance of living is
      lessening.
   You say a word of thanks to the *xwm kab* spirits
   So that you can go on your way to meet your ancestors.

130. Now the spirits of the house poles [*ncej dab ncej qhua*]
   Extend their arms to block your road.
   They stretch out their fingers to hold your arms and say,
   "Why did you not ask your parents to seek help from the shaman?"

131. You will answer,
     "A long time ago, there was no sickness on earth
     And no illness on the land.

132. "Now cruel hearted Ntxwj Nyoog
     Released the illness down to the earth people who liked to die."
     Those who knew how to pick up the seeds
     Picked them up and stuck them in their pockets.
     You did not know how to pick them up.
     You picked up the seeds and stuck them in your liver.

133. Others knew how to pick them up and stick them in their
         pockets.
     When you picked them up, you put them in your heart.
     Therefore, now you put on the new outfits and come along.
     The spirits of the poles will ask,
     "There is much illness on earth.
     Why did you not ask your parents to get help from the
         shaman?"

134. Then you must answer,
     "Nine times my parents and my brothers had the shaman come
         and try to find my soul.
     Nine kinds of medicine could not heal my sickness."
     Then you could no longer breathe,
     And your throat was drying.
     You stopped breathing,
     And your throat was drying.

135. Then you must say that you waited for your brothers to carry
         you from the bed to the floor.
     You waited for your brothers to boil water to wash your body.
     You waited for your brothers to place you on the floor.
     You waited for your brothers to boil water to wash your face.
     Now you must say thanks to the spirits of the poles,
     So that you can go on your way to meet your ancestors.
     [End of one level]

136. Now the spirits of the side door[*dab rooj lis*]
     Will extend their arms to block your road.
     They will stretch their fingers to block your path.
     They will ask,
     "You are a person of the earth.
     Where do you want to go?"
     You will answer,
     "There is a lot of illness on the earth,
     So I must go."

137. The spirits of the side door will say,
     "Why did you not ask you brothers and your parents
     To seek help from the shaman to heal you?"
     Then you will answer,
     "Nine shamanic trances could not find my soul.
     Nine kinds of medicine could not heal my sickness."

138. Now your left hand is hitting the black rocks.
     Your hand is slapping the stone.
     There are many spirits you must give thanks to
     So that you may go.
     Then the spirits of the side door will let you go.
     You can find the way to meet your ancestors.
     [End of one level]

139. A long time ago,
     There was no illness on earth and no dying on the land.
     Because bad-hearted Ntxwj Nyoog released the seeds of illness and dying
         on the earth,
     You must, therefore, put on the new outfits and march on your way.
     Your mouth and tongue are drying.

140. You come from the side door to the front door
     And must pay back your spirits.
     You come from the front door to the side door.
     You will lie down and repay the spirits.
     When you are dead, you must dress up to go.

You will leave your parents behind.
Your brothers and sisters are crying because you are dead.
Your parents and relatives are wailing because you have disappeared.

141. You have dressed up and will arrive at the slope.
Your relatives are wailing because you are dead.
You have dressed up and will arrive at the forest.
You will leave behind you parents to wail because you are dead.

142. Now Txawj Nkiag has arrived with his wisdom.
Txawj Nkiag will send you to the slope.
He will send you, Tub Nraug Laj, to meet your grandmother.
He will send you, dead son, to the valley to meet your grandfather.
[End of one level]

143. He will offer you three cups of wine
And will send you to meet your ancestors.
If you take them, you will get to them.
Now you will come and be heading on your way.
It is the earth spirits of the side door that will allow you to go.
You will then be on your way to meet your ancestors.

144. It seems like you were born to live on earth.
However, you do not live forever.
It is because of Ntxwj Nyoog's bad heart.
It is because Ntxwj Nyoog is cruel.

145. When you went to work in your field,
You picked up Ntxwj Nyoog's sickness on your hands.
When you were working,
You picked up Ntxwj Nyoog's dying seeds on your hands.

146. You have put on good outfits to go.
Then you will climb to get your "mandate for life" paper.
Then you can descend to be reborn on earth.
You will wander around the plain.
You go climb Nyuj Vaj Tuam Teem's silver ladder.

147. When you wander around over there,
You go climb Nyuj Vaj Tuam Teem's golden ladder.
You must remember this in your heart.
You must remember this in your liver.

148. You must remember to go and get your "mandate for life" paper from
Nyuj Vaj Tuam Teem.
Come back to be reborn on earth [*rov los thawj xeeb*],
So that you will have a good life.

149. When you climb the sky ladder,
One day you climb one step,
Two days you climb two steps,
Three days you climb three,
Four days you climb four steps,
Five days you climb five.

150. Six days you climb six steps,
Seven days you climb seven,
Eight days you climb eight steps,
Nine days you climb nine,
Ten days you climb ten steps,
Eleven days you climb eleven,
Twelve days you climb twelve steps,
Thirteen days you climb thirteen steps.
In one cycle of thirteen days,
You climb to the top of one Teem Txwv.
Remember to go ask for your paper from Nyuj Vaj Tuam Teem.
When you have your good paper,
You will return to be reborn
Into a human being on earth.
That will be the right way.

151. You must remember to climb.
One day you climb one step,
Two days you climb two steps,
Three days you climb three,

Four days you climb four steps,
Five days you climb five,
Six days you climb six steps,
Seven days you climb seven,
Eight days you climb eight steps,
Nine days you climb nine,
Ten days you climb ten steps,
Eleven days you climb eleven,
Twelve days you climb twelve steps,
Thirteen days you climb thirteen steps.
You remember this in your liver.
When you climb to the top of the second Teem Txwv,
Remember to get your "mandate for life" paper from Nyuj Vaj Tuam Teem.

152. It seems like one day you climb one step,
Two days you climb two steps,
Three days you climb three,
Four days you climb four steps,
Five days you climb five,
Six days you climb six steps,
Seven days you climb seven,
Eight days you climb eight steps,
Nine days you climb nine,
Ten days you climb ten steps,
Eleven days you climb eleven,
Twelve days you climb twelve steps,
Thirteen days you climb thirteen steps.
Then you reach the top of the third Teem Txwv.

153. You must remember to get your paper.
Should you get a cow paper,
You would be afraid that a human being would use you to plow.
Should you get a horse paper,
You would be afraid that another would ride you.
Should you get a pig paper,
You would be afraid that you would be sacrificed.
Should you get a dog paper,

You would be afraid that others would beat you.
Should you get a bird or insect paper,
You would be afraid of the rain and the sunlight.

154. You must remember to go and get your paper
From the paper house at Nyuj Vaj Tuam Teem's desk.
Then you dive into Nyuj Vaj Tuam Teem's ocean
So that you can obtain the paper to be reborn as a leader.
After you get your paper from Nyuj Vaj Tuam Teem,
Txawj Nkiag will lead you back to earth
To be reborn on the land.
You must remember to go down to earth.

155. One day you descend one step,
Two days you descend two,
Three days you descend three steps,
Four days you descend four,
Five days you descend five steps,
Six days you descend six,
Seven days you descend seven steps,
Eight days you descend eight,
Nine days you descend nine steps,
Ten days you descend ten,
Eleven days you descend eleven steps,
Twelve days you descend twelve steps.
In one cycle of thirteen days,
You will remember you have descended.
You will have already passed one Teem Txwv.

156. Now you remember in your heart:
One day you descend one step,
Two days you descend two,
Three days you descend three steps,
Four days you descend four,
Five days you descend five steps,
Six days you descend six,
Seven days you descend seven steps,

Eight days you descend eight,
Nine days you descend nine steps,
Ten days you descend ten,
Eleven days you descend eleven steps,
Twelve days you descend twelve steps.
In one cycle of thirteen days,
You have come down two Teem Txwv to earth.

157. Then again:
One day you descend one step,
Two days you descend two,
Three days you descend three steps,
Four days you descend four,
Five days you descend five steps,
Six days you descend six,
Seven days you descend seven steps,
Eight days you descend eight,
Nine days you descend nine steps,
Ten days you descend ten,
Eleven days you descend eleven steps,
Twelve days you descend twelve steps.
In one cycle of thirteen days,
You have already descended to the land.
You have arrived on earth.

158. It seems that Txawj Nkiag has shown you
How to get your paper from Nyuj Vaj Tuam Teem's desk.
Now you have returned to earth.
Remember in your heart that you are on earth now.

159. Txawj Nkiag already took you to exchange your paper from Nyuj Vaj
       Tuam Teem's palace.
Now Tsawj Nkiag will take you back to earth.
Remember in your heart
That he will send you to be reborn again.
You should be reborn as a leader
So that you will live a good life.

160. [Now three cups of wine are offered to the dead person]
     Take these three cups of wine to drink.
     Txawj Nkiag will take you to get your fine clothing
     So that you will be able to go and meet your ancestors.

161. Now you have put on a nice outfit,
     And you will go to find your birth shirt [placenta].
     Now the chanter will lead the person
     From one village to another, calling it by name.
     He will lead the dead person
     Back to the village where the person was born.
     There the person will be able to find the buried birth shirt
     And will then be reborn as a human being.

162. One person, three souls, and seven shadows.
     Since you have gone, your body is dead
     But not your souls.
     One of your souls will go to put on the rebirth shirt.

163. You will go to get your rebirth shirt
     From the village in which you were born.
     In order to get there,
     You must go from village to village
     Until you reach the place where you were born.

164. When you were alive, you ate part of the forest.
     You used part of their firewood.
     You drank from their stream.
     Now that you will go,
     The spirits or owners of that particular place
     Will extend their arms to block your way
     And stretch their fingers and hold your arms.

165. Since you have wasted part of their forest
     And used some of their firewood,
     As you pass their territory,
     You will use your paper money to pay and give thanks to them.

Use your incense and paper money to pay your tolls
So that the guards will let you through to your ancestors.
[The chanter burns three pieces of paper money near the dead person's head.]

166. Your mother and father and your brothers and sisters
Give you paper money.
You will take it with you.
You will use it to pay your tolls
And anything else you must pay for along the way
So that you will have a good journey.

167. If you come to a big river, remember these words,
Now that you are going to obtain your rebirth shirt from your
birth village.
When you arrive at the river and the river is very wide,
Even if you go to the upper part of the river,
You could not cross it.
Even if you go to the lower part of the river,
You could not cross it.

168. You must take your money and your incense
And pay the fare of the spirit boat.
Then the spirits will take you to the other side
So that you will have your way to go.
The spirits will send you across to the other slope
So that you will have a road to march on.
[Paper money is burned for the dead person.]

169. Now that you have given thanks to the spirits of the land,
You will go to obtain your rebirth shirt to put on.
If you are a woman, your rebirth shirt is at the bedpost.
If you are a man, your rebirth shirt is at the main pole.
You must come to look for your rebirth shirt to wear.
You must search around the fire for your shirt.

170. You must look around from the side door to the front door.
You must look around the poles.

You will then find your rebirth shirt
So that you will have it to put on and wear.
Then Txawj Nkiag will take you to be reborn on earth.
You would be reborn a cow but fear people would use you to plow.
You would be born a dog but fear people would beat you.

171. You would be reborn a pig but fear you would be killed.
You would be born a horse but fear you would be ridden.
You would be born a chicken but fear people would cut you.
You should be reborn a human being so that you will have a good life.
When you are on your way to rebirth,
You should not follow the upper road;
That is the road people use to look for food.
You should not use the lower road either,
Because that is the road people use to look for their clothing.
You should follow the middle road;
That is the road for you to look for a new mother and father.

172. If you want to be reborn a chief and leader,
You would be heading into the middle and shaking to the sides.
Then you would come out to the cattle fields of the chief.
You would shake in the liver
So that you would come out to be the new son of the chief in the court.
If you follow the middle road
You would jump onto the desk of the chief.

173. You would then jump and come out at the court
So that in your next life you will become the new son of the chief.
[End of one level]

174. [Wine is offered to the dead person.]
Now we give you three drinks of wine.
Then you will jump on your path and look for your ancestors.

175. Now you are a human being on earth.
One body, three souls, and seven shadows.
Your body and your shadows are all dead.

One of your souls will put on new outfits
And go to look for your ancestors.

176. Now that you are going to look for your ancestors,
I will give you a bag to carry, your sack to hold.
You will climb up to the sky.
You will march around the field.
Txawj Nkiag will lead you to climb Ntxwj Nyoog's silver ladder.
You will walk around the field.
Then Txawj Nkiag will take you to climb Ntxwj Nyoog's golden ladder.

177. You should remember that one day you climb one level,
Two days you climb two levels,
Three days you climb three,
Four days you climb four levels,
Five days you climb five,
Six days you climb six levels,
Seven days you climb seven,
Eight days you climb eight levels,
Nine days you climb nine,
Ten days you climb ten levels,
Eleven days you climb eleven,
Twelve days you climb twelve levels.
In one cycle of thirteen days,
You climb to the top of Teem Txwv to Nyuj Vaj Tuam Teem's land.

178. When you get there, Nyuj Vaj Tuam Teem will ask you,
"Since you are a human being on earth, why have you come?
They say that earth is a good place to find food and clothing."
You will answer,
"If the leaves do not fall, the forest will not grow.
If no one dies, there will be no place on earth to plow.
If the leaves do not fall, the forest will not be clear.
If no one is sick and dies, there will not be a place on earth to dwell."

179. So, now you have put on your new outfits and come.
You will say that you do not have anything at all;

231

You have only the sound of the reed pipes and the gong
And the wailing and crying of the people so that you have come.

180. Then Nyuj Vaj Tuam Teem will say,
"Open up your Showing the Way procedure for me to see."
You will answer that you do not have any eating or drinking papers,
So when you die, you will not return.
There are procedures for showing the path and pointing the way.
So when you die, you will not return home.
You will tell this to Nyuj Vaj Tuam Tuam Teem so that you will be able
to go on.
[The chanter takes the bamboo horns and points to the dead person.]

181. You should remember that one day you climb one level,
Two days you climb two levels,
Three days you climb three,
Four days you climb four levels,
Five days you climb five,
Six days you climb six levels,
Seven days you climb seven,
Eight days you climb eight levels,
Nine days you climb nine,
Ten days you climb ten levels,
Eleven days you climb eleven,
Twelve days you climb twelve levels.

182. In one cycle of thirteen days,
You will arrive at Ntxwj Nyoog's rocky gate.
You have put on the new outfit, and you must go.
You will leave your parents and relatives crying on earth.
As you open Ntxwj Nyoog's gate,
You will turn and see that your parents and relatives are crying
on the land.

183. Now you have climbed up to Ntxwj Nyoog's gate.
When you open it, let in the cries.
When you take a look, you will see the gigantic village of your ancestors.

When you open the gate, do not let it make a noise.

When you take a look,

You will see that your grandparents live in a big village [lit., "as big as eight to nine folds"].

184. When you arrive at Nyxwj Nyoog's land,

You will see others peeling garlic and onions.

You should not help them.

You should say that you hurt your fingers and you cannot.

When they ask you to help them peel onions,

You must say that your fingers and toes are hurt and bleeding,

And you cannot help them to peel onions.

[As the chanter says these words, he ties a red thread on the dead persons fingers to represent blood.]

185. When you arrive at caterpillar rocky mountain,

You will see the caterpillars jumping as big as deer.

186. You pull out your hempen shoes and put them on.

When you see the caterpillars jumping as big as pigs,

Reach out and pull on your shoes,

So that you will have a way to meet your grandmother and grandfather.

[The chanter points to the dead person with a piece of firewood.]

187. Then you arrive at the dragon and tiger rocky mountain and valley.

The dragon's mouth will open to swallow you.

You will use this knot of hemp to stick into its mouth.

Then the rocky mouth will be closed.

It will open to bite you.

The you will put this hemp into the mouth.

Then it will be closed.

Your path will then be open to see your ancestors.

[Three knots of hemp are then prepared and put into the hands of the dead man.]

188. Here are your hemp knots,

Which you will throw into the dragon and tiger's mouth

So that you will have your way to meet your ancestors.
Now you have arrived at Ntxwj Nyoog's sour and salty river.
You will find a man and his wife guarding the river.
The wife is holding the bitter water;
The husband is holding the salty water.
They will ask,
"You are a human being from earth.
Why have you come?
Since you have come,
You must drink the bitter and salty water."

189. You must tell them that you have a good mother and father on earth.
You have good brothers and sisters,
And domestic animals on the land.
You are coming to pay your debts to the Chinese.
You must say your mouth is bleeding, so you cannot drink,
So the spirits of the river will make way for you to pass.
You will have your way to meet your ancestors.
[The chanter covers the dead man's mouth with a red cloth, symbolizing blood.]

190. Now Txawj Nkiag will give you your bag to carry, your sack
to hold,
And your umbrella for you to carry to protect you.
You will climb to the sharp and rocky mountain.
You will hear the dragons' and tigers' groans
Coming from above to block your road.
Do not be afraid,
Because they are the sounds of your parents and relatives,
Whom you left behind at home.

191. When you arrive at the sharp rocky mountain,
You will hear the dragons and the tigers groaning
To block your path.
Do not be afraid
Because they are the sounds of your parents and relatives,
Whom you left behind at home.

192. When you arrive at the hot slope and warm valley,
     Others will take out their paper umbrellas to protect themselves.
     When you arrive at the warm slope and the hot valley
     And you see others pull out their umbrellas,
     You should reach for your umbrella to protect yourself, too,
     So that you will be able to find your way to your ancestors.
     [The chanter takes the bamboo horns and points to the red cloth
          that covers the dead person's face.]
     Here is your fan.

193. Now that you have put on your fine clothing
     And have passed the caterpillar mountain and valley,
     You have passed the sharp dragon and tiger mountain;
     You have passed the hot slope and warm valley;
     You have passed the cloudy slope and windy.
     Now Txawj Nkiag will take you to meet your grandmother
          and grandfather.

194. Now you have put on fine clothing to go.
     You will take your chicken with you.
     Your chicken will be in front of you, and you will follow your chicken.
     When there is a sunny day, you will hide under your chicken's wing.
     On a rainy day, you will hide under your chicken's tail.

195. When your chicken combs his wings, fix your shirt.
     When your chicken combs his legs, fix your leggings.
     When your chicken combs his tail, fix your shoes.
     When your chicken combs his head, fix your turban.
     When your chicken combs his waist, you fix your belt.
     Let your chicken go in front, and follow him.

196. When you arrive at the cold sky and dark land,
     The sunny sky and dried land, the dried world,
     If their rooster crows and your rooster answers,
     Those are not your ancestors' coffins.
     If their rooster crow and your rooster replies
     Those are not your ancestors' graves.

197. If your rooster crows and their rooster answers,
     Those are your ancestors' coffins.
     If your rooster crows and their rooster replies,
     Those are your ancestors' graves.
     Should their rooster crow and your rooster answer,
     It means that they will trick you into jumping off the rocky
         mountain.
     Should their rooster crow and your chicken reply,
     It means they will trick you to jump off the cliff.

198. When you arrive and see the happy faces who are waiting for you
         in the south,
     They are not your ancestors;
     They are the ones who would take you to trade for food and clothing.
     When you arrive and see the happy faces who are standing to the
         north,
     They are not your ancestors.
     They are the ones who would take you to trade for something to eat.

199. When you arrive and see the unhappy faces who extend their arms
         to you,
     Jump into their laps.
     When you see the unhappy faces,
     Jump into their laps,
     For they are your grandmother and grandfather.
     When you arrive, your grandmother and grandfather will ask,
     "You are a human being on earth.
     That is the best place to live.
     Why have you come?"

200. "Since you have come, what have you brought with you?"
     You will tell them you have nothing.
     The only thing you have is your procedure for showing the way
         [cwj qhuab kev].
     Your ancestors will ask you to show it to them.
     Unfold your procedure for showing the way.
     Your procedure for showing the way is good according to custom.

201. Your living threads are broken [*koj tsuj tu hlab npuag*].
Now that you have come to the world of cold and darkness,
You will not return home.
Your grandparents will ask,
"Who brought you here?"
You will reply that he is someone you could not know.
His ears are as big as the fan,
And his eyes are as big as the cup.
Your grandparents will ask,
"Could we find his trail and go after him?"
You will say that there is no way to find the trail and go after him,
Because he came this year, and he already left last year.
When he came he came inland, he returned by water.

202. Your grandparents will ask,
"Can we ride a horse or cow to go after him?"
You must answer that you cannot follow him.
You should not follow him,
Because you might fall into a trap.
You must say this
So that you can have a way to meet your grandparents.
[The chanter throws the bamboo horns to see if the dead person has
    heard, then picks them up and holds them in his hand.]

203. Txawj Nkiag will send you to this point only.
Take three cups of wine for you to drink.
Then you will let one soul go back to the land of the living.
Now reply when I throw the horns.
[The chanter throws the bamboo horns onto the ground. If both pieces
    of the *txhib ntawg* open, the ritual is finished. If one turns up and one
    turns down, the chanter continues.]

204. Do not be afraid.
Hold these chicken eggs for comfort.

205. Find a chicken or pig to sacrifice.
Txawj Nkiag sends you to this point only.

Put on your hempen shoes and go to the other side.
Txawj Nkiag is not going to that side,
Because Txawj Nkiag does not have any hempen shoes.

206. You will close your eyes and ears and head
     To stay with your grandmother and grandfather.
     On a new day,
     You will change your bodily form
     And become a beautiful butterfly.

"QHUAB KEV"

(SHOWING THE WAY)

HMONG TEXT

1. Ntawm no mus yog zaj qhuab kev hais txog peb Hmoob kev cai muaj ib tug tuag mas thov ib tug tuaj qhuab kev yog zaj uas xa tus tuag kom nws mus cuag poj cuag yawm kom nws mus txog rau dab teb

2. zoo li niam nov ntuj ntsig teb hav caj sim vos yog raug tau lub ntuj los nyob Tub Nraug Laj cev los mus txoos neej hav caj teb sim vos raug lub ntuj los txoos yuav raug tau Tub Nraug Laj cev ntsig los mus ntob

3. zoo li niam nov koj tuag tseeb tuag dag hos tuag tiag mus tuag cuav ua ciav koj tuag dag ces koj sawv lis tsis los mus ntaus qaib ntaus npua ncig vaj ncig loog tuag tiag ces tig ntsej los mloog qi los nuam Txawj Nkiag yuav hu nkauj dab lus taum pub koj mloog

4. niam ua lub zam lim zim txog tim toj es leej hlob saib yog koj hos niam ua lub zam lim zim txog tim ub ua ciav leej yau saib tij tog koj tsis sub niam nov ces koj tuag tiag koj tij ntsej los mloog tig muag los nuam Txawj Nkiag yuav hu nkauj dab lus taum pub koj mloog no na ntawm no tag ib qib ntawm no tag ib quag

5. zoo li hnub txheej tshoj thaum ub ntuj teb txhawv twg tuaj hos ntiaj teb txhawv
   lawm Ntxwj Nyoog qab vag zeb tuaj nes ntuj cag txhawv twg los ntuj cag txhawv
   lawm Ntxwj Nyoog qab vag lag los

6. leeg twg pom dej ntxheb qab nkawm twg pom dej cag tsev yog tau puj mab pom
   tau dej ntxheb qab yog tau puj suav pom daj cag tsev nim nov yog tau puj suav
   nkaus raj lis zim mus kwv coj los txog hais tau niaj ib tshob tuaj nruab yias tooj
   hos yias tooj npau sis vooj

7. hos hais tau niaj ib tshob tuaj nruab yias hlau yias npau sis auv nrhaub dej txiag
   sov li so tuaj nruab tsuag ua tub tuag tus dej mus ntxuav muag muab dej txiag
   tov ua dej so ntxuav tub tuag qhov muag mos qam nyoos rov lawm yaj ceeb koj
   kwv koj tij li pom koj tseeb

8. zoo nim no ces zoo muab dej txiag tov lawm dej so qam so ntxuav tub tuag qhov
   muag mos qam nyoo rov lawm yaj nrag yog lawm kwv tig li pom koj tag ntawm
   no tag ib qib qhov no tag ib quag

9. ntawm no mus yuav muab dej rau koj ntxuav muag tso yuav xa koj mus cuag
   poj cuag yawm zoo nim ces yuav muab tau tus dej ntxheb los ntxuav tub tuag
   qhov muag dawb

10. mos qam nyoo rov lawm yaj ceeb tub tuag lub ntsej lub muag tas tub tuag yuav
    rag nees lis ntws rov lawm Lwm Yeeb zoo li tub tuag qhov muag dawb mos qam
    nyoos rov lawm yaj nrag zoo niam nov tub tuag yuav rag nees ntws rov lawm
    Yeeb Nrag

11. zoo nim nov ces yog tau hnub txheej txhoj thaum ub ua ciav Txawj Nkiag tuaj
    txog tub txawg tuaj poob zoo li tus poov xab txawm tsis muaj hos poov cawv
    txawm tsis tau cav tau tias poov xab nyob twg tuaj hos cav tias poov xab

12. nyob pem Ntxwj Nyoog qab tsaus ntab yuav cav tau tias poov cawv nyob twg
    los zoo li Nkauj Iab Nraug Oo tias poov cawv nyob pem Ntxwj Nyoog gab tsaus
    muv nim nov yuav tso leej twg mus muab poov xab pem Ntxwj Nyoog gab tsuas
    muv muab poov xab coj los txoj

13. zaum nov yuav tso Nkauj Li Kwm mus muab poov xab pem Ntxwj Nyoog qab
tsuas ntab muab poov cawv pem Ntxwj Nyoog qab tsuas muv zoo nim nov ces
Nkauj Mog mus muab poov xab pem Ntxwj Nyoog qab tsuas ntab rov los poob
Nkauj Mim mus muab poov cawv pem Ntxwj Nyoog qab tsuas muv rov los txog
nim nov ces

14. muab poov coj los nrom qam nroos tuaj rau nruab vab ib hnub ob taig kis cawv
qab cawv lis meej mus xws zib htab ua lawm tub tuag tus cawv mus qhuab kab
zoo li muab poov cawv coj los nrom qam nros tuaj nruab le ib hnub ob taig kis
cawv qab cawv li meej mus xws zib mes ua lawm tub tuag tus cawv mus qhuab
kev zoo li ntawm no mus tag ib qib qhov no mus tag ib quag

15. zoo li nim no ces Txawj Nkiag nqig tuaj poob tub txawg nqis tuaj txog yuav muab
poov cawv nrom nroo tuaj tom taj ua lawm tub tuag tus cawv mus qhuab kab
yuav muab poov cawv nrom nroo tuaj tom txuas zoo li muab poov cawv mus
ua tub tuag tus cawv tuag

16. zoo li nim nov ces muab poov cawv coj los ua txuj hos muab poov xab coj los
ua civ noob txheej tshoj thaum ub muab poov xab poov cawv li nraim ua tub
tuag nyoog qas nraim mus cuag poj nis

17. ntawm no mus tag ib qib qhov no mus tag ib quag tuav peb txog cawv rau koj
haus tas tso yuav coj koj mus cuag poj cuag yawm no zoo li nim no ces Txawj
Nkiag nqis tuaj tub txawg nqis tuaj poob ua cas noob maj raug tsis muaj hos
noob ntuag raug tsis tau

18. cav tias noob nyob twg thiaj muaj hos noob ntuag nyob twg li tshuav yog tau
noob txheej tshoj thaum ub maj zaj nab peb hlis tshav zaj luav peb hlis cua ntiaj
teb no noob maj tuag tu caj hos noob ntuag tuag tu ces nim no cav tau tias noob
maj nyob pem Ntxwj Nyoog

19. toj zeb zag cav tias noob ntuag nyob pem Ntxwj Nyoog toj zeb zuag nim nov cas
tub txib los tsis muaj hos tub Khai los tsis tau yog tau Nkauj Iab Nraug Oo yuav
tso tau Niam Kag mus muab noob maj pem Ntxwj Nyoog zeb zag niam nkauj
quag mus muab noob ntuag pem Ntxwj Nyoog tej zeb zuag

20. muab noob maj rov los txog muab noob ntuag rov los txog ua ciav nim no muab maj nrom nroo rov lawm ntiaj teb ib hlis peb caug nyoog noob maj nqis xiav teb muab noob ntuag nrom nroo tuaj nruab ha ib hlis peb caug nyoog noob ntuag nqis xiav hav

21. zoo li nim no ib hlis peb caug nyoog Nkauj Iab Nraug Oo mus hlais niaj ib kawg coj los txog muab niaj ib ntshuas coj los ua rau tub tuag npua muab lawm niaj peb ntshuas coj los ntaus rau tuag ua ciav qas ntswg los tsis nthuav muab rau tub tuag rau coj mus tsuj lawm Ntxwj Nyoog toj kab ntsuab qas luj tsis xuab qas ntswg los tsis ntxias muab rau tub tuag rau coj mus tsuj lawm Ntxwj Nyoog toj kab nplias

22. zoo li nim nov ces muab noob maj noob ntuag coj los ua rau koj leej tub tuag npua koj ntim lub txiaj zam li zim txog tim toj hos muab noob maj noob ntuag ua rau koj leej tub tuag npua mus cuag poj nis

23. zoo li muab niaj ib ntsuas ua rau tub tuag npua tub tuag ntim lub txiaj zam lis zim txog tim rawm muab noob maj noob ntuag ua rau tub tuag npua mus cuag nkawm no qhov no mus tas ib qib ntawm no mus tas ib quag

24. tav nov koj mus txog pem Ntxwj Nyoog toj zej ntsig rawm kab no nim kab ntsig kab nos dhia rhees luaj thav yaj ces koj tes lauj muab koj khau maj hos

25. koj mus txog pem Ntxwj Nyoog toj kab ntsig rawm kab nos kab ntsig nos dhia rhees luaj thav npua koj tes nas mus muab koj khau ntsuag ces koj li tau kev mus cuag poj cuag yawm no na

26. niam no ces yog nkauj qaib ha nkauj seev qas yees tuaj qab roob txiv lau qaib ua lau seev qas yees tuaj nram qab ha nkauj qaib ua nkauj seev qas yees tuaj xya xyoo ua nkauj nqis tuaj tsis muaj tub txiv lau qaib ua nkauj ua lau qas ntxiag los xya niaj hos ua lau nqis muaj kiv

27. niam no poj qaib seev qas yees los mus nteg qe poj qaib seev qas yees ib
   hnub
ib hnub ntej ho
ib hnub nteg ib lub
ob hnub nteg ob lub

peb hnub nteg peb lub
plaub hnub nteg plaub lub
tsib hnub nteg tsib lub
rau hnub nteg rau lub
xya hnub nteg xya lub
yim hnub nteg yim lub
cuaj hnub nteg cuaj lub
kaum hnub nteg kaum lub

28. zoo li ib tsug kaum peb hnub ces nteg tau kaum peb lub zoo li niam no poj qaib seev qas yees las puag qe poj qaib seev qas yees los puag lawm niam ib hlis peb caug nyoo cas daug tau niam peb tib tug zoo li poj qaib ces kom poj qaib tub seev qas yees tuaj tsev peg dau seev li ntxaig saib tsis zoo dav seev li ntxaig los muab lawm niaj ib tug lawm

29. zoo li poj qaib coj poj qaib tub seev qas yees rheeb ncig lis khuav tuaj tsev taug yog tau niaj mub li plis siab tsis zoo niaj mub li plis muab lawm niaj muab lawm ib tug lawm tshuav niaj ib tib tug niam no poj qaib tub hlob tiav txuj hos poj qaib tub mus phov thab ntiaj teb leej hlob leej yau las cem tias yog ntiaj teb tub tuag tug qaib mus qhuab kab

30. zoo li poj qaib kuj hlob mus tiav ci yog lawm poj qaib tub mus phov tsev ntiaj teb leej hlob leej yau los cem tias yog tub tuag tus qaib mus taw kev ua cia niam no yuav muab txiv lau qaib nplis lis nplos ua lawm kom ua lawm koj qaib, yog qaib liab plhis plaub nplis plaub qas plho tuaj nruab cub yog qaib yog qaib ntsim muab ua koj tub tuag tau qaib mus npog ntim

31. zoo li niam no zoo li koj qaib ces yog koj qaib kais yuav muab phlis plaub lis phlo tuaj nruab cub ua lawm tub tuag tus qaib mus npog tais zoo li txiv lau qaib qua qas luam txiv lau qaib qua qas laws txog ntuj sua teb tom qab yog koj tub tuag tug qaib mus qhuab kab txiv lau qaib qua qas laws txog lawm txiv laus qaib quas qas laws txog lawm ntuj sua teb tom pes yog tub tuag koj tus qaib mus taws kev no

32. ntawm no mus tas ib qib qhov no mus tas ib quag ntsuav peb txog cawv rau koj haus tso yuav muab koj qaib rau koj coj mus cuag poj cuag yawm no na ntawm no yuav muab koj siab qaib laig rau koj li tau kev mus cuag poj cuag yawg

33. noj ces txij koj ib leeg noj ho haus ces koj ib leeg haus ploj ces koj ib leeg ploj tuag ces koj ib leeg tuag noj tsis taus nchuav nruab taub haus tsis taus los nchuav nruab rag noj tsis taus los ua tiag nqas haus tsis taus los ua tiag ris yuav coj mus pub poj pub yawg noj yuav mus dia koj yawg, kwv tij nyob tub tuag teb no

34. zoo li niam no ces yog tau noob txheej tshoj thaum ub ntiaj teb tsis muaj mob yog teb cais raug tau tsis muaj nkeeg

35. yog tau Ntxwj Nyoog siab tsis ncaj hos tso lub mob lub tuag nqis rov ntiaj teb es tub tuag li tau kev tuag los mus yog tau Suav tsuj ab tis ua ab koj kwv koj tig chaws niam qas zias tuaj nruab hlab yog tau Suav tsuj kim tis ua kim koj kwv koj tig muab tau Suav tsuj niaj ib tib ntsim zoo li qas tsi nyob ncaws tauj ho yog tau koj kwv koj tig muab Suav tsuj lawm niaj ib tib pab coj mus ua koj tub tuag tus ntaub mus npog ncauj ho

36. zoo li qas tsi nyob nres Ntxhiav yog tau hnub txheej tshoj thaum ub noog pej noog haud nyob ncaws Ntxhiav koj kwv koj tig yuav muab ntaub tsuj niaj ib tib fab coj los ua koj tub tuag tus ntaub mus npog hniav no

37. zoo li niam nov ces yog tau ntiaj teb tim qas tsi teb cais tim qas cas yog noob txheej tshoj thaum ub ntiaj teb raug tsis muaj mob teb cais raug tsis muaj kheeg yog tau peb ntiaj teb yog tau peb ntiaj teb nyiam ploj hos ntiaj nrag nyiam tuag yuav mus muab niaj tsab los pam ua qauv quaj hos

38. muab niam cuam los ua pam ua qauv nyiav muab tawv nyuj los tawv phij dub ua nruas ntaus muab plhaub mag ua qeej tshov ntaus cuaj qws nrov lawm cuaj suab zoo li deeg qas daws txog Ntxwj Nyoog lub ntuj ntsuab ntaus cuaj qws nrov cuaj zag deeg qas daws Ntxwj Nyoog lub ntuj dag

39. Ntxwj Nyoog nrug rooj ntug los saib nrug lub rooj teb rov los xyuas zoo li yog ntiaj teb nyiam ploj hos ntiaj nrag nyiam tuag ua ciav Ntxwj Nyoog tso niaj mos ntsuab tuaj tshuaj ntiaj teb es tso mos muv tuaj xyuas ntiaj nrag niaj mos ntsuab rov mus poob zoo li mos muv rov mus txog Ntxwj Nyoog tsa

40. ncauj qhub hais tias ntiaj teb tim qas tsi yuav nrov deeg nqa daws txog kuv txiv yawm Ntxwj Nyoog lub rooj lub ntuj dag ua ciav niaj mos ntsuab tias vim ntiaj teb nyiam ploj hos ntiaj nrag nyiam tuag

41. nuab niaj cab tua ua nruab kab muab niaj cuam tua ua tuaj nruab ke muab niaj
    tsab coj los pam ua qauv quaj os muab niaj cuam coj los pam ua qauv nyiav tawv
    nyuj ces tawv nyuj dub ua nruas ntaus hos muab plhuab mag ua qeej tshuab las
    ua qeej tshov

42. ntaus cuaj qws nrov cuaj suab li deeg qas daws txog koj txiv yawg Ntxwj Nyoog
    lub rooj lub ntuj ntsuaj no ntaus cuaj qws nrov cuaj zag Ntxwj Nyoog nrov ntxhe
    qas ntws txog txiv yawg Ntxwj Nyoog lub rooj vag Ntxwj Nyoog tso lub mob
    nqis ntiaj teb

43. zoo li niam no tso lub tuag poob thav ntiaj nrag ua cov tswm nyov tso lub mob
    los xya niaj ho ntiaj teb nyob ntsiag txiaj hos Ntxwj Nyoog tso lub tuag los lawm
    xya xyoo ntiaj teb nyob ntsiag moos

44. Ntxwj Nyoog li qhib lub rooj ntug los saib ntuj lub rooj teb los xyuas ua ciav
    Ntxwj Nyoog lub mob khuam ntav ntuj tso lub tuag los kuam ntav teb nian nov
    ces Ntxwj Nyoog muab txiab tooj txiav lis qawv lub mob ri lis hawv muab txiab
    hlau txiav lis qo lub tuag ri lis ho lawm ntiaj teb

45. zoo li lub mob lub tuag khuam nkaus tus ceg ntoo maj hos lub tuag khuam nkaus
    tus ceg ntoo tov ua ciav niam no ces Tub Nraug Laj ua teb lis zim txog tej yas
    kab luag txawj khaws luag khaws li nkaus Ntxwj Nyoog lub mob lub tuag ntsaws
    khaws luag tej nqaws tiab

46. zoo li Tub Nraug Laj li koj tsis txawj khaws zoo li khaws tau Ntxwj Nyoog lub
    mob ntsaj hos ntsaws nkaus tej nruab siab no zoo li niam no luag txawj khaws
    luag khaws tau Ntxwj Nyoog, lub mob lub tuag ntsaws nkaus tej nqaws awv Tub
    Nraug Laj ces tsis txawj khaws yuav khaws tau Ntxwj Nyoog lub tuag ntsaws
    nkaus tej nyuag ntshua plawv

47. koj ua teb li zim tuaj tej ya kab ua ciav tsaws tau Ntxwj Nyoog lub mob lub mob
    poob qa nkaus rau koj tej quav npab koj ua teb li zim rau tej yas kev Ntxwj Nyoog
    lub tuag tau poob qas nroos rau koj quav tes ces niam no tub nraug laj li koj ces
    yuav ua mob qag ntxiag tuaj nruab siab

48. ua noos qas ntxiag tuaj nruab cev rov los txog zoo li koj los pw hau qaug lias txaj
    no hau qaug lias ncoo zoo li nim nov ces koj kwv koj tig leej tub tig sab laj tuaj

tom tag ho cav tau leej twg ntxooj neeb tseeb tav no koj kwv koj tij ces sab laj tuaj tom txuas leej twg li ntxooj neeb zoo cav tau Txiv Muam Mab li ntxooj neeb tseeb cav tau Txiv Nuam Suav neeb zoo

49. koj kwv koj tij tes lauj tuav cwj xyab tuav tswm sab lauj nas tuav lawm tswm ntawv txog Txiv Muam Mab Txiv Nuam Mab tias xyoo no koj tuaj tsis tsum ncaij ho tawm plaws lub nrauj lam tias tus nees txaij ho Txiv Muam Suav tias tub kwv xyoo no koj tuaj txis tsum nyoog tsis txum thaud hos ntawm no tawm plaws Tub Nraug Laj tus nees nraug no

50. ua ciav tub tij rov los txog tom toj hos ua ciav tub tij nhov tias Tub Nraug Laj nrog Ntxwj Nyoog lub mob si puag ntsaj ho tub kwv rov los txog tom ncoo yog tau Tub Nraug Laj yuav nrog Ntxwj Nyoog lub mob nroo

51. zoo li no ces yog tau tub tij siab tsis kheev tub kwv siab tsis nqig tub tij tias cav tau leej twg ntxooj neeb tseeb cav tau nkawd twg ntxooj neeb zoo koj kwv koj tij tes lauj tuav tswm xyab lauj nas tuav tswm ntawv ntoj neeb tsog Txiv Muam Mab

52. Txiv Muam Mab tias kwv tij txhia xyoo koj tsis ntoj kuv Txiv Muam Mab nyob txoj kev deb xyoo no koj ntoj neeb nthuav ntawv txog kuv Tub Nraug Laj tus ntsuj plig pw lis ko tuaj nruab qhov hleb Txiv Muam Suav tias tub kwv txhia xyoo koj tsis ntoj neeb Txiv Muam Suav· nyob lawm txoj kev dav xyoo no koj ntoj neeb tuaj txog txiv nraug laj tus plig pw li ko nruab qhov ntxa tu tub tij siab tub tij rov li niab tu tub kwv plawv tub kwv rov li zawv tub tij los txog tom taj hos ua ciav yog tau Tub Nraug Laj li koj zaj mob nyob tsis kaj hos

53. yog zaj mob sib puag ntsaj ho tub kwv los txog tom ncoo Tub Nraug Laj li koj lub mob tsis zoo yuav nrog Ntxwj Nyoog zaj mob sib puag nroo los mus tsis zoo ua cia tub tij tias cav ntiaj teb no leej twg ntxooj neeb tseeb nkawd twg ntxoog neeb zoo

54. cav tau tooj nchai Siv Yis ntxooj neeb tseeb ntiaj teb no tooj nchai Siv Yis ntx-ooj neeb zoo niam no ces koj kwv koj tig tes lauj tuav tswm xyab lauj maum nas tuav cwj ntaw ntoj neeb txog tooj nchai Siv Yis raws tooj nchai Siv Yig nqis tuaj poob tooj nchai Siv Yis ntauj taws nqis tuaj txog muab cwj neeb txhos lis ntso

55. ncoj neeb sis plho zoo tswb neeb nrov lam lug nqis nto toj hos ciav yog xyoo no poob qas nroo Tub Nraug Laj xyoo ploj ua ciav tooj nchai Siv Yis muab cwj neeb

txhos lis ntsaws ncoj neeb tej sis thawv tswb neeb nrov lam lug nqis nto tsuag
xyoo no ua ciav poob nroo Tub Nraug Laj li koj nrog Ntxwj Nyoog zaj mob sib
puag tuag

56. ua ciav niam no ces yog tau ntiaj teb tim li cas qas cais tim li tsi yog tau hnub
txheej tshoj thaum ub ntiaj teb tsis mob ntiaj nrag raug tau tsis muaj nkeeg

57. ntiaj teb tsis tau ploj ho teb cais tsis muaj tuag noob txheej tshoj thaum ub ces
nqaij yog lawm nqaij toog txhav yog txhav hlau niam no ces nqaij los yog nqaij
ciab zib txha los yog txha plhaub mag yog vim tau noob txheej tshoj thaum ub
niag neej tswv yim loj es niag neej muab niaj dab coj mus muag noj ho

58. niag neej tswv yim ntau niag neej ces muab niaj dab coj mus muag haus niam
no niag neej ces muab niag dab coj mus muag,noj tas tshuav niam ob tib tug zoo
li niam dab mus nug txuj lawm Puj Saub teb nug ci lawm Puj Saub chaw Puj
Saub mus qhuab kev Yawm Saub mus qhia npe

59. zoo li Puj Saub mus qhub txuj ho zoo li niam dab coj mus Poj Saub yawm mus
qhia lus tias niam neej ces tswv yim loj niag neeg ntxias niag dab coj mus muag
noj ho niag neej tswv yim ntau niag neej ntxais niag dab coj mus muag haus niam
no niag dab tshuav neb ob tib tug neb nce li hlo pem Ntxwj Nyoog toj zeb zag
sua loj ho

60. tsuab Ntxwj Nyoog peb teg hmoov tshauv hmoov xua nqis tsuj rov txog lawm
yaj ceeb neb mus nrog niag nphoo hmoov tshauv nam zog mus nrog niag dab
nphoo hmoov xua zoo li niam no niag dab rov zoj los txog niag dab nce hlo txog
Ntxwj Nyoog toj zeb zag nrom suas loj hos tsuab zoj lawm Ntxwj Nyoog peb teg
hmoov tshauv niag dab nce hlo mus txog Ntxwj Nyoog toj zeb zuag tsuab zoj
lawm Ntxwj Nyoog peb teg hmoov xua niaj dab rov zoj los txog niam dab

61. tias niag neej nes yog vim noob txheej tshoj thaum ub nej tswv yim loj es nej
muab peb niam dab coj mus muag noj ho nej tswv yim ntau nej muab peb dab
coj mus muag haus niam no ces txav zog tuaj peb nphoo hmoov tshauv nam zog
tuaj peb nphoo hmoov xua niam neej hais tias niag dab nej xub nphoo tuaj hos

62. niam dab tias niam neej nej tswv yim loj ces nej xub nphoo tuaj hos ua ciav niag
neej nphoo niaj peb teg mus niaj dab nraim ntshis tuaj nraum rooj ho niam no

niag dab nphoo niag niaj peb teg tuaj ces niag neej qhov muag plooj hos zoo li
niag neej nphoo niaj peb teg mus niag dab traim ntshis nraum ntsa niag dab
nphoo niaj peb teg tuaj ces ntshe niag neej qhov muag nplas

63. zoo li nim no ces dab pom neej hos neej tsis pom dab niag dab tias niag dev niam
tom nruj nrawv tuaj tod vaj hos txav zog tuaj peb nphoo hmoov tshauv nam zog
los peb nphoo hmoov xua hnub tsheej tshoj thaum ub niag ces tswv yim loj es
niag neej muab peb niag dab coj mus muag noj hos

64. zoo li niam neej ces tswv yim ntau niag neej muab peb niag dab coj mus muaq
haus niag neej ces yuav ntxias peb niag dab txog ntuj sua teb tom qab muab niam
dab coj mus noj tus caj ho niam neej ces muab niam dab ntxias txog ntuj sua
teb tom pes muab niam dab coj mus muag noj nqis tu ces

65. zoo li niam mo ces tshuav lawm wb niaj ob tib tug txav zog tuaj peb nphoo hmoov
tshauv nam zag tuaj peb nphoo hmoov xua niam dev tias nian dab niam muaj
tes ces nej xub nphoo tuaj es niag dab tias yog li nej tsav zog tuaj peb sib nphoo
hmoov tshauv nam zog los tuaj peb sib nphoo hmoov xua niag dab ces nphoo
niam peb teg tuaj ces niag dev nraim ntshis tuaj nraum rooj ho

66. niag dev qhov muag ces tsis plooj hos niag dab nphoo niam peb teg mus niag
dev nraim ntshis tuaj nraum ntsa niag dev qhov muag tsis plas niag dab tias niag
dev zaum no ces puas pom peb niam dev hais tias tsis pom nej hos niam no ces
niam dev tom nruj nrawv tuaj tom vaj niag dab yuav tias niag dev ua cas nej
yuav tom nruj nrawv tuaj tom vaj hos niam dev tias yog vim niag niam dab coj
peb ntiaj teb tib neeg mus tsuj li

67. niam no niam dev ces tom nruj nrawv rov lawm ntiaj teb niam dab tias niaj dev
cas niam yuav tom nruj nrawv rov lawm ntiaj teb niam dev tias tos peb tom nruj
ntawv rov ntiaj teb los yog vim nej es coj tau peb ntiaj teb tib neeg nce hlo lawm
Ntxwj Nyoog lub rooj vag zeb

68. zoo li nim no dev pom dab dab tsis pom dev zoo li niam no ces niam neej ces
nam zaj tuaj tom nphoo hmoov tshauv txav los los nphoo hmoov xua zoo li niam
neej nphoo niaj peb teg mus niam dab nraim ntshis tuaj nraum ntsa niam dab
nphoo niaj peb teg tuaj ces niam neej qhov muag nplas

69. zoo li niam neej nphoo lawm peb teg niag dab nraim ntshis tuaj nraum rooj ho
nim no ces niam dab nphoo niaj peb nphoo niag neej qhov muag plooj niaj peb
zaum no ces ntiaj teb neeg no ces yog dab pom neej hos neej ces tsis pom dab niam
no ces niam dab ntxias niam neej mus txog ntuj sua teb tom qab muab niam neej
coj mus muag noj hos nqis tu ncaj hos niam dab yuav muab niam neej ntxias
txog ntuj sua teb tom pes niag dab muab niam neej ntxias coj mus muag tu ces

70. zoo li zaum no ces niam dab ntxias niam neej mus txoj kev pem toj es niam dab
ntxias niam neej coj mus muag noj hos niag dab ntxias niag neej mus txog kev
nram hav niag dab ntxias niag neej coj mus muag hnav no ntawm no mus tas
ib qib qhov no mus tas ib quag

71. zoo li nim nov ces ntuj ntsig teb ha caj sim voos noob txheej tshoj thaum ub
raug tau lub ntuj ntsig Tub Nraug Laj li koj cev los txoos zoo li nim nov ces ntuj
teb ntsim hav caj sim vos noob txheej tshoj thaum ub raug tau lub ntuj los yog
raug tau tub nraug laj li koj cev los nyob cas nim nov ces yog tau noob txheej
tshoj thaum ub zaj nab peb hlis tshav

72. zaj luav peb hlis cua ntiaj teb no ces ntuj qhuav lis qhawv tuaj xya niaj teb qhuav
lis qho los xya xyoo noob xyoob tuag tu caj hos noob ntoo tuag tu ces ntiaj teb
do qas cuas los xya niaj ntiaj nrag do qas cuas los xya xyoo

73. Nkauj Iab Nraug Oo hais tias nyob twg li txawm noob xyoob qhov twg li txawg
noob ntoo Nkauj Iab Nraug Oo hais tias noob xyoob nyob pem Ntxwj Nyoog
qab cooj qaib noob ntoo nyob pem Ntxwj Nyoog qab nkaug npuas

74. zoo li nian nov ces tub txib los tsis muaj hos tub khaiv los tsis tau yuav tso leej
twg mus muab noob xyoob nkawm twg yuav mus muab noob ntoo

75. Nkauj Iab Nraug Oo hais tias Nkauj Tseeg Lis Tseev mus muab noob xyoob pem
Ntxwj Nyoog qab cooj qaib tso Puj Tseeg Lis Tseev mus muab noob ntoo lawm
pem Ntxwj Nyoog qab nkuag npuas

76. Poj Tseeg Lis Tseev ya lis plho mus ntsib Ntxwj Nyoog nkawm tub yug nyuj hos
ua ciav Ntxwj Nyoog nkawm tub yug nyuj hais tias txhia xyoo koj tsis ntoj ua
ciav txhia niaj koj tsis khiav

249

77. zoo li xyoo no koj yuav tuaj mus dab tsi Puj Tseeg Lis Tseev hais tias yog ntiaj teb peb hlis tshav yog zaj luav cua yog xya niaj es teb do teb li dus los xya xyoo

78. zaun no Nkauj Iab Nraug Oo tso kuv tuaj mus muab noob xyoob pem Ntxvj Nyoog qab cooj qaib mus muab noob ntoo qab nkuag npuas noob xyoob muaj los tsis muaj nes noob ntoo tshuav los tsis tshuav ua ciav Ntxwj Nyoog nkawm tub yug nyuj hais tias noob xyoob tshuav lawm niaj ib tib re noob ntoo tshuav lawm niaj ib tib rau

79. Puj Tseeg Lis Tseev ya plho mus txog pem Ntxwj Nyoog qab nkuag npuas muab zoj niaj ib tib re noob xyoob nqa lis ncuv tuaj ntawm ncauj muab zoj noob ntoo ib tib rau nqa lis ncuv tuaj htawm taw

80. Puj Tseeg Lis Tseev ya plho rov los txog ntiaj teb Nkauj Iab Nraug Oo hais tias Puj Tseeg Lis Tseev koj muab noob xyoo hua lis hawv tuaj nram roob muab noob ntoo hua lis hawv tuaj nruab hav Puj Tseeg Lis Tseev ya plho muab hua lis hawv tuaj nruab roob muab noob ntoo hua lis hawv tuaj nruab hav ua ciav ib hlis peb caug nyoog

81. nim nov noob xyoob ua kaus poob noob ntoo mus ua kaus hlav ua ciav noob xyoob tuaj peb tug noob ntoo tuaj niaj peb tsob

82. ua ciav nim nov noob xyoob hlob tiav txuj hos muaj ib yog Nas Kos tug muaj ib tug ces yog suav tug Suav coj mus fiab vab muaj ib tug ces cia Txawj Nkiag nqis tuaj txog muab txiav zoj muab txhij zog ob tog txhij muab phua lis plho

83. ua ob sab ces Txawj Nkiag muab coj los ua koj leej tub tuag tus cwj mus qhuab kab zoo li nim nov ces noob ntoo hlob mus tiav txuj muaj ib tug ces cia nas kos kaws tuaj saum ntsis muaj ib tug ces yog mab yog suav tug niaj Mab Suav txiav coj mus ua hai lawm

84. zoo li nim nov ces muaj ib tug ces yog Hmoob tug luag txiav coj mus ua thoob ua rhawv rau dej hos zoo li nim nov ces muaj ib tug ces cia Txawj Nkiag nqis tuaj txog muab txiav lis ntho muab hliav zoj ua plaub ceg

85. muab phua zoj ua ob deg ua koj tub tuag tus cwj mus taw ke ua tus cwj Puj Saub
mus qhia lus tus cwj Puj Saub qhia tub tuag kev ntawm no mus tas ib qib qhov
no mus tas ib quag

86. zoo li nim nov ces neej hav teb ntsig caj sim voos yog tau noob txheej tshoj thaum
ub yog raug tau lub ntuj cev los nyob nim nov yog raug tau tub nraug laj li koj
cev los mus txoos

87. zoo li nim nov neej hav teb ntsig caj sim vos yog noob txheej tshoj thaum ub
yog raug tau lub ntuj los txoos nim nov ntsig tau tub nraug laj li koj cev los nyob
zoo li nian nov ces noob ntoo ces tuaj lawm niaj ib tib tsob tub txib nqis tsis
muaj hos tub khai nqis tsis tau

88. Txawj Nkiag hais tias txib tau kev zej nqa rab ntaj hos muaj peb tug nce hlo toj
peg xub tshav txiav lis nrawv niaj ib tug nkaug lis nkuav tuaj nram tiaj hos

89. nkaug lis zoj tuaj nram tus nim no coj los ua tub tuag tus nees zaj nees txaij lis
ntxhub yuav muab zoj niaj ib rab ntaj txiav lis nrawv nkaug lis zoj tuaj rau nram
tus coj los tsim zoj ua nees txaij nees kua eeb

90. rau tub tuag caij rag lis ntw mus lawm lwm yeeb yog tus nees txaij nees kuav pav
yuav caij rag lis ntw lawm yeeb nrag qhov no tas ib qib ntawm no tas ib quag zoo
li nim nov ces tub txawg nqis tuaj txog Txawj Nkiag nqis tuaj txog ua cas noob
qoob nqis tsis muav hos niv nov noob loo txawm tsis tau ces yuav hais tias

91. yuav hais tias ua li noob qoob nyob qhov twg thiaj li muaj noob loo los txawm
tsis tau yuav hais tias ua li noob qoob noob loo nyob qhov twg lis muaj

92. Txawj Nkiag hais tias ua li noob qoob nyob qhov twg li muaj hos ua li noob loo
thiaj li tshuav nes hais tias noob qoob ces nyob pem Ntxwj Nyoog toj zeb zag
noob loo ces nyob pem Ntxwj Nyoog rawm zeb tso thiaj li muaj li tshuav nes

93. hais tias tub txib los tsis muaj nes tub khai los tsis tau nes hais tias yuav tso leej
twg mus muab noob qoob pem Ntxwj Nyoog rawm zeb tso

94. yuav tso nas tsuag mus muab noob qoob mus nqa noo loo nas tsuag phwb lis
nuag mus ntsib Ntxwj Nyoog nkawm tub yug nyuj hos Ntxwj Nyoog nkawm

tub yug nyuj yuav hais tias koj yuav tuaj mus dab tsi ua ciav txhia niaj koj tsis ntoj txhia xyoo koj tsis khiav

95. nas tsuag yuav hais tias txhia niaj kuv tsis ntoj los vim tsis muaj kab txhia niaj kuv khiav los vim tsis muaj kev xyoo no ces yog tau noob qoob txawm tsis muaj hos noob loo los txawm tsis tau Txawj Nkiag nqis tuaj txog tub txawg nqis tuaj poob noob qoob los tsis muaj noob loo los tsis tau

96. zoo li xyoo no Nkauj Iab Nraug Oo li txib kuv tuaj muab noob qoob noob loo pem Ntxwj Nyoog toj zeb zag zoo li noob qoob muaj los nes noob loo thuav los tsis tshuav Ntxwj Nyoog tub yug nyuj hais tias noob qoob tshuav lawm niaj ib re noob loo ces tshuav lawm niaj ib tib rau

97. nas tsuag phwb lis nuag mus muab noob qoob nqis los poob mus muab noob loo nqis los txog yuav muab noob qoob nrom qam nroos tuaj nruab ke ib hlis peb caug nyoog noob qoob nqis xiav teb

98. muab noob loo nrom qam nroos tuaj nruab hav ib hlis peb caug nyoog noob loo nqis xiav hav zoo li puv tsib hlis peb caug noob loo hlob tiav txuj hos puv tsib hlis peb ces noob qoob mus hlob txiav ci

99. zoo li nim nov ces cuaj leeg los ntxheb khob yim leej los ntxheb taig muab noob loo los ua tub tuag tus mov laig zoo li cuaj leeg los ntxheb taig yim leej los ntx- heb khob

100. zoo li muab noob qoob nrom qam nroos tuaj tim toj muab coj los ua tub tuag tus hno kho tshaib muab noob loo nrom qam nroos tuaj tim roob muab coj los laig rau tub tuag niaj peb dia tuaj tim rawm tub tuag li tau kev mus cuag yawm no na

101. ntawm no mus tas ib qib qhov no mus tas ib quag poj kab yawg kev mus no na tsis quab nog tsis quab see koj txais koj lis tau nov na thaum twg laig ces hais li ntawm no rau tus tuag

102. zoo li nim nov ces nplooj lwg qav tsim lim kaws quav toj quav taug ri lis hawv poob li nthav Ci Txuj thiab Tuj Nplug nkaw noob neej nqis ntiaj teb tej ntshua plawv ces

103. zoo li nim nov ces quav toj quav taug ri li hawv tuaj tim toj hos zoo li noob txheej tshoj thaum ub ces txawj tuag nqis txawj feb nim nov ces Ci Txuj thiab Tuj Nplug ces tsim noob neej rau ntiaj teb ces txawj tuag tsis txawj rov

104. zoo li nix nov ces nplooj lwg qav tsib lim kaws quav toj quav taug ri ii hawv tuaj tim toj zoo li ntiaj teb tib neeg mus sib pus ploj nim nov ces nplooj lwg qav tsin lim kaws quav toj quav taug ri li hawv tuaj tim tog poob nthav noob neej nqis ntiaj teb

105. zoo li noob txheej tshoj ntuj thaum ub ces txawj tuag nqis txawj rov zoo li nim nov ces Ci Txuj thiab Tuj Nplug nkaw siab tsis zoo nplooj lwg qav tsim lim kaws quav toj quav taug yuav pus ntiaj teb tib neeg tuag ces yuav tsis txawj rov zoo li leej twg tuag ces yuav khaws tau nploog lwg qav tsim lim kaws txoj kev ploj nas

106. ntawm no mus tag ib qib qhov no mus tag ib quag tuav peb txog cawv rau koj haus tas tso yuav xa koj mus cuag poj cuag yawg no na noj txij ib leeg noj haus ces txij koj ib leeg haus noj tsis taus rau nruab taub haus tsis taus rau nruab rag noj tsis tag ua tiag nqa haus tsis taus los ua tiag pus coj mus pub poj yawg noj pub poj yawg haus

107. yuav mus dia poj dia yawg lawm ntuj tsiag teb tsaus yuav dia poj dia yawg lawm ntuj tshav teb nqhuab li sawv muab noj mus ua neej tshiab neej lig no na qas txhiab nyob tsim nuj qas txhis nyob tsim nqi no

108. nim no ces koj zoo li hnub txheej tshoj thaum ub Poj Saub tsim noob neej los nyob tsim noob tsav los rau ntiaj teb tsim lub ntuj los txoos tsim lub teb los poob tsim tau nkauj hnub tuaj peb caug lub nraug hli lawm peb caug nkawm nkauj hnub kav peb caug hnub nraug hli kav peb caug nyoog zoo li kav tau ntiaj teb leej twg muaj tsug cia zoo txuj ho nkawm twg muaj ci cia zoo ci cav tau yaj yuam muaj txug cia zoo txuj ho cav tau yaj yig muaj ci cia

109. zoo ci yog tau yaj yuam rab hneev tooj ncai muaj peb caug hlau zoo li nim rab hneev hlau mus peb caug nta coj mus tua nkauj hnub tua lawm nees nkaum cuaj lub nraug hli tua tau nees nkaum cuaj nkawg nkauj hnub tshuav ib tib lub nraug hli ces tshuav ib tib leeg Nkauj Hnub ces ntshai nkauj hnub nraim qas ntshis tuaj npoo ntuj ho

110. ntuj tsaus qas nti los xya niaj ho tshuav Nraug Hli nraim qas ntshis tej npoo
teb zoo li tsaus ntuj qas nraim los lawm xya xyoo tuj lug yog ntiaj teb yuav mloog
txuj rau Poj Saub mloog rau Saub Yawm pluj lug hais tias Tuj Nplug thiab Ci
Txuj neb rov mus txog neb tso txiv nyuj mus hu Nkauj Hnub li lawm tuaj

111. neb tso txiv nees mus hu Nraug Hli li tawm los Nkauj Hnub tias zoo li Nkauj
Hnub ces tuag lawm nees nkaum cuaj lub zoo li Nraug Hli tuag lawm nees
nkaum cuaj nkawg nim no Nkauj Hnub tsis tawm tuaj Nraug Hli tsis tawm
los Ci Txuj thiab Tuj Nplug rov los txog los tso txiv nyuj mus hu Nkauj Hnub
tias txiv nyuj lub suab luj hos

112. tso txiv nees mus hu Nraug Hli tias txiv nees lub suab heev ces Nkauj Hnub
nraim ntshis tsis tawm tuaj Nraug Hli nraim nkoos tsis tawm los ntuj yuav
tsaus qas nti los xya niaj teb yuav tsaus qas nti los xya xyoo

113. ua ciav nim no Ci Txuj thiab Tuj Nplug nug txuj lawm Poj Saub nug ci rau
Saub Yawm poj saub mus qhuab kev Saub Yawm mus qhuab kab Puj Saub mus
qhub tsug Saub Yawm mus qhub tias zoo li Ci Txuj thiab Tuj Nplug

114. neb yuav kom Nkauj Hnub tawm tuaj ces Nraug Hli tawm los neb mus txog
neb kom Nkauj Mog mus hu Nkauj Hnub niam peb suab tuaj hauv ntuj es
Nkauj Hnub li tawm tuaj hos kom Nkauj Mim mus hu peb los tuaj qab ntug
ces Nraug Hli li tawm los

115. zoo li Ci Txuj thiab Tuj Nplug rov los txog kom Nkauj Mog mim mus hu niam
peb suab txhais taug tuaj hos ua ciav Nkauj Hnub nrai qas ntshis tsis tawm
tuaj hos Nkauj Mim mus hu niam peb zag txhais peg los Nraug Hli nraim qas
ntshis tsis tawm los

116. nim no lub teb tsaus li nti los xya xyoo Ci Txuj thiab Tuj Nplug hmoog txuj
lawm Poj Saub mloog ci rau saum Saub Yawm ua ciav Poj Saub tias Ci Txuj
thiab Tuj Nplug neb kom Nkauj Hnub li tawm los ces tso txiv lau qaib taw luaj
ko diav nrog ntuj txiv thooj siab hu Nkauj Hnub li tawm tuaj hos

117. zoo li neb rov mus txog neb tso txiv lau qaib taw luaj ko tawv nrog ntuj txiv
thooj plawv hu Nraug Hli li tawm los zoo li nim nov ces Ci Txuj thiab Tuj Nplug
rov los txog zoo li Ci Txuj thiab Tuj Nplug kom txiv lau qaib qua niaj peb zag

118. txhais peg tuaj ces ua ciav Nkauj Hnub tawm plaws tuaj hos zoo li txiv lau qaib
qua niaj peb zag qab ntug los zoo li Nraug Hli tawm plaws tej npoo teb zoo li
nim nov ces lub ntuj yuav kaj nrig los xya xyoo Nkauj Hnub yuav pus ntiaj
teb ua noj hos

119. zoo li xya niaj ces Nraug Hli yuav los kav ntiaj nrag ua hnav zaum no ces lub
ntuj kaj nrig los xya niaj hos lub teb kaj nrig los xya xyoo zoo li noob txheej
tshoj thaum ub Nkauj Hnub tawm tuaj hos zoo li tawm pem ceeb tsheej ib
Nkauj Hnub tawm pem ceeb tsheej yog Nkauj Hli nraim

120. lis ntshis tej npoo ntuj hos ntiaj teb yuav tsaus los xya niaj hos Nraug Hli yuav
nraim lis ntshis tej npoo teb los tau xya xyoo zoo li lub ntuj tsaus lis nti los tau xya
xyoo ces ntiaj teb ntsiag niaj hos lub teb tsaus lis nti los tau xya niaj lub teb nyob
ntsiag to ntiaj teb tsis tau kev mus ua noj ntiaj nrag tsis tau kev mus ua haus hos

121. zoo li nim nov ces Nkauj Hnub tawm qas plaws rov los kav plaub fab muaj ib
fab cia rau ntiaj teb Ci Txuj thiab Tuj Nplug mus ua noj hos muaj ib fab cia
kav rau tub tuag mus cuag poj ho Nkauj Hnub ces kav niaj ib fab cais rau ntiaj
teb mus ua haus muaj niaj ib fab ces Nkauj Hnub tawm tuaj kav rau tub tuag
mus cuag yawg no nas qhov no mus tas ib qib ntawm no mus tas ib quag

122. zoo li nim nob ces neej hav teb ntsig hav caj sim voos yog raug lub ntuj los
nyob zoo li xyoo no yog raug tau lub Tub Nraug Laj li koj cev txiaj zam los
mus txoos neej hav teb ntsig cam sim voos yuav raug tau lub ntuj li txoos raug
tau Tub Nraug Laj li koj cev los mus nyob

123. zoo niv nob ces koj ntim lub txiaj zam lis zim yuav los mus yog tau ntiaj teb
zoo ua noj hos teb li cais zoo ua haus koj ntim lub txiaj zam li yeev yuav los
mus ces cas txiv dab rooj paim yuav ua daj lis ris tav lawm koj kab ua nros lis
yas chua lawm koj npab tias koj yog peb ntiaj teb mus tu tsiaj es ntiaj nrag tib
neeg mus tu txhuv koj ntim lub txiaj zam li zam yuav

124. mus tus tsi koj yuav hais tias yog tau ntiaj teb tus mob nkeeg mob teb cais mob
nkeeg ntau ces niv nob kuv thiaj li yuav los mus ces zoo li ces niam txiv dab
rooj lis pain yuav daj lis ris tias koj yog ntiaj teb tib neeg mus tu tsiaj es ntiaj
nrag tib neeg mus tu txhuv ntiaj teb mob nkeeg hlob ntiaj nrag mob nkeeg
ntau cas koj tsis kom koj kwv koj tig ntooj neeb saib cas koj tsis kom koj niam

koj txiv ntxooj neeb kho koj yuav tias cuaj hauv neeb los raws tsis tau yim hauv tshuaj los raws tsis cuag

125. niv nob koj tes lauj tuav yees ntab lauj nas npuaj ntawm plab tes lauj tuav ntawm cev koj lauj nas nplawm ntawm tes ces koj kwv tij ntxooj neeb txog txiv muam mab los tsis kaj hos nthuav tsawv txog Txiv Nuam Suav los tsis zoo

126. raws tau tooj nchai Siv Yis ntxooj neeb qas thawv tswb neeb nrov lam luj lug tej toj xyoo no poob nroos lub xyoo ploj hos tooj nchai Siv Yis ntxooj neeb lis tsawv tswb neeb nrov lis lug txog tej hauv tsuag xyoo no yog poob tag Tub Nraug Laj li koj lub xyoo tuag

127. zoo niv nob ces tes lauj tuam zeb dub lauj nas tuam zeb daus zoo li hlab tsuj hlab npuag ces ntau ces koj li ntim lub txiaj zam lis yeev yuav los mus ces koj yuav ua niam txiv dab rooj paim ib los tsaug ces koj li tau kev mus cuag poj cuag yawg nob nas ntawm no mus tas ib qib qhov no mus tas ib quag niv nob ces koj ntim lub txiaj zam lis yeev los mus txog lawm niam txiv dab xwm kab los yej ces nkawm niam txiv dab xwm yuav ua daj lis ris tav lawm

128. koj kab ua dos li yas huas lawm koj npab tias luag cav tias ntiaj teb zoo ua noj teb cais zoo ua haus koj yuav los mus ua tus tsi zoo li koj hais tias ntiaj teb tus mob nkeeg coob ntiaj nrag tus mob nkeeg ntau yog tau Ntxwj Nyoog siab tsis ncaj Ntxwj Nyoog siab tsis zoo tso lub mob nqis lawm koj tej quav npab tso lub tuag poob nthav koj quav tes koj tes lauj nas npuaj

129. tuav lawm xyoob yim vim koj cev xeeb soob lauj nas tuav ntawm hlau vim yog koj lub cev xeeb yau koj ua niam txiv xwm kab ib los tsaug ces koj li tau kev mus cuag poj cuag yawg no nas

130. zoo li nim no ces niam txiv ncej dab ncej qhua ua daj lis ris tav lawm koj kab ua dos lis ris huas lawm koj tes hais tias cas koj tsis kom koj kwv koj tig ntx-ooj neeb saib koj niam koj txiv ntxooj neeb kho koj hais tias noob txheej tshoj thaum ub ntiaj teb raug tsis muaj mob teb cais raug tsis muaj nkeeg

131. nim nov ces yog tau Ntxwj Nyoog siab tsis zoo yog ntiaj teb nyiam ploj yog lawm ntiaj nrag nyiam tuag Ntxwj Nyoog tso lub mob nqis ntiaj teb thiaj li tso lub tuag nqis ntiaj nram luag txawj khaws ntsaws ntso luag tej nqaws tiab

132. hos koj ces tsis txawj khaws ces khaws tau Ntxwj Nyoog lub mob ntsaws ntso
koj tej hlab siab luag txawj khaws ces luag khaws Ntxwj Nyoog lub mob ntsaws
ntso luag tej nqaws awv

133. koj ces tsis txawj khaws yuav khaws tau Ntxwj Nyoog lub mob ntsaws koj tej
hlab plawv nim no koj thiaj ntim lub tsiaj zam li yeev los mus niam txiv ncej
dab ncej qhua yog tus mob nkeeg coob hais tias yog lawm ntiaj nrag tus mob
nkeeg ntau

134. niam txiv ncej dab ncej qhua ua cas koj tsis kom koj kwv koj tig koj niam koj
txiv ntooj neeb saib nthuav yaig xyuas koj hais tias cuaj hauv neeb los kho tsis
tau yim hauv tshuaj los kho tsis cuag hos zoo li nim nov ces koj txoj pa yaj lis
ntxhub koj ncauj qhuav nkig lis nkub koj txoj pa yaj lis tshuav koj ncauj qhuav
nkig lis nkuav

135. zoo li koj hais tias koj tos koj kwv koj tig nqa koj saum txaj rov pem teb tos koj
kwv koj tig rhuab dej los ntxuav koj cev tos koj kwv koj tig nqa koj rov tom
txuas koj tos koj kwv koj tig rhuab dej los rau koj ntxuav muag tas ces koj yuav
los mus ces koj yuav ua niam txiv ncej dab ncej qhua ib los tsaug ces koj li tau
kev mus cuag poj cuag yawg no nas

136. ntawm no mus tas ib qib qhov no mus tas ib quag zoo li niam txiv dab rooj lis
tag ua daj lis ris tav lawm koj kab ua dos lis yas tav lawm koj kev hais tias koj
yog ntiaj teb tib neeg mus tu tsiag hos koj yuav los ua tus dab tsi koj hais tias
ntiaj teb tus mob nkeeg ntau ces koj yuav los mus

137. zoo li niam txiv dab rooj tag hais tias koj tsiv kom koj kwv koj tig ntxooj neeb
saib koj tsis kom niam koj txiv ntsooj neeb kho koj hais tias cuaj hauv neeb los
kho tsis tau hos yim hauv tshuaj los kho tsis cuag

138. zoo li nim nov ces koj tes lauj npuaj zeb dub koj tes lauj npuaj zeb daus koj
hlab tsuj hlab npuag ntau koj thiaj li yuav los mus no na niam txiv dab rooj
lis tag li tso koj kab li tso koj ke koj li tau kev mus cuag poj cuag yawg no na
qhov no ces tas ib quag ntawm no tas ib qib

139. zoo li nim nov ces noob txheej tshoj thaum ub ntiaj teb raug tsis muaj mob
teb cais raug tsis muaj tuag vim Ntxwj Nyoog siab tsis zoo tso lub mob tso lub

257

tuag nqis ntiaj teb koj thiaj ntim lub txiaj zam lis zim ncig yeev ncauj qhuav
koj nplaig nkig lis nkuav

140. koj los taj rau tom txhuas koj yuav los pauj qhua koj los tom txuas rau tom taj
koj yuav los pw lis ko mus pauj dab no nas zoo li koj tuag tas koj yuav ntim
lub txiaj zam lis zim yuav los mus koj tseg koj niam koj txiv tseg koj kwv koj
tig quaj zig qees ua ciav yog koj tuag koj niam koj txiv koj kwv koj tig nyiav
zig qees yog koj ploj

141. zoo li leej twg yuav hlub nkawm twg yuav tshua koj ntim tau lub txiaj zam lis
yeev txog tim toj hos koj kwv koj tig quaj nyiav qas laws yog koj ploj hos zoo
li koj yuav ntim lub txiaj zam lis zim txog tim tsuag koj yuav tseg koj niam koj
txiv quaj nyiav yog lawm koj tuag

142. zoo li nim no cas Txawj Nkiag nqis tuaj txog ces tub txawg nqis tuaj poob
ces txawj nkiag yuav xa tub tuag txog tim toj es xa Tub Nraug Laj li koj mus
cuag poj hos yuav xa tub tuag mus txog tim rawm xa tub tuag rov mus cuag
yawg no nas ntawm no mus tas ib gib qhov no tas ib quag yuav tuav peb txog
cawv rau koj tso yuav xa koj mus cuag poj cuag yawg no nas koj txais ces koj
tau

143. nim nov ces koj yuav los mus yog ntiaj teb dab rooj tag tso lawm koj kev koj
lis tau kev mus cuag poj hos koj li tau mus cuag yawm

144. zoo li koj los ua sim neej no rau ntiaj teb koj nyob tsis taus laus yog vim Ntxwj
Nyoog siab tsis zoo Ntxwj Nyoog siab tsis ncaj hos

145. koj ua teb txog tej yas kab koj khaws tau Ntxwj Nyoog lub mob dai koj tej quav
npab koj ua teb lis zim txog tej yas kev khaws tau Ntxwj Nyoog lub tuag dai
nkaus tej yas tes

146. Koj ntim tau lub txiaj zam li yeev los mus ces koj nce hlo mus muab ntawv niaj
ntawv xyoo rov ntiaj teb los mus thawj xeeb ces koj ncig yeev rov nram tiaj hos
koj mus nce Nyuj Vaj Tuam Teem tus ntaiv nyiaj hos

147. zoo li koj ncig yeev tuaj nram ub koj mus nce Nyuj Vaj Tuam Teem tus ntaiv
kub koj nco ntsoov tuaj nruab siab cim ntsoov tuaj

148. nruab plawv koj nco ntsoov mus muab ntawv niaj ntawv xyoo pem Nyuj Vaj
     Tuam Teem rov los thawj xeeb rau ntiaj teb no lis tau zoo

149. koj mus nce ntaiv ntuj ces
     ib hnub koj nce ib qib
     ob hnub koj nce ob qib
     peb hnub koj nce peb qib
     plaub hnub koj nce plaub qib

150. tsib hnub koj nce tsib qib
     rau hnub koj nce rau qib
     xya hnub koj nce xya qib
     yim hnub koj nce yim qib
     cuaj hnub koj nce cuaj qib
     kaum hnub koj nce kaum qib
     kaum ib hnub koj nce kaum ib qib
     kaum ob hnub koj nce kaum ob qib
     kaum peb hnub koj nce kaum peb qib

     koj nce ib lub Teem Txwv ub taug kaum peb hnub ces koj nce nto ntaiv ntuj
     hos koj nco ntsoov mus thov ntaub thov ntawv pem Nyuj Vaj Tuam Teem kom
     tau zoo ntaub zoo ntawv koj mam li rov los ua neej rau ntiaj teb thiaj li zoo
     poj kab yawg kev ces mus li

151. zoo li koj nco ntsoov
     ib hnub rov nce ib qib
     ob hnub nce ob qib
     peb hnub nce peb qib
     plaub hnub nce plaub qib
     tsib hnub nce tsib qib
     rau hnub nce rau qib
     xya hnub nce xya qib
     qib yim hnub nce yim qib
     cuaj hnub nce cuaj qib
     kaum hnub nce kaum qib
     kaum ib hnub nce kaum ib qib
     kaum ob hnub nce kaum ob qib

kaum peb hnub ces koj nco ntsoov tuaj nruab siab yog koj nce nto ob lub Teem
Txwv koj nco ntsoov mus muab ntaub niaj ntawv xyoo pem Nyuj Vag Tuam Teem

152. zoo li ib hnub koj rov nce ib qib
ob hnub nce ob qib
peb hnub nce peb qib
plaub hnub nce plaub qib
tsib hnub nce tsib qib
rau hnub nce rau qib
xya hnub nce xya qib
yim hnub nce yim qib
cuaj hnub nce cuaj qib
kaum hnub nce kaum qib
kaum ib hnub nce kaum ib qib
kaum ob hnub nce kaum ob qib

ib tsug kaum peb hnub ces koj nce nto peb lub Teem Txwv

153. koj nco ntsoov mus nuab ntaub nuab ntawv xyoo koj muab ntawv nyuj los
ntshai luag laij koj muab ntawv nees los ntshai luag caij koj mus muab ntawv
npua los ntshai luag tua koj muab ntawv dev los ntshai luag ntaus koj mus muab
ntawv kab noog los nag ntub tshav ntuj kub no

154. zoo li koj nco ntsoov mus nuab lawm hauv Nyuj Vaj Tuam Teem tsev ntaub tsev
ntawv rooj ntaub rooj ntaw ces koj phwb lis nuag tuaj nruab tiv txwv thiaj li tau
ntawv nom ntawv tsawv no koj muab tau ntaub muab tau ntawv ntawm Nyuj
Vaj Tuam Teem tau lawm ces nim no Txawj Nkiag yuav coj koj nqis rov lawm ntiaj
teb rov thawj xeeb rau ntiaj nrag koj nco ntsoov nqis rov rau ntiaj teb no zoo li

155. ib hnub koj nqis ib qib
ob hnub nqis ob qib
peb hnub nqis peb qis
plaub hnub nqis plaub qib
tsib hnub nqis tsib qib
rau hnub nqis rau qib
xya hnub nqis xya qib
yim hnub nqis yim qib

cuaj hnub nqis cuaj qib
kaum hnub nqis kaum qib
kaum ib hnub nqis kaum ib qib
kaum ob hnub nqis kaum ob qib

ib tsug kaum peb hnub ces koj nco ntsoov tuaj nruab siab koj nqis dhau ib lub
Teem Txwv lawm

156. nim no ces koj cim ntsoov tuaj nruab plawv tias
ib hnub koj nqis ib qib
ob hnub koj nqis ob qib
peb hnub ces nqis peb qib
plaub hnub nqis plaub qib
tsib hnub nqis tsib qib
rau hnub nqis rau qib
xya hnub nqis xya qib
yim hnub nqis yim qib
cuaj hnub nqis cuaj qib
kaum hnub nqis kaum qib
kaum ib hnub nqis kaum ib qib
kaum ob hnub nqis kaum ob qib

ib tsug kaum peb hnub ces koj nqis dhau ob lub Teem Txwv rov los ntiaj teb

157. zoo li koj rov nqis
ib hnub nqis ib qib
ob hnub nqis ob qib
peb hnub nqis peb qib
plaub hnub nqis plaub qib
tsib hnub nqis tsib qib
rau hnub nqis rau qib
xya hnub nqis xya qib
yim hnub nqis yim qib
cuaj hnub nqis cuaj qib
kaum hnub nqis kaum qib
kaum ib hnub nqis kaum ib qib
kaum ob hnub ces nqis kaum ob qib

puv ib tsug kaum peb hnub ces koj nqis los txog ntiaj nrag nqis los poob ntiaj teb hos

158. zoo li Txawj Nkiag coj koj mus thov tau ntaub niaj mus muab tau ntawv xyoo pem Nyuj Vaj Tuam Teem rooj ntaub rov los txog rau ntiaj nrag lis cais lawm hos koj nco li ntsoov tuaj nruab siab

159. zaum no Txawj Nkiag xa koj mus hloov tau ntaub xyoo ntawv niaj pem ceeb tsheej Nyuj Vaj Tuam Teem phav tsuj phav npuag tas lawm ces Txawj Nkiag pus koj rov los poob ntiaj teb nrag qas li cais cim lis ntsoov tuaj nruab plawv Txawj Nkiag yuav xa koj mus thawj xeeb dua koj mus thawj suav nom sua txwv koj lis tau zoo no nas

160. ntawm no rov ua txoj caw rau tus tuag tuav peb txog cawv rau koj haus tau yuav coj koj mus muab tsho tsuj tsho npuag hnav ces koj li tau kev mus cuag poj cuag yawg no nas tus qhuab kev rov tuav tshib ntawg kev cai pam tuag ntawm Hmoob yuav xa tus tuag mus ua tsaug teb ua tsaug chaw nws yug los lub teb chaws twg nws ho mus nyob pes tsawg lub teb chaws ces yuav tau

161. xa mus ua tsaug kom txhua cov tab chaws uas nws tau los ua neej nyob los lawm txog thaum nws tuag zoo li nim no ces koj yuav ntim tau lub txiaj saub zam lis yuav los mus muab koj tsho tsuj tsho npuag hnav koj los ua neej thawj xeeb ib zaug rau ntiaj teb no koj los ua neej ib zaug tshwm sim rau li teb chaws yug nyob lub zos thiab teb chaws twg ces hais lub npe teb chaws ntawd koj yuav mus muab koj tsho tsuj tsho npuag hnav koj thiaj

162. li tau kev mus thawj xeeb ib tug neeg peb tug ntsuj peb tug plig xya tus duab koj yuav los ces koj lub cev tuag tas ntsuj plig tuag tsis tas muaj ib tug ntsuj plig yuav mus nuab tsho tsuj tsho npuag hnav

163. koj yuav sua roj sua hneev rov qab mus muab tsho tsuj tsho npuag lawm lub npe teb chaws uas thaum yug tau nws thaum nws tuag lawm ces hais qhia rau ua tsaug teb chaws uas nws ua neej los mus lawm rov mus cob hauv lub zos thaum nws yug ntawm

164. koj los noj tsuag luag ib ntsug zoov koj rauv tas luag ib ntsug taws koj haus tu luag ib tug dej nim no koj yuav los mus ces niam sab seej thwj tim xeeb teb

xeeb chaw ua daj lis ris tav koj kab ua dos lis nyas ntsuas koj npab ua daj lis ris
tav kev ua dos lis nyas ntsuas koj tes koj los noj tsuag luag ib ntsug teb rauv tas
luag ib ntsug zoov nuj

165. koj yuav los mus koj yuav muab nyiaj txiag xyab ntawv coj ua sab seej thwv
tim xeeb teb xeeb chaw thwv xeeb thwv yaj ib los tsaug ces koj muaj nyiaj txiag
xyab ntaw lo tuam teeb thooj koj muab nyiaj txiag xyab ntawv los poj mab
yawm sua xeeb teb xeeb chaw tuam peeb choj ces luag tso koj kev koj li tau kev
mus cuag poj cuag yawg no nas ces muab peb daig xav txheej

166. coj los hlawv rau ntawm tus tuag ib sab ces hais ua suab laig dab koj kwv koj
tig koj niam koj txiv muab nyiaj txiag xyab ntaw rau koj coj mus ua tsaug teb
tsaug chaw koj coj mus muas kev mab kev suav lawm yeeb tim nrag nyob tsim
nuj coj mus kev lawm yeeb tim teb nyob tsim nqis

167. yog muaj dej loj ces hais ntxiv li no nim no ces koj mus muab tsho tsuj tsho
npuag rov lawm koj qub teb qub chaw koj mus txog ntawm dej yog dej hlob
tis ua hlob loj tis ua loj ces koj lug loo tuaj hauv dej los koj hla

168. tsis dhau koj lug loo tuaj qab deg los hla tsis dhau koj yuav muab nyiaj txiag
xyab ntaw mus ntiav poj mab yawm sua lub nkoj dab poj mab yawm sua li xa
koj ntab yeev rau tim ntug koj thiaj li tau kev mus poj mab yawg sua yuav xa
koj ntab lis yees rau tim toj koj li tau kev ntoj tas li no muab peb daig xav txheej
hlawv rau tus tuag ces koj tau kev mus cuag poj cuag yawg no nas

169. zoo li nim no koj ua luag tsaug teb tsaug chaw tas ces koj yuav mus nrhiav
koj tsho tsuj tsho npuag hnav koj yog ib ntxhais ces koj tsho tsuj tsho npuag
nyob ntawm ncej txag koj yog ib leeg tub cag ces koj tsho tsuj tsho npuag nyob
ntawm ncej tas ces koj yuav los mus nrhiav koj tsho tsuj tsho npuag hnav koj
yuav muab koj tsho tsuj tsho npuag ces koj phwb lis nuag qab cub dhau qab
cais

170. koj phwb lis nuag rooj tag dhau rooj paim koj phwb lis nuag ncej dab dhau
ncej qhua koj yuav phwb lis nuag muab tau koj tsho tsuj tsho npuag koj li tau
tsho tsuj tsho npuag hnav koj li tau tsho tsuj tsho npuag npua ces Txawj Nkiag
yuav coj koj mus thawj xeeb lawm ntiaj teb thawj xeeb lawm ntiaj nrag koj
yuav mus thawj ua nyuj los ntshai luag laij ua dev los ntshai luag ntaus

171. mus ua npua los ntshai luag tua ua nees los ntshai luag caij mus ua qaib los ntshai luag hlais koj yuav mus thawj ua leej tib neeg los ntshai khwv fab lwm sim ces koj tau nom tau tswv ces koj tau zoo koj yuav los mus thawj xeeb ces koj tsis txhob los mus txoj kev pem toj yog poj mab yawm sua txoj kev mus nrhiav noj koj yuav mus txoj nram hav ces yog poj mab yawm sua txoj kev mus nrhiav hnav koj yuav mus txoj kev nruab nrab li yog txoj kev mus nrhiav niam txiv li

172. yog txoj kev mus thawj xeeb ua suav nom suav tswv zoo li koj yuav phwb qas nuag tuaj nruab nrab deeg qas daws tuaj ob cag koj li tawm plaws suav nom leej tub tsw nyuj nees nrag deeg qas daws tuaj nruab siab koj li tawm plaws suav nom leej tub tshiab nyuj nees kiab mus txoj nruab nrab ces koj li dhia rhee rau suav nom lub rooj khw koj tawm plaws fab lwm sim ces yog suav meej nom tus tub tsw

173. nim no koj dhia qas rhees ces koj tawm plaws pem ncauj kiab fab lwm sim ces koj tawm plaws suav meej nom leej mus tub tshiab no nas ntawm no tas ib qib qhov no tas ib quag qhov no rov qab ua txoj caw duav

174. nim no os yuav tuav peb txog cawv rau koj haus tso yuav qhia koj kab koj mus nrhiav koj poj koj yawm no nas

175. zoo li nim no koj yog ib tug leej tib neeg txawm rau ntiaj teb ib tug peb ntsuj xya tus duab koj ntsuj duab ntsuj cev tuag tas tshuav koj ntsuj plig tuag tsis tas muaj ib tug ntsuj plig yuav ntim lub txiaj zam lis yeev los mus nrhia poj nrhia yawg zoo li koj yuav los mus nrhia poj nrhia yawm ces yuav muab koj hnab rau koj ris muab koj seev koj nqa koj nce lis hlo txog pem ntuj ub mus txog suav yeeb yaj kiab coj koj mus cuag poj cuag yawm

176. ces koj nco ntsoov tuaj ntawm ncauj tsuj nthi tuaj ntawm taw nco ntsoov tuaj nruab plaw koj yuav nce rov mus cuag koj poj koj yawm pem ntuj ub koj ncig lis yeev tuaj nram tiaj Txawj Nkiag yuav coj koj mus nce Ntxwj Nyoog tus ntaiv nyiaj koj ncig lis yeev tuaj nram tus Txawj Nkiag yuav coj koj mus nce Ntxwj Nyoog tus ntaiv kub

177. zoo li koj nco qas ntsoov
    ib hnub koj nce ib qib
    ob hnub ob qib
    peb hnub peb qib

plaub hnub plaub qib
tsib hnub tsib qib
rau hnub rau qib
xya hnub xya qib
yim hnub yim qib
cuaj hnub cuaj qib
kaum hnub kaum qib
kaum ib hnub kaum ib qib
kaum ob hnub kaum ob qib

ces puv ib tsug kaum peb hnub ces koj nce nto ib lub Teem Txwv rov pem
Nyuj Vaj Tuam Teem teb

178. zoo li koj mus Nyuj Vaj Tuam Teem hais tias koj yog ntiaj teb leej tib neeg koj
yuav los ua tus tsi luag tsuas cav ntiaj teb zoo ua noj ntiaj nrag zoo ua haus koj hais
rau niam txiv Nyuj Vaj Tuam Teem hais tias nplooj tsis zeeg cas zoov tsis hlob ntiaj
teb leej tib neeg tsis muaj mob muaj tuag ces tsis txuas nyob zoo li nplooj tsis zeeg
zoov tsis kaj ntiaj teb leej tib neeg tsis muaj mob muaj tuag ces ntim tsis tag nplooj
zeeg zoov lis hlob ntiaj teb leej tib neeg txawj mob txawj tuag thiaj txaus nyob

179. nplooj zeeg zoov li kaj ntiaj teb leej tib neeg txawj mob txawj tuag thiaj li ntim
tas koj thiaj li yuav ntim lub txiaj zam lis yeev los mus koj tias dab tsi los koj
tsis tau yam twg los koj tsis muaj tau lawm zaj qeeg kus zaj nruas tau lawm kev
quaj kus kev nyiav ces koj yuav los mus

180. nim no Nyuj Vaj Tuam Teem li yuav hais tias nthuav koj cwj qhuab kab los
pub peb xyuas Nyuj Vaj Tuam Teem hais tias koj ntawv noj tsis muaj lub ntawv
haus tsis muaj npe cwj qhuab kab nraug ua kab ces koj txawj tuag tsis txawj
fib qab cwj qhuab kev nraug ua kev ces koj txawj tuag tsis txawj fib tsev koj
yuav hais li no ua Nyuj Vaj Tuam Teem tsaug ces koj li tau kev [mus muab tus
txib ntawg ib yom rau tus tuag]

181. zoo li koj yuav nco lis ntsoov
ib hnub nce ib qib
ob hnub nce ob qib
peb hnub nce peb qib
plaub hnub nce plaub qib

tsib hnub tsib qib

rau hnub rau qib

xya hnub xya qib

yim hnub yim qib

cuaj hnub cuaj qib

kaum hnub kaum qib

kaum ib hnub kaum ib qib

kaum ob hnub kaum ob qib

kaum peb hnub nce kaum peb qib

182. zoo li koj yuav nce hlo txog Ntxwj sib pes Nyoog lub rooj vag zeb koj ntim lub txiaj zam lis yeev los mus koj yuav tseg tau koj niam koj txiv koj kwv koj tij quaj zom qas zaws rau ntiaj teb koj yuav mus qhib Ntxwj sib pes Nyoog lub rooj vag koj tij ntiaj xib lees saib yuav pom koj niam koj txiv koj kwv koj tij quaj zom zaws rov lawm ntiaj nrag

183. nim no koj nce nto Ntxwj Nyoog lub rooj vag koj mus qhib Ntxwj Nyoog tseev kom quaj koj tig ntiaj lees saib tom ntej yuav pom koj poj koj yawm cuaj cuag yim pes tsawg zos luaj koj mus qhib Ntxwj Nyoog lub rooj vag tsis tseev kom nrov koj tig ntiaj xib lees saib rov tom ntej yuav pom koj poj koj yawm nyob cuaj caum yim pes tsawg zos no nas

184. zoo li koj ntim tau lub txiaj zam lis yeev mus txog Ntxwj Nyoog chaw tev qij tev dos luag kom koj nrog luag tev qij koj tsis txhob nrog luag tev koj hais tias mob koj ntiv tes koj tev tsis tau luag tias kom koj nrog luag tev dos koj hais tias mob koj ntiv taw koj hais tias mob koj ntiv tes ntiv taw los ntshav ces koj tev tsis tau no nas thaum hais qhov no ces muab ib txog xov liab khi tus tuag ntawd nti tes

185. nim no koj mus txog pem Ntxwj Nyoog toj kab ntsig dawm kab ntsig kab no dhia luaj thav yaj ces koj lauj

186. muab koj khau maj niaj kab ntsig kab nos dhia rhees luaj thav npua ces koj tes muab koj khau ntuag rau koj li tau kev mus cuag poj cuag yawm [thaum hais txog qhov no muab tus txhib ntawg ib yom rau tus tuag thiab]

187. zoo li nim no koj mus txog luag toj zeb zag peg zeb tso ncauj zeb zag rua lis hlo yuav nqos koj koj yuav muab cos maj cos ntuag ntsaws lis ntiag ncauj zeb

zag tsov lo ncauj zeb zag li qhaws hlo koj mus txog ncauj zeb zag dawm zeb
tsov ncauj zeb tsov rua ncauj lis vos yuav tom koj ces koj muab koj cos maj
cos ntuag ntsaws lis ntso rau ncauj zeb zag tso lis qhaws nkaus koj li tau kev
mus cuag poj cuag yawg no nas [thaum hais qhov no tas lawm npaj peb lub
cos maj cos ntuag cia mas muab rau tus tuag txhais]

188. tes ces hais tias koj cos maj cos ntuag nyob ntawm no koj muab koj cos maj
cos ntuag ntsaws rau zeb zag tsov lo koj li tau kev dhau mus cuag poj cuag
yawm no nas zoo li nim no koj mus txog Ntxwj Nyoog tus dej iab dej daw ob
niam txiv zov dej iab dej daw leej niam tuav dej iab leej txiv tuav dej daw yuav
hais li zoj tias koj yog ntiaj teb leej tib neeg koj yuav los mus ua tus tsi koj yuav
los mus ces koj haus dej iab dej daw tso koj mam li mus

189. ces koj tias ntiaj teb koj tshuav zoo niam zoo txiv ntiaj nrag koj tshuav zoo kwv
zoo tij zoo tsiaj zoo txhuv koj yuav los mus pauj nuj pauj nqi rau niaj mab niaj
sua koj qhov ncauj los ntshav ces koj tsis haus ces koj tsis taus ces koj yuav los
mus ces ob niam txiv dab zov dej iab dej daws li tso koj kev lis plhuav koj li tau
ke mus cuag poj cuag yawm no nas [thaum hais tias tas li no lawm muab ib
daim ntaub liab coj los npoj rau tus tuag lub qhov ncauj]

190. zoo li nim no Txawj Nkiag muab koj hnab rau koj ris muab koj seev rau koj
nqa muab koj kaus rau koj kwv koj yuav nce lis hlo mus txog toj zeb zuag koj
hnov niaj txiv zaj tsiv tsov nyooj qas laws pem ceeb tsheej los tav koj kab koj
tsis txhob ntshai yog koj niam koj txiv koj kwv koj tij ua koj pag ua koj xau
tuaj tom qab koj mus txog toj zeb zuag koj hnov niaj txiv zaj tsiv tsov nyooj
qas laws los tav koj kev koj tsis txhob ntshai yog koj kwv koj tij koj niam koj
txiv ua koj pag coj xau tuaj tom tsev

191. nim no koj mus txog toj tshav kub dawm tshav ntaiv luag muab luag kaus ntaub
kaus ntawv coj los kwv koj mus txog toj tshav ntaiv dawm tshav kub luag muab
luag kaus ntawv kaus ntaub kwv ces koj muab koj kaus ntaub kaus ntawv los
kwv luag muab luag kaus roos ces koj kaus roos koj ces koj li tau kev mus cuag
poj cuag yawm no nas

192. thaum hais tag ntawm no ces muab lub kaus rau tus tuag txhais tes koj kaus
ces nyob ntawm no muab koj kwv koj thiaj li tau kev mus cuag poj cuag yawg
no tos zoo li nim no koj mus txog toj tsaus huab dawm tsaus cua ces luag muab

luag ntxuam los ntxuam ces koj muab koj ntxuam los ntxuam cua koj thiaj li
tau ke mus cuag poj cuag yawm [no tos ces muab tus txhib ntawg ib yom rau
daim ntaub npog ncauj] koj ntxuam nyob ntawm no

193. zoo li nim no koj ntim tau lub txiaj zam lis yeev los mus dhau toj toj kab ntsig
dawm kab nos toj zeb zuag dawm zeb tsov koj los dhau toj tshav kub dawm
tshav ntaiv toj tsaus huab dawm tsaus cua tas ces Txawj Nkiag yuav coj koj
mus cuag poj cuag yawm no nas

194. koj yuav ntim lub txiaj zam lis yeev los mus ces koj coj koj qaib mus koj qaib
ua koj ntej koj lawv koj qaib qab tshav ntuj ces koj nkaum koj qaib tis los nag
ces koj nkaum koj qaib tw

195. koj qaib ntsis tis ces koj kho lawm koj tsho koj qaib ntsis hlaub ces koj kho
ntsig koj qaib ntsis taw ces koj kho koj khau koj qaib ntsis hau ces koj kho lawm
koj phuam koj qaib ntsis duav ces koj kho lawm koj siv no nas koj qaib ua koj
ntej ces koj lawv koj qaib qab koj mus

196. txoq lawm ntuj tsiag teb tsaus ntuj tsha teb nqhuab ntuj nqhua teb nkig yog
luag qaib qua koj qaib teb tsis yog koj pog koj yawm hauv muas hleb yoq luaq
qaib qua koj qaib xa tsis yog koj pog koj yawm hauv nuag ntxa

197. koj qaib qua luag qaib teb thiaj li yog koj pog koj hauv muag hleb koj qaib qua
luag qaib xa ces li yog koj poj koj yawm hauv muag ntxa luag qaib qua koj qaib
teb ces yog luag yuav ntxias koj mus dhia tsuas zeb koj·qaib teb luag qaib qua
ces yog luaq yuav coj koj mus dhia tsua

198. koj mus txog tus uas ntsej muag luag lis nyav tuaj nram hav tsis yog koj poj
koj yawm yog luag yuav coj koj mus muas noj muas hnav koj mus txog tus
ntsej muag luag lis nyav tuaj pem toj tsis yog koj poj koj yawm yog luag yuav
coj koj mus muas noj no

199. koj mus txog tus ntsej muag doog lis nciab nthuav nqaws tiab koj dhia rhees
rau tej nqaws tiab tus ntsej muag doog lis nkawv ces koj dhia rhees rau tej nqaws
awv ces yog koj poj koj yawm koj mus txog koj poj koj yawm hais koj tias koj
nyob ntiaj teb koj yog leej tib neeg ntiaj teb zoo ua noj teb cais zoo ua hnav

200. koj yuav los mus koj tau tus tsi koj los koj tau tus dab tsi koj hais tias dab tsi los tsis tau tsuas tau tus cwj qhuab kab lus qhuab kev koj poj koj yawm hais tias nthuav koj cwj qhuab kab los peb saib nthuav koj cwj qhuab kev los rau peb xyuas cwj qhuab kab nraug ua ke cwj qhuab ke mus nraug ua kab

201. koj hlab tsuj tu hlab npuag ntaug koj los nyob ntuj tsiag teb tsaus ntuj no teb ntsim koj los ib sim neej tsis fib qab tsis fib tsev koj poj koj yawm hais koj tias yog leej twg xa koj tuaj koj hais tias xyov yog txiv yawm txiv qas tsi xa koj tuaj ntsej luaj ntxuam muag luaj khob xa koj tuaj koj poj koj yawm hais tia ua li nim no tsoj qab puas tsoj tau taug lw puas taug cuag koj hais tias tsoj qab los tsoj tsis tau taug lw los taug tsis cuag lawm luag tuaj xyoo no luag twb rov lawm tsaib no lawm tus qhuab kev muab tus txib ntawg pov rau saum daim txiag thaum nws tuaj nruab nqhuab rov nruab dej lawm

202. koj poj koj yawm hais tias caij nees raws puas tau rag nyuj raws puas cuaj koj hais tias rag nees los tsis tau rag nyuj los tsis cuag txhob tsoj qab nyob tsam mus mag luag nta tsis txhob taug lw nyob tsam mus mag luag hneev ces koj hais li no koj thiaj li tau kev mus cuag poj cuag yawm no nas tus qhuab ke muab tus txib ntawg pov rau saum daim txiag ces rov khaws tus txib ntawg los tuav ces hais ntxiv li no

203. Txawj Nkiag xa koj li no yuav rau peb txog cawv koj haus tso koj ntaus ib ntsug plig rov tom qab no yog yaj ceeb neeg ces yuav yaj kuam [hais li no tas muab tus txhib ntawg pov rau saum daim txiag yog ob sab ntxeev ces cia li ib sab ntxeev xwb ces hais tias]

204. tsis ntshai os muab qaib qe los nqee ces zoo

205. nrhiav qaib nrhiav npua los kho ces zoo os

206. Txawj Nkiag xa koj txog txij no ces koj khau maj koj ntuag rau ces koj mus tim ub Txawj Nkiaj tsis muaj khau maj ntuag ces mus tim no

207. koj yuav qos ntsej qos muag mus dai poj dai yawm ntuj tshiab ces plhis lis plho ua kab npauj kab xi

FLOWER VILLAGE DEMOGRAPHICS

FLOWER VILLAGE WAS originally established around 1947, across the spur of the hill a short distance from its present location. Its original site is now inhabited by a small group of Mien (Yao) people, northern Thai hill dwellers who are closely related to the Hmong, especially linguistically.[1]

The majority of villagers (58 percent) moved to Flower Village looking for land; the first inhabitants were members of the Muas clan and came from the border of Laos. According to the Hmong, Flower Village and its environs have particularly fertile land. That 31 percent of the inhabitants live there due to marriage reflects the patrilocal residence rule. Another 1 percent came to the village because they had been ill elsewhere; Hmong who suffer from repeated health problems of any kind will relocate to avoid trouble with a spirit in the original house, or will move to a different house within the same village—a phenomenon I observed twice during my fourteen-month stay. The shamans say that those whose problems continue after such a move are in danger, perhaps due to the influence of a bad spirit. In such cases, the family usually moves quite a distance away.

Over the course of the next decade, other clans moved into the village; 36 percent of the population was born elsewhere. Scholars who have studied the structure of Hmong villages (Cooper 1984:47–55; Geddes 1976:91–93;

Tapp 1989a:21–26) have found that in earlier times all of the inhabitants were members of a single clan. In keeping with the rules of clan exogamy and patrilocal residency, daughters—"other people's women"—frequently moved far from their natal village when they married. In Flower Village today, young women often are able to marry men who live within their natal village, as several different clans are in residence there. Thus, they do not marry into a family of strangers, as frequently happens, and they are able to maintain warm and close relationships with their natal families and their neighbors. The Muas, the original inhabitants of Flower Village, represent the largest clan (41 percent), followed by the Hawj (27 percent), Vwj (16 percent), Yaj (4 percent), Thoj (3 percent), Vaj (1 percent), and miscellaneous other clans (8 percent).

In 1988 there are 248 males and 239 females in Flower Village. Over half of the population (52 percent) was under fifteen years of age (see table D.1). There were more male children than female between the ages of two and ten, but this is not a significant gender difference.

TABLE D.1

Age Distribution in Flower Village, 1988

Age (years)	Males (248 total)	Females (239 total)
0–1	6.0%	9.2%
2–5	16.9%	13.8%
6–10	16.5%	16.3%
11–15	12.9%	12.5%
16–20	14.1%	11.7%
21–35	18.9%	19.7%
36–50	9.3%	12.1%
51+	5.2%	4.6%

In Western countries, having 50 percent of the population under the age of fifteen would be considered problematic, an economic burden to society, but in Hmong society, young people are an asset because they contribute to production at a very early age. The small elderly population in the village reflects the shorter life span as compared to more developed countries.

Flower Village has large households, the size of which is comparable to that reported in other studies on the Hmong (Lee 1981; Tapp 1989a:21). The most common household size was seven to nine people (31 percent), followed by four to six (27 percent), and ten to thirteen (20 percent). Only 14 percent of the households consisted of one to three people, and these were single-generation households—a widowed man living alone, and a widowed woman and her unmarried retarded son. The 8 percent of households with fourteen to sixteen family members were either multigenerational or included many children. The overwhelming majority of Flower Village households had two or more generations (95 percent), and within that number 36 percent contained three generations, and 1 percent contained four. This leaves a high percentage of two-generation nuclear families (58 percent), which are composed of parents and children. This may reflect the short life span of grandparents, or a change in family structure as children marry and move to their own dwellings (Kunstadter 1984). Most of the nuclear families live next door to one another and are related, so they function as extended families.

All of the inhabitants of Flower Village were White Hmong with the exception of one Green Mong family—a couple and their four children who ran a small general store. Five in-married women were Green Mong as well. Although intermarriage between Green Mong and White Hmong was becoming more common during my fieldwork, it was not the norm. White Hmong women told me it is difficult for them to marry Green Mong men because they do not know how to prepare for Green Mong rituals, nor can they make batik, a textile art in which Green Mong women excel.

CHRISTIANS IN FLOWER VILLAGE

Flower Village has a small Protestant church, which ten of the sixty-four families attended. Although these families were not the central subject of my research, there are several points I wish to address regarding them. It has been reported in the literature that recently whole villages have adopted Christianity at once, perhaps because this allowed them to dispense with costly Hmong kinship rituals and to attain literacy by attending missionary schools (Cooper 1984:68–69; Tapp 1989a:99–100). In Flower Village, only ten families over a period of several years adopted Protestantism. They were not all of the same lineage or clan, and many of them, when asked why they converted, gave "a true belief in the Christian God" as their motivation. Many members of the fifty-four other families, some of whom were related to the Christians, said they would not convert and they did not trust missionaries. The Christians of Flower Village were not always the poorest of the village people, as has been suggested, although two of the families I interviewed did acknowledge that it was easier to be Christian because they did not have to spend money on animals to sacrifice for rituals. I often saw them, however, sacrificing pigs together on Christian holidays, which they did inside the small church, not in their own patrilineal houses. All lineage members and affines, Christian and non-Christian, were invited to these feasts, and many of them accepted the invitation.

One of the poorest Christian families in Flower Village had a married daughter and son-in-law living in their household. The couple's child, a daughter, was born under their roof, an unusual but not unheard-of situation (Cooper 1984:40–43). The family told me that, in the Christian fashion, they did not carry out rituals such as soul calling when the child was born, although they did bury the child's placenta under the bed.

The desire for literacy among the converts to Christianity has been well documented by Tapp (1989a:121–30), and the data I collected in Flower Village support his argument. Six of the ten Christian families had children in school in the valley and, according to my informants, these children had been sponsored by the missionaries who converted them. One of the girls who had received a sixth-grade education—unusual because girls do not often leave the village before marriage—was chosen Miss Hmong in a beauty pageant in the town of Chiang Rai. Her parents, who proudly showed me her photograph, attributed her good luck and subsequent marriage to an educated man to their conversion to Christianity.

A SHAMANIC HEALING

IN THE UNITED STATES

THE SHAMANIC RITUALS I observed in Flower Village were much the same as the one described here. The main differences were that this case study occurred in the United States—and that I was the patient.

I was diagnosed with a serious illness when I returned home after my fieldwork in Thailand. I had surgery, and the doctors told me it had gone well, but I was still frightened. Even when I was home and was supposed to be resting, I paced the floor and couldn't lie still without medication. One of my Hmong informants in Providence suggested that a Hmong shaman in the city come and conduct a ritual for me. I had seen many people in Flower Village recover their health, or at least their serenity and good spirits, after a shaman had interceded for them, and so I was glad to ask for a shaman's help.

For the first part of the ritual, the shaman went into trance at his own home, to diagnose the problem. This was a quieter, quicker journey than the one described below. The shaman did not leap onto his "horse" (a wooden bench) but only sat on it, shaking gently and chanting. When he had finished this diagnostic journey to the spirit world, he told me and my husband that because my husband's ancestors had been neglected, they had taken one of my souls. (We were never sure which soul; it was difficult to get that information from the shaman.)

The second part of the ritual occurred in our home, in front of the fireplace. The shaman killed a chicken and sent its soul to ask the ancestors if there was anything we had done that was not respectful to them. He looked at the chicken's feet and into its beak and throat and said that my husband's parents in the otherworld needed spirit money and food to eat; if we sent it to them, I would be cured. The shaman's wife taught my children to fold spirit money into two hundred small boats, some male and some female, depending on how the boats were folded. The shaman sacrificed another chicken on the kitchen floor and examined it. Then he sat on his "horse," tied a dark cloth over his face, and began to journey to the otherworld to find my stolen soul. He chanted, rang his finger bells, and made a hair-raising blindfolded leap onto his horse, just as the shamans in Flower Village had always done.

After the shaman finished the journey, my husband and my son burned all the paper boats in the fireplace while the shaman said the words of offering to my husband's parents. Then the shaman took a hoop-shaped rattle and drew it down over my head. Hmong are small people, and the shaman could draw this rattle down to the feet of a sick Hmong, but I am larger, so it sat on my shoulders.

The shaman tore a narrow strip of red cloth from the red ties on his black mask. He rolled the cloth even thinner, into a long piece of red string that he wound around and around my wrist and tied there for protection. I was to wear the red string until it fell off of its own accord.

Meanwhile my daughters and the shaman's wife had cooked the chickens. At the end of the ritual, my husband and I were served and ate first, and then the rest of the family ate with the shaman, his wife, and his assistant.

I felt much better and more relaxed after the ritual. It helped me that my whole family had been there, that all my children had lent emotional support. Afterward I could sleep again, I could relax without medication, and I even began to feel optimistic about life—or at least less terrified than before.

The shaman never asked for payment; he knew he would be compensated. We paid him in rice, chickens, and cash, as shamanic ritual certainly wasn't covered by my health insurance.

After a couple of months the shaman performed another, smaller ritual to thank the spirits, for I had gotten well. Paper money was burned, several chickens were killed, and the shaman read the bones and claws and pronounced me well.

HEALTH CARE AND GENDER ISSUES

OF HMONG IN THE UNITED STATES

I BEGAN MY FIELD research in hopes of discovering how Hmong cultural beliefs affected women's reception of Western health care during childbirth. A comparison of the two birth systems makes it clear why Hmong women in the early days of their migration to the United States regarded a hospital delivery as frightening and inexplicable. Socialized to be modest, they were forced to accept the ministrations of strangers, who were often males; they were not at home, where the lineage spirits offered protection; because they had to give up the placenta and blood from the birth, instead of carefully burying it, their child was put at risk for health problems in the land of light and difficulty in returning to the land of darkness; they were offered fruit juice and other "cold" food, which could cause them to be ill in old age and slowed their return to balance and good health following the birth. The entire hospital experience was complicated by language difficulties; in the absence of translators, no explanations could be given to the women who had to undergo what they perceived as invasive, humiliating, and even dangerous procedures.

Conditions surrounding health care for the Hmong in the United States had improved by the time I finished my fieldwork: my first Hmong informants in the Providence clinics were working as translators and mediators in the hospitals, and Hmong women had learned English. When the hospital staff understood why Hmong women would not eat hospital food, they allowed husbands to bring in the fresh rice and chicken soup with herbs that constitute the Hmong postpartum diet. In some instances women requested, and were given, the placenta to take home, but Hmong informants in the United States have told me that the Showing the Way chant has the power to guide a soul to its birth shirt, even if the soul does not know where it is. My informants also stated that it was impossible to bury the birth shirt when living in a tenement house with no garden, but most of them did not seem worried by this.

Hospitals all over the country have begun to integrate issues of health care for Hmong and other Southeast Asians. In 1999, for example, while giving a talk in Wisconsin on epilepsy among the Hmong, I was invited to visit a clinic to speak with doctors and Hmong health-care workers about the Hmong concept of birth. Peter Kunstadter (1985, 1990, 1997) has conducted research in California and Thailand on comparative health issues, and hires Hmong as his research assistants in both countries; his work is valuable and helpful for understanding Hmong fears and the new illnesses they have contracted in this country, such as heart disease, strokes, and gout. Films have been made to explain Hmong fears about health care and hospitals, such as *Between Two Worlds: The Hmong Shaman in America,* produced by Taggart Siegel and Dwight Conquergood (1986); *The Best Place to Live,* produced by Peter O'Neill and Ralph Rugoff (1982); and *Contraception Information for Hmong Couples,* produced at the University of Minnesota (1992). Hospitals in Wisconsin and Minnesota allow shamans to come in and perform healing rituals—which are shorter and quieter than usual—at the patient's bedside. As well, Hmong children who have grown up and been educated in this country can mediate for their families.

Hmong women do not find giving birth in hospitals as terrifying as they used to; and often they come in to deliver their babies and leave the next day.[1] But coming to a hospital to be treated for an illness is another story. Hmong think hospitals are places to die, and they believe that surgery or taking blood will weaken and deform the body throughout incarnations. Since decisions regarding medical treatment are considered a family matter, all family members go to the emergency room, which they tend to use as a primary care facility in terms of Western biomedicine; the actual primary care for many Hmong is still done by shamans, herbalists, and families. Many Hmong women in the United States grow their own medicinal plants and rely on home remedies, as do many Americans, unless they are seriously ill.

As Anne Fadiman has pointed out, some fears concerning health care are universal and cannot be ascribed to a particular culture. In the case of Hmong in this country, the natural fear of illness is exacerbated by the strangeness of the culture in which they find themselves.

GENDER ISSUES

Hmong in Southeast Asia have faced many changes due to the incursion of Western and Thai culture. For Hmong in the United States, the changes have been more drastic, a natural consequence of living within a Western culture instead of confronting it from a distance. Many Hmong have now lived in the United States for twenty-five years, and the changes in their culture are apparent, especially in the area of gender equality. Women have more agency, they work outside of the home, and they are formally educated. As women's roles change, the relationships between men and women change. Further research might provide important insights into domestic violence in Hmong communities.

But the outcome of changing roles for Hmong women is not always tragic. I recently attended a celebration for a Hmong friend who was my research assistant in Thailand. Like several other younger Hmong women, Mee Moua went to graduate school and earned her law degree. She became a lawyer and a lobbyist, and recently she was the first Hmong person to be elected to the state legislature—the Senate—in Minnesota. The *New York Times* article about her was titled "The Soul of a New Political Machine Is Hmong."[2]

NOTES

1. The WIC program provides supplemental food for low-income mothers and their children. It is administered by the Department of Agriculture's Food and Nutrition Service and is distributed by individual states.

2. Funds for research on the Hmong in Providence were provided by the Ethnic Family Life Project of the Office of Adolescent Family Life, Department of Health and Human Services.

3. An episiotomy is a surgical incision of the vagina to widen the birth outlet, considered by some to be an unnecessary procedure. The chorionic membrane is the outermost of two membranes enveloping the fetus.

4. See Jordan 1983 for a cross-cultural comparison of birthing systems.

5. The Hmong National Development Program is an umbrella organization that grew out of earlier programs run by the Office of Refugee Resettlement, U.S. Department of Health and Human Services. In the late 1980s, General Vang Pao began the Lao Family Association, which has branches all over the United States. Several women's groups, such as the Hmong/Lao Women's Association and Women's Allied Health Network (WAHL) educate and assist women in difficult

or crisis situations. Hmong Allied Health Network Support assists people with questions and health issues.

6. See Symonds 1992, 1997b, and 1998.

INTRODUCTION: CONDUCTING RESEARCH IN A HMONG VILLAGE

1. See Mead and Newton 1967:142–244; McClain 1975:38–56; Muecke 1976:377–83; MacCormack 1982:1–23; Jordan 1983:3–12; Kay 1982:1–24; Fruzzetti 1982:24–25, 101; Fruzzetti and Oster, 1976:97–132; Newman 1969:112–35, 1972, 1985; Laderman 1983:172; Martin 1992:54–67; Davis Floyd 1988:153–72 and 1990:175–89.

2. Hanks 1963; Hart et al. 1965; Mougne 1978:68–108; Manderson 1981:509–20, Laderman 1983.

3. Anne Fadiman (1997:1–11) opens her book—which was published after I began my study—with a description of a Hmong birth that is consistent with my observations, as does Pranee Liamputtong Rice's *Hmong Women and Reproduction* (2000:87–104) which deals comprehensively with reproductive issues in Thailand and Australia.

4. Other anthropological studies on the Hmong in Southeast Asia have mentioned birth in passing (Cooper 1984:15, 145; Tapp 1989a:67–68). Howard Radley, in his dissertation on the Green Mong in Thailand, recounts that a shaman informed him that "a child receives 32 bones from its father at birth" and reports that Hmong "distinguish between the male principle of a child: the bones, and the female principle: the flesh" (1986:245). Although the bone/flesh dichotomy is common in many Southeast Asian and other cultures (Leach 1954:13–14, 20; Boddy 1989:66–67, 67n29; Lévi Strauss 1969:393–405; Fox 1971:219–252; Traube 1986:93), the White Hmong in Flower Village seemed unaware of it. For more on Hmong/Miao social structure, see Ruey Yih-Fu 1960:152–53; Radley 1986:125–32; Lee 1981:75–86; Tapp 1989b:19.

A few of the studies on Hmong refugees in the United States mention birth. In an oral history, May Xiong, a Green Mong woman living in the United States, and Nancy Donnelly (1986:201–44) discuss the problems she had giving birth during the war in Laos. Potter and Whirren (1984:48–62) and Hahn and Muecke (1984) investigate cultural aspects of birthing, whereas Rumbaut and Weeks (1986:428–65) present quantitative data on fertility. All of the authors presenting data on Hmong reproduction are impressed by the consistently high fertility rates.

5. This section appeared in an earlier form in *The Political Economy of* AIDS,

edited by Merrill Singer (Farmingdale, N.Y.: Baywood Publishing Company, 1998).

6. Hmong and Mien (Miao/Yao) speak linguistically related languages. Linguists are not in agreement on the genetic roots of this language family. On the Hmong in China, see Tapp 2001 and Schein 2000.

7. Ibid.

8. The 1990 census on the populations of Chinese nationalities reported 7,398,035 Miao (*Beijing Review* 33, no. 52 [Dec. 24–30, 1990]: 34, quoted in Schein 200:70).

9. By "traditional" I do not mean to imply that cultures are static; I am speaking only of aspects or "themes" of Hmong culture that are discernable over time.

10. Tapp (1990:113) asserts that the two "dialects" of Green Mong and White Hmong in Southeast Asia should be considered subdialects of the main Chuan-qiandian dialect of Hmong in China.

11. See Alting von Geusau (1986:41–77) for a discussion of the terms used for minorities.

12. The council arranged affiliation with the Tribal Research Institute of Chiang Mai, and the staff kindly gave me suggestions for possible research sites and assisted me with paperwork.

13. Funding for the Southeast Asian Summer Studies Institute was kindly provided by a Foreign Language and Area Studies Grant (FLAS).

14. On agricultural calendars, see Cooper et al. 1996:31–39; Lemoine 1972c:50–69; Tapp 1989b:47–51.

1 / HMONG COSMOLOGY: A BALANCE OF OPPOSITES

1. Mickey 1947, de Beauclair 1960, Graham 1937, Morechand 1968, Lemoine 1972b and 1983a.

2. On universalism of sexual asymmetry, see Ortner 1974:67–68; Rosaldo 1974:17–42; and Lamphere 1974. On gender symmetry and sexual equality, see Leacock 1976:11–35; Sanday 1981; and Sacks 1977:211–34.

3. Unlike another group of mountain dwellers, the Akha, who can recite the names of ancestors for many generations back during ritual feasting (Kammerer 1986:122–24; Hanks 1974:114–27; Alting 1983:252), the Hmong remember, name, and offer food to ancestors from only three or four generations past. All other ancestors are called simply "the ancestors" *(cuag poj cuag yawm)*.

4. I agree with the findings of Tapp (1989a:172–73) and others that ethnic categories are fluid and not static. See Leach 1954:281 and Moerman 1965:1215–30.

5. See Lemoine 1972b, 1983a, 1988; Radley 1986; and Cooper 1984:28–33. A good example is Lemoine's *L'initiation du mort chez les Hmong* (1983a), from research in a Green Mong village in Laos. One of the funeral chants Lemoine records is remarkably similar to a chant I heard in the White Hmong Flower Village in northern Thailand, although certain aspects of the chant are stressed in one text and glossed over in the other.

6. As it would be cumbersome to repeat "the Hmong believe" in every other sentence, for the most part I simply report these beliefs here.

7. On the construction of houses and symbolic meaning in other societies of Southeast Asia, see Izikowitz and Sorensen 1982:1–6; Cunningham 1973:204–38; Tambiah 1969:423–29; Turton 1978:113–32; and Kammerer 1986.

8. See Tapp 1989a:63–64. On other considerations when building a Hmong house, see Lemoine 1972c:99–113; Cooper 1984:29; and Radley 1986:235–38.

9. Most men cannot afford to marry more than once, but if a man has more than one wife, usually he and his wives all sleep together. In one of the homes I visited often, however, the wives slept separately, each with her own children.

10. Puj and Yawm Saub, or Grandmother and Grandfather Saub, are responsible for fertility and reproduction (see appendix B, verse 108). See Radley 1986:262–65 for a different discussion of Saub, and Mottin 1982:33–43 and Lemoine 1983a:18 for similarities.

11. As well as these two altars, Tapp (1989) tells of a medicine altar *(dab tshuaj)* for herbalists. I did not see any in Flower Village, although years later I did see one in a Green Mong village in Nan Province.

12. In Flower Village the Showing the Way chant states that death came when a tiger and gibbon were killed (see appendix B, verse 41).

13. Nyuj Vaj Tuam Teem, the assistant of Ntxwj Nyoog, sits behind a desk and gives out new papers or mandates for life (see chap. 4). See Tapp 1989a:60.

14. Chindarsi 1976:30; Tapp 1989b:120*n*6; Lemoine 1997.

15. Names for souls given here are from Lemoine 1997.

16. Epilepsy also is considered a sign that one may become a shaman, as the shaking of an epileptic seizure is similar to the shaking of a shaman in trance.

17. Hmong are very careful about this; in Providence, I spoke to firemen and policemen to explain why Hmong burned paper money and also to tell them never to walk between the shaman and the altar when a shaman is in a trance.

18. For more about the shaman's helping spirits, see Culhane-Pera et al. 2003.

19. Anna-Leena Siikala (1987:201–15) writes that the Siberian shamans' role is also nonpolitical, which may be taken as circumstantial evidence for the theory that the Hmong originated in Siberia (quoted in Lemoine 1997:144).

20. The people in Flower Village told me that illnesses can also be caused by curses and ghosts *(raug dab)*, but I never saw any cases attributed to either during my stay, and do not know how they would be treated.

21. See Zanker et al. 1989 for a description of this program.

22. The patient was grateful for my extemporaneous doctoring and afterward became quite helpful to me, even letting me observe the birth of her child.

23. Lemoine 1972c:184–86 and 1997; Tapp 1989b:164–65.

24. In practice, "good" burials are performed for everyone. If a person was not a good Hmong, died badly (see chap. 4), or remained unmarried, the funeral service is simply shorter; but there are very few unmarried Hmong men or women.

25. Here and elsewhere, I have used people's real names only with their permission.

2 / MOTHERS, DAUGHTERS, AND WIVES

1. Annette Weiner (1976), Lina Fruzzetti (1982), and Henrietta Moore (1988) have faced similar problems in their work. Rather than importing an analytical model, all of these scholars have based their interpretations on "the community question"—that is, on what people have told them rather than on their preconceived assumptions.

For recent studies on gender see also Chatterjee 1993, Fruzzetti and Perez 2002, and Ray 2000.

2. For more discussion of women's roles, see Cooper 1984:135–47; Donnelly 1994; Johnson 1985; Lemoine 1972c:113; and Vang and Lewis 1990.

3. Sometimes the brother's son marries the sister's daughter; but it is preferred that the brother's daughter marry his sister's son. In this way the bride-price passes from one generation to the next through the males.

4. Hmong believe that emotions are felt through the liver *(daim siab)* and that it is the seat of the affections. The liver is divided into the good part *(daim nplooj siab zoo)* and the bad part *(daim nplooj siab phem)*; if the bad part rules, then the person has a "bad" or "difficult" liver. In this instance a bad liver describes a man whose ill-nature leads him to violence; a bad liver can also cause someone to be depressed, lonely, evil, indecisive, timid, discouraged, or nauseated, just to name

a few "liverish" qualities. Conversely, someone with a good liver is good-natured, courageous, affectionate, at peace, and so forth.

5. See Catlin 1982:173; Yang et al. 1980; Johns 1986:5–11; Mottin 1980b.

6. The divorced woman I knew did not sing either.

7. This does not mean that women never sing; a young girl who sings well will often sing at home, for her family. In America, Hmong women—with permission from their husbands and families—often sing love songs, as do men. Many of these songs from Laos and Thailand are available on tape, with rock music added as a background.

Traditional Hmong musical instruments are no longer played; although there is a type of Jew's harp, I did not see it used much. In Thailand now the boom box is the fashion.

8. Although beauty in women is not a virtue, it is a consideration. Hmong definitions of beauty may be slightly different from Westerners'. When a young man and his father go to look for a marriageable girl, they prefer a girl with strong legs (which means she can work hard) and shiny, "strong" hair. They also look for a pretty face. Tribal beauty pageants are held in Thailand now.

9. This is a fairly standard bride-price, but taking a long time over negotiations is also standard.

10. The difficult sister-in-law probably moved next door. When extended families grow too large for a single household, sons build a new house nearby.

3 / BIRTH: THE JOURNEY TO THE LAND OF LIGHT

1. On beliefs about colostrum, see Morse 1989, Gunnlaugsson and Einarsdottir 1993, and Rice 2000.

2. Hmong legends say that Hmong come from a land of ice and snow or from Mongolia (Tapp 1989b:183–85; Mottin 1984:99).

3. For a girl, this line would be left out. She will leave the lineage at marriage, and thus has no connection to the central house post and the natal ancestors.

4. The bamboo soul resides in the marrow of the backbone (Lemoine 1997:146).

5. "Merchants" are the Chinese.

6. The Hmong believe that because they have lost their ability to write (Tapp 1989b:122–30), they must seek answers or "words" inside the bones, heads, and

tongues of chickens. The grandfather is hoping that the chicken parts will augur well for the child's future.

7. Many of the Hmong birth and post-birth practices are also Chinese practices (Tapp, personal communication). Barbara Pillsbury (1978:15) writes about Chinese postpartum practices in what she terms "Doing the Month." Both she and Nicholas Tapp state that modern urban Chinese women still observe these practices.

8. See, e.g., Hart 1965:34–40; Manderson 1981:509–20; Laderman 1983:174 Mougne 1978:68–108.

9. Manderson 1981:509–20; Mougne 1978:68–108; Hanks 1963:71–77; Rajadhon 1965:115–204; Muecke 1976:377–83; Keyes 1977:158.

10. A similar myth in which Siv Yis changes into a young woman is presented in Charles Johnson's collection of translated Hmong myths and legends, *Dab Neeg Hmoob* (1985:41–45).

11. Sometimes Kab Yeeb is a deity incorporating a spirit couple, similar to the "motherfather" of ancestors; at other times Kab Yeeb seems to be a deity incorporating both sexes in a single spirit.

12. Kunstadter (1996) has found that, due to family planning efforts by the Thai government, there has been a drop in birth rate among the Hmong, although families are still large.

13. Children of the same father are considered members of one family and are addressed by the same terms, "brothers" *(kwv tij)* or "sisters" *(viv ncaus)* (Lee 1981:13), even if they have different mothers. A father is addressed by all of his children by the same term, whereas mothers are addressed as "older mother" (first wife), "younger mother" (second wife), and so on.

14. I believe that the high infant mortality rate may in fact be underestimated. Considering the secrecy that surrounds birth, it is likely that I was not informed of all the instances of miscarriage and stillbirth, especially those that occurred before women in Flower Village became comfortable with me.

4 / DEATH: THE JOURNEY TO THE LAND OF DARKNESS

1. There are several accounts of the Showing the Way chant from various locations and groups of Miao/Hmong, for example: in China, Clark 1904, Graham 1937, Beauclair 1960, Mickey 1947; in Laos, Mottin 1982, Morechand 1968, Lemoine

1972b; and Bertrais 1973. See also Falk 1996 and Morrison 1997 on the playing of reed pipes at funerals, and descriptions of "The Song of the Expiring of Life" (Qeej tu Siav), which is played on reed pipes.

2. Lemoine gives a full and detailed account of Green Mong mortuary rituals and provides a French translation of the Showing the Way chant. The chant itself, although not the analysis, has been translated into English by White (Lemoine 1983b).

3. See Chindarsi 1976:60 and Thao 1986:370. There is some ambiguity about when the soul receives the "mandate for life." Hmong also told me that the third soul receives the "mandate for life" not at death but just before it embarks for the land of light, during the soul calling ritual on the third day of a newborn's life.

4. I have been told by other Hmong that some households burn the cloth used for washing the dead and watch to see if it develops stripes as it burns, which would be a sign that the deceased soul will return in the form of tiger. Nusit Chindarsi (1976:65) states the cloth is examined in order to determine the deceased's future gender.

5. It is not always clear whether one or two souls go all the way to the village of the ancestors. As with anything concerning various souls, there are discrepancies among accounts; one Hmong informant said there was no way to be 100 percent consistent.

6. The second and third souls (see chap. 1).

7. Throughout the Showing the Way chant, the chanter refers to himself in the third person. Perhaps this is a form of distancing to alleviate the risk he takes in going so near the land of darkness.

8. There are many spirits and deities in the Showing the Way chant, and not even the Hmong know who all of them are.

9. Lemoine's chant tells of the toad who brought sickness and death to the world (1983b:17–20). All of the chants discuss the toad (or frog), some in more detail than others (see appendices B and C, verses 102–5).

10. Jacques Lemoine (1983a:47–48) also discusses Lady Sun and Lord Moon, noting that in China the moon is yin, female, and the sun yang, male. Tapp also suggests that the Hmong use of the sun as female and the moon as male is done in opposition to the Chinese (1989a:48). Eberhardt in his discussions of Chinese folklore states that only in societies where women are considered very important are they identified with the sun (1965). Hmong told me that the moon goes out at night, which only men can do, whereas the sun warms and nurtures the earth.

11. Although some Hmong say that this is where the soul gets the "mandate for life" paper, others say that the third soul doesn't get the "mandate for life" until the soul-calling ritual on the third day after birth.

12. Jacques Lemoine states that Hmong have an "ancestral mass" and that the soul is reincarnated in the same lineage (1983a:107). Nicholas Tapp writes that Hmong souls must return in the same clan (1986a:85).

13. The song the wife sings to her dead husband is improvised around traditional themes.

14. A few years ago I attended the funeral of a Hmong man in Minnesota. At that time the dead man's son repaid $1,000 that my husband and I had lent to the dead man some ten years earlier, when he was having trouble getting established in this country. Although we hadn't mentioned the debt or asked that it be repaid, it was on the list of debts, and the dead man's son insisted that we accept repayment, or else his father would never arrive safely in the village of the ancestors in the land of darkness.

15. See Radley (1986:485–92) and Chindarsi (1976:148–57) for various translations of this traditional, and improvised, chant. (As this section lasted all night, I fell asleep during parts of it.)

16. Howard Radley (1986:365) and Nicholas Tapp (1989a:85) write that a woman carrying a torch led the procession.

17. There is always an even number of pipers at a funeral—two or four, never one or three. Tooj had four pipers at his burial because he was an old and respected man.

18. See Chindarsi 1976:90–91 for a list describing how parts are distributed.

19. Sometimes the rice cakes are given to the eldest sister. I was unable to determine the significance of these special cakes.

20. See also Bloch and Parry 1982:15–18 for general discussion, and Turton 1978:121, Walker 1983:235, and Radley 1986:333–34 for specifics.

21. That all the seeds for crops seem to have been *retrieved* from the land of darkness hints that these seeds may once have existed in the land of light. Perhaps the seeds were removed to the land of darkness when humans made the connection between the two worlds, bringing death into the land of light by killing a tiger and a gibbon.

22. Ntxwj Nyoog is one of the deities who judges the returning vital soul and gives it the chance to be reborn as a human being—or refuses the soul that chance, which may account for some of his fearsomeness.

23. A shaman's helping spirits are not wild, nor do they have anything to do

with death. Even tame spirits linked with death, such as ancestors of one's own lineage, can be harmful to the living who come too near the land of darkness.

EPILOGUE: HIV/AIDS AND THE HMONG IN THAILAND

1. Dr. Vichai Poshyachinda coined the term "natural pathways" to describe how people view and understand sexuality (personal communication).

2. Microbicides are creams, gels, suppositories, or sponges inserted into the vagina before sexual intercourse. Microbicides prevent transmission of HIV and other STDs by creating a chemical barrier between the virus and the vaginal wall, either by changing the pH of the vagina or by preventing replication of the virus.

Cultural issues regarding the body will create obstacles to the use of microbicides. Some women have been taught not to touch their genitalia, much less insert anything into their vaginas. In parts of Africa, men prefer dry sex and women use herbs before having intercourse to ensure this state. Also, microbicides kill sperm as well as the HIV virus, which is a problem for people who want children. Much current research is attempting to discover how women and men will accept this method of female-controlled prevention when it has been perfected.

APPENDIX D: FLOWER VILLAGE DEMOGRAPHICS

1. The Mien language is in the linguistic subfamily Hmong/Mien (Miao/Yao), a branch of the Sino-Tibetan family, or Austro/Tai.

APPENDIX F: HEALTH CARE AND GENDER ISSUES
OF HMONG IN THE UNITED STATES

1. Some Hmong women still do not get prenatal care, which they regard as unnecessary, since pregnancy is considered a normal, healthy state that does not require a doctor's intervention.

2. "The Soul of a New Political Machine Is Hmong." *New York Times,* February 2, 2002: A-13.

BIBLIOGRAPHY

Abadie, Maurice

    1924   *Les Races du Haut-Tonkin de Phong-Tho a Lang-Son.* Paris: Société d'Éditions/Géographiques, Maritimes et Coloniales.

Abu-Lughod, Lila

    1986   *Veiled Sentiments: Honor and Poetry in a Bedouin Society.* Berkeley: University of California Press.

Ahern, Emily Martin

    1975   "The Power and Pollution of Chinese Women." In Wolf and Witke 1975:193–214.

Alting von Geusau, Leo

    1983   "Dialects of Akhazan: The Interiorization of a Perennial Minority Group." In McKinnon and Bhruksasri 1983:243–77.

Ardner, Edward

    1975   "Belief and the Problem of Women." In Shirley Ardner 1975:1–19.

Ardner, Shirley, ed.

    1975   *Perceiving Women.* London: Malaby Press.

Atkinson, Jane M., and Shelly Errington

    1990   *Power and Difference: Gender in Island Southeast Asia.* Stanford, Calif.: Stanford University Press.

Beauclair, Inez de

1960   "A Miao Tribe of Southeast Kweichow and Its Cultural Configuration."
        Bulletin of the Institute of Ethnology (Academica Sinica, Nanking, Taipei)
        10.

1970   *Tribal Cultures of Southwest China.* Taipei: Orient Cultural Service.

Bernatzik, Hugo Adolph

1970 [1947] *Akha and Miao: Problems of Applied Ethnography in Farther India.* Trans.
        Alois Nagler. New Haven, Conn.: Human Relations Area Files.

Bertrais, Yves

1964   *Dictionnaire Hmong (Meo Blanc).* Vientiane: Mission Catholique.

1978   *The Traditional Marriage among the White Hmong of Thailand and Laos.*
        Chiang Mai: Hmong Centre.

Bertrais, Yves, in collaboration with Yaj Diav and Zoov Ntxheb

1973   *Kab Ke Pam Tuag* (Funeral rites). Vientiane: n.p.

Beyrer, Charles, et al.

1997   "Widely Varying Prevalence and Risk Behaviors and HIV Infection among
        the Hilltribe and Ethnic Minority Peoples of Upper Northern Thailand."
        AIDS Care 9, no. 4:427–39.

1998   *War in the Blood: Sex, Politics and AIDS* in Southeast Asia. London: Zed
        Books, Ltd.

Binney, George A.

1971   *The Social and Economic Organization of Two White Meo Communities in
        Northern Thailand.* Washington, D.C.: Advanced Research Publication
        Agency, Department of Defense.

Blanc, Marie-Eve, Laurence Husson, and Evelyne Micollier, eds.

2000   *Sociétés asiatiques face au sida.* Paris: L'Harmattan.

Bliatout, Bruce Thowpaou

1988   "Hmong Attitudes towards Surgery: How It Affects Patient Prognosis."
        Migration World 16, no. 1:25–28.

1991   "Hmong Healing Practitioners." *Hmong Forum* 2:58–66.

Bloch, Maurice, and Jonathan Parry

1982   "Introduction." In *Death and the Regeneration of Life,* idem, eds., 1–44.
        Cambridge, U.K.: Cambridge University Press.

Boddy, Janice

1989   *Wombs and Spirits: Women, Men, and the Zar Cult in Northern Sudan.*
        Madison: University of Wisconsin Press.

Bohannan, Paul, and Mark Glazer, eds.

1973   *High Points in Anthropology*. New York: Knopf.

Bourdieu, Pierre

1977   *Outline of a Theory of Practice*. Cambridge, U.K.: Cambridge University
        Press.

Bradley, David

1983   "Identity: The Persistence of Minority Groups." In McKinnon and Bhruk-
        sasri 1986:46–55.

Brindenthal, R., and C. Koontz, eds.

1976   *Becoming Visible: Women in European History*. Boston: Houghton Mifflin.

Brummelhuis, Han ten, and Gilbert Herdt, eds.

1995   *Culture and Sexual Risk: Anthropological Perspectives on AIDS*. Amsterdam
        and Philadelphia: Gordon and Breach.

Catlin, Amy

1982   "Speech Surrogate Systems of the Hmong: From Singing Voices to Talk-
        ing Reeds." In Olney and Downing 1982:170–97.

Catlin, Amy, and Dixie Swift, eds.

1987   *Textiles as Texts: Arts of Hmong Women from Laos*. Los Angeles: The
        Women's Building.

Chatterjee, Partha

1993   *The Nation and Its Fragments: Colonial and Postcolonial Histories*. Prince-
        ton, N.J.: Princeton University Press.

Chen Qiguang and Li Yongsui

1981   "Hanyu Miao-Yaoyu tongyuan lizheng" (Some examples of the genetic
        affinity between Han and Miao-Yao). *Minzu yuwen*, no. 2:13–26.

Chindarsi, Nusit

1976   *The Religion of the Hmong Njua*. Bangkok: Siam Society.

1983   "Hmong Shamanism." In McKinnon and Bhruksasri 1983:187–93.

Clarke, Samuel R.

1911   *Among the Tribes in Southwest China*. London: China Inland Mission.

Cohen, Eric

1989   "International Politics and the Transformation of Folk Crafts: The Hmong
        (Meo) of Thailand," part 1. *Journal of the Siam Society* 77:69–82.

Cohen, Paul J.

1984   "Opium and the Karen: A Study of Indebtedness in Northern Thailand."
        Journal of Southeast Asian Studies 15, no. 1:150–65.

Collier, Jane F., and Sylvia Yanagisako

1987   *Gender and Kinship: Essays toward a Unified Analysis.* Stanford, Calif.: Stanford University Press.

Conquergood, Dwight, Paja Thao, and Xa Thao

1989   *I Am a Shaman: A Hmong Life Story with Ethnographic Commentary.* Southeast Asian Refugee Studies Occasional Paper, no. 8. Minneapolis: University of Minnesota, Center for Urban and Regional Affairs.

Cooper, Robert

1983   "Sexual Inequality among the Hmong Highlanders of Thailand." In McKinnon and Bhruksasri 1983:174–86.

1984   *Resource Scarcity and the Hmong Response: Patterns of Settlement and Economy in Transition.* Singapore: Singapore University Press.

Cooper, Robert, Shav N. Sooj, and Kiab Lis

1998   "Rape: Perceptions and Processes of Hmong Customary Law." Paper presented at the First International Workshop on the Hmong/Miao in Asia, Centre de archives d'outre mer, Aix-en-Provence, France. September 11–13.

Cooper, Robert, Nicholas Tapp, Gary Yia Lee, and Gretel Schwoer-Kohl

1996 [1991] *The Hmong.* Bangkok: Art Asia Press.

Count, Earl

1960   "Myth as Worldview: A Biosocial Synthesis." In Stanley Diamond 1960: 580–627.

Crystal, Eric

1987   "Buffalo Heads and Sacred Threads: Hmong Culture of the Southeast Asian Highlands." In Catlin and Swift 1987:14–22.

Culhane-Pera, Kathleen Ann

1987   "Description and Interpretation of a Hmong Shaman in St. Paul." Unpublished paper. Department of Anthropology, University of Minnesota.

1989   "Analysis of Cultural Beliefs and Power Dynamics in Disagreements about Health Care of Hmong Children." M.A. thesis, University of Minnesota.

Culhane-Pera, Kathleen A., D. E. Vawter, P. Xiong, B. Babbit, and M. Solberg, eds.

2003   *Healing by Heart: Clinical and Ethnical Case Stories of Hmong Families and Western Providers.* Nashville, Tenn.: Vanderbilt University Press.

Cunningham, Clarke

1964   "Order in the Atoni House." In Needham 1972:204–38.

Davis Floyd, Robie E.

1988   "Birth as an American Rite of Passage." In Michealson 1988:153–72.

1990   "The Role of Obstetrical Rituals in the Resolution of Cultural Anomaly." *Social Science and Medicine* 31, no. 2.

Diamond, Norma

1988   "The Miao and Poison: Interactions on China's Frontier." *Ethnology* 27, no. 1:1–25.

1995   "Defining the Miao: Ming, Qing, and Contemporary Views." In Harrell 1995:92–116.

Diamond, Stanley, ed.

1960   *Culture in History: Essays in Honor of Paul Radin.* New York: Columbia University Press.

Donnelly, Nancy D.

1994   *The Changing Lives of Refugee Hmong Women.* Seattle: University of Washington Press.

Doore, Gary, ed.

1988   *Shaman's Path: Healing, Personal Growth and Empowerment.* Boston and London: Shambhala.

Douglas, Mary

1966   *Purity and Danger: An Analysis of the Concepts of Pollution and Taboo.* London: Routledge and Kegan Paul.

Downing, B., and D. Olney, eds.

1982   *The Hmong in the West: Observations and Reports.* Minneapolis: Center for Urban and Regional Affairs, University of Minnesota.

Durkheim, Emile

1952   [1897] *Suicide.* London: Routledge and Kegan Paul.

Durrenberger, E. Paul

1971   "The Ethnography of Lisu Curing." Ph.D. diss., University of Illinois at Urbana-Champaign.

Eberhard, Wolfram, ed.

1965   *Folk Tales of China.* Chicago: University of Chicago Press.

Eberhardt, Nancy, ed.

1988   *Gender, Power and the Construction of Moral Order: Studies from the Thai Periphery.* Center for Southeast Asian Studies Monograph, no.4. Madison: University of Wisconsin-Madison.

Ebihara, May

1977   "Residence Patterns in a Khmer Village." *Annals of the New York Academy of Sciences,* no. 293:51–68.

Eliade, Mircea, ed.

1987   *The Encyclopedia of Religion.* Vol. 13. New York: Macmillan.

Elias, Christopher J., and Lori Heise

1993   "The Development of Microbicides: A New Method of HIV Prevention for Women." Working papers, no. 6. New York: The Population Council.

Errington, Shelly

1990   "Recasting Sex, Gender, and Power: A Theoretical and Regional Overview." In Atkinson and Errington 1990.

Etkin, Nina, ed.

1998   *Reviews in Anthropology.* University of Hawaii, Manoa: Gordon and Breach.

Fadiman, Anne

1997   *The Spirit Catches You and You Fall Down.* New York: Farrar, Straus and Giroux.

Falk, Catherine

1996   "Upon Meeting the Ancestors: Hmong Funeral Rituals in Asia and Australia." *Hmong Studies Journal* 1, no. 1. http://members.aol.com/hmongstudies/hsj.html.

Farham, Christie A., ed.

1987   *The Impact of Feminist Research on the Academy.* Bloomington: Indiana University Press.

Feuchtwang, Stephan

1974   *An Anthropological Analysis of Chinese Geomancy.* Vientiane: Vithagna.

Fox, James J.

1971   "Sisters' Child as Plant: Metaphors in an Idiom of Consanguinity." In Needham 1971:219–252.

Freedman, Maurice

1966   *Chinese Lineage and Society: Fukien and Kwangtung.* London: Athlone Press.

1969   *Geomancy.* London: Proceedings of the Royal Anthropological Institute of Great Britain and Ireland, 5–15.

Fruzzetti, Lina

1982   *The Gift of a Virgin.* New Brunswick, N.J.: Rutgers University Press.

Fruzzetti, Lina, and Akos Oster

1976   "Seed and Earth: A Cultural Analysis of Kinship in a Bengali Town." *Contributions to Indian Sociology,* n.s., no. 10:97–132.

Fruzzetti, Lina, and Rosa Perez

2002   "The Gender of the Nation: Allegoric Femininity and Women's Status in
        Bengal and Goa." In *Mirrors of the Empire: Towards a Debate on Portugese
        Colonialism and Postcolonialism.* Special issue of *Ethnográfica.* Lisboa, Por-
        tugal: ISCTE.

Geddes, William R.

1970   "Opium and the Miao: A Study in Ecological Adjustment." *Oceana* 41, no.
        1:1–11.

1976   *Migrants of the Mountains: The Cultural Ecology of the Blue Miao (Hmong
        Njua) of Thailand.* Oxford: Clarendon Press.

Goldstein, Beth

1986   "Resolving Sexual Assault: Hmong and the American Legal System." In
        Hendricks et al. 1986:135–43.

Gollub, Erica L.

1995   "Woman-Centered Prevention Techniques and Technologies." In O'Leary
        and Jemmott 1995:43–82.

Good, Byron

1977   "The Heart of What's the Matter: The Semantics of Illness in Iran." *Cul-
        ture, Medicine and Psychiatry* 1:25–58.

Graham, David Crockett

1923   "A Ch'uan Miao Tribe of Southern Szechuen." *Journal of the West China
        Border Research Society* 1:1–56.

1926   "Critical Note: The Ch'uan Miao." *Journal of Religion* 6, no. 3:302–7.

1937   "The Ceremonies of the Ch'uan Miao." *Journal of the West China Border
        Research Society* 9:71–119.

1954   *Songs and Stories of the Ch'uan Miao.* Washington, D.C.: Smithsonian Insti-
        tution Miscellaneous Collection, vol. 123, no. 1.

Grandstaff, Terry B.

1979   "The Hmong, Opium and the Haw: Speculation on the Origin of Their
        Association." *Journal of the Siam Society* 67:2, 170–79.

Gua, Bo

1975   "Opium, Bombs and Trees: The Future of the Hmong Tribesmen in North-
        ern Thailand." *Journal of Contemporary Asia* 1:70–80.

Gunnlaugsson, Geir, and Jonina Einarsdottir

1993   "Colostrum and Ideas about Bad Milk: A Case Study from Guinea-
        Bissau." *Social Science and Medicine* 36, no. 3:383–88.

295

Hahn, Ann, and Marjorie Muecke

1987　"Current Problems in Obstetrics, Gynecology and Fertility." In *The Anthropology of Birth in Five U.S. Ethnic Populations: Implications for Obstetrical Practice.* Chicago: New Year Medical Publishers Inc.

Hainsworth, Geoffrey E., ed.

1981　*Southeast Asia: Women, Changing Social Structure and Cultural Continuity.* Ottawa: University of Ottawa Press.

Hang, Doua

1986　"Tam Tuab Neeq: Connecting the Generations." In Johns and Strecker 1986:33–41.

Hanks, Jane R.

1960　"Reflections on the Ontology of Rice." In Stanley Diamond 1960:298–301.

1963　*Maternity and Its Rituals in Bang Chan.* Data Paper no. 51. Ithaca, N.Y.: Cornell University Southeast Asia Program.

1974　"Recitation of Patrilineages among the Akha." In Smith 1974:114–27.

1988　"The Power of Akha Women." In Eberhardt 1988:13–32.

Hanks, Jane R., and Lucien M. Hanks

2001　*Tribes of the North Thailand Frontier.* Yale Southeast Asian Studies, no. 51. New Haven, Conn.: Yale University Southeast Asia Studies.

Harrell, Stevan, ed.

1995　*Cultural Encounters on China's Ethnic Frontiers.* Seattle: University of Washington Press.

Hart, Donn V.

1969　*Bisayan Filipino and Malay Humeral Pathologies: Folk Medicine and Ethnohistory in Southeast Asia.* Southeast Asia Program, Data Paper no. 76. Ithaca, N.Y.: Southeast Asia Program, Cornell University.

Hart, Donn V., R. J. Coughlin, and Phya Anuman Rajadhon

1965　*Southeast Asian Birth Customs: Three Studies in Human Reproduction.* New Haven, Conn.: Human Relations Area Files Press.

Hayami, Yoko

1992　"Ritual and Religious Transformation among the Sgaw Karen of Northern Thailand: Implications on Gender and Ethnic Identity." Ph.D. diss., Brown University.

1993　"Internal and External Discourse of Communality, Tradition and Environment: Minority Claims on Forest in the Northern Hills of Thailand." *Tonan Ajia kenkyu* (Southeast Asian studies) (Kyoto) 35:558–79.

Hearn, Robert

1974   *Thai Government Programs in Refugee Relocation and Resettlement in Thailand*. Auburn, N.Y.: Thailand Books.

Heberer, Thomas

1989   *China and Its National Minorities: Autonomy or Assimilation*. Armonk, N.Y., and London: M. E. Sharpe.

Heimbach, Ernest E.

1969   *White Hmong-English Dictionary*. Ithaca, N.Y.: , Southeast Asia Program, Cornell University.

Hendricks, Glenn L., Amos S. Deinard, and Bruce T. Downing, eds.

1986   *The Hmong in Transition*. New York and Minneapolis: Center for Migration Studies and Southeast Asian Refugee Studies Project, University of Minnesota.

Hertz, Robert

1960   [1907] "A Contribution to the Study of the Collective Representation of Death." In idem, *Death and the Right Hand*, trans. R. and C. Needham, pp. 29–86. Glencoe, Ill.: Free Press.

Hicks, David

1976   *Tetum Ghosts and Kin*. Palo Alto, Calif.: Mayfield Publishing Co.

Hill, Ann

1988   "Women without Talents Are Virtuous." In Eberhardt 1988:53–72.

Huntington, Richard, and Peter Metcalf

1979   *Celebrations of Death: The Anthropology of Mortuary Ritual*. Cambridge, U.K.: Cambridge University Press.

Hutheesing, Otome Klein

1990   *Emerging Sexual Inequality among the Lisu of Northern Thailand*. Leiden, New York, Copenhagen, and Cologne: E. J. Brill.

Hymes, Dell, ed.

1969   *Reinventing Anthropology*. New York: Pantheon Books.

Izikowitz, Karl G.

1982   "Introduction." In *The House in East and Southeast Asia: Anthropological and Architectural Objects*, K. G. Izikowitz and P. Sorensen, eds., pp. 1–6. Monograph Series 30. London: Curzon Press.

Jay, Nancy

1992   *Throughout Your Generations Forever: Sacrifice, Religion, and Paternity*. Chicago: University of Chicago Press.

Jay, Robert

1969   "Personal and Extrapersonal Vision in Anthropology." In Hymes 1969:
367–81.

Johns, Brenda

1986   "An Introduction to White Hmong Sung Poetry." In Johns and Strecker
1986:5–11.

Johns, Brenda, and David Strecker, eds.

1986   *The Hmong World.* New Haven, Conn.: Council on Southeast Asian Studies, Yale Center for International and Area Studies.

Johnson, Charles

1985   *Dab Neeg Hmoob: Myths, Legends and Folk Tales from the Hmong of Laos.*
St. Paul, Minn.: Linguistics Department, Macalester College.

Jonsson, Hjorleifur

1998a   "Dead Headman: Histories and Communities in the Hinterland." In
Trankell and Summers 1998:192–212.

1998b   "Forest Products and Peoples: Upland Groups, Thai Politics, and Regional
Space." *Sojourn* 13:1–37.

2000   "Minority Identity and the Location of Difference in the South China Bor-
derlands." *Ethnos* 65:1.

Jordan, Brigitte

1983   *Birth in Four Cultures: A Cross Cultural Investigation of Childbirth in Yuca-
tan, Holland, Sweden and the United States.* Montreal: Eden Press.

Jupp, J., ed.

1999   *The Australian People: An Encyclopedia of the Nation, Its People and Their
Origin.* 2nd ed. Canberra: Angus and Robertson.

Kammerer, Cornelia Ann

1983   "Constructed Meaning: An Analysis of the Akha House." Paper presented
at the Annual Meeting of the American Anthropological Association,
December, Chicago.

1986   "Gateway to the Akha World: Kinship, Ritual, and Community among
Highlanders of Thailand." Ph.D. diss., University of Chicago.

1988a   "Shifting Gender Asymmetries among Ahka of Northern Thailand." In
Eberhardt 1988:33–51.

1988b   "Of Labels and Laws: Thailand's Resettlement and Repatriation Policies."
Cultural Survival Quarterly 12, no. 4:7–12.

1989   "Opium and Tribal People in the Golden Triangle." Paper presented at the annual meeting of the American Anthropological Association, November 17, Washington, D.C.

1994a   "Structural Vulnerability, AIDS Prevention, and Care: AIDS among Akha in Thailand." Paper presented at the Conference on Sociocultural Dimensions of HIV/AIDS Control and Care in Thailand, January, Chiang Mai.

1994b   "Population Control, STDs, and AIDS Prevention in Thailand: 'Studying Up' from the Tribal Periphery." Paper presented at the annual meeting of the American Anthropological Association, December, Atlanta, Georgia.

Kammerer, Cornelia Ann, Otome Klein Hutheesing, Ralana Maneeprasert, and Patricia V. Symonds

1995   "Vulnerability to HIV Infection among Three Hilltribes in Northern Thailand: Qualitative Anthropological Issues." In Brummelhuis and Herdt 1995:53–75.

Kaufman, Howard K.

1960   *Bangkhuad: A Community Study in Thailand.* Monographs of the Association for Asian Studies, no. 10. Locust Valley, N.Y.: J. J. Augustin.

Kay, Margarita

1982   *Anthropology of Human Birth.* Philadelphia: F. A. Davis Company.

Kesmanee, Chupinit

1989   "The Poisoning Effects of a Lovers' Triangle: Highlanders, Opium and Extension Crops, a Policy Overdue for Review." In McKinnon and Vienne 1989:61–102.

Keyes, Charles

1971   "Buddhism and National Integration in Thailand." *Journal of Asian Studies* 30, no. 3:551–68.

1977   *The Golden Peninsula: Culture and Adaptation in Mainland Southeast Asia.* New York: Macmillan.

1984   "Mother or Mistress but Never a Monk: Buddhist Notions of Female Gender in Rural Thailand." *American Ethnologist* 11:223–40.

Kirsch, Thomas

1973   *Feasting and Social Oscillation: Religion and Society in Upland Southeast Asia.* Southeast Asia Program, Cornell University, Data Paper no. 92. Ithaca, N.Y.: Department of Asian Studies, Cornell University.

1975   "Economy, Polity and Religion in Thailand." Skinner and Kirsch 1975: 172–96.

1983   "Buddhism, Sex Roles, and the Thai Economy." In Esterik 1983:17–41.

1985   "Text and Context: Buddhist Sex Roles/Culture of Gender Revisited."
        American Ethnologist 12:302–30.

Kirton, Elizabeth S.

1985   "The Locked Medicine Cabinet: Hmong Health Care in America." Ph.D.
        diss., University of California at Santa Barbara.

Kunstadter, Peter

1983   "Highland Populations in Northern Thailand." In McKinnon and Bhruk-
        sasri 1983:15–45.

1984   *Demographic Differences in a Rapidly Changing Mixed Ethnic Population
        in Northwestern Thailand.* Research Paper Series 19. Tokyo: University Pop-
        ulation Institute, KUPRI.

1985   "Health of Hmong in Thailand: Factors, Morbidity and Mortality in Com-
        parison with Other Ethnic Groups." *Cultural Medical Psychiatry* 9, no.
        4:423–37.

1996   "Aspects of Change in Hmong Society: Economy, Demography, Gender
        Status and Marriage." Paper presented at the Sixth International Confer-
        ence on Thai Studies, 14–17 October, Chiang Mai University.

Kunstadter, Peter, Sally L. Kunstadter, and P. Ritnetikul

1990   "Demographic Variables in Fetal and Child Mortality: Hmong in Thai-
        land." Paper presented at the annual meeting of the Association for Asian
        Studies, April, Chicago.

Kunstadter, Peter, and Prasit Leepreecha

1997   "Morbidity of Hmong Refugees in Fresno, California, Compared with
        Non-Refugee Hmong in Thailand." Paper presented at the annual meet-
        ing of the Population Association of America, Washington, D.C.

Kunstadter, Peter, C. Podhisita, Prasit Leepreecha, and Sally L. Kunstadter

1991   "Rapid Changes in Fertility among Hmong in Northern Thailand." Paper
        presented at the annual meeting of the Thai Population Association,
        November, Chiang Mai.

Laderman, Carol

1983   *Wives and Midwives: Childbirth and Nutrition in Rural Malaysia.* Berke-
        ley and London: University of California Press.

Lamphere, Louise

1974   "Strategies, Cooperation, and Conflict among Women in Domestic
        Groups." In Rosaldo and Lamphere 1974:1–42.

1987   "Feminism in Anthropology: The Struggle to Reshape Our Thinking about
        Gender." In Farham 1987:11–33.

Larchrojna, Somphob

1975 "Karen Medicine." M. A. thesis, Sydney University.

1986 [1983] "Pwo Karen, Spirits and Souls." In McKinnon and Bhruksasri 1983:169–73.

Lartequy, Jean, with Yang Dao

1979 *La fabuleuse aventure du peuple de l'opium.* Paris: Presses de la cité.

Leach, Edmund

1954 *Political Systems of Highland Burma: A Study of Kachin Social Structure.* Boston: Beacon Press.

1961 *Rethinking Anthropology.* London School of Economics Monograph on Social Anthropology 22. London: Athlone Press.

Leacock, Eleanor B.

1976 "Women in Egalitarian Society." In Brindenthal and Koontz 1976:11–35.

Lebar, Frank M., Gerald C. Hickey, and John K. Musgrave

1964 *Ethnic Groups of Mainland Southeast Asia.* New Haven, Conn.: Hmong Relations Area Files.

Lee, Gary Yia

1981 "The Effects of Development Measures on the Socio-Economy of the White Hmong." Ph.D. diss., University of Sydney.

1987a "Ethnicity and the State: Historical Overview of the Hmong in Lao Politics." Paper presented at the International Conference on Thai Studies, July 3–6, Australian National University, Canberra.

1987b "Minority Politics in Thailand: A Hmong Perspective." Paper presented at the International Conference on Thai Studies, July 3–6, Australian National University, Canberra.

1999 "The Hmong." In Jupp 1999:535–36.

Leepreecha, Prasit

1998 "Ntoo Xeeb: Cultural Revival on Forest Conservation of the Hmong in Thailand." Paper presented at the First International Workshop on the Hmong/Miao in Asia, September 11–13, Centre de archives d'outre mer, Aix-en-Provence, France.

2001 "Kinship and Identity among Hmong in Thailand." Ph.D. diss., University of Washington.

Lehman, Frederik

1963 *The Structure of Chin Society.* Urbana: University of Illinois Press.

Lemoine, Jacques

1972a "Les Ecritures du Hmong." *Bulletin des Amis du Royaume Lao* 7–8:123–65.

1972b   "L'initiation du mort chez les Hmong." *L'Homme* 12: 1–3.

1972c   *Un Village Hmong vert du haut Laos: Milieu technique et organisation sociale.* Paris: École pratique des hautes études, Centre national de la recherche scientifique.

1983a   *L'Initiation du mort chez les Hmong.* Bangkok: Pandora Press.

1983b   *Showing the Way.* Trans. Kenneth White. Bangkok: Pandora Press.

1986   "Shamanism in the Context of Hmong Resettlement." In Hendricks 1986:337–48.

1988   "The Bridge: An Essential Implement of Hmong and Yao Shamanism." In Doore 1988:63–72.

1997   "The Constitution of a Hmong Shaman's Power of Healing and Folk Culture." *Shaman* 4, nos. 1–2:143–65.

Lévi-Strauss, Claude

1969   *The Elementary Structures of Kinship.* Trans. James Harle Bell, John Richard von Sturmer, and Rodney Needham. Boston: Beacon Press.

Linton, Ralph

1973   "Status and Role." In Bohannan and Glazer 1973:187–200.

Lombard-Salmon, Claudine

1972   *Un Exemple d'acculturation chinoise: la province de Gui Zhou au XVIIIe siècle.* Paris: École française d'Extrême–Orient.

Lyman, Thomas A.

1990   "The Mong (Green Miao) and Their Language," part 1. *Journal of the Siam Society* 78:63–65.

MacCormack, Carol, ed.

1982   *Ethnography of Fertility and Birth.* London: Academic Press.

MacCormack, Carol, and Marilyn Strathern, eds.

1980   *Nature, Culture and Gender.* Cambridge, U.K.: Cambridge University Press.

Malinkowski, Bronislaw

1948   *Magic, Science and Religion, and Other Essays.* New York: The Free Press.

Manderson, Lenore

1981   "Roasting, Smoking and Dieting in Response to Birth: Malay Confinement in Cross Cultural Perspective." *Social Science and Medicine* 15(B): 509–20.

Maneeprasert, Ralana

1989   "Women and Children First: A Review of the Current Nutritional Status in the Highlands." In McKinnon and Vienne 1989.

Mark, Lindy L.

1967   "Patrilineal Cross-Cousin Marriage among the Magpie Miao: Preferential or Proscriptive." *American Anthropologist* 69:55–62.

Martin, Emily

1992 (1987) *The Woman in the Body: A Cultural Analysis of Reproduction.* Boston: Beacon Press.

Maspero, Henri

1981   *Taoism and Chinese Religion.* Trans. F. A. Kierman, Jr. Amherst: University of Massachusetts Press.

McClain, Carol

1975   "Ethno-Obstetrics in Ajijic." *Anthropological Quarterly* 48, no. 1:38–56.

McCoy, Alfred W.

1990 [1972] *The Politics of Heroin in Southeast Asia.* New York: Harper and Row.

McKinnon, John, and Wanat Bhruksasri, eds.

1983   *Highlanders of Thailand.* Singapore: Oxford University Press.

McKinnon, John, and Bernard Vienne, eds.

1989   *Hill Tribes Today: Problems in Change.* Bangkok: White Lotus-ORSTOM (Tri-ORSTOM Project).

Mead, Margaret, and Niles Newton

1967   "Cultural Patterning of Perinatal Behaviour." In Richardson and Guttmacher 1967:142–244.

Michaud, Jean

1997   "From Southeast China into Upper Indochina: An Overview of Hmong (Miao) Migrations." *Asia Pacific Viewpoint* 38, no. 2:119–30.

Michealson, K., et al., eds.

1988   *Childbirth in America.* South Hadley, Mass.: Bergen and Garvey.

Mickey, Margaret Portia

1947   *The Cowrie Shell Miao of Kweichow.* Papers of the Peabody Museum of American Archaeology and Ethnology 32, no. 1:1–94. Cambridge, Mass.: The Museum, 1947.

Milner, G. B., ed.

1978   *Natural Symbols in South East Asia.* London: School of Oriental and African Studies, University of London.

Mills, James

1922   *The Lhota Naga.* London: Macmillan.

1926   *The Ao Naga.* London: Macmillan.

Mills, Mary Beth

1997 "Contesting the Margins of Modernity: Women, Migration, and Consumption in Thailand." *American Ethnologist* 24, no. 1:37–61.

Moerman, Michael

1965 "Ethnic Identification in a Complex Civilization: Who Are the Lue?" *American Anthropologist* 67:1215–30.

Mohanty, Chandra

1990 "Cartographies of Struggle." In *Third World Women and the Politics of Feminism,* ed. Chandra Mohanty, Ann Russo, and Lourdes Torres, 1–47. Bloomington: Indiana University Press.

Moore, Henrietta L.

1988 *Feminism and Anthropology.* Cambridge, U. K.: Polity Press.

Moran, Mary

1991 *Civilized Women: Gender and Prestige among the Glebo of Liberia.* Ithaca, N.Y.: Cornell University Press.

Morechand, Guy

1968 "Le chamanisme des Hmong." *Bulletin de l'École française d'Extrême-Orient* 54:53–94.

Morrison, Gayle

1997 "Hmong Qeej Speaks to the Spirits." *Hmong Studies Journal* 2, no. 1. http://members.aol.com/hmongstudies/hsj.html.

Morse, Janice M.

1989 "Cultural Variations in the Behavioral Response to Parturition: Childbirth in Fiji." *Medical Anthropology* 12:35–54.

Mottin, Jean

1978 *Elements de grammaire Hmong blanc.* Bangkok: Don Bosco Press.

1979 *Fêtes de nouvel an chez les Hmong blanc de Thaïlande.* Bangkok: Don Bosco Press.

1980a *The History of the Hmong (Meo).* Bangkok: Odeon Store Ltd.

1980b *55 chants d'amour Hmong blanc: 55 zaj kwvtxhiaj Hmoob dawb.* Bangkok: Don Bosco Press.

1982 *Allons faire le tour du ciel et de la terre: le chamanisme de Hmong vu dans les textes.* Bangkok: White Lotus.

1984 "A Hmong Shaman's Seance." *Asian Folklore Studies* 43:99–108.

Mougne, Christine

1978 "An Ethnography of Reproduction: Changing Patterns of Fertility in a Northern Thai Village." In Stott 1978:68–108.

Muecke, Marjorie A.

1976   "Health Care Systems as Socializing Agents: Childbearing the North Thai and Western Ways." *Social Science and Medicine* 10, nos. 7–8:377–83.

1981   "Changes in Women's Status Associated with Modernization in Northern Thailand." In Hainsworth 1981:53–65.

Mukhopadhyay, Carol, and Patricia Higgins

1988   "Anthropological Studies of Women's Status Revisited: 1977–1987." *Annual Review of Anthropology* 17:461–95.

Murdock, G. P., ed.

1960   *Social Structure in Southeast Asia.* Wennergren Foundation for Anthropological Research, Viking Fund Publication in Anthropology no. 29. Chicago: Quadrangle Books, 1960.

Narayan, Kisrin

1986   "Birds on a Branch: Girlfriends and Wedding Songs in Kangra." *Ethos* 14, no. 1:47–75.

Needham, Rodney

1967   "Percussion and Transition." *Man* 2:606–14.

1972   *Right and Left: Essays on Dual Symbolic Classifications.* Chicago: University of Chicago Press.

Needham, Rodney, ed.

1971   *Rethinking Kinship and Marriage.* Association of Social Anthropologists, monograph 11. London: Tavistock Press.

Newman, Lucille

1969   "The Folklore of Pregnancy: Wives' Tales in Contra Costa County, California." *Western Folklore* 28:112–35a

1972   *Birth Control: An Anthropological View.* Module 27. Reading, Mass.: Addison-Wesley.

Newman, Lucille, ed.

1985   *Women's Medicine: A Cross-Cultural Study of Indigenous Fertility Regulation.* New Brunswick, N.J.: Rutgers University Press.

O'Leary, Ann, and Loretta Sweet Jemmott, eds.

1995   *Women at Risk: Issues in the Primary Prevention of AIDS.* New York and London: Plenum Press.

Olney, Douglas P., and Bruce T. Downing, eds.

1982   *The Hmong in the West.* Minneapolis: Southeast Asian Refugee Studies Project, Center for Urban and Regional Affairs, University of Minnesota.

Ortner, Sherry

1974　"Is Female to Male as Nature Is to Culture?" Rosaldo and Lamphere 1974:67–87.

1994　"Resistance and the Problem of Ethnographic Refusal." *Comparative Studies in Society and History* 37, no. 1:173–93.

Pillsbury, Barbara L.

1978　"Doing the Month: Confinement and Convalescence of Chinese Women after Childbirth." *Social Science and Medicine* 12, no. 1B:11–22.

Poshyachinda, Vichai

1996　"Shifting Borders, Shifting Identities: New Perspectives on Thai Homosexuality." Paper presented at the Thai Studies Sixth International Conference, October 14–17, Chiang Mai.

Potter, Gayle, and Alice Whirren

1981　"Traditional Hmong Birth Customs: A Historical Study." In Olney and Downing 1981:48–62.

Quincy, Keith

1988　*Hmong: History of a People.* Cheney: Eastern Washington University Press.

Radcliffe-Brown, Andrew R.

1964　*The Andaman Islanders.* New York: The Free Press.

Radley, Howard M.

1986　"Economic Marginalization and the Ethnic Consciousness of the Green Hmong (Moob Ntsuab) of Northwestern Thailand." Ph.D. diss., Corpus Christi College, Oxford University.

Rajadhon, Phya Anuman

1965　"Customs Connected with the Rearing of Children." In Hart et al. 1965:115–204.

Ratliff, Martha

n.d.　"Vocabulary of Environment and Subsistence in the Hmong-Mien Protolanguage." In *Proceedings of the First International Symposium on the Hmong/Miao in Asia,* Centre de archives d'outre mer, Aix-en-Provence, France. September 11–13.

Ray, Sangeeta

2000　*Engendering India: Woman and Nation in Colonial and Postcolonial Narratives.* Durham and London: Duke University Press.

Reiter, R. R.

1977　*Towards an Anthropology of Women.* New York and London: Monthly Review Press.

Rice, Pranee Liamputtong

2000　*Hmong Women and Reproduction.* Westport, Conn., and London: Bergin and Garvey.

Rice, Pranee L., and Lenore Manderson, eds.

1996　*Maternity and Reproductive Health in Asian Societies.* Amsterdam: Harwood Academic Publishers.

Richardson, Stephen A., and Alan Guttmacher, eds.

1967　*Childbearing: Its Social and Psychological Aspects.* Baltimore: Williams and Wilkins Company.

Rosaldo, Michelle Z.

1974　"Women, Culture and Society: A Theoretical Overview." In Rosaldo and Lamphere 1974:17–42.

1980　*Knowledge and Passion: Ilongot Notions of Self and Social Life.* Cambridge, U.K.: Cambridge University Press.

Rosaldo, Michelle Zimbalist, and Louise Lamphere, eds.

1974　*Woman, Culture and Society.* Stanford, Calif.: Stanford University Press.

Ruey, Yih-fu

1958　"Terminological Structure of the Miao Kinship System." *Bulletin of the Institute of History and Philology, Academia Sinica* (Taipei) 29, no. 2:613–39.

1960　"The Magpie Miao of Southern Szechuan." In Murdock 1960:143–55.

1962　"The Miao: Their Origin and Southward Migration." In *Proceedings of the International Association of Historians of Asia, Second Biennial Conference,* Taipei, Taiwan.

Rumbaut, Ruben, and John R. Weeks

1986　"Fertility and Adaptation: Indochinese Refugees in the United States." *International Migration Review* 20, no. 2:428–65.

Sacks, Karen

1977　"Engels Revisited: Women and the Organization of Production and Private Property." In Reiter 1977:211–34.

Sanday, Peggy

1981　*Female Power and Male Dominance: On the Origins of Sexual Inequality.* Cambridge, U.K.: Cambridge University Press.

Sargent, Carolyn F.

1989　*Maternity, Medicine, and Power: Reproductive Decisions in Urban Benin.* Berkley and Los Angeles: University of California Press.

Savina, Françoise

1924 *Historie de Miao*. Hong Kong: Imprimerie de la Société des missions-étrangères.

Schein, Louisa

2000 *Minority Rules: The Miao and the Feminine in China's Cultural Politics*. Durham, N.C., and London: Duke University Press.

Schneider, Jane, and Annette Weiner, eds.

1989 *Cloth and Human Experience*. Washington and London: Smithsonian Institute Press.

Scott, James M.

1969 *The White Poppy: The History of Opium*. London: Funk and Wagnall Co.

Siikala, Anna-Leena

1987 "Siberian and Inner Asian Shamanism." In Eliade 1987:201–15.

Singer, Merrill, ed.

1997 *The Political Economy of AIDS*. Amityville, N.Y.: Baywood Press.

Skinner, G. William, and A. Thomas Kirsch, eds.

1975 *Changes and Persistence in Thai Society: Essays in Honor of Lauriston Sharp*. Ithaca, N.Y.: Cornell University Press.

Smalley, William A., Chiakoua Vang, and Ghia Yee Yang

1990 *Mother of Writing: The Origin and Development of a Hmong Messianic Script*. Chicago: University of Chicago Press.

Smith, R. J., ed.

1974 *Social Organization and the Applications of Anthropology: Essays in Honor of Lauriston Sharpe*. Ithaca, N.Y.: Cornell University Press.

Stott, P., ed.

1978 *Nature and Man in Southeast Asia*. London: School of Oriental and African Studies.

Strathern, Marilyn

1972 *Women in Between: Female Roles in a Male World, Mt. Hagen, New Guinea*. London: Seminar Press.

1980 "No Nature, No Culture: The Hagen Case." In MacCormack and Strathern 1980:174–222.

1988 *The Gender of the Gift: Problems with Women and Problems with Society in Melanesia*. Berkeley: University of California Press.

Strecker, David

1986 "Proto-Hmongic Finals." Paper presented at the 19th Conference on Sino-Tibetan Languages and Linguistics, Columbus, Ohio.

1987   "The Hmong Mien Languages." *Linguistics of the Tibeto Burman Area* 10, no. 2:1–11.

Sutthi, Chantaboon

1983   "Highland Swidden Cultivation." Tribal Research Center, Department of Public Welfare, Ministry of the Interior. (Mimeo in Thai)

1989   "Highland Swidden Cultivation: From Better to Worse." In McKinnon and Vienne 1988:107–42.

Symonds, Patricia V.

1990   "Women and Birth in a Thai Highland Community." In *Proceedings of the 4th International Conference on Thai Studies,* vol. 1:375–81.

1991   "Cosmology and the Cycle of Life: Birth, Death, and Gender in a Village in Northern Thailand." Ph.D. diss., Brown University.

1993   "Cosmology and the Cycle of Life: Hmong Views of Birth, Death, and Gender in a Mountain Village in Northern Thailand." *Journal of the National Research Council of Thailand* 25, no. 2 (July December):1–15.

1996   "Cosmological Aspects of Birth among the Hmong." In Manderson and Rice 1996:103–23.

1997a   "Blessing in a White Hmong Community in Northern Thailand: Invocation and Sacrifice." In Tannenbaum and Kammerer 1997a:98–115.

1997b   "The Political Economy and Cultural Logics of HIV/AIDS among the Hmong in Northern Thailand." In Singer 1997b:205–26.

1998   "Following Cultural Pathways for the Prevention of HIV/AIDS: Notes from the Field." Paper presented at the First International Workshop on the Hmong/Miao in Asia, Centre de archives d'outre mer, Aix-en-Provence, France. September 11–13.

2000   "Suivre les chemins culturels dans le cadre de la prévention du VIH/sida chez les Hmong de Thaïlande." In Blanc et al. 2000:367–94.

Symonds, Patricia V., and Cornelia Kammerer

1992   "AIDS in Asia: Hill Tribes Endangered at Thailand's Periphery." *Cultural Survival Quarterly* 16, no. 3:23–25.

Symonds, Patricia V., and Brooke G. Schoepf

1998   "HIV/AIDS: The Global Pandemic and Struggles for Control." In Etkin 1998:189–209.

Tambiah, Stanley J.

1969   "Animals Are Good to Think and Good to Prohibit." *Ethnology* 8:423–29.

1970   *Spirit Cults in North-East Thailand.* Cambridge, U.K.: Cambridge University Press.

1985   *Culture, Thought and Social Action: An Anthropological Perspective.* Cambridge, Mass.: Harvard University Press.

Tannenbaum, Nicola

1995   *Who Can Compete Against the World? Power-Protection and Buddhism in the Shan Worldview.* Ann Arbor, Mich.: Association of Asian Studies.

Tannenbaum, Nicola, and Cornelia Kammerer, eds.

1997   *Merit and Blessing in Mainland Southeast Asia.* New Haven, Conn.: Yale University Press.

Tapp, Nicholas

1986a   "Geomancy as an Aspect of Upland-Lowland Relationships." In Hendricks 1986:87–95.

1986b   *The Hmong of Thailand: Opium People of the Golden Triangle.* London: Anti-Slavery Society.

1988   "The Hmong: Political Economy of an Illegal Crop." In Taylor and Turton 1988:230–40. New York: Monthly Review Press.

1989a   "Hmong Religion." *Asian Folklore Studies* 48:59–94.

1989b   *Sovereignty and Rebellion: The White Hmong of Northern Thailand.* Singapore: Oxford University Press.

1990   "Milieu and Context: The Disappearance of White Hmong." *Proceedings of the International Conference on Thai Studies, Kunming, China, 1990.* Vol. 3:108–20.

2001   "The Hmong of China: Context, Agency, and the Imaginary." *Sinica Leidensia* 51.

Tasanapradit, Porn, and Usanee Perngparn and Vichai Poshyachinda

1986   *Hill Tribe Population and Family Planning.* Proceedings of National Research Dissemination Seminar Organized by Family Health Division, Department of Health, Ministry of Public Health, Chiang Mai Province 3–5 September 1986. Bangkok: Institute of Health Research, Chulalongkorn University.

Taylor, J. G., and A. Turton, eds.

1988   *Ethnic Histories and Minority Identities.* New York: Monthly Review Press.

Tedlock, Dennis

1983   *The Spoken Word and the Work of Interpretation.* Philadelphia: University of Pennsylvania Press.

Thao, Xoua

1984   "Southeast Asian Refugees of Rhode Island: Hmong Perception of Illness." *Rhode Island Medical Journal* 67:323–30.

1986   "Hmong Perceptions of Illness and Traditional Ways of Healing." In Hendricks et al. 1986:365–78.

Thitsa, Khin

1980   *Providence and Prostitution: Image and Reality in Buddhist Thailand.* London: Change International Reports.

Thompson, Stuart E.

1988   "Death, Food, and Fertility." In Watson and Rawski 1988:71–108.

Tooker, Deborah E.

1988   "Inside and Outside: Schematic Replication at the Levels of Village, Household, and Person Among the Akha of Northern Thailand." Ph.D. diss., Harvard University.

Trankell, I. B., and L. Summers, eds.

1998   *Facets of Power and Its Limitations: Political Culture in Southeast Asia.* Uppsala: Uppsala Studies in Cultural Anthropology.

Traube, Elizabeth G.

1986   *Cosmology and Social Life: Ritual Exchange among the Mambai of East Timor.* Chicago and London: University of Chicago Press.

Tribal Research Institute, Thailand

2000   *Tribal Population Summary in Thailand.* Chiang Mai: Service and Publicity Section, Tribal Research Institute.

Turner, Victor

1967   *The Forest of Symbols.* Ithaca, N.Y.: Cornell University Press.

1969   *The Ritual Process: Structure and Anti-Structure.* Chicago: Aldine.

1986   *The Anthropology of Performance.* New York: Performing Arts Journal Publications.

Turton, Andrew

1978   "Architecture and Political Space in Thailand." In Milner 1978:113–32.

Van Esterik, Penny, ed.

1982   *Women of Southeast Asia.* Center for Southeast Asian Studies, Occasional Paper no. 9. Dekalb, Ill.: Northern Illinois University.

Van Gennep, Arnold

1960   [1909] *The Rites of Passage.* Trans. Monika B. Vizedom and Gabrielle L. Caffe. Chicago: University of Chicago Press.

Vang, Lue, and Judy Lewis

1990   [1984] *Grandmother's Path, Grandfather's Way.* Rancho Cordova, Calif.: Zellerbach Family Fund.

Vang, Ntxhi

1992   "Symbols Used in Hmong Funeral Ritual." Unpublished manuscript.

Vernant, Jean-Pierre

1980   *Myth and Society in Ancient Greece.* Trans. by Janet Lloyd. Sussex: Harvester Press; Atlantic Highlands, N.J.: Humanities Press.

Walker, Anthony

1983   "The Lahu People: An Introduction." In McKinnon and Bhruksasri 1983:227–37.

Wang Fushi

1985   *Miaoyu jianzhi* (A sketch of the Miao language). Beijing: Nationalities Press.

Watson, James L.

1982   "Of Flesh and Bones: The Management of Death Pollution in Cantonese Society." In Bloch and Parry 1982:155–86.

Watson, James L., and Evelyn S. Rawski, eds.

1988   *Death Ritual in Late Imperial China.* Berkeley: University of California Press.

Weiner, Annette B.

1976   *Women of Value, Men of Renown: New Perspectives in Trobriand Exchange.* Austin: University of Texas Press.

Westermeyer, Joseph

1982   *Poppies, Pipes, and People: Opium and Its Use in Laos.* Berkeley: University of California Press.

White, Kenneth, trans.

1983   *Kr'ua Ke, Showing the Way: A Hmong Initiation of the Dead.* Recorded and trans. into French by Jacques Lemoine, pp. 41–76; trans. into English by Kenneth White, pp. 7–40. Bangkok: Pandora.

Wolf, Margery

1972   *Women and the Family in Rural Taiwan.* Stanford, Calif.: Stanford University Press.

Wolf, Margery, and Roxane Witke, eds.

1975   *Women in Chinese Society.* Stanford, Calif.: Stanford University Press.

Xiong, May, and Nancy Donnelly

1986   "My Life in Laos." In Johns and Strecker 1986:201–44.

Yang Dao

1975   *Les Hmong du Laos face au développement.* Vientiane: Siaosavath.

1982   "Why Did the Hmong Leave Laos?" In Downing and Olney 1982:3–18.

1993   *Hmong at the Turning Point.* Minneapolis: World Bridge Associates.

Yang, Kou, Vang Peng Yang, and Touly Yang

1980   *Khaws Kwvtxhiaj Hmoob* (A collection of Hmong traditional songs). Long
Beach, Calif.: Asian Pacific Outreach Inc.

Zanker, Stanley

1989   *Health in the Hills: The MOPH's Attempts to Provide Comprehensive Health
and Family Planning Services for the Ethnic Minorities.* Project paper
report B. Bangkok: Ministry of Public Health.

INDEX

Page numbers in italic refer to figures